The Political Economy of
Rural Poverty

The Political Economy of Rural Poverty

The case for land reform

M. Riad El-Ghonemy

R

Routledge
London and New York

First published 1990
by Routledge
11 New Fetter Lane, London EC4P 4EE
29 West 35th Street, New York, NY 10001

© 1990 M. Riad El-Ghonemy

Phototypeset in 10pt Times by
Mews Photosetting, Beckenham, Kent
Printed and bound in Great Britain by
Mackays of Chatham PLC, Chatham, Kent

British Library Cataloguing in Publication Data

El-Ghonemy, M. Riad *1924–*
    The political economy of rural poverty:
    the case for land reform
    1. Developing countries. Land tenure, related
    to poverty in agricultural communities
    I. Title
    333.33'5'091724

    ISBN 0-415-04082-5
        0-415-04083-3 pbk

Library of Congress-Cataloging-in-Publication Data

El Ghonemy, Mohamad Riad. 1924–
    The political economy of rural poverty: the case for land reform
/M. Riad El-Ghonemy.
        p.   cm.
    Bibliography: p.
    Includes index
    ISBN 0-415-04082-5
        0-415-04083-3 pbk
    1. Land reform – Developing countries – Case studies. I. Title.
HD13333.D44.E38   1989
333.3'1–dc19   88-36484
                                                                  CIP

Contents

Contents

Part 2 The analytical issues

Contents

Figures

Tables

Tables

Acronyms and abbreviations

BMR	Basic metabolic rate
CIDA	Inter-American Committee for Agricultural Development, Washington D.C.
CLR	Complete Land Reform
CPE	Centrally Planned Economies
CPI	Consumers' Price Index
ECLA	United Nations Economic Commission for Latin America, Santiago, Chile
ECWA	United Nations Economic Commission for West Asia, Baghdad
FAO	The Food and Agricultural Organization of the United Nations, Rome, Italy
GDP	Gross Domestic Product
GFCF	Gross Fixed Capital Formation
GNP	Gross National Product
IDB	Inter-American Development Bank, Washington, D.C.
IFPRI	International Food Policy Research Institute, Washington, D.C.
ILO	International Labour Organization, Geneva, Switzerland
IMF	International Monetary Fund
LC	Land Concentration
LDC	Less Developed Country
MNC	Multinational Corporation
OECD	Organization for Economic Cooperation and Development
PLR	Partial Land Reform
UNESCO	United Nations Educational, Scientific and Cultural Organization
UNICEF	United Nations International Children's Fund

Acronyms and abbreviations

UNRISD	United Nations Research Institute for Social Development, Geneva
US AID	United States Agency for International Development
WB	World Bank
WCARRD	World Conference on Agrarian Reform and Rural Development
WHO	World Health Organization

Acknowledgements

I am greatly indebted to the Agricultural Economics Unit at Queen Elizabeth House, Oxford University and to George Peters in particular. At his invitation, I have been fortunate in receiving invaluable administrative assistance, and the intellectual insight into fundamental development problems through the seminars and discussions with the faculty and the graduate students. I also owe George Peters thanks for calling my attention to a number of gaps in the preparation of the statistical analysis and in my judgement about the analytical apparatus of the neo-classical economics, although he may still object to what I say.

Most of the findings on the relationship between land distribution, nutrition, poverty and rates of agricultural growth which appear in the book were part of two seminars which I gave in 1986 and 1988. I have greatly benefited from the suggestions and criticisms that I have received from Godfrey Tyler, who read the entire draft of the manuscript. He helped weed out obscurities and clarify the presentation of data. In the course of writing the book, he has been a tireless sounding-board on a wide range of issues. Tony Mollett kindly read the drafts of Chapters 4 and 5, and offered valuable comments. Alan Maunder offered helpful comments on Chapter 3 which clarified the discussion on the institution of property rights. Within Queen Elizabeth House, I received helpful suggestions and criticisms from Frances Stewart, who read an earlier draft of Chapter 5 which I presented as a paper at the Conference of The Development Studies Association, University of Birmingham, in 1988.

I am grateful to Hans Singer, for his continued encouragement and interest in the subject of this book, particularly during my visiting fellowship at the Institute of Development Studies, University of Sussex. Laurence Smith and Richard King provided most helpful comments on Chapters 3 and 5, and their generous invitation to me to give seminars at the University of Glasgow, Scotland and North Carolina, USA, respectively, offered me the opportunity to talk to their graduate students. I

Acknowledgements

am obliged to Agit Singh and David Lehmann, Development Studies, University of Cambridge who, during my invited lecture, gave me the opportunity to clarify a number of issues discussed in Part One of the book. I am also indebted to the anonymous reviewers who, among other things, pointed out the importance of discussing the theory of the state in Chapter 3 and suggested many improvements to the original manuscript. Alan Jarvis, editor of social sciences at Routledge has been very patient, and a source of useful ideas in the course of preparing the manuscript.

I offer special gratitude to the Food and Agricultural Organization of the United Nations (FAO), in which I served and learned a good deal from my colleagues and from the farmers in the many developing countries which I visited and in which I worked. The Statistics Division and the Publications Division were kind enough to authorise the use of several data. My deep appreciation to James Riddell and Hans Meliczek in the Human Resources Division and to L. Naiken and C. Morojele in the Statistics Division who provided me with much material. I am indebted to Eugenia Loyster and Bill Thiesenhusen of the Land Tenure Centre, University of Wisconsin, who generously helped with the background material on the interest of the United States' Government in land reform questions.

I acknowledge with gratitude the intellectual influence of Kenneth Parsons, Professor Emeritus, University of Wisconsin, on my recognition of institutional arrangements as a central issue in agricultural development. Since our joint field study on land tenure in the Middle East during the second half of 1955, I have admired his commitment to the twin challenges of land reform for the mitigation of rural poverty, and to economists for advice on practical decisions on these issues.

Needless to say, none of the above scholars, institutions and organisations has any responsibility for the contents of this book, for which I am solely accountable.

I am grateful to Julia Knight of Queen Elizabeth House for her administrative support, understanding and generosity. Theo Palaskas and J.D. Talamini offered assistance in the statistical analysis of data in Chapter 5, for which I am grateful. Robert Fletcher was very helpful in improving the linguistic style of the manuscript in Part One and Part Two. My deep thanks to the staff of the Agricultural Economics Unit Library, Sheila Allcock, Rosie Bonello, Joan Chaundy, Felicity Ehrlich. Jillian Mathews and Sarah Stockes helped with the typing of the early manuscript. I am indebted to Juliette Majot for her interest in the subject matter, and her tireless assistance in editing, word processing and laying out the numerous tables in the manuscript; without her efficiency, I could not have submitted the manuscript on time. Finally, my wife Marianne has suffered from my long absences and preoccupation throughout the gestation of this book. Without her endless support, this study would have been delayed.

M.R. El-Ghonemy
Queen Elizabeth House
University of Oxford

Introduction: the aims and analytical procedures

Among the major issues in development policy, malnutrition, poverty, and inequality in the distribution of wealth and opportunities are well known to interested observers. However, it is on the inter-relationship between them and the role of the state in quickly alleviating poverty and inequality not by the market mechanism, but through land reform that different schools of thought and ideologies conflict. Since 1980, this conflict has been further intensified to the disadvantage of land reform policy and the rural poor. We have set out to investigate these questions which we consider vital to a large part of humankind.

The concerns

This book springs from three concerns. The first arises from my observations as a participant in the conceptual debate and practical programmes for alleviating poverty in developing countries (LDCs) over the past 40 years. Though once the very foundation of rural development and social and political stability, land reform has suffered a recent decline both as a policy issue and in development thinking. Simultaneously, since 1980, I have witnessed a swing away from land reform in the analytical reasoning behind foreign assistance priorities of most powerful donor countries and international aid giving agencies. Ironically, this swift change occurred soon after the governments of all developing nations and the governing bodies of international organisations had, in 1979, officially committed themselves to take action 'to realise' equitable distribution of land, 'to implement' land distribution with speed and 'to quickly eliminate' under-nutrition before the year 2000.[1] Yet, by 1988, all authoritative statistics on the aggregate level indicate deterioration, not improvement. As documented in Chapter 1, the numbers of the rural poor, the landless, and the malnourished have all increased, as has the concentration of land distribution and inequality in the distribution of wealth in many LDCs. The persistent neglect of agriculture, particularly the food producing sector has resulted in an alarming trend of falling

1

food productivity in most LDCs. This contradiction between rhetoric and reality points to a moral crisis in policy commitment to reduce both poverty, and the gross disparity of incomes.

The second concern – one that is related to the first – is academic and analytic. During my University seminars, students have expressed interest in the institutional and political determinants of rural poverty and inequalities. At the same time, they seemed to be frustrated by the difficulty in applying the analytical apparatus of economic theory to understanding the social organisation of agrarian economies. The difficulty lies in the separation of theoretical economics from applied economics, and the further separation of politics, history and institutions from neo-classical economics. The latter has converted economics from a social science to Newtonian mechanics, distancing its concern from realities of social and political arrangements. This intellectual segregation has led to a distorted understanding of the multi-disciplinary issues of rural development policy formulation.

Most perplexing to students is the economic justification of government intervention by land reform policy as an alternative to the uncertain and imperfect market. Of particular concern is regulation of the distribution of income to alleviate poverty during the lifetime of the currently poor individuals. In training young economists, too much emphasis has been placed on quantitative analysis of efficient allocation of resources by the free play of the market equating returns at the margin, at the expense of distribution and welfare considerations. Students tend to write their theses on commodity-orientated subjects using sophisticated models based on restrictive assumptions. Such a quantitative approach to approximating real conditions seems to be considered as more 'elegant' and more academically prestigious than an inquiry into the process of social change such as land reform and institutional arrangements governing production, exchange, distribution and consumption in rural areas of LDCs. This tendency is worrying because upon completion of their training, most graduates from LDCs actually work in governmental posts on inter-dependent and practical development problems.[2]

The third concern springs from swift swings in international developments witnessed since the beginning of this decade. Structural adjustments of national economies and liberalisation of trade have become the dominant preoccupation in the face of mounting debts, inflation, trade, and balance of payments deficits in many LDCs. Concurrently, attention has been diverted away from land reform and the problems of poor cultivators and landless workers which are part of these structural problems. While we recognise the need to expand exporting capacity and to ease the balance of payment deficits, coping with the severe economic recession should not serve as an excuse for LDCs' policy makers to delay land reform implementation, to cut off resources for land reclamation and land settlement schemes, or to maintain subsidised public goods and services in rural areas. Such actions have already compounded the problems of the rural poor in many property-market economies as documented in a recent study.[3]

Furthermore, where justice in property rights in land once featured prominently among questions of international human rights among the super powers, it has, in a sense, been sacrificed in the pursuit of improved international relations and a probable narrowing of the gap in ideological conflicts. Land reform as a policy issue has virutally disappeared as a fundamental development issue in international debate in the United Nations forums, only to be replaced by ambiguous integrated rural development programmes and environmental concerns which avoid landed property distribution issues. Recent adjustments in centrally planned socialist economies have, through price incentives, encouraged peasants to individually sell part of their surplus produce in the market and to expand private investment. Unfortunately, these types of adjustments have been misinterpreted as a retreat from complete land reform. In fact, social ownership of land and of the major means of production continue in these economies. Distorted interpretations of such adjustments in literature and in the Western media contribute to the declining support of land reform.

But the nearness of events, the scarcity of documented evidence on the consequences of recent changes, and the use of value judgements all contribute to the difficulty in exploring issues in contemporary history. Yet many of us have witnessed these post-1980 changes, and while they are still fresh in our minds it would be fatuous to ignore them, shying away in procrastination, and vainly hoping that time will provide us with a more complete record on which to base our conclusions more accurately. We cannot afford to await perfection in documenting a trend which, should it continue, holds dire consequences. Even before the post-1980 changes, an FAO study, 'Agriculture: Towards the Year 2000' estimated a rise in the absolute numbers of the seriously under-nourished persons and the rural poor between the base year 1975 and the terminal year 2000. In its analysis under 'If trends persist', the study states:

> The mockery which a continuation of a past food-consumption trends and income distribution would make of universally accepted social objectives is most clearly brought out in the estimates of numbers of seriously under-nourished people . . . the total would rise from an average 435 million (1974 –76) to 590 million by the year 2000. (FAO, 1981: 21)

Projections of the number of landless workers were not made because of variations in population pressure on cultivated land, intensity of land use and changes in the demand for labour outside agriculture. However, the study estimates that if current trends in agricultural population growth

3

and existing patterns of land distribution in 90 developing countries persists, the number of both mini-land holders and landless households would increase from 167 million in 1980 to about 220 million in the year 2000 (FAO, 1981: 88). The message conveyed by this study is clear. The alleviation of absolute poverty and under-nutrition requires redistributing existing productive assets and increasing food productivity. This means in practice that hungry rural people must have access to the means of growing their own food. Without recognising the legitimacy of this approach, and by perpetuating the post-1980 shifts in policy formulation, the alarming trend of increased poverty and under-nourishment will be compounded into the next century.

The aims

This book aims to help policy makers, development practitioners and students of development gain a better understanding of basic concepts relevant to contemporary rural development problems facing LDCs. It alerts readers to the problems perpetuated by a partial understanding of rural poverty determinants as well as the consequences of ignoring the association between poverty and the concentration of wealth and income in a few hands. Although the book is written for those with training in economics, the material can also be understood by the general reader. Professional economic jargon has been avoided as far as possible. We have focused on a combination of abstract and empirical analysis of the experiences of a sample of developing countries. This focus and the presentation of the author's experience in developing countries are in response to the recommendations of the anonymous reviewers of the manuscript, and the publisher. The reader may notice that most of the observations made are based on the author's own experience as a University teacher, and practitioner in the rural development programmes of his native Egypt, and internationally, with the Food and Agriculture Organization of the United Nation (FAO).

By sharing these experiences with a wide readership, the author's intention is to clarify the analytical and policy issues of land reform in the process of rural development under different kinds of economies, political organisation and social arrangements. The following is a sample of the critical questions we address:

1. Is land reform a prerequisite to a rapid reduction of rural poverty and to rectification of social injustice and political instability? If so, under what agrarian system? If it is not a sufficient condition in itself, what are the complementary prerequisites for reducing poverty and simultaneously contributing to agricultural growth and national development?

2. Does any scope of land reform alone realise these changes and pro- vide landless peasants with accessible opportunities for enhanced abilities, secured employment and command over food?
3. Can poverty be quickly reduced and the rate of agricultural growth be increased through land reform irrespective of the country's average income per head and the prevailing operative ideologies?
4. Is rural poverty a matter of resource allocation determined by price mechanisms, and therefore responsive to the working of a free market? Or is poverty a structural problem of unfavourable institutional settings (including the power structures) in agriculture?
5. Does the break-up of large privately owned farms (as usually demanded by land reformers and peasant organisations) disrupt production and reduce the marketed surplus, particularly of food- grains? If so, under what circumstances? On the other hand, will the redistribution of large privately owned farms to beneficiaries under diverse institutional arrangements and production organisations raise productivity of land and labour and thus realise potential gains?
6. Is the realisation of high rates of agricultural growth and techological advance conditional upon the dominance of large farms and multinational corporations?
7. Are the institutions of property rights, authority of the state, and the power-based transactions within or outside the 'market' suscep- tible to analysis by relevant tools of economic theory?
8. What are the current dilemmas facing policy makers with respect to instituting land reform and making IMF–induced fiscal and structural adjustments which affect food production and the rural poor?

These and similar questions are empirically analysed and their functional links are explained in the following chapters. Also, the terms of 'land reform', 'agrarian reform', 'rural development', 'poverty', 'institutions', 'exploitation', 'power', 'opportunities', 'command over food', 'under- nutrition' and 'agrarian system' are defined in the course of the study.

Why focus on the political economy?

We have emphasised 'political economy' in the title of this book, and accordingly, the economic activities of owners and tillers of land in production relations and exchange are examined in their political and historical contexts. This study attaches great importance to the inter- relationship between the land-based *political power* and the role of the state on the one hand, and their indivisible function in the *economic pro- cess* on the other. By political power, we simply mean the balance of diverse conflicting interests and incentives to action which influence the choice of policy. This choice is a reflection of the 'balance sheet' of the vested interests of landlords, middlemen, tenants and wage-dependent landless workers, as well as the political interests of those who rule the country. Low or high ceilings on private landed property, its nationalisation or payment of full, part, or no compensation to affected landowners, prohibition of tenancy or control of farmland rent – all constitute the net product of a practical calculus of conflicting interests.

The political economy as a branch of social science enables us to study the empiricism of these issues as well as the sample of questions listed earlier. Our study is an inquiry into the changes in social organisation of agrarian economies over time in an historical and political contexts. Within this framework the study of land reform and poverty in rural areas is an investigation of the dynamic social change in a number of interacting economic and non-economic factors. These factors are not confined to the conventional economics of resource ownership and use in the agricultural sector of the economy. Instead, they are extended to the chain of social arrangements which govern the production, exchange, distribution and the consumption of goods and services. Thus our concern is not restricted to resource allocation problems in agricultural production, but includes the institutional framework. By institutional framework, we mean the organised rules and transactions established by law (or custom with the force of law) which determine the rights, duties, and actions of the individual's business life in the society. We are concerned with the working rules of law and custom which secure, in a given time and place, property rights in land, power relations, and the authority of the state in modifying the iniquitous land tenure arrangements and regulating the market distributional function on the grounds of public interest. For a realistic analysis of development problems, a distinction needs to be made betweeen the role of the State in protecting private property in capitalist systems, and its collective power in assigning rights in land use under central planning and collective management of socialist economies.

It is apparent that a study of a distribution of wealth – which in agrarian economies is represented primarily by land and related material assets and the effect this has on social and production relations – cannot be subjected to a single-track analysis. It requires the use of relevant analytical tools from the body of economic theory, political science, an historical approach and also moral and ethical reasoning. It also necessitates supplementing the economic factors (employment, income, investment, saving, marketable surplus, etc.) with equally important institutional factors (land tenure, class power relations, custom-determined credit arrangements, government bureaucracy, political organisation, etc.). This comprehensive scheme is best served by the science of political economy which has been segregated into narrow specialised areas of analysis. For each area, a partial analytical apparatus is developed, based on sets of restrictive assumptions and extracted from observations in certain conditions at a given time in history.

The diverse analytical reasoning behind the concept of exploitation illustrates this point. The conception is differently formed by individual scholars with varying backgrounds and within each author's unique system of analysis abstracted from different social conditions of production relations and property rights. The analytic reasoning behind each interpretation seems to be consistent with the social conditions studied and each conclusion reached. In Chapter 5 we discuss briefly the different meanings of exploitation based on different notions of the institution of private property rights including one's own labour and its product. These notions range from that of Locke in the Seventeenth Century, to those of Ricardo and Marx in the Nineteenth Century, to those conceived by Nozick and Roemer in the present century. From their different conclusions (and there are many more), independently reached by different systems of analysis, we can see the importance of first understanding the underlying assumptions and the prevailing socio-economic conditions from which the principles were abstracted before employing them indiscriminately.

With regard to the use of the neo-classical analytical system of thought in the study of land reform and poverty we can partly employ relevant tools on efficiency of resource use in agriculture related to the size of farms under different land tenure arrangements, and the working of land, credit, and labour markets. In our study, we shall explore the process of monopolisation of land and other means of production in a private property-market economy. We cannot, therefore, limit the inquiry to 'pure' economic theory. Because institutional factors are considered 'non-economic', unquantifiable and unpredictable, factors such as land tenure arrangements, power relations in transactions, custom-determined rules of conduct, and the government administrative and legal systems are excluded from conventional models. Some economists treat them as constraints to growth, residuals or externalities. By excluding institutional arrangements, the assumptions used often at variance with real economic experience of developing countries. As the sub-discipline of development economics has brought forward, this experience suggests that income disparity, low productivity and consumption levels of the poor are rooted in the 'non-economic' factors which have been put aside by the neo-classical analytical system.

Limitations are apparent in the different theories and hypotheses which explain inequality in *personal* (individual or household) income distribution in LDCs. For instance, the concern of the Ricardian and neo-classical theories of *functional* income distribution is restricted to shares of capital and labour. Another weakness of this analytical system is the manner in which it treats farmers as two homogeneous sub-groups of capitalists or profit-makers, and wage-earners. Subsistence peasants who are self-employed and the main food producers are thus overlooked. There are also limitations and conflicting interpretations of the several theories on utility and welfare, particularly with regard to government intervention to redistribute land and income with preference for the immediate alleviation of poverty as against relying on the market to alleviate poverty in the far distant future.[4] To study the impact of government intervention via land reform upon the time trend of poverty incidence, we are concerned with changes in personal (individual or household) income and consumption distribution. Understanding these changes is necessary for estimating the proportion and number of people whose income or consumption falls below a minimum subsistence level known as the poverty line.

We view land reform as effective policy leading rural development when it quickly reduces poverty incidence by redistributing the skewed pattern of *privately* owned land, transferring monopoly profit of landlords to the existing poor cultivators, and by creating accessible opportunities for the rural poor. Obtainable opportunities include: access to the productive assets of land, credit, and water; and ability to increase productivity in order to contribute to and benefit from agricultural growth, to live longer and healthier lives, to improve skills and literacy, and above all to gain self-respect.

Unlike changes in agricultural production, reducing the incidence of poverty among the current generation by redistributing wealth cannot be left to natural laws. This distinction was clearly made by John Stuart Mill in his *Principles of Political Economy*. The distribution or redistribution of wealth, in his words is:

> a matter of human institution solely. The things [material wealth] once there, mankind individually or collectively can do with them as they like. They can place them at the disposal of whatsoever they please and on whatever terms. . . . If private property were adopted, we must presume that it would be accompanied by none of the initial inequalities and injustice . . . the division of the produce would be a public act. The principle might either be that of complete equality, or of apportionment to the necessities or deserts of individuals, in whatever manner might be comfortable to the ideas of justice prevailing in the community. (Mill, 1848: 350, 352)

The analytical procedures

Our analysis rests on two premises. The first is that each kind of social and economic organisation has different sets of rules and political motives.

A private enterprise economy, whether with State- controlled or free market mechanism, is different from a centrally planned and managed economy having communal or social ownership of productive assets. The second is that rural development is realised if in the country's time trend in poverty incidence, the numbers of the absolutely poor in the countryside diminish as quickly as possible. Keeping in mind Mill's reasoning for the State act to modify the rules governing the distribution of wealth, we examine quantitatively, and qualitatively the dynamics of social change which generate or quickly alleviate poverty within the peculiar circumstances of each country. Only then can we understand the characteristics of each agrarian economy which obstruct or enhance rural development. To facilitate our empirical exploration, we first conceptualise the development problems.

The elements of the problems are described in three related hypotheses:

1. In less developed countries, land ownership is more commonly secured by institutional means than by the market mechanism.
2. The lower the concentration of land ownership/holdings, the lower the level of absolute poverty in rural areas, (irrespective of the level of a country's average income per head).
3. Realising high rates of agricultural growth is not conditional upon high land concentration and the dominance of large estates.

In delineating these relationships, we follow two analytical approaches: an historical review is combined with a narrative of the institutional arrangements to explain the factors underlying the economic process; and a qualitative statement is combined with a quantitative analysis of cross sectional data (correlation and regression methods).

In our analysis, a selected sample of developing countries is studied on a country-by-country basis in order to understand the policy choice under varied agrarian systems and different arrangements of the institutions of property rights in land and other means of production. To capture the dynamic changes with respect to agricultural growth, equity and poverty, the study covers a post-land reform period of 30 years on average. This is followed by an inter-country comparison of 14 countries, including five case studies. An explanatory framework is suggested for the classification of countries into broad and homogeneous categories according to the scope of change in the pattern of land distribution. The broad categories are:

(a) a complete land reform policy;
(b) a partial policy, dividing the agrarian system into reform and non-reform sectors; and

(c) no redistribution of *privately* owned land, leaving the market and
     political power structures unaltered.

In this empirical review and comparison, no preference is implied for
one approach over the other. Rather the intention is to show, as objectively as the data permit, how the scope of change affects income
distribution, food productivity, the incidence of rural poverty, and the
quality of life (literacy, nutrition and life expectancy). We identify the
dynamic forces operating elsewhere in the national economy and in the
international labour market, and their effects on the sustainability of the
initial gains from land reform are examined.

To observe the speed and extent of reduction in the incidence of
poverty and its characteristics, two factors are introduced: time (inter-
temporal comparison) and the demographic characteristics of each
country (population growth rates and fertility rates). Poverty estimates
made at specific points in time are compared provided they are
nutritionally-based, reliable and consistent in the criteria used for
measurement. Although this approach offers a rather crude base for comparison, we hope it will help to draw some broad lessons of interest to
policy makers, development analysts and students of development
problems.

Content and scope of the study

This study is divided into three parts. *Part One* explores the perplexity
surrounding the shift away from the crucial policy issues of land reform,
poverty and gross inequalities in opportunities. It presents a profile of
the agricultural dimension of poverty. It investigates whether there have
been fundamental changes during the period 1980–5 (as compared to
1960–80) in levels of malnutrition, food productivity, or land distribution, which could justify complacency. *Part Two* sets the conceptual
frame of reference for the analysis of a variety of countries' experiences
presented in the rest of the book. *Part Three* examines a sample of LDCs'
empirical evidence on the origin and effects of policy choice for tackling
the problems of rural under-development within their historical contexts.
By way of guidance to the reader, we present a synthesis of the content
of each chapter.

Chapter 1

The first chapter presents a descriptive profile of rural poverty and the
demand and supply sides of its agricultural dimension. Two questions
are examined: how poverty and low productivity of the agricultural
labour force constitute a single problem; and how the state's neglect

of agriculture in the allocation of investment has reduced the productive capacity of agriculture and that of agricultural workers. The time trend (1950–84) in the distribution of landownership/holdings is presented. Inter-temporal comparison of changes in 1960–85 is based on aggregative results of agricultural censuses, food surveys, and compiled LDCs' data of food production and estimates of incidence of poverty and landlessness.

Chapter 2

This chapter explores first, the sharp swing in development thinking, particularly in the system of economic analysis and policy prescriptions for solving rural development problems; and second, the shift away from the pre-1980 focus on land reform, equitable distribution of income and on poverty-orientated policies of powerful aid-giving countries, influential development assistance agencies and international lending institutions. This discussion traces the ideological elements of the shift, and then appraises the apparent dilemmas facing policy makers in many LDCs with respect to: their choice, commitment and implementation of land reform policy under different forms of political power; and second, their choice of structural adjustment policies as induced by the International Monetary Fund (IMF) in alliance with the World Bank and foreign creditors. Examples of country experiences in these two situations are presented.

Chapter 3

The conceptual elements of the institution of property rights, power relations and the authority of the state are presented, and an explanation is offered of how they condition the policy choice. Land reform and rural development as used in this book are defined. The chapter explains poverty as both an agricultural problem and a structural phenomenon, and distinguishes between rural development and rural betterment. The determinants of gains and losses and difficulties in measuring the distributive consequences of land reform are examined. Relevant principles of the theories of the state, utility and welfare, entitlement and justice are discussed in terms of their application to government intervention to restrict property rights in land. We proposed a schema for the understanding of the relationships between access to land, employment, command over food-intake, and the decreased risk of malnutrition.

Chapter 4

This chapter examines the analytical issues and available empirical evidence on allocative efficiency and on employment in both capitalist and socialist agriculture. Two questions are posed. The first is, would the break-up of large farms in capitalist agriculture raise land productivity, increase employment, and realise potential gains to society as a whole? The second question probes the consequences of the indiscriminate use of efficiency criteria in judging the performance of large farms in different ideological and economic contexts.

Chapter 5

The fifth chapter begins by conceptualising institutional monopoly as a primary source of generating poverty and inequality in agrarian economies characterised by land concentration. It examines the meaning of exploitation and identifies barriers to agricultural growth and alleviation of poverty in private property-market economies where land represents a high proportion of total wealth. The differences between these barriers to entry and those associated with industry are explained. The three hypotheses presented earlier are tested. Institutional means for owning or holding land are distinguished from the mechanics of the land market in economic terms and these means are then identified in the historical experience of pre-1952 Egypt and that of Kenya; two countries with scarce cultivable land, capitalist agriculture and long colonial rule. Through the review of their experiences, we attempt to explain the dynamic process of monopolisation of factor and product markets. We then identify the implications this has for agricultural growth, food production, and for creating the conditions of poverty in rural areas. A statistical analysis using correlation and regression methods follows a model. The analysis is based on available data from 20 LDCs.

Chapter 6

The empirical discussion is advanced. Five case studies of countries which have implemented land reforms are presented according to a suggested set of criteria. China and Cuba represent central planning socialist approaches to land reform, while South Korea, Iraq, and Egypt represent land reform based on private property in a capitalist agriculture. These case studies examine the origin of land reform and its design, and the scope of its coverage. They also examine the implementation capability of state institutions. Emphasis is placed on the diverse initial agrarian conditions, natural endowments, forms of agricultural production organisation and institutional arrangements. In each case, the impact of land reform is assessed in terms of the distribution of land and income, food productivity and the pace in reducing poverty incidence.

Chapter 7

Here is found an exploration of the central question of whether both the pace and extent of the reduction in poverty incidence are conditional upon land reform and its scale. If not, what other policy instruments can realise this objective, and under what agrarian conditions. An inter-country quantitative analysis is conducted, and encompasses the demographic characteristics of each country. Using data on the speed in poverty reduction from country experiences, the conceptual distinction between rural development and rural betterment presented in Chapter 3 is applied.

Chapter 8

This final chapter draws some conclusions in the light of the conceptual framework presented in Part Two and the empirical evidence from country experiences studied in Part Three. It assesses retrospectively how the choice of political economy has contributed to the inquiry of the subject of this book. After outlining the findings of the study which should be of particular interest to policy-makers and rural development analysts, we challenge some assumptions on poverty reduction and suggest guiding principles for evaluating the impact of land reform. The prospects for activating land reform policies are examined in the context of the realities presented and in the face of the current economic crises, persisting poverty and falling food productivity in many LDCs.

Data sources, including the author's field studies in Egypt, Iraq and Mozambique are cited throughout the text. Available estimates of poverty incidence in 64 developing countries are presented in Appendix A and the inter-temporal comparison appears in Chapter 7. The technicalities of measuring the variables of poverty, landlessness, land concentration and rates of agricultural growth are presented in Appendix B.

Notes

1 This official commitment by governments and international organisations was in their adoption of the 'Declaration of Principles' and the 'Programme of Action' at the 'World Conference on Agrarian Reform and Rural Development' held in Rome between 12 and 20 July 1979. See FAO publication on the Conference Proceedings in *Report*.

2 This is based on a study by the American Agricultural Economic Association on the MSc and Ph.D graduates in agricultural economics from US universities between 1969 and 1979. The study shows that 30 per cent of the graduates were from developing countries, 40 per cent of them held University positions. Fifty per cent worked in their governments and 10 per cent worked in International Organisations. The

survey of the Institute of Development Studies at the University of Sussex, UK. *Register of Research in the UK, 1981–83*, show that out of 1,272 theses for MSc and Ph.D or D.Phil in development studies, only 30 were on subjects directly or indirectly related to land reform and land tenure issues. This record covers 32 colleges and universities without a disaggregation of graduates' countries into developed and LDCs.

3 See *Adjustment with a Human Face*, a study by UNICEF, edited by G.A. Cornia, R. Jolly and F. Stewart' Vol. I, 1987 and Vol. II, 1988.

4 On the reasoning behind government intervention to redistribute income/consumption vs. the uncertainty in gains by the currently poor see J. Graaf (1958), *Theoretical Welfare Economics*, Cambridge University Press; W.J. Baumol (1952), *Welfare Economics and the Theory of the State*, Harvard University Press; and, E.S. Phelps (1965), 'A critique of neutralism', published as Chapter 4 in *Fiscal Neutrality Toward Economic Growth*, McGraw Hill.

Part 1

Puzzles and dilemmas

Chapter one

Persistent poverty and crippled agriculture: a single problem

Rural poverty measured in terms of the proportion and the absolute number of rural populations living in deprivation remains staggeringly high in most LDCs. Although the primary source of rural employment and subsistence in many countries, agriculture continues to be crippled. Poverty in rural areas, combined with stagnant or deteriorating output in agriculture constitute one single problem, linked by the very low productivity of a large section of the labour force in agriculture, particularly in food production per head. This deficiency in productive capacity of human resources in agriculture forges the crucial link in a chain of poverty. In other words, the crippled state of agriculture, and the inferior standard of living of the rural poor are testament to the denied opportunities for positive change to realise potential gains.

The incidence and scale of poverty

This section broadly examines the scale of deprivation in LDCs' rural areas, aiming to show that the post-1980 scale of absolute poverty and the human misery which it generates, in no way justifies complacency or neglect by the international community.

This study is based on data on the proportion and number of the rural population living in absolute poverty, as defined and estimated by 64 developing countries. The population of these 64 countries represents about 90 per cent of the total population of all LDCs. Estimates are made at one point in time during 1977–85, and in a few cases, countries have inter-temporal estimates since the 1950s. Although useful, these estimates have several limitations, and so require caution in their use. Some of these qualifications are listed below:

1. Different countries may use different methodologies; in particular, they may use different cut-off points to identify the 'poverty line' below which individuals or households are considered poor.
2. The proportion of the total expenditure of individuals or household

taken up by food consumption compared to other necessities may vary from one measure to another.

3. The use of a single poverty line for the country as a whole conceals:
   (a) the degree of inequality in the distribution of income/consumption among the poor;
   (b) the occupational categories of the poor as hired agricultural workers, share croppers, very small holders of land or livestock, nomads, artisan fishermen, forestry workers, female heads of households, etc; and
   (c) the age and sex composition of the members of poor households.

4. Clear categorisation of the poor, particularly the landless and the undernourished is often considered politically dangerous and inconvenient for those in power. This information is, therefore, often intentionally unpublished or underestimated.

With these limitations in mind, the author compiled the available estimates for 60 countries used in 1985 for the preparation of *The Dynamics of Rural Poverty* (FAO, 1986a: Table 1.1). Since 1985, estimates for China, Turkey, Iraq and the Ivory Coast have been added and necessary corrections and updating of the estimates for the other 60 countries have also been made (see Appendix A). In our sample of 64 countries, the total number of the rural poor is estimated at 767 million persons.

Of the 64 countries, only 14 had a 'low' incidence of poverty (below 30 per cent).[1] At the other extreme, 34 countries suffered 'high' poverty incidence of 50 per cent and over. Classified by region, sixteen are in Africa, ten in Latin America, four in Asia and three in the Middle East. Of the 767 million rural poor, nearly 70 per cent are concentrated in seven countries, mostly Asian: India (266 million), China (60 million), Bangladesh (56 million), Indonesia (52 million), Nigeria (40 million), Brazil (26 million), and Pakistan (24 million). However approximate these estimates of the scale of poverty may be, it is undeniable that this degree of poverty incidence in the rural areas of 64 countries is intolerably high.

Most of these hundreds of millions of people are likely to be illiterate and in ill health; though all rural poor are not necessarily malnourished, malnourished (or undernourished) people are almost always poor. In 1981, the total number of persons undernourished or at high risk of it in 98 developing countries was estimated by the FAO. At two levels of minimum average calorie requirements per person, the estimation was 335 million at the low level of 1.2 BMR (basic metabolic rate) and 494 million at the less conservative level of 1.4 BMR.[2] A clear association is apparent between this estimate of malnutrition in 98 countries, and our estimates of the rural poor in 64 countries. This approximate association can be attributed to the high proportion of the rural poor in LDCs and their high proportionate expenditure on food is high, (about 70–75 per cent). A similar association can be seen in 1974/5 when the Fourth World Food Survey (FAO, 1977) estimated the number of malnourished people in 98 developing countries at 455 million. The World Bank, using US$150 as minimum income per head, estimated the number of absolute poor in developiᵤ g countries at 770 million (World Bank, 1978: Table 34). Assuming that 70 per cent of them were in rural areas, the rural poor amounted to nearly 550 million in 1975. Compared to our estimate in 1985, there is a substantial rise of rural poverty.

Since 1961, and at aggregate level, a trend towards a rise in the number of malnourished people has emerged. Using the same cut-off points (1.2 and 1.4 BMR) for estimating the incidence of malnutrition in 1969–71 and 1979–81, the Fifth World Food Survey (FAO, 1985b: Table 3.1: 26) shows the number (in millions) in developing market economies under A (1.2) and B (1.4) as follows:

	Africa		Far East		Latin America		Middle East		Total	
	A	B	A	B	A	B	A	B	A	B
1969–71	57	81	208	303	36	53	23	34	325	472
1979–81	70	99	210	313	38	56	16	25	335	494

Within these regions, the worst incidence was in the 36 countries classified by the United Nations as the least developed countries, 25 of which are in Africa where malnutrition increased in proportion and in numbers. The increase in the numbers of malnourished in Africa, the Far East, and Latin America reflects institutional constraints working against the vulnerable low income groups' acquisition of food-intake. It also reflects the role of the growth in population compounded by governments' failure in their development programmes to ensure that the rising demand for food is matched by an increase in *per capita* supply of food from domestic food production and importation.

But who are these poor and undernourished in *rural* areas? Surveys and area studies identify:

(a) small farmers in ecologically poor areas where conditions are unfavourable to the production of food;
(b) casual and regularly hired agricultural landless workers not receiving grain-wage equivalents who must therefore rely heavily on the market to acquire their entire grain food;
(c) pregnant and lactating rural women; and

(d)   young children whose undernutrition is higher among girls than boys below the age of five.

The landless workers, whose income is wage-based and whose calorie-intake is market-dependent, are at serious risk of malnutrition. As net buyers of food, they are vulnerable to unstable food consumption not merely because of the seasonality of food production (particularly before harvest time), but also because they are often displaced by mechanisation and capital-intensive technologies. In times of famine, they are, of course, most vulnerable, facing serious malnutrition, and low chances of survival.

Despite variations in definition, the total number of landless worker *households* in agriculture is estimated at 168 million in 1979. Increasing by 12 million households during the period of 1980-5, the total number in developing countries with private property-market economies reached nearly 180 million (FAO, 1987b). Differentiated by gender, the picture of landless poor becomes more focused. Women, who account for approximately one half of the landless worker population in some countries, run higher risks of malnutrition than do men, for reasons endemic to their society. Traditionally used as cheap labour, they are the first to be displaced by labour-saving technology and, in most non-socialist agriculture, they are denied legitimacy and entitlement in access to land and credit. In addition to the nutritional demands of pregnancy and lactation, their labour in agriculture often entails high-calorie loss activities, such as walking long distances to fetch water for household consumption. With inadequate nutrition, this large part of the agricultural workforce is effectively denied the opportunity to increase productivity, and in turn, the families' income. It is puzzling why, despite the lip service paid to women's rights by many politicians and policy makers, sex discrimination based on the traditionally, inferior position of rural women working in agriculture continues today.[3]

As poverty, inferior environmental conditions, and inappropriate agricultural policy generate malnutrition, illiteracy fuels the problems of the rural poor, among whom it is particularly high. The UNESCO statistical yearbook data in 1985 (differentiated only between rural and urban areas for 21 countries) show that in 12 of them, rates were as high as 50 to 90 per cent. In all 21 countries, illiteracy rates in rural areas were 2.5-3.0 times higher than those in urban areas. Once again, the disadvantageous position of women is manifested in their very high rate of illiteracy, between 60 and 98 per cent.

Regrettably, country statistics and international development indicators do not break down national averages on calorie supply per head, literacy, mortality or life expectancy into rural and urban categories; this in itself indicates insufficient concern for rural poverty. In the absence of such data, a few individual country studies must be relied upon.[4] These indicate that:

(a) child and infant mortality rates in rural areas are, on average, 2–4 times higher than those in urban areas, and 5–6 times those of the national average;
(b) on average between 100 and 150 per 1,000 young children in rural areas die before reaching the age of two; and
(c) that illiteracy and infant mortality rates are roughly more than three times higher among the landless workers than among medium and large land owners.

These high rates persist in rural areas of many developing countries despite the notable progress made towards improved health services, and a decline in the infant mortality rates over the past two decades.

All these depressing statistics suggest considerable lost opportunities for potential productive capacity of hundreds of millions of rural poor and their children, and inevitably, for their countries. Or, put a different way, when opportunities are denied, human capital is lost, and potential gains in productivity are never realised. The figures illustrate the real consequences of neglecting human resources in rural areas, and governmental denial of opportunities in their respective societies. One manifestation of such neglect can readily be seen in the inadequate access to basic public services by the rural poor. The large section of the rural population which is illiterate and undernourished, is inhibited by its inability to participate in local organisations. It is also inhibited, unable to stand up to corrupt government officials and to the exploitative attitude of landlords and moneylenders.

Inevitably, the most tragic victims of poverty are the children of poor households who suffer while their parents hope in vain that their children will escape their own poverty trap. In the author's experience, only luck and persistence saved him from the fate of Egypt's 11 million illiterate in rural areas:

At the age of six, I had to walk five kilometres to and from the nearest primary school, trading my native dress for a western uniform that my father could ill afford. When I was ten I had to drop one year of schooling because I caught malaria, bilharzia and trachoma. When I finally graduated to high school, I had to make a daily round trip of 50 km by donkey and local train.

This experience of the 1930s is still shared today by millions of rural children in developing countries.

21

Crippled agriculture and declining food production

The preceding section outlines the denial to the poor of their human rights to secure basic necessities leading to deficient productive capacity. This state of productive capacity is represented by the very low level of productivity and consumption per head. Since the majority of the poor in rural areas depend on agriculture and associated non-farming activities for their employment and income, it is important to characterise the supply and demand sides of the agricultural dimension which generate conditions of the under-utilisation of labour.

There are two sets of elements in the agricultural dimension of poverty. The first includes the natural physical endowments and technologies utilised in the process of agricultural production. The second set is encompassed in the institutional framework of land tenure rights, the distribution of farm-sizes, the structure of power (based on the institution of property), and the state policy shaping the character of output growth and distribution of income in agriculture. It is important to recognise one other set of elements in the character of the national economy; the growth of agricultural population and the corresponding change in demand for agricultural labour and products operating in the rest of the economy and the international labour market.

The paradox of decreasing demand for an increasing supply of agricultural labour

In a capitalist system of industrial development, industry does not permit new entrants of labour unless their contribution to output (marginal productivity) is equal to or higher than their wages. The balance of the labour force left unabsorbed by other sectors, must, therefore, remain in agriculture, which, like an already saturated sponge, attempts to contain the fast growing numbers of entrants at the expense of a declining productivity per head of agricultural workers.

In this section, aggregative data is used to judge intertemporal changes (1960–85). Although this aggregation conceals the inter-country and within countrywide variations in resource endowments, social systems and the initial conditions before 1960, the data in Tables 1.1 and 1.2 are telling. As acknowledged earlier, the statistics available from many developing countries are shaky, and the data on labour productivity in agriculture are not always secure. The term 'labour force' is conceptually and statistically crude, and not uniformly applied in country censuses, many of which underestimate the number of women.

Table 1.1 shows that agriculture accounts for 72 per cent of the total labour force in low-income countries and 44 per cent in middle income countries (grouped by World Bank Development indicators). In the

Table 1.1 **Performance of agriculture in developing countries, 1960–85**

		1965–80 %	*1980–5* %
Population: average annual growth rate %			
Low income economies – total		2.3	1.9
excluding China and India		2.7	2.7
Middle income economies		2.4	2.3
Agricultural labour force as percentage of total			
Low income economies	1960	77	
	1980	72	
Middle income economies	1960	61	
	1980	44	
Annual growth rate %	1970–81	1.4	1.5
GDP Average annual growth rate %			
Low income economies – total		4.8	7.3
excluding China and India		3.2	2.8
Middle income economies		6.5	1.7
† *Agricultural GDP growth rate %*			
Low income economies – total		2.7	6.0
excluding China and India		2.0	1.9
Per capita	1960–70	0.3	
	1970–80	0.3	–1.1
Food production Total	1960–70	2.9	
	1970–80	2.8	2.5
Per capita agricultural labour force	1960–70	0.4	
	1970–80	0.4	
‡ *Arable land* per capita agricultural population (hectares)	1974–76	0.36	0.34
Annual rate of growth percentage of above	1968–80	–0.25	0.56
	1971–73 to 1980–82	–1.9	

Sources: * World Development Report 1987, Development Indicators, except annual growth rate of labour force which are taken from FAO, 1987a, *Country Tables*, Rome: 334 and 336.
       † World Development Report, 1982: 41.
       ‡ FAO, *Production Year Book*, 1985, in Table 2, FAO [C 87/19] period, 1971–3 and 1980–2 from FAO, SOFA, 1985, Table 1–6.

early 1980s, the share of agriculture in total output (GDP) was 35 per cent and 20 per cent respectively. These percentages suggest a serious structural imbalance, disadvantageous to the rural poor. During 1960–80, industry in developing countries was able to absorb an annual rate of only 0.5 per cent of a total labour force whose annual growth was 2.3 per cent. This trend in slow absorption of the labour force outside the agricultural sector, and the corresponding slow proportionate decline of the agricultural labour force (with an increase in absolute size) compounds the problems of the poor.

Given these structural characteristics, increasing employment opportunities must be created within rural areas by combining the intensification of agricultural land and labour use, with non-farm activities requiring no specialisation or development of high skills (Booth and Sundrum, 1985). Low-income LDCs facing an extensive incidence of poverty in agriculture, trapped by institutional obstacles and high population growth, cannot imitate the historical experience of the now industrialised developed countries, for their initial conditions of economic growth differ significantly (see Chapters 5 and 6). Just how different these conditions are can be seen in Table 1.1. According to the data, the labour force in agriculture grew at the average annual rate of 1.4 per cent in all developing countries in the period 1960–85.

This contrasts sharply to the dynamic growth and structural changes over time experienced in developed capitalist countries, where the growth in the agricultural labour force was −3.0 per cent. As regional averages, Africa experienced 1.8 per cent growth, Asia, 0.9 per cent, the Middle East and Latin America, 0.7 per cent. These regional averages, however, hide a wide variation among countries within each region. For example, the annual rate in 1960–85 was 0.4 per cent in Brazil, 0.9 per cent in Egypt, 1.4 per cent in India, and as high as 3.0 per cent in Kenya. With the persistent growth of the labour force in agriculture coupled with the sluggish growth of agricultural GDP, output per head declined from the annual average rate of 0.3 per cent in 1960–80 to a negative 1.1 per cent in 1980–5. This downward trend in gross income per head of agricultural labour force can also be deduced from the trend in real wages in agriculture. It is true that data on wage rates, number of working days per year and consumers' price index (CPI) are not always secure, (particularly as many peasants and landless workers do not consume all the commodities included in this Index). It is also true that small farmers and share croppers are mostly self-employed, relying on their family labour to produce their own food. Nevertheless, the available data on *real* wages in agriculture for 12 countries in 1970–84 can help to explain the declining low incomes of hired agricultural workers in these countries. Real wages (agricultural wages deflated by CPI for each country) declined in eight of the twelve developing countries (ILO, several issues of *Year-book of Labour Statistics* cited in FAO, 1987a: Table 7).

Deteriorating food productivity

Food, particularly cereal, is the single most important commodity produced by agriculture. This may appear obvious to most of us, but it does not appear obvious to policy makers in several LDCs. How else can we explain the neglect of the production of cereals and meat represented as food production in Tables 1.1 and 1.2?

Population growth (in both rural and urban areas) and the income elasticities of different socio-economic groups determine whether domestically produced food is sufficient to feed a given population, and if it is not, whether the deficiency is to be made up by import (including food aid).[5] In this way, food is different to other agricultural commodities. Apart from the obvious biological need which it fills, it is a source of *security*, contributing to self-respect and dignity for individuals, and for their countries. This may explain why so many developing countries insist that self-sufficiency in food production be set as a major policy objective, irrespective of the comparative advantage of utilising their agricultural resources. This has been one of the long-debated issues in development which have come to the fore as a consequence of the prevalence of under-nutrition and frequent famines.

Despite the ideals of food self-sufficiency and food security, the empirical evidence during the 25 year period 1960–85 is distressing: of 128 developing countries, only 38 experienced food production per head of total population which continuously kept up with population growth over the entire period. The remaining 90 countries include 27 whose percentage of undernourished people increased between 1969–71 and 1979–81 (FAO, 1985b: Table 2.2 and Appendix 1). Some are highly populated, (such as Nigeria, Mexico, Turkey, Egypt, Colombia and Ethiopia), and in 24 countries, over 50 per cent of the rural population live in absolute poverty.

Breaking the aggregate data on food production given in Table 1.1 into regions, Table 1.2 shows that Africa experienced the most serious decline because it was continuous, throughout the long period 1960–85. Even the countries of the Middle East and Latin America, which did relatively well in the 1960s and 1970s failed in 1981–5 to keep pace with population growth. It is remarkable that in Asia, with the most populated countries in the world, productivity improved substantially. We note from Table 1.2 that when the CPE are added to developing countries with private property-market economies, the food productivity rates rose from 0.5 and 0.2 per cent to 0.9 and 1.4 per cent respectively. It is for this reason that the data on total and per head food production throughout the period are given in Table 1.3 for developing countries with egalitarian agrarian systems, irrespective of their political ideological systems.

Table 1.2 **Food productivity in developing countries by regions, 1960–85**

	Annual rates of population growth		Food production per head growth rates	
	1960–80 %	*1981–5* %	*1960–80* %	*1981–5* %
Africa				
(excluding South Africa)	2.8	3.0	−0.7	−1.1
Middle (Near) East	2.8	2.7	0.5	−1.5
Latin America	2.6	2.3	0.9	−0.5
Far East – Asia, developing	2.3	2.1	0.7	1.5
All developing market economies	2.5	2.4	0.5	0.2
All developing countries including Asian (CPE)	2.4	2.0	0.9	1.4

Note: CPE stands for Centrally Planned Economies or the Countries with Socialist agriculture and communal land tenure.

Sources: FAO, 1987, *Country Tables*, Rome: 320–34.

Table 1.3 **Food production in developing countries with egalitarian agrarian systems, 1960–85**

	Annual rate of growth					
	Total food production			Per head		
	1960–70	*1971–80*	*1981–90*	*1960–70*	*1971–80*	*1981–5*
Albania	3.2	4.6	2.6	0.4	2.1	0.4
China	5.8	3.1	6.0	3.4	1.3	4.7
Cuba	4.3	3.0	2.1	2.2	1.8	1.5
Kampuchea	3.2		12.6	0.7		9.7
Laos	6.0	2.6	6.5	3.3	0.7	4.2
Libya	7.0	5.3	11.9	2.9	1.2	7.7
North Korea		5.7	4.2		3.0	1.7
South Korea	4.0	4.8	3.7	1.5	3.0	2.1
Vietnam	1.3	3.4	5.1	−0.8	1.0	3.1

Source: FAO, *Production Year Book* 1985 and *Country Tables* 1987, Rome

Breaking down the data further, and relating it to poverty, Table 1.4 gives the data for 19 African countries with available estimates of poverty levels, 50 per cent and above. Having the largest population in Africa (81 million in 1980), Nigeria deserves an explanation. Nigeria deserves an explanation. Nigeria has a relatively high GNP per head (US$770 in 1983), thanks to her oil revenue, large natural agriculture endowment, and location in the humid West African region. Its agricultural production and equity performance, however, is dramatically low: the estimated incidence of poverty in rural areas ranged between 40 and 60 per cent in 1978–85; the quality of life in terms of the life expectancy and infant mortality is as inferior as that of many low-income economies. In addition, there has been a negative rate of change in both agricultural GDP per head of the labour force in agriculture (−0.3) and *per capita* food production during the period 1970–84.

These indicators are all linked to a state of neglected agriculture, with 68 per cent of the total labour force in agriculture and 80 per cent of the population living in rural areas. Even without statistical analysis, data given in Table 1.4 shows the association between poverty and the very low productivity which affects a substantial portion of the rural population. Of the 19 countries, 13 have negative growth in agricultural GDP per head of the labour force, and three have positive growth (0.3 and 0.4). The large size of the agricultural labour force sharing a mean value at 78 per cent is higher than the weighted average of all low-income developing countries (72 per cent in 1980). Fourteen countries had negative growth rates of food production per head and in three others, (Burundi, Chad and Tanzania) the margin was between 0.1 and 0.4. These high rates of population growth, require aggregate food production annual growth rates of, at least 3.5 per cent to meet the rising demand for food. This compares with the present average of 1.5 per cent. Certainly there is justification for growing concern with many LDCs' failure to produce enough food to match their growing population.

The deficient institutional framework of agriculture

Apart from the inferior quality of life of the majority of the labour force in many LDCs and the exogenous factors of weather (especially in Africa), how can we explain the deficiency in agriculture's productive capacity of human and physical resources? Should climate and population growth bear the brunt of blame in all developing countries whose productivity declined in 1960–85? In the light of remarkable technical advances for bringing land, water, even human fertility under the control of applied science, it is incredible that climate and population are still identified as the lone culprits.

Leaving for the moment the impact of the recent cycles of world economic recessions, there is another explanation for declining

27

Table 1.4 Productivity of agricultural labour force in 18 African countries with rural poverty levels at 50 per cent and over, 1970–84

Country	Rural poor as percentage of rural population	Labour force in agriculture — As percentage of total 1980	Labour force in agriculture — Annual rate of growth 1970–80	Gross agricultural production — Annual growth 1970–84 %	Gross agricultural production — Per capita growth rate 1970–84 %	Food production — Annual growth rate 1971–80 %	Food production — 1980–84 %	Food production — Per capita growth rate 1970–84 %
Benin	65	70	0.6	2.9	0.3	2.85	2.88	-0.9
Botswana	55	70	1.1	-0.1	-3.7	-3.55	0.97	-2.3
Burundi	85	93	1.2	2.2	0.4	2.30	2.68	0.4
Chad	56	83	0.9	0.9	-1.3	2.48	-1.46	0.1
Ethiopia	65	80	1.4	1.6	-0.7	2.03	-0.98	-0.6
Ghana	55	56	1.9	-0.1	-3.0	-1.75	1.47	-3.8
Kenya	45–55	81	3.2	2.8	-1.3	2.09	3.51	-0.8
Lesotho	55	86	1.6	-0.1	-2.4	0.85	-0.27	-1.0
Madagascar	50	81	1.8	1.6	-1.1	1.38	2.48	-0.6
Malawi	85	83	1.4	3.4	0.4	1.51	2.49	-0.1
Nigeria	58	68	2.7	2.2	-1.3	2.88	0.95	-1.9
Rwanda	90	93	3.0	4.2	0.8	4.78	2.96	0.6
Sierra Leone	65	70	0.1	1.5	-0.1	1.19	0.33	-1.2
Somalia	60	73	3.2	1.1	-4.3	0.93	0.19	-2.4
Sudan	70	71	1.9	2.3	-0.7	3.45	2.93	-2.5
Swaziland	50	74	1.2	4.28	2.76	3.48	3.33	2.7
Tanzania	60	86	2.3	3.8	0.3	5.79	-0.33	0.4
Zaire	80	72	0.8	1.9	-0.9	1.64	3.30	-1.1
Zambia	52	73	2.2	2.1	-1.0	2.83	1.40	-1.7

Sources: Levels of rural poverty in the second column are from 'World Bank Social Indicators Data Sheets', June 1984, except those for Nigeria (Collier, forthcoming), and Somalia (Tyler, G.J., F.A.O. Rural Poverty Study Series No. 7, August 1983). All estimates of poverty incidence refer to the percentage of rural population falling below a country-specific absolute minimum income required for meeting basic human needs and not only the minimum food requirement. The two estimates of Kenya are a very specific absolute minimum income required for meeting basic human needs and not only the minimum food requirement. The two estimates of Kenya are a very specific absolute minimum income required for meeting basic human needs and not only the minimum food requirement made between 1977 and 1979. Whilst the World Bank estimate was 55 per cent, others were lower depending on the cut-off point – see Diana Hunt *The Impending Crisis in Kenya* – Chapter 3, Gower, 1984. The data in the rest of the columns are compiled from *Atlas of African Agriculture*, FAO, Rome, 1986.

productivity; the intricate obstacles set by the institutional framework of production, exchange, and distribution. Their influence in many LDCs, takes different forms: creating a state of under-utilisation of labour, land and technology in agriculture and inhibiting the character and volume of investment needed to raise the demand for labour. In turn, this influence contributes to the very low levels of productivity and consumption of a large section of the existing workforce.

To support this explanation, the same methods used in the preceding section will be used, namely, analysing aggregate data, presenting examples of a few countries, and leaving the conceptual and statistical analysis to follow in Chapters 3 and 5. Data used in this section refer to the institution of property rights in land and the related size distribution of land holdings. They also refer to the institution of power manifested in a combination of land-based rural power and authority of the state in the selection and enforcement of public policy. The latter concerns:

(a) the character and volume of public expenditure on agriculture and its share relative to other sectors of the national economy; and

(b) the choice of policies with respect to pricing agricultural inputs and products, and the land tenure regulatory arrangements.

Increasing land concentration and polarisation

In this section, we are primarily concerned with land-holding units in which the scale and use of the means of production are at work. Consider first the aggregate features of the size distribution of land holdings (owned, rented, share-cropped or a combination of these tenure arrangements). Data on holdings are given in country agricultural censuses, which uniformly report area and size distribution. Although the coverage of countries varies, the completed results of censuses for 1950, 1960 and 1970 are considered in this study. The available results for 16 countries which completed the most recent census during 1978–84 were compiled by the author.[6] In addition, there are a few results of the 1984 surveys on land ownership in Egypt and Iraq. The compiled results are presented in Table 1.5. They suggest three generalities: first, that there is rising inequality in the distribution of land holding; second, that there is an increasing polarisation in agrarian structure; and third, that it is small constrained farms which produce most of the food grain.

The results of agricultural censuses during the period 1945–84 show a rising inequality in distribution of land holding. The share of small-holdings (below 5 hectares) increased, while the corresponding areas did not. Contrarily, the actual size of large holdings grew over the same period. The share of the former increased in number of total holders

Table 1.5 **Changes in the concentration of size distribution of land holding in 23 developing countries, 1950–84***

Countries ranked in descending order of number of agricultural population per hectare of arable land	1980	Land concentration Index – Gini coefficient			
		1950s	1960s	1970s	1980–4
Egypt†	7.8	0.61 (1950)	0.38 (1965)	0.45 (1975)	0.43 (1984)
Bangladesh	7.2		0.47 (1960)	0.57 (1970)	0.55 (1984)
				0.42 (1977)	
Kenya	6.0		0.82 (1960)	0.74 (1971)	0.77 (1981)
Nepal	5.9		0.57 (1961)	0.69 (1971)	0.61 (1982)
Korea, South	5.8	0.72 (1945)	0.39 (1960)	0.37 (1970)	0.30 (1980)
Indonesia	4.1		0.62 (1963)	0.72 (1973)	
Saudia Arabia	4.1			0.79 (1972)	0.83 (1983)
Sri Lanka	3.4		0.66 (1960)	0.51 (1973)	0.62 (1982)
Philippines	3.2	0.51 (1948)	0.50 (1960)	0.51 (1971)	0.53 (1981)
India	2.7	0.68 (1954)	0.59 (1961)	0.64 (1971)	0.62 (1978)
Pakistan	2.5		0.63 (1963)	0.52 (1973)	0.54 (1980)
Dominican Republic	1.8	0.79 (1950)	0.80 (1960)	0.79 (1971)	
Thailand	1.7		0.46 (1963)	0.41 (1970)	0.46 (1978)
Colombia	1.6	0.85 (1954)	0.86 (1960)	0.86 (1971)	
Honduras	1.3	0.73 (1952)		0.78 (1974)	
Costa Rica	1.2	0.79 (1950)	0.78 (1963)	0.83 (1973)	
Panama	1.2	0.72 (1950)	0.74 (1960)	0.78 (1971)	0.84 (1981)
Turkey	0.9		0.63 (1963)		0.58 (1980)
Paraguay	0.9		0.93 (1960)		0.94 (1981)
Iraq	0.7	0.88 (1957)		0.65 (1971)	0.39 (1982)
Venezuela	0.6		0.94 (1961)	0.92 (1971)	
Brazil	0.5	0.83 (1950)	0.84 (1960)	0.84 (1970)	0.86 (1980)
Uruguay	0.3		0.82 (1961)	0.83 (1970)	0.84 (1980)

Note: *Countries for which data on size distribution of land holdings are available for at least two points of time. Years in parentheses refer to date of census or survey.

   † Egypt's index refers to land ownership (several editions of Statistical Yearbook).

Sources: Unless otherwise indicated below, Gini coefficient for 1960, 1970 and 1980 is calculated by FAO Statistics Division, Rome, based on results of World Agricultural Censuses. The 1950s Coefficient is calculated by the author from available results of agricultural census except South Korea (1945), for which the calculation was based on data in *Land Reform in South Korea*, US Agency for International Development, Spring Review, June 1970: 7, Table 3. *Kenya* (1960) from Berry and Cline, 1979, Table 3–3, Index for 1970 is calculated by the author from Statistical Abstract 1971 of Kenya, Table 84. *Turkey* (1963) from Berry and Cline, 1979. *Bangladesh* (1960 and 1970) from ILO ACRD IX 1979 'Poverty and employment in rural areas', Table VII. Also *Thailand* (1970). *Bangladesh* (1984) calculated by the author from Bagladesh Census of Agriculture 1983–4 Vol. I Table 5. *Iraq* (1982) refers to Gini index of land ownership calculated from data in A.S. Alwan 'Agrarian systems and development in Iraq' in *Land Reform*, FAO, 1986: 25, Table 2. *Indonesia* (1973) calculated from the results of agriculture census. Data on number of agricultural population per one hectare of arable land are taken from FAO *1987 Country Tables* corresponding to each country.

of land from 60 per cent in 1950 to 66 per cent in 1970, whereas their share in *total area* remained almost constant at 6 per cent suggesting a process of continued fragmentation and a fall in average size. In fact, the results of the 1970 census analysed in FAO (1984) show 33 developing countries with a high index of concentration of land holding (Gini coefficient at 0.5 and over), 17 of which were Latin American, where the concentration was 0.7 and over in 15 countries.[7] The few available results of the last census of 1980 show that the index of concentration in Latin America has *not* improved and it has even worsened between the 1970s and 1980 in Panama, Paraguay and Uruguay, all having a very high concentration at a Gini coefficient of 0.8 and 0.9. As shown in Table 1.5, concentration has also increased between 1970 and 1984 in other regions (Kenya, Saudi Arabia, Bangladesh, Sri Lanka, the Philippines, and Thailand). Over the entire period (1945–84) concentration has fallen sharply in the three countries which carried out major land reforms (Egypt, Iraq and South Korea).

The increasing land concentration noted above has been associated with a rise in the minute holdings which become smaller and smaller while attempting to accommodate more and more peasants. Concomitantly, large farms in the size group of 200 ha and over have increased in average size (particularly in South America), accounting for 58 per cent of total area in 1950 and 66 per cent in 1970. Their share in total number of holdings was a tiny fraction of about 5 per cent. This size group includes the multinational corporations and large plantations.

This process of polarisation in agrarian structures is associated with extensive tenancy, absentee ownership of land, indebtedness and rising landlessness. In the recent past, these features of polarisation emerged in African countries south of the Sahara, where traditional communal land property gave way gradually to individual ownership and foreign-owned plantations linked with multinationals (e.g. Nigeria, Kenya, Malawi and Madagascar).

In fact, landlessness increased faster than growth rates of the agricultural labour force in many countries, irrespective of the variation in their intensity of population pressure on land. This seems to suggest the tendency of mini-holders to lose their lands and become landless workers relying for their livelihood on wage labour, increasing their vulnerability to several uncertainties, noted earlier. The growth in landlessness, relative to the labour force in agriculture, can be seen from Table 1.6 giving a few examples for which we have some estimates.

This continued rise in landless agricultural workers is evidence of their lack of access to land. Significant numbers of these entrants into landlessness are likely to add to the number of the rural poor in their respective countries, unless their real wages increase and the number of their working days rises.

Table 1.6 **Growth rates in landlessness and labour force in agriculture in five developing countries, 1960–70**

		Brazil	Indonesia	Morocco	Panama	Philippines
Landless workers*						
As percentage of	1970	25	23	21	21	15
agricultural labour force	1980	39	36	33	30	37
Annual average rates of growth	1970–80	1.4	1.3	1.2	0.9	2.2
Labour force in agriculture†						
Annual average rates of growth	1970–80	−0.3	0.6	1.1	−0.2	1.8

Note: Estimates of landlessness in Indonesia refer to Java
Sources: * For 1970, *Yearbook of Labour Statistics*, ILO, Geneva.
                † 1987 *Country Tables*, FAO, Rome.

Neglect of production of food grains on small farms

The results of the agricultural censuses since 1950 reveal two features with respect to land use: first, the completed 1970 census shows that countries characterised by a higher percentage of large holdings tend to have little cropland, and more land under pastures or left temporarily fallow. (In South America, for example, this fallow land represents nearly 65 per cent of total area holdings. In contrast, the percentage of cropland to total area of holdings was 92 per cent in Asia and the Middle East, two land-scarce regions where the area cultivated by temporary crops (mostly food crops) was 86 per cent.) Second, it is small-holders of less than one hectare who are the primary growers of food grain. The 1970 agricultural census, for example, shows that this group of landholders produced 74 per cent of total harvested wheat, 68 per cent of rice, and 60 per cent of maize (FAO, 1981a: Tables 6 to 6.9). This high intensity of food cropping in small farms has been realised despite several institutional constraints in the supply of credit and technical services by government. Once again, it is women who are particularly constrained in many LDCs, where they are denied access to institutional credit and technical services. Although agricultural censuses do not disaggregate farm holders by sex, household surveys estimate female heads of household at 15–20 per cent, with 50–60 per cent of working time on food-producing farms worked by women. These percentages rise in rural areas with widespread migration of male heads of the households, (Dey, 1980, Palmer, 183, and Safilios-Rothschild, 1982, 1983), yet, women as significant producers of food crops, livestock and dairy products are virtually invisible to policy makers and technocrats in most LDCs.

Distorted public investment in agriculture

The realities of the size distribution of holdings and their cropping intensity helps to explain how the powerful political lobby influences the selection and enforcement of public policies in agriculture. Governments and their technocrats are not neutral. Rather, they tend to represent the interests of those groups on whose power governments depend for their tenure in office.

In many contemporary developing countries, policy-makers and their technical planners underestimate the importance of agriculture. About 250 years ago, François Quesnay, the leader of the Physiocrats addressed the subject saying:

> Everything that is disadvantageous to agriculture is prejudicial to the state and the nation, and everything that favours agriculture is profitable to the state and the nation. . . . It is agriculture which furnishes the material of industry and commerce and which pays both. . . .
>
> (Alexander Gray, 1931: 102)

This argument for the accentuation of France's agriculture in the early 1700s is still very relevant today to many LDCs. In economic terms, there is no justification for under-estimating agriculture or for not recognising its capital needs in order to accelerate agricultural growth rates. The principle of this long established relationship were formulated by the Harrod-Domar Model in the 1940s.

The question is: to what extent is agriculture neglected by policy makers despite the rhetoric to the contrary. Thanks to the intellectual efforts made over the past thirty years by a number of economists, we can estimate the level of inadequacy of investment. For instance, we can estimate agriculture's needs of capital if we know the share of agriculture in total gross domestic product (GDP), the desired rate of growth of agricultural output, the expected capital-output ratio (incremental output yielded from incremental capital invested in agriculture) and the percentage of national saving in GDP (Rajkrishna, 1982, Lipton 1977). There are methodological limitations for the use of capital-output ratio as argued by Paul Steeten, 1972.[8]

We can also estimate the degree of inadequacy by relating the share of agriculture in Gross Fixed Capital Formation (GFCF) to its share in GDP and the labour force.[9] The wider the gap between shares, the higher the extent of neglected investment. This can be illustrated using data of Egypt (as a developing country) and the United Kingdom (as a developed country).

Share of agriculture	Egypt		UK	
	1976 %	*1982* %	*1976* %	*1982* %
In gross domestic product	29	20	3	2
In total labour force	50	46	2	2
In GFCF (calculated from United Nations National Account Statistics, 1982)	7.0	7.1	2.6	2.7

The example suggests the extent to which agriculture in Eygpt was denied its adequate share in capital investment in 1976 and 1982. By calculating the capital-output ratio (4:1) and the planned annual rate of growth of agricultural GDP at 4 per cent, the share of agriculture in GDP at 20 per cent, and the share of domestic saving at 15 per cent of total GDP, Egyptian agriculture should have received at least 21 per cent of total investment in 1982 instead of the actual, insufficient share of 7.1 per cent. The low rate of investment resulted in an annual rate of growth of agricultural GDP at 2.5 per cent in 1980–3. The example also suggests that as the structure of production in the economy is diversified and its GNP per head rises in real terms, the share (in percentage) of agriculture in total output, labour force and total investment falls proportionately. Nevertheless, GFCF includes capital formation from both *private* and *public* expenditure, excludes public *current* expenditure (e.g. subsidies granted in the form of cheap fertilisers, insecticides etc.) and government expenditure on agricultural extension and research.

The use of the share of agriculture in total public expenditure is useful in measuring the adequacy of meeting the investment needs of agriculture. In addition to current expenditure, it includes capital expenditure (e.g. investment in irrigation, drainage, land reclamation and food storage). Public expenditure is also an indicator of the extent of government commitment to agriculture and the priority it attaches to it. *Planned* expenditure, however, promises something much different than the benefits accrued to small land holders from *actual* expenditure. According to empirical evidence, this is a warning to heed; in countries where the size distribution of land ownership is highly unequal, a relatively small number of landlords, middlemen, and traders tend to capture most of the benefits from public expenditure.

To relate public expenditure to poverty, the author previously analysed data collected in a unified format from 48 developing countries according to their public expenditure on agriculture during the period 1978–82 (El Ghonemy, 1984). The *per capita* allocation of public expenditure on agriculture was related to levels of rural poverty for 31 countries. The data on government expenditure was converted to US$ at the official rate of exchange for each country, although in some instances, the domestic currency was over-valued. With this limitation in comparison, it was found that in all 48 countries, the average share of public expenditure in agriculture was about 10 per cent compared to the much higher shares in GDP (between 30 per cent and 40 per cent) and the labour force (average 73 per cent). Importantly, the level of allocation to agriculture was inversely related to the level of poverty in the 31 countries, i.e., the higher the poverty, the lower the allocation per head of agricultural population. In the 20 countries with high poverty incidence (50 per cent and over) the average allocation per head in terms of US$ weighted by the size of the agricultural population was US$13, as compared to the average of US$37 for the 14 countries with low poverty incidence (less than 30 per cent). Not surprisingly, the actual expenditure was lower than the planned targets by a margin in the range of 15–35 per cent in most countries for which information was available.

Actual investment, as low as it might be, is not entirely financed by domestic sources. Most LDCs rely on foreign aid and grants to finance their investment in agricultural and rural areas. For example, in his 1986 field study of the Yemen Arab Republic, the author estimated that 90 per cent of government expenditure in agriculture came from 20 donor countries and the balance was from the domestic resources allocated to the Ministry of Agriculture. Even with this heavy reliance on foreign resources, the expenditure per head of agricultural population was only equivalent to one US$. This is very low indeed, considering the decline in real terms in the growth rate of total agricultural product from 3 per cent in 1980 to 0.6 per cent in 1986 and a drop in *per capita* food production below the 1970s level. It is also low when compared to another private property–market economy such as India, whose allocations were four times as much per head, although its average income per head is only half that of Yemen.

However relative or absolute neglect is measured, these disappointing statistics show why agriculture and the food producing sector in particular is crippled. They are disappointing because the cumulatively low, negative growth in *per capita* food output in LDCs cannot continue if poverty, food shortage and the horrendous incidence of malnutrition are to be substantially alleviated. But investment in irrigation, land reclamation, large drainage schemes, supply of technical knowledge and research cannot be expected from the private sector. It should be expected from their governments.

In many LDCs, financing investment in agriculture is fraught with difficulties. Rich landlords usually resist adequate taxation and tend to evade payment if the laws were passed under their formidable power; landlords who are absentee owners together with their insecure tenants are not interested in investing in land productivity. On the other end of the scale, small owners who would be interested in increasing productivity do not have the capacity to invest in irrigation and drainage. Furthermore, private traders and urban businessmen cannot be relied upon for undertaking the needed volume and proper pattern of investment in agriculture. These internal vested interests on the one hand, and capital-starved small farmers on the other, may explain the reliance of many governments of LDCs on foreign assistance and capital flow from multinationals operating in agriculture, whatever the attached strings may be. It also explains the course taken by many governments which are unable, for political reasons to tax (or collect) from farmers directly. Taxation of agriculture as a whole is implied by indirect taxation of marketed surplus through a distorted price policy which lowers producers' prices to support urban resident consumers.

The supply of chemical fertiliser is an important public investment towards increasing demand for labour and raising productive capacity of existing stock of land. Despite notable progress in the 1970s, there has been a dramatic decline in the annual rate of fertiliser consumption in *all* developing countries (market ad socialist economies) from 11 per cent to 3.9 per cent in the first part of the present decade (FAO, 1985c; Table 1.7). However, this aggregate average conceals a wide variation between and within countries. Variations are to be found in terms of: cropping intensity by quality of land, size of holding, the preferential allocation of fertiliser between food crops and exportable non-food crops and inter-country differences in poverty levels. For instance, while the decline was 3.5 per cent in Asia, it was 17 per cent in Latin America. Furthermore, our study, (El-Ghonemy, 1984) reveals an inverse relationship between the level of poverty incidence and fertiliser consumption per unit of crop land. The average was as low as 5 kilograms per hectare in high poverty countries, whereas it was 13 kg/ha in low poverty countries. The average was even lower for food crops (3 kg/ha) than it was for exportable food crops (80–100 kg/ha) in the sample of the 19 poor African countries in Table 1.4. These widely differing rates in the use of fertiliser indicate the low application of fertiliser in food production and the resulting stagnation and failure to meet increasing demand. The peasants of one hectare or less who produce food already know the methods to increase the yield and they presumably want to increase it.

Small farmers constitute a large proportion of food producers, and they could substantially increase food production, if they were not constrained by institutional obstacles (this point will be examined further in Chapter 4). The institutional obstacle course is both familiar and frustrating: expensive credit and its rationing by title to land which deprives many tenants; the isolation of many peasants never reached by agricultural technical personnel; disincentives arising from governmental policy on agricultural pricing with pronounced preference for exportable cash crops. Further to institutional obstacles, widespread illiteracy among the great mass of small farmers (women in particular) and an already low expenditure on education, tend to reduce the potential scope of investment in technical change. This is likely to lower the effective return on investment in agricultural research-cum-extension services.[10]

The dilemma in pricing policy

Constraints imposed by pricing policy on food production have been the concern of many scholars and international agencies.[11] Recently, their connection to poverty was closely examined in Indian agriculture, where an immense database dates from the 1950s. Desai and Parthasarathy (in Mellor and Desai, 1985) examined the relationships within temporal changes in land tenure systems. In explaining the downward trend in absolute poverty, their conclusions attached maximum importance to changes in the size distribution of holding; and tenancy regulation which favoured the poor peasants during the period 1956–70. Ahluwalia (1978 and 1985) on the other hand, examined agricultural growth rates and consumer prices relative to poverty, and concluded that rural poverty fluctuated with the performances of the food sector in agriculture and the price of food consumed by the poor.

The impact of pricing policy on farmers' incentives and rewards suffers from generalisation. The generic term 'farmers' is misleading without a specification of their different occupational categories. Subsistence farmers, for example, having no marketed surplus do not benefit from either a rise or a fall in food prices, except when they hire out their own family labour to other farmers. The landless agricultural workers, being net buyers of food, are likely to be harmed by a rise in food prices together with their fellow poor in urban areas. Small farmers who do not grow food crops and do not own livestock must also rely on the market to provide their food requirements. On the other hand, small farmers cultivating mixed crops, medium and large farmers and commercialised plantations are likely to benefit most from a rise in agricultural products' prices. Consequently, income distribution probably worsens. Disincentive arising from low prices may lead those large producers to keep a substantial area of their farms out of production. Although it seems affordable in the short term, it continues at the expense of a reduced total output and declining unemployment of the landless workers.

Generalisation is, therefore, misleading and empirical examples are always helpful, hence two illustrations: how relative changes in the prices of products and material inputs in Bangladesh adversely affected small

37

farmers' income; and in Egypt, how pricing policy shows that low prices of crops procured by the government, combined with subsidies granted for inputs led to a net transfer of income from farmers to consumers. (This implies an indirect taxation of food crops' producers and a heavy indirect taxation of agriculture as a whole.)

In the case of Bangladesh, the government, through its Agricultural Development Corporation (BADC), controls the distribution of fertilisers (mostly through grants from donors). Since 1973 prices of chemical fertilisers rose at an annual rate of 23 per cent (as a result of gradual withdrawal of subsidies). In 1974–84, prices of paddy rice increased at the annual rate of only 12 per cent. This distortion in prices has led to a decline in the income of the small farmers (holding less than 2.5 acres) who represent 70 per cent of total landholders and cultivate 30 per cent of total farm area. It has also resulted in a 30 per cent reduction of the consumption of fertilisers by *all* farmers whose demand for the use of this crucial yield-increasing and labour-using input was unfulfilled (Hussein, 1985).

Through pricing policy in Egypt, the government controls the price level and procurement of the entire crops of cotton, and sugar cane, as well as parts of the marketed surplus of wheat, rice and beans. The government also allots the area to be cultivated. Procurement prices are fixed each year at levels 20–50 per cent below world market prices. In their comprehensive study, von Braun and de Haen (1983) estimated the crop producers' losses and the consumers' gains at 1975 price levels after making the necessary adjustments for: subsidies granted to the producers for their utilised inputs (fertilisers and pesticides) and subsidies granted to consumers (cheap food prices and cheap raw cotton delivered to domestic factories). The results are summarised in Table 1.7.

Table 1.7 **Farmers' income loss and consumers' gain from pricing policy in Egypt, 1980**

	Producers' price as percentage of World price		*Total income loss to crop producers*	*Total income gain to consumers*
	1975	*1980*	*In million Egyptian Pounds at 1975 price level 1980*	*1980*
Wheat	35.3	41.5	72.2	43.8
Rice	14.5	42.0	139.9	118.9
Cotton	20.0	50.0	319.2	187.8
Sugar	26.8	41.2	90.6	125.6
Beans	53.1	55.6	8.6	11.3

Source: Based on data given in:
Von Braun, J. and de Haen, H. *The Effects of Food Price and Subsidy Policies on Egyptian Agriculture* Research report 42, International Food Policy Research Institute, November, 1983, Tables 13, 14, 22, and 23.

Clearly, the farmers and the agricultural sector have suffered the consequences of the deliberately designed agricultural pricing policy. The brunt was borne by the small farmers, (holding less than 5 acres) who represent 92 per cent of total land holders in Egypt, and who cultivate 65 per cent of total farm area.[12] The loss should be seen not only in terms of depressed incomes from low prices, but also in the opportunity cost, i.e., incomes which farmers could have gained from higher prices provided by the world market and from their free choice to change areas of crops. In a sense, the total loss by crop producers estimated at 630 million Egyptian pounds in 1980 could be considered as an excessive indirect tax; a subsidy paid by farmers to benefit the vocal urban consumers and the manufacturing sector processing raw cotton and sugar cane. As agriculture received about 300 million Egyptian pounds (at 1975 prices) in 1980, including 100 million pounds for subsidised agricultural inputs, the estimated total loss of income by farmers substantially exceeds government expenditure on agriculture. For the economy as a whole, this represents a net taxation of agriculture.

These two examples of price policies, in Egypt and Bangladesh, seem to represent what is actually happening in many developing countries. There is sufficient evidence from developing countries to show some common institutional arrangements which work against the peasant realisation of income and output gains from pricing policy. They are:

(a) unequal access to subsidised inputs and market information;
(b) indebtedness to moneylenders and local traders who combine lending with compulsory purchase of crops at pre-determined prices;
(c) the multiplicity of intermediaries in the market and a hierarchy of officials who may defraud poor peasants;
(d) high rates for irrigation water charged by pump owners who control water rights in certain rural localities; and
(e) the traders' and middlemen's practice of hoarding food grain in the expectation of a further rise in prices, thus harming the rural poor who rely heavily on the market for their entire calorie intake.

It is an ironic paradox that while LDCs' governments pay lip service to the high priority accorded to agriculture and the welfare of the peasants, their public actions continue to cripple both.

Still, at this point in our study, many of the relationships and their potential implications for policy remain tentative. More empirical evidence, and further conceptual and statistical examination in the following chapters clarify these implications.

Notes

1   The developing countries having an incidence of absolute rural poverty
    below 30 per cent of total rural population are: China, South Korea,
    Mauritius, Tunisia, Jordan, Egypt, Argentina, Nicaragua, Turkey, S.
    Yemen, Guatemala, Sri Lanka, Iraq and Ivory Coast.
2   BMR stands for Basic Metabolic Rate, which is an estimated minimum
    dietary energy requirement using a safe range within which individuals
    can adjust their body weight in response to changes in energy intake
    without danger to health. The range is $1.2 \times$ BMR and $1.4 \times$ BMR.
    The difference represents a 7 per cent variation for adults of the same
    age and weight as empirically observed (FAO, 1985b: 19-21).
3   Perhaps one of the significant features of development thinking over the
    last decade has been the systematic arguments to indicate the
    underestimated role of women in development. The international fora
    have gradually succeeded in bringing the issues involved to the attention
    of policy makers in developing countries. Among the several arguments
    for the important role of women in agriculture see Safilios-Rothschild
    (1983); McSweeney (1979). FAO's document 'The role of women in
    agricultural development', (1983a) 'Women in developing agriculture'
    Chapter 2 of *The State of Food and Agriculture 1983*, FAO (1983b) and
    *Rural Labour Market Issues Relating to Labour Utilization,
    Remuneration and the Position of Women* ILO (1983).
4   Examples of these country studies are: Kelley *et al.* (1982),
    Egypt: Population and Development in Rural Egypt, results of field
    research in a sample of 3,830 households in provinces of Egypt, carried
    out by Allen C. Kelley, Atef M. Khalifa and M. Nabil El-Khorasaty.
    The study shows whereas the national average mortality was 18 per
    thousand and infant mortality was 108 per thousand, the survey results
    reveal that these rates were as high as 63 and 260 respectively in the
    villages surveyed.
    India: The 1978 All-India Infant Mortality Rate Survey indicated a death
    rate of 139 per thousand among infants born to illiterate mothers in
    rural areas, but only 64 where mothers had completed primary eduction.
    Kenyan statistics show a death rate of 101 among infants of illiterate
    mothers, compared to 82 among those whose mothers had one to six
    years of education.
    Bangladesh: In Companiganj, a similar pattern was found, infant deaths
    among the landless were estimated at 155 per thousand, with a child
    death rate of 25. Among households with three acres of land, however,
    death rates dropped sharply to 85 (infants) and 18 (children). A study in
    the Matlab area of Comilla District, in 1977 (UN – 1984, Souza:
    146–58) offers an interesting analysis of the combined impact of
    education *and* land tenure status on health. Among uneducated small
    land-owners the child death rate was measured at 23, while among
    landless agricultural workers it was 32.8 per thousand of children (1–5
    years).
5   This tendency towards a growing dependence on the unstable world

market of food commodities is manifested in the rising scale of food imports which expanded in 1970–80 at an annual rate of 10–12 per cent. Cereal imports, in particular, have sharply risen by nearly 50 per cent between 1974 and 1985 (excluding food aid). The rise was experienced by most LDCs irrespective of their GNP per head level. For 1986–7 the US Department of Agriculture estimated a further rise in cereal imports by developing countries of some two million tons.

6 I am grateful to the Statistics Division of FAO for providing me with the results of the census from 15 countries completed by June 1987. The results of the Bangladesh Census 1983–4 were obtained by the author from Volume I published by the Bangladesh Bureau of Statistics, May 1986.

7 The Gini coefficient is a measure of concentration or inequality which ranges from 0 to 1; the larger the index, the greater the inequality. Thus a Gini at 0 represents perfect equality and 1 represents perfect inequality.

8 Capital/output ratio is widely referred to in the literature on investment and is used in development planning. Nevertheless, it is arbitrary and ambiguous. Paul Streeten (1972) examined the limitations in its use: aggregation of diverse forms of capital as a homogeneous quantity; strong assumptions used with regard to its separation from human capital, institutions, management and organisations, attitude to work which influences output; and problems of measurement (valuation of capital and output due to changing levels of prices) time-lag between investment and output yielded, confusion between using average and incremental ratios, assumptions about rate of growth of the labour force, use of public expenditure on health, education and nutrition as consumption . . . etc. Streeten concludes that, given these difficulties and ambiguities, its usefulness in development planning is doubtful. *The Frontiers of Development Studies*, Chapter 6. However, based on Szepanik's study of 17 developing countries, Lipton (1977: Table 8.1) found that in 11 of them, agriculture has fallen far short of adequate investment. He also showed that the marginal capital productivity in agriculture is not smaller than that of other sectors, as is widely assumed.

9 Gross Fixed Capital Formation is a valuation of investment in land improvement and reclamation, irrigation, drainage, farm buildings and equipment. GFCG in agriculture is given for some developing countries in the United Nations' *National Account Statistics* which is issued annually.

10 Two related points are raised here. The first concerns the importance of primary education for the realisation of the effective benefits from the results of agriculture research. With the exception of socialist economies (China, Cuba, North Korea, etc.), statistics on education show that between 30 per cent and 50 per cent of children in many developing countries are denied opportunities for primary education. T.W. Schultz's research has shown that primary schooling is the least costly and most profitable of all schooling as rural children can still do

an appreciable amount of farm work. See his work: *The Economic Value of Education* (1963) and *Investing in People* (1981). The other point deals with the estimated internal rate of return from investment in agricultural research. Since agricultural research is carried out in most developing countries by government institutions, and since the application of the results from research takes a long time, governments are reluctant to allocate sufficient resources with preference for reliance on technology developed by foreign agents. If *all* farmers use the results reached by extension services, the widespread and full effects on productivity and incomes would likely make the internal rate of return in the region of 30–70 per cent. See Ruttan (1982) and Thirtle and Bottomley (1988).

11 There is an extensive literature on the subject of agricultural prices. On its importance to incentives in the allocation of resources see The World Bank – *World Development Report 1986* – Part II, and FAO Study 'Agricultural price policies' Document no. C 85/19, Rome 1985. On its implications for equity and poverty, see, for example, Mellor (1975); The Bulletins of the International Food Research Institute (IFPRI) on specific country experiences; Lipton (1977) *Why Poor People Stay Poor*, particularly Chapter 13 'Price twist'; Ghai and Smith *Agricultural Prices Policy and Equity in Sub-Saharan Africa*, particularly Chapters 5 and 8 on 'Practice and impact'; and Mellor and Desai (ed) (1985) *Agricultural Change and Rural Poverty*. This study shows the relations between prices, agricultural growth and poverty in India, and the views of Desai, Parthasaraty and Ahluwalia in the text are taken from this study.

12 In his study on 'The impact of agricultural policies on income distribution', Ahmad Ibrahim shows that small landholders grow more of the price-controlled traditional crops and less of the non-controlled profitable crops (vegetables and fruit) than larger farmers; a practice which has widened inequality in income distribution among farmers. See Tables 7.A.2 and 7.A.3 in Abdel Malek and A.Tignor (eds) *The Political Economy of Income Distribution in Egypt*, Holmes and Meier, 1982.

Chapter two

The ideological shift and dilemmas facing governments

This chapter explores the puzzle: granted that the conditions generating gross inequalities and poverty incidence in rural areas of most LDCs have remained fundamentally unchanged (or are even worse in some cases), how can we explain the post-1980 shifts in development thinking, particularly with regard to land reform policy issue.

To probe this question, we first examine how the problems and policy issues raised in the preceding chapter have been considered by the economists of various periods in their systems of analysis and in furnishing policy advice to developing countries. This is followed by an attempt to identify the factors which contributed to the post-1980 swing in policy prescriptions of international development agencies and donor countries. We focus upon the changing views on government intervention in regulating the market mechanism and the possible implications this has on land reform and poverty reduction. Finally, this chapter examines the dilemmas facing policy makers in LDCs over instituting land reforms, and in their response to the policy prescriptions of external agencies with regard to economic imbalances and inflation. Our concern is with the effects which the IMF-induced financial and economic adjustments are likely to have on the food producing peasants and other rural poor.

Our thesis rests on five propositions:

1. Economics is a social science providing policy choice for problem-solving.
2. The merit of any theorising on economic phenomena is in its relevance to effective poverty problem-solving in LDCs.
3. The understanding of rural development problems in their totality in different settings within an historical context of each country is necessary for meaningful anti-poverty policy prescriptions.
4. The exclusion or inadequate understanding of the institutional framework of agricultural production and exchange leads to deficient understanding of the cumulative causal chain of rural poverty and falling food productivity.

5. The content of the policy prescriptions of analysts, donors, and international assistance agencies is a function of whatever ideology is held by the prescribers and the test of these ideologies is in their actions.

The puzzle in the analytic reasoning behind policy prescriptions

Policy prescriptions for resolving rural under-development problems are partially based on analytical reasoning. Controversy in the professional debate on the reasoning behind policy prescriptions is bound to persist with regard to development issues such as changes in the institution of private rights in land property; limitation of free enterprise in agriculture; and the extent of government intervention in the regulation of the market mechanism and the distribution of wealth. The analytical arguments surrounding these issues influence policy prescriptions in many developing countries through providing them with aid, policy advice, training their young professionals and assessment of their development strategy and programmes. In some cases, the development analysts from donor agencies and rich countries go so far as to condition the terms of aid through the LDCs' acceptance of the donor's perception of just how the LDCs should solve their own domestic problems.

While examining these controversial questions, we need to explore the historical changes in the system of thought with respect to the analysis of the production organisation and the distribution of wealth in agriculture.

From comprehensiveness to the break-up of development issues

The realism in the comprehensive understanding of development issues was the prudent approach followed by the founders of social philosophy and political economy during the 18th and 19th centuries. Their common sense led them to refrain from separating analytical reasoning from observations on social organisation of economic phenomena operating within the laws and customs of society. They did not ignore the institution of land tenure or its political context as habitually followed by contemporary neo-classical economists. Instead, their intellectual construction was rooted in concern about economic phenomena and social organisation embedded in the age-old feudal land tenure systems in Britain and Ireland, and the share-cropping arrangements in France and other parts of the Western Europe of their day. Thus, they did not generalise.

By looking towards the concern of the trinity of economic thought, Adam Smith, Malthus and Ricardo followed by John Stewart Mill, and

Karl Marx, we realise that they had clear vision of the entire economic, social and political forces interwoven in the principles or doctrines which they formulated. They did, of course, reach different conclusions, particularly with respect to adjusting the institution of private property and rent from land, the influence of demographic factors and customs on subsistence levels, the function of the market order and the extent of regulation by the State.

My understanding of their writings is that they abstracted their principles from a number of agrarian events witnessed during the 18th and 19th centuries, from which they also formulated their thoughts on political economy. Initially, there were emerging changes in the factor-market resulting from the invention of machinery which gave a spur to capital-labour substitution and the rural de-population through migration of agricultural labourers. Next, their concern turned to the rapid expansion of giant agricultural corporations in the European colonies which superimposed European conceptions of land property, tenancy and transactions, combined with native forced labour to produce high value cash crops exported to their mother countries.

Also reflected in their writing, was their concern for the changing conception of captitalism in agriculture. This was based on changes in the institution of property in land from the unlimited and arbitrary authority of the British sovereign which granted large estates in exchange for feudal obligation, and defined the contractual rights and duties of landlords and tenants; a process which lasted six centuries until it was settled in 1834 by British Parliamentary legislation. This was accompanied by the series of 'Poor Laws' (1535–1834) for the relief of the destitute and unemployed poor in Britain. The economic effects and the morality of this approach to poverty gave rise to condemnation by both Adam Smith and Karl Marx. Finally, there was the ugly feudal tenure system in Ireland, combined with the displacement of a large number of handloom weavers leading to the Irish famine of 1845–51, which took the lives of one million poor peasants. Deep in poverty indebtedness and out of despair, tenants, poor landless workers and cottiers who were evicted by feudal landlords, land grabbers, bailiffs, large estate managers, trader-speculators (in potatoes and cereal exchange) as well as moneylenders, launched the unprecedented 'land wars' in Ireland. They continued for 13 years, from 1879 to 1892.

Against this sketched background, and within the historical context of agrarian episodes came many economic principles on which present economic thoughts are chiefly based. The founders of economics observed, understood, and analysed the interlocking socio-political forces and the working of class conflicts among landlords, tenants, workers and traders in the dynamics of the economy. Although all agreed that

45

the evils of the old feudal tenure relations should not happen again, they differed widely on the role of the State in the protection of reform of production relations in agriculture – on subsistence wages, and on land taxation.

For example, Adam Smith and Malthus advocated the 'harmonic' functioning of the market forces as a 'law of nature'. Although Adam Smith was against absentee landowners, monopoly with regard to corn and rising rents, neither did he favour an elaborate apparatus of government control on the individual strivings for self-interest. In his words, 'I have not great faith in political arithmetic' (Smith, 1776: 50). He criticised the fixed rates of land tax irrespective of rising rents being extracted by landlords from their tenants. He stressed the disadvantages of rents in kind and services and condemned these arrangements for being 'frequently hurtful to the tenant and to the community . . . high rents and church tithe . . . 'left the tenants poor and beggarly . . .' (Smith, 1776: 783).

It was Ricardo's corn model that explained the origin of rent from land and the determinants of the landlord profit in agriculture characterised by a scarcity of land and diminishing returns. He also provided an explanation of the accumulation of surplus and the functional distribution of income from realised growth. This led to the understanding of the monopoly power of the landlords in receiving high rents from land under both controlled and free trade. Ricardo did not favour restrictions on this monopoly power exercised by the landlords. John Stewart Mill, however, as a scholar and Member of Parliament, called for more action because he saw the distribution of wealth in the man's making depending on the Law of Society (Book II, Chapter 1). He viewed the state as a mechanism for restraining the evils of unrestricted *laissez-faire* and for helping the large proportion of society who cannot help themselves. He argued for government intervention to abolish the right of primogeniture in land property, to tax the increases in rent from an established base year and to protect, by law, the rights and security of the tenants in general and Irish tenants in particular. In 1879 he formed the Land Tenure Association in Britain, to which he was subsequently elected President. His intellectual efforts inspired the enactment of the Landlord and Tenant Act followed by the first Agricultural Holding Act in 1875 and Tenants Compensation Act of 1890.

The assault on private property in land came from Karl Marx who called for the introduction of property in common by the collective power of the masses (workers' state). He viewed the state as the instrument of capitalists' monopoly power and the government as 'an executive committee for managing the common affairs of the whole bourgeoisie'. He viewed the capitalist mode of production in the British and French land tenure systems as responsible for the exploitation of labourers and tenants by landlords, the rising class struggle and social disintegration of the economy. Marx condemned the 'laws of nature' and the sacredness of private property. He considered the combination of rent from land, interest and profit received by landlords and lending agents as appropriated by means of monopoly power.

With the strength of the marginal analysis school in the second half of the last century and the leap of the neo-classical economics in this century, the comprehensive understanding of the complex socio-political forces in shaping economic phenomena in agriculture has been broken up into narrow areas of concern. Economics as one branch of social science has been divided into theoretical and applied disciplines. In the marginal analysis school of thought, land is treated as just a divisible factor of production, like seeds, fertiliser, tractors, credit and labour. The theoretical apparatus has distanced itself from political economy based on elements of social organisation in the *dynamics* of growth and shifted towards *static* equilibria of physical commodity relations. Thus, economics has become dominated by a 'single paradigm of maximization of resource allocations' via the market (Gordon, 1965 and Coats, 1969). However, not all neo-classical economists consider the market as a distributive mechanism because of the separation of efficiency of resource allocation from income distribution and because of emerging market power of the monopolists. There are some who are concerned with externalities to resource efficiency and monpolistic competition. The concerns were initiated by the work of Chamberlain and Robinson in the early 1930s.

In short, the conversion of economics as a social science into a Newtonian-type approach primarily concerned with economic administration of scarce resources has distorted rural development issues. The institution of land tenure, authority of the state and land-based power are excluded. These issues as well as class conflicts and human motivations are left to anthropologists, psychologists, sociologists, political scientists, and historians. The separation of theoretical economic under rigid assumptions from applied economics, and the further separation of politics and institutions from economics has weakened its strength in problem-solving and in the comprehensive understanding of rural under-development. The low income and consumption levels of the poor peasants were rooted exactly in what had been put aside; the complexity of institutional-cum-sociopolitical forces underlying the distribution of productive assets, notably land and the corresponding power structure.

The experience of developing countries in the post-war era proved the inadequacy of this narrow approach to understand and tackle the problems of rural poverty, and gross inequalities. Experience has shown that the use of a standardised criterion of economic growth as a development objective in an unregulated market economy of poor countries could not reduce poverty at a socially acceptable rate. It was recognised that solutions for poverty and other rural under-development problems were not to be found primarily in technical change, foreign aid and material capital investment. On this conjuncton, Seers (1969) wrote:

> It looks as if economic growth may not merely fail to solve social and political difficulties; certain types of growth can actually cause them. . . . It looks like a preference for avoiding the real problems of development. (In Uphoff and Ilchman, 1972: 123)

Towards broadening the narrow analytical system

It was inevitable that the boundaries of the analytical apparatus of neo-classical economics, had to be expanded and new analytical tools had to be found. This concern did not arise from intellectual curiosity. Instead, it was based on sufficient evidence accumulated from the interaction with different settings in developing countries after the Second World War. Economists and other social scientists from academic institutions, international organisations and donor countries were called upon by LDCs' governments to examine their development problems; to assist in formal planning techniques; to furnish advice on the formulation and implementation of land reform and rural development programmes and to train their national personnel in these fields (e.g., Taiwan, Japan, North Korea, India, Bolivia, Chile and Iraq during the 1940s and 1950s). The author was substantially involved during the 1950s and 1960s with the programmes of Egypt, Ecuador, Iraq and Paraguay and for a short time in Cuba.

From their encounter with poverty, landlessness, small farmers' institutional constraints, dual economic structure of agriculture (modern and traditional subsistence) and systems of government which were shaped during the colonial period in most LDCs, development economists fostered active roles for government intervention and purposeful planning for development. The aim was to respond to the rising development needs of the LDCs to realise their overriding objective of food security and a rapid alleviation of mass poverty. The analytical apparatus lying behind policy formulation was to combine the principles of economics with statistics and to have a full appreciation of social organisation, institutions and political power shaping the economy within the historical context of each country. The thrust was the question of income distribution which required a more active role of governments in the redistribution of productive assets and accrued income towards a large section of the population living in absolute poverty. It has been argued that these policy prescriptions accelerate economic growth from a wider participation of a large section of LDCs' agricultural labour force. Increased income and productivity would then result from greater access to land and technology, and effective demand for goods and services would also increase. Their income and consumption would grow at rates proportionately higher than those of the rich.

Ideas on institutional economics originated by Thorstein Veblen and John Commons earlier in the present century with respect to the importance of human values and attitudes were of use to this expanded analytical approach, as well as to the clarification of the meaning of property and security of expectation in transactions backed by law. Equally valuable were the ideas of John M. Keynes (1935) and Michal Kalecki (1954) on the combined merits of macro-economic analysis and the role of the government in economic management and greater public expenditure. This combination determines the volume of aggregate employment and effective demand necessary to resolve capitalism's instability and unemployment in the midst of plenty. The relevance of Keynes' theory to land reform lies in his strong support of government intervention and of land reform's expected contribution to increasing employment and purchasing power (Singer, 1985).

As the conventional system of analysis expanded, new concepts were formulated, including meeting basic needs, redistribution with growth, participation, entitlement, development planning for economic policy cumulative causation of poverty, the efficient and innovative abilities of small farmers, food security, social cost-benefit analysis, etc. Clearly, the use of the expanded analytical apparatus has required interdisciplinary contributions from economists, statisticians, political scientists, anthropologists, sociologists, psychologists, nutritionists, experts in health, education and systems of government. There is extensive literature on the subject of the relevance of the development economics approach to LDCs.[1]

This post-war orientation in development thinking has strengthened the case for a speedy assault on poverty, and for the removal of institutional barriers in order to accelerate rural development. Nevertheless, not all development economists are pre-land reform. They do not all agree that redistribution of private landed property and the corresponding rural power are necessary for the reduction in poverty and alleviation of inequalities. In her defence of heterogeneity, Frances Stewart says:

> Developing countries themselves are not homogeneous . . . because of differences in customs, colonial experience, geography and culture. No single development economics is likely to be appropriate to all (Stewart, 1971: 324).

There is a consensus on the merits of development planning as a technique for rapidly expanding the productive potential of LDCs to attain desired growth within a defined period of time. However, the nature of land reform precludes it from appearing in advance by planning technocrats in their designs of development plans. In this way, it is utterly different from planning education and health services, import-substitution, taxation and land reclamation. The experience of Egypt, Cuba, Iraq, South Korea, Syria and South Yemen indicates that planning for the distribution of income from investment and output growth started *after* land reforms were instituted and the power structure altered. This lesson was confirmed by David Morowitz in his careful review of 25 years' experience in 26 developing countries during the period 1950–75. He says:

> The historical experience suggests that it simply may not be possible to grow first and redistribute later, because the structure of growth may largely fix the pattern of distribution, at least until much higher levels of *per capita* income are approached. That is to say, if greater equality of income is to be an objective in the medium term, it may be necessary to tackle it as a first priority by land reform, mass education . . . rather than leaving it until after growth has taken place. (Morowitz, 1977: 41).

Where the consistent political will to alleviate poverty exists development plans at their best can determine public investment priorities to benefit, within a time frame, the pre-defined categories of the rural poor, and backward agricultural areas. However, without starting from a base of an egalitarian agrarian system, reducing poverty in relative and absolute terms would take several decades, perhaps a generation.

The current relapse

A missing piece of the puzzle is why the conceptual contribution of development economics did not win the entire field of development thought in the economic profession. Why has it been treated as an appendix to general economics (basically abstracted from industrial countries)? Why has this conceptual contribution been persistently attacked by pro-classical eocnomists who continue to influence policy makers of many LDCs and who have managed to keep the strategic positions in the IMF, World Bank and the rich Western governments.

In fact, attack and counter-attack is not new in development theory. It was triggered in the first half of the present century by the analytical arguments and perceptions of Veblen, Commons, Mitchell, Keynes,

Knight, Kalecki and Myrdal, whose conceptual contributions were intended to expand the neo-classical theoretical apparatus. Their experience provided insight into the cumulative causes of development problems; it prompted them to include relevant social arrangements and to shift their emphasis from the narrow and static micro-focus of efficiency to the dynamic macro-economic focus of development. Combined with this was an understanding of the political elements in government intervention to regulate the market mechanism. Recently, the assault on this broadened approach has gained strength, as presented by Deepak Lal in his *The Poverty of 'Development Economics'* (1983), and counter-argued by Stewart (1985) and Toye (1987).

As we understand the main views (which are relevant to rural development) held by opponents, they rest on a central theme of the efficient allocation of resources through: a minimal government intervention; dominance of a private sector free of price control by the state; pro-multinationals, plantations, large and medium private farmers and progressive small farmers; export-led agricultural production to relieve pressure on balance of payments; greater investment in training; and discouraging import-substitution policy. Thus, the emphasis is on the supply side and the monetary management of the economy. It is neither on the demand structure (especially the low effective demand of the poor), nor on the institutional order which crippled agriculture and its food production sector. In agriculture, the overriding concern is output growth, irrespective of distributional consequences and at the cost of the food-producing peasant and wage-based agricultural worker. Small tenants, sharecroppers, and landless labourers wishing to own land can supposedly borrow credit on the market in competitive agriculture. Thus land reform is negated.

The opponents attribute any malfunctioning of the economy to government systems of planning and regulations of the free functioning of the market mechanism (fostered by development economists), not to its imperfect functioning in developing countries nor to the institutional obstacles, defective land tenure system and related land-based market power in agriculture.

Ironically, the writings and policy advice of this counter-movement present the current performance of South Korea and Taiwan as paradigms of success of the advocated development policy. Empirical studies trace their current performance back to 1945–53 when major land reforms and the restructuring of their rural power and economies were effectively implemented. The early restructuring has substantially reduced landlessness; raised productivity, consumption and real wages; and induced technical change. It also realised greater equalities in the distribution of income and services; provided the peasants with the institutional framework required for production incentives. These

51

institutional changes, in turn, generated higher agricultural GDP growth (see Chapter 6). Hence, egalitarian agrarian systems in South Korea and Taiwan combined with directing compensations (which were paid to ex-landlords), towards non-agricultural investment have contributed to financing industrialisation in its first phase and they have led to greater export earnings (Fei *et al.*, 1979, Adelman, 1978, 1984, and Dong Wan and Yang Boo, 1984).

It is also ironic that the national economies of South Korea and Taiwan have been controlled by an archetype of an authoritarian system of government characterised by successful development planning and efficient management. Planning for development to help economic policy has been followed by most LDCs after India's lead in the early 1950s, but with different structure and content. Planning was conceptually promoted by leading economists, notably Arthur Lewis, Jan Tinberger and Ragnar Frisch, who were awarded the Nobel Prize for their contributions to development theory and planning. Thus land reform and development planning, have, in a sense, been victims of their success. This success was realised in South Korea and Taiwan, by the very means which are currently attacked by the pro neo-classical economists.

After independence from the long period of colonial rule, LDCs are in a race against time, and a struggle against persisting malnutrition and poverty. If they find it necessary to remove institutional barriers in agriculture and to plan investment, the type of economic growth, and the distribution of benefits, economists and the international financing agencies should not question their right to do so. Toye rightly says:

> It could be asked by what authority do pro-classical economists, who pose as value-free social scientists, presume to specify what objectives a developing country should have? As policy advisors, they claim to be technicians who can appropriately prescribe the efficient means to achieve given ends. None of this provides an intellectual basis from which to challenge particular preferred ends of policy (by developing countries). . . . (Toye 1987: 25)

How then can we explain these dramatic shifts in development thinking? We learnt from Aristotle that puzzles or perplexities arouse interest and that wondering leads to a search for an explanation. It may perhaps be argued that we are perplexed by the unperplexing. But aren't violent swings of approaches to practical policies on the rapid alleviation of gross inequalities, under-nutrition and mass poverty worthy of exploration?

One explanation is in the seeming lack of agreement on the fundamental elements constituting 'development' and its policy content.

There is also no coherent theory on income distribution on which all economists agree (see the reviews by Ranadive, 1978; Bigsten, 1983; and Anand and Kanbur, 1984). Despite the intellectual efforts invested since the 1950s on theorising development supported by hard evidence from LDCs' past experience, there have been continuous shifts of analytic reasoning and focus over the recent decades. Both advocates and opponents are heavily armed with professional arguments in their intellectual war. The debate continues, enriching literature and discussion at annual meetings of the professional economists.

There is another possible explanation which is related to the first. It originates in the domain of ideology with regard to the institution of property, the roles of the market and the state in the distribution of wealth. Economists and other social scientists think and respond to development problems within a framework of beliefs, driven by a set of motives and intentions. Such disguised ideomotion – impossible to identify independently – is, of course, derived from their own societal values, particularly its preference on the ideology governing the institution of property. The mental state is reflected in explaining *why* and *what* is accepted or rejected from a wide range of concepts, and policy ideas in respect to particular circumstances of developing countries. In blending these together, the analyst is not value-free, despite claiming the contrary. Depending on the degree of value judgements used, his or her choice of analytical principles (abstracted from capitalist-based or Marxist economies, then supported by data collected and fitted into the framework of arguments) influence conclusions reached. In turn, they affect the recommendations to be made on such practical problems as institutional means to hold agricultural land, employment of the agricultural landless workers, production organisation related to the size distribution of farms, subsidising prices or commodities consumed by the poor, and the allocation of imported scarce means of production between landlords and peasants.

However, vigorous statistical analysis tends to reduce the degree of bias. Still, the degree of freedom of rural development analysts is reduced by whatever ideology is held by whoever commands the major source of their incomes whether academic institutions, development assistance agencies, or the government.[2] After insight gained from his long involvement in development problems of poor countries, Gunnar Myrdal was concerned about this ideological parenting, writing:

> Social scientists are human, some as we know well, are all too human; and they are part of a social system and a culture. Our research interests, the particular approach we choose, the course we follow in drawing inferences and organizing our finding, are not determined by facts alone. . . . Our lack of curiosity about our own peculiar

53

behavior as researchers should be surprising . . . our behavior can be easily ascertained from our writing. (Myrdal, 1968, Vol. I: 6)

Our discussion suggests that the analytical approach to understanding under-development in its totality has suffered from two relapses. The first after the neo-classical economists' abrupt break with the comprehensive system of the political economy established by the prudent founders of economics in the 18th and 19th centuries. This has resulted in chopping the analytical tools into separate fragments. The second, recently occurred, accompanying rising financial and trade problems since 1979, and a change in ideologies of the powerful industrialised countries in their policies for development aid. Furthermore, the total understanding of the cumulative causation of poverty and the institutional determinants of malnutrition and gross inequality in rural areas has been distorted in two ways: the first is discarding the political power structures which influence government action.

The second is operational. The design of rural development projects, and the definitions of their social objectives are, in most cases, ambiguous. This ambiguity results in reducing the potential for rural development as programmes and projects are designed to administer delivery of material and services in politically-chosen areas. These areas can often have a heterogeneous rural class with conflicting interests and needs. Thus, most of the powerless rural poor and the real issues in land tenure and related power structures tend to get passed by. Yet, within this confusion, developing countries will continue to look for advice from economists and other social scientists.

The puzzle of shifting international assistance prescriptions

Although land reform is primarily the responsibility of the sovereign governments of developing countries, donor countries and international financing agencies (IA) have a powerful influence on their policy-makers. They do play an important catalytic role in shaping LDCs' policies on resource use and income distribution, despite their relatively low share in total investment. They rely mostly on the use of both linguistic devices and the financial instruments of power.

It is useful to start with the central issue addressed here in the form of a hypothesis: 'the shift in the content of policy prescriptions provided in the foreign assistance to LDCs corresponds to shifts in the internal ideologies of the prescribers and not necessarily to changing conditions of rural poverty in LDCs'. The assumptions on which the exploration of this proposition is based are as follows:

1. The content of the donor and IA's policy prescriptions for how to approach LDCs' rural development problems and what should be or should not be done, is a function of the former's set of ideologies and internal politics.
2. The technical functionaries (including economists) employed by the donors and IAs are intellectually conditioned by their employers/institutions' ideologies, even if in the functionary's set of beliefs, the policy prescriptions are irrelevant.
3. The test of the donors and IAs' ideologies is in their action.
4. The prescriptions to tackle the LDCs' rural under-development problems cannot be separated from their distributional consequences.
5. The prescriptions can be broken down into two broad categories: that favouring a *laissez-faire* policy of the dominant free play of market mechanism in agriculture leaving the concentration of land, incomes and power unchanged; and pro-land reform policy and reduction in gross inequalities and poverty in rural areas through government intervention.
6. If the policy prescriptions ignore the central problems of poverty, malnutrition, declining food productivity and gross inequalities, the prescriptions are either irrelevant or pursuing the vested interests of the prescribers.

Because the term ideology is ambiguous and does not possess a meaning on which all its users agree (Corbett, 1965), and because we have little competence in international politics, this discussion will be limited to the identification of the elements in the shift in international development assistance in respect to land reform and poverty over the period 1950–86. To make the discussion manageable, it shall be confined to three IAs considered very powerful in the world today: the United States Agency for International Development (AID), the World Bank (WB) and the collective influence of the major industrialised countries known as the Group of Seven. Unfortunately, data on the Soviet Union and its allies in the Socialist bloc in respect of their external assistance to LDCs in the sphere of agriculture and land reform is not accessible.

The ideological complex

There is a complex of three sets of beliefs: the donors and IAs, the recipient country and the employed technocrats, including economists and other social scientists. Among these three parties, there may be harmony, or conflict. The influence of the third set, however, should be reduced, or even excluded, as it consists of national and international civil servants who are expected to articulate whatever ideology their employers possess.

Perhaps no other policy issue is more susceptible to this ideological complex than land reform and related income redistribution and production-organisation. The articulation for or against land reform is at the heart of this complex, manifested in the ideological preference for private individual property or social ownership with collective farming. Will donors and IAs justify or argue against the imposition of a ceiling on private property and limitation of the entrepreneur's freedom in renting out land or lending credit? Will they recommend State intervention as an alternative to a market determination of input and product prices, wages and profit in agriculture? If a limitation of private property is to be supported, and the principle of expropriation of land is to be justified, will donors and AIs also support the extension of the same limitations to foreign plantations including subsidiaries of multinationals? Will an ideal of equity in opportunities and the economic freedom be an alloy of ideals, and contradiction if it is to be extended to the landless workers and the rural poor?

The ideological shift in the US stance on land reform

After the Second World War, the United States' foreign development assistance vigorously pursued land reform as a major redistributive and stabilising policy. Past experience suggests three possible explanations, within capitalist ideology, for this strategy. The first is moral. To satisfy the American ideology founded by Thomas Jefferson and Abraham Lincoln according to which the entitlement to holding agricultural private property is considered a prerequisite to democracy and market economy. This conception was instituted early in 1862 by the Homestead Act (Family Farm). The second motive is political: to counter potential communist movements among the desperately poor peasants in LDCs. The third is economic: to secure rural stability conducive to American private investment in LDCs' agriculture and to expand the internal market for American manufactured goods. The growth of production and potential rise in the incomes of land reform beneficiaries are anticipated to lead to an increase in their effective demand.

If our interpretation is correct, we can understand the vigorous intervention of the USA in instituting land reform programmes in Japan, Taiwan and South Korea, and in their provision of financial support for implementing land reform in Southern Italy as part of the Marshall Plan for Europe. This successful experience in the late 1940s and early 1950s encouraged the United States to pursue its pro-land reform policy and to extend its assistance to LDCs. To integrate this ideology into the Federal Government functions, President Truman entrusted its implementation to the newly established Technical Cooperation Administration (TCA). As one of its first acts, the TCA held the first World Conference on Land Tenure (Madison, Wisconsin, 1951). The Conference was instrumental in disseminating subtle ideas on land reform based on professional reasoning and empirical evidence.

However, where the land reform programmes were designed and intended to expropriate large foreign-owned estates including those of American multinational corporations, US support was absent, frustrating the land reforms, as occurred in Guatemala and the Philippines in the 1950s (for a detailed account, see Olson, 1974). Within this framework of inconsistency between ideals and realities, a new initiative was promulgated by President Kennedy in 1961 when he immediately stated his ideals in his inaugural address: 'If a free society cannot help the many who are poor, it cannot save the few who are rich . . . our pledge is to assist free governments in casting off the chains of poverty.' The concern of the Kennedy administration was primarily focused on the implications of high land concentrations in Latin America, combined with absentee landlords and increasing numbers of landless workers who had virtually no chance of acquiring land on their own through the defective market mechanism. There was also a fear of the potential response of peasants' movements in some Latin American countries following the successful revolution in Cuba and its Soviet-backed land reform policy. This concern was expressed in President Kennedy's words:

> . . . there is no place in democratic life for institutions which benefit the few while denying the needs of the many, even though the elimination of such institutions may require far reaching and difficult changes such as land reform and tax reform and a vastly increased emphasis on education, health and housing![3]

The events which followed, suggest that his statement was not merely political rhetoric, but a genuine commitment. Four initiatives were taken in the early 1960s:

1. The creation of the 'Alliance for Progress' programme in which land reform, combined with social services, was central, and for which the US Congress allocated US$500 million.
2. The establishment of the Inter-American Development Bank (IDB) in which the USA's contribution amounted to 45 per cent of the IDB's capital on the proviso that the funds were to be used for social progress including land settlements and reforms.
3. The establishment of the Land Tenure Center at the University of Wisconsin for training, research and for furnishing policy advice to LDCs' governments.
4. The issue of the Foreign Assistance Act 1961 and the creation of the Agency for International Development (AID) to implement the programme.

Sections 102 and 103 of the Act are directed to land reform and it is useful to quote a few lines which indicate the perception of the US government of the time:

> The principle purpose of bilateral development assistance is to help the poor majority of people in developing countries to participate in a process of equitable growth through productive work and to influence the decisions that shape their lives, with the goal to increase their incomes . . . the establishment of more equitable and more secure land tenure arrangements is one means by which the productivity and income of the rural poor will be increased.

This powerful reasoning was articulated by the American Secretary of Agriculture at the 'USAID Spring Review on Land Reform', Washington DC, June 1970, and the World Conference on Agrarian Reform and Rural Development, Rome, 1979 in which the author participated.

In 1980, the Republican party came to power, and under the Reagan administration, the official stance shifted to the opposite pole. Compare the preceding expressions of pro-land reform policy to the new official direction in foreign aid to developing countries published in 1986 under the title *Policy Determination on Land Tenure*. The dramatic shift is apparent: no support to government intervention in private land redistribution, but the distribution of *public lands* in settlement schemes and cadastral surveys to be financially aided; land to be purchased in the open market by American assistance if needed; and the supply of inputs for production must be done through the private sector if provided by the American aid, etc. This new perception was reiterated in November 1987, when the American Delegation to the FAO Conference held in Rome insisted that the market mechanism and not the instituted land reform should realise equal distribution of land.

What, then, has happened to the American ideals set forth earlier to help the poor majority participate in equitable growth through secure land tenure and more equitable distribution of land? Two American scholars, Gary Olson (1974) and John Montgomery (1984), analysed the changes in US foreign policy and offered some explanations. Apart from the special circumstances of US involvement in the land reforms of Japan, Taiwan, South Korea, Southern Italy and Bolivia, it seems that progress in land reform was not made a *condition* for American aid. This contrasts to the Swedish government's conditional assistance to Ethiopia in the early 1970s. Professor Montgomery believes that the decline in the use of foreign aid to foster land reform does not represent a fundamental retreat from the Americans' ideals, as the ideals behind expanding opportunities for the landless peasants, the ideology of realising the peasants' hopes for democracy and the American fear of communism remain intact. He also harkens back to the influence of the Americans' disappointment with their involvement in land reforms in Vietnam, Chile and some Central American countries (Montgomery, 1984: 133-7).

We suggest two more interpretations. One is that not all ideals, even those stated in the US Constitution have been completely implemented within the USA itself as the equal opportunities for all citizens. Even after the passage of the Civil Rights Act 1964, the American government have been unable to realise the full extent of the ideals with regard to America's black community. This inability persists in terms of unemployment rates, average income, incidence of poverty and the black community's dependence on government transfer payments. This inconsistency was first analysed by Myrdal (1944) in his *American Dilemma*, and recently by Vronam (AER, May 1986). The other interpretation is the growing good relations between the USA, the Soviet Union and China when the latter's agressive attitudes towards land reform recently softened in the international community. It seems that this emerging framework for international co-operation works against the question of land reform. Poverty and land reform are not part of the human rights disputes, or those world issues which preoccupy the super powers.

Whatever the reasons might be, land reform as a policy issue in American foreign policy is dead under the ideology of the Republican party as implemented by the Reagan administration. This complete turn around presents a sharp contrast to the ideology pursued in the 1950s, 1960s and 1970s under the Democratic party administrations of Presidents Truman, Kennedy, Johnson and Carter.

The puzzle behind the World Bank's shifting policy

In the domain of international development assistance and lending, the World Bank (WB) is certainly a powerful institution, influencing the thinking of policy-makers and the planning technocrats in many LDCs. As a multilateral assistance agency in the United Nations system, WB has a comparative advantage in collecting data and in undertaking field research on fundamental issues in rural development. This advantage is reflected in the WB's intellectual contribution to the understanding of the relationships between economic growth, income distribution and meeting the basic needs of the poor. Under the leadership of McNamara, a close associate of the late President Kennedy, the WB accorded high priority to agriculture in general, and land reform and rural poverty in particular, between 1972 and 1980. It was the golden age, so to speak, of these rural development policy issues, both intellectually and operationally. With persuasive arguments and empirical reasoning, the WB showed in its celebrated publications how rapid alleviation of poverty via an increase in productivity, employment and the purchasing power of the poor peasants would come through.

59

... in developing countries, land represents a high proportion of total wealth ... inegalitarian patterns of land-ownership are a major source of income inequality ... the owners of land possess political and economic power which can be exercised in ways that harm the interests of the bulk of the rural people ... agricultural development cannot do all it might to improve rural life *if* the distribution of land-ownership is highly skewed. (Agricultural Sector Paper: 30–5)

In its guidelines for lending and granting assistance to developing countries, the WB stated 'In countries where increased productivity can effectively be achieved *only* subsequent to land reform, the Bank *will not* support projects which do not include land reform' (Land Reform Policy Paper, 1974: 11). In the 1970s, nearly 55 per cent of the total World Bank lending to agriculture went to poverty-orientated rural development projects. This does not mean that all funds invested in these projects reached the poor and directly benefited the landless workers.[4]

As US foreign policy on aid to LDCs shifted, the WB's emphasis on egalitarian agricultural development faded away by the turn of the 1980s. Its development perception had suddenly changed, and its lending and assistance had declined, despite continuing talk about concern for poverty. In 1986 and 1987, the share of the 'Agriculture and Rural Development' sector in total WB loans and field operations was far below its annual average in 1977–81, particularly in Asia and Africa where rural poverty is concentrated. Apart from this regional decline, lending for rural development (poverty-orientated projects) as a percentage of the total agricultural sector fell from its 1977–9 level of 52 per cent to 29 per cent to 1983–5. The regional change, based on data calculated from the WB 1986 and 1987 Annual Reports is shown in Table 2.1.

Table 2.1 **Regional change in the World Bank allocation for agriculture and rural development 1977–87**

Annual Average	1977–81 %	1986 %	1987 %	Percentage change in 1987 over 1977–81
East Asia and Pacific	33	15	13	−20
South/Eastern Asia	40	36	10	−30
Southern Africa	32	20	28	−4
Western Africa	38	21	23	−15
Latin America	23	41	23	0

Why were concerns for land reform and greater equality in income distribution short-lived? Two questions need to be asked: Why is this swift conversion in the WB's perception for development? and what is the new prescription? The answer for the first question is to be found

in the World Development Reports 1982–7 and in the heading of an article
appearing in the WB's *Research News*, 1985. It reads, 'The World has
changed, so has the Bank'. But to what fundamental changes since the
turn of the 1980s does the Bank refer? What changes would justify such
a dramatic shift? In our specific concern for agriculture and the conditions of the rural poor, we see that far from fundamental changes, there
has been little basic change, and that the technical institutional obstacles
have, since 1960, continued into the 1980s in most LDCs. We have seen
in Chapter 1 that land concentration actually *worsened* in many LCs and
that low food productivity has also been alarmingly persistent. Institutional obstacles to growth and technical change in the declining food
producing sector also continue. The number of the poor and malnourished
has considerably increased. As Toye says: 'The inadequacy of development (in LDCs) has always to be related to some particular cause.' These
causes are to be found in 'structural inequalities in international economic
relations, the lack of internal political will or ability to redistribute assets
and income, and the neglect of popular participation in development.
A novel set of policies would have to lay its stress elsewhere' (Toye,
1987: 48).

The WB's new policy prescription is based on a market mechanism
freed from government intervention and planning for development. This
is intended to ensure that resources are used more efficiently by the
private sector, leaving the pattern of the distribution of land, income
and power unchanged. 'Unemployment and poverty are to be alleviated
by creating a policy environment which will encourage foreign and
domestic private investment' and makes markets and incentives work
(World Development Report, 1986: 43). Yes, markets and incentives
can work in LDCs, but under what conditions of social organisation,
and in which institutional systems and legal frameworks? In fact, the
Western conception of a free exchange in factor markets does not even
exist in many rural areas of LDCs. Where the distribution of land ownership and opportunities is highly skewed, the market works for the benefit
of traders, large and medium farmers and multinational corporations,
while most probably harming the poor peasants and the landless workers.
The rural poor make up the socio-economic group most likely to be hard
hit by the WB's post-1980 policy package; for how can small peasants
and landless workers respond to price incentives and profit opportunities
from technical change if they have neither the secure tenure of land,
nor legitimate access to land and credit? Consider the reasoning of the
World Bank itself, as it was forcefully presented in the 1970s, *prior* to
its shift in policy.

A redistributive land reform can go a long way towards a solution
(to rural poverty problems) in a relatively short period. Without

such a reform, however, it is difficult to see much prospect of major advances in reducing poverty in rural areas. . . . (World Bank 1977: 116)

The low productivity and malnutrition of a major section of the agricultural labour force lies, therefore, not in the scarcity of productive resources in agriculture, but in how these productive assets are owned and used under prevailing institutional arrangements.

What of worsening foreign debts, terms of trade and balance of payments? Could these conditions justify the sharp turn in World Bank policy? Though increased in scale, they are long-standing problems, and though it is necessary to solve them, they cannot be solved solely in terms of a financial medicine. The problems represent a long-term structural imbalance which should be resolved within a long-term perspective broad enough to realise sustained rural *development* and not only economic *growth*. Given the available empirical evidence, the World Bank's new policy of production adjustment is likely to exacerbate the already skewed distribution of income and power in favour of the medium and large farms closely integrated with the international market via exports and the multinationals.

Problems were compounded in the 1980s by the policies of the major Western industrialised countries themselves, whose leaders have spurred on WB's current preoccupations. These policies include offering LDCs excessive lending facilities in the 1970s, followed by an unprecedented rise in interest rates in real terms, and an over-appreciation of the exchange value of the US dollar. Concurrently, demand for LDCs' primary agricultural products was reduced both in volume and in prices, and a slow-down in the OECD member countries' annual economic growth rates from an average 4.7 per cent in 1965–73, (before the sharp rise in oil prices in 1973) to 2.8 per cent in 1974–80 and to 2.5 per cent in 1986. The slow-down led to rising unemployment in their economies. Between 1980 and 1985, industrialised countries also reduced their annual rate of concessional external assistance to LDCs. As creditors and importers of primary products, they were also unwilling to open their markets to goods produced by their debtors from LDCs.

Candidly, the real power behind the WB's swift change in direction lies in the post-1980 changes in the internal politics and development philosophy of Western industrialised governments which themselves govern the WB's overall policy. There is an obvious correlation between the American foreign policy outlined earlier and of the World Bank in respect to land reform and concern for inequalities and poverty in LDCs. A similar parallel seems to exist with respect to the change in the pre-1980 development ideologies of the governments of the UK's Labour party, contrasted with those of the Conservative party government under the leadership of Mrs Thatcher.[5] The influence of the American and British governments lies in their voting power in the affairs of the WB (along with other members of the Group of Seven) and their respective shares in the WB's capital stock. The broad lines of WB and IMF policies on assistance to LDCs seem to follow the collective decision made in the round of summit meetings attended by the Group of Seven, which includes Canada, West Germany, France, Italy, Japan, UK, and the USA. The representatives of the USA, and the UK, ensure that the WB's and IMF's operational programmes are consistent with the interests of their governments' policy goals. The influence of the Group of Seven is obvious, considering their control of 49 per cent of the voting power and 51 per cent of the WB's capital stock in 1986. The USA holds the greatest share at 21 per cent of total capital stock, and 20 per cent of total voting power in the WB, entitling her to hold senior posts, including the Presidency.

So, another piece of the puzzle behind the sharp turn away from the pre-1980 stance is found. But the puzzle still remains incomplete with respect to the assertive WB reasoning that the bank has changed because the development problems of LDCs have changed. The assertion seems inconsistent, and even contradictory to the economic justification forcefully argued by the WB of the 1970s explained earlier. One explanation may lie in the domain of morality and the ideological complex suggested at the start of this section.

Our discussion suggests the following:

1. Land reform as a policy issue in rural development with a focus on redistribution of wealth and income has been a victim of changes in the operational ideologies of the major countries and international institutions entrusted with development aid to poor countries.
2. That the shift cannot be attributed to complacency about improvements in LDCs' conditions of poverty and their horrendous proportions of malnutrition, landlessness and declining food productivity.
3. That the stated hypothesis in the introduction tends to be confirmed.
4. That the identified shifts and their proclaimed reasonings are likely to confuse students of development policy, disturb progress toward poverty alleviation made by LDCs' development efforts in the 1970s, and could compound the dilemmas facing policy makers in many developing countries.

Dilemmas facing developing countries

To respond to the complex set of problems characterised in the fore-going sections, LDCs are faced with a number of dilemmas. For the purpose of this study, two questions are explored in this section: the political path to institute major land redistribution programmes, and the choice of responses to financial and trade difficulties within the context of each country's distribution of land and power. We will focus on the implications of these dilemmas for the reduction of poverty and income distribution with emphasis on sustained growth of food production.

The dilemma over land reform

The structure of power, which coincides with the distribution of land property and income in many LDCs' rural areas, determines the pace at which justice and tangible evidence of poverty alleviation can be realised. The question is: what form of government can effectively realise this restructuring, whether by choice and negotiation or by obligation? The question carries a number of implications, perhaps clarified by David Hume in 1750, when he said 'For forms of government let fools contest, whatever is best administered is best'.

Historical experience suggests two broad governmental forms and approaches: a government brought by the force of a military action or by a popular revolution of the peasants; and a representative government deciding on land reform by a parliamentary majority within constitutional procedures and the rule of law. Under the former, a small group having the power of force and authority, dissolve parliament, abolish the existing constitution and combine legislative and executive power. The ideology is formulated and implemented with respect to land reform with the assistance of a chosen group of liberal intellectuals and progressive technocrats. The perceptible assumptions of this group of reformers are: that they represent the aspirations and collective frustrations of the mass peasants and landless workers; that they act for the public interest against prevailing vested interests of landlords, money lenders and middlemen supported by a corrupt administration; that their reform ideologies exhibit an alternative to the abused concept of private property and economic liberty practised in the prevailing social order of semi-feudal character; that the existing land-based power structure resisted fundamental changes required to rapidly reduce poverty, and gross inequalities in opportunities.

The dilemma faced is this: the military and revolutionary approach brings rapid and tangible results, but whatever mistakes are made, whatever moral irregularities are committed by the new bureaucracy, they are unaccountable to representative organisations of people, whose freedom of expression is suppressed. Abstinence from public criticism tends to be the rule and not the exception. Consequently, liberties and democratic procedures, (in the Western tradition) are sacrificed. On the other hand, under a democratic order of majority, redistribution of private land and property is slow and tends to bring only a partial solution. It first requires a process of lengthy studies, followed by negotiations, leading to compromise. It is equally susceptible to moral irregularities by the bureaucracy and the attitudes of the urban elite who are sympathetic to landlords' interests. Just which of the two paths is most appropriate is a matter of each country's internal balance of class interests and distribution of power.

History tells us that the military and the authoritarian approach to instituting land reform has dominated during the present century, beginning with the Mexican Revolution of the peasants under the leadership of Emilio Zapata in 1911, followed by the Bolshevik revolution of Soviet Russia, 1917–23. Since the Second World War a series of land reforms having different ideologies and scope of change were implemented as a direct consequence of external forces or domestic military action (*coups d'état*). Land reforms in Japan, Taiwan, South Korea in 1945–52 were initiated with the direct involvement of the USA during their occupation. A similar approach was followed by Soviet power in North Korea, Vietnam, Laos and Eastern European countries. Working with popular movements, authoritarian regimes instituted major land reform programmes in China, 1949–56, Egypt 1952 and 1961, Bolivia 1953, Iraq and Syria 1958, Cuba 1959, Algeria 1962–70, Peru 1963 and 1969, South Yemen 1968, 1970, Ethiopia 1975, Mozambique 1976–80 and Nicaragua 1979. This is not an exhaustive account. Iran, under the authoritarian power of the Shah, instituted a redistributive reform (1962–71) out of choice, convenience and obligation. Several Latin American countries have done, then undone, their half-hearted land reform programmes and there is still too much empty talk about reforms. It would be incorrect to infer that all totalitarian regimes and military rulers are in favour of redistributive land reforms. Many are not. Some have allied with big land owners and industrialists, e.g. Paraguay, Bangladesh, Pakistan (1977–88) and Chile after 1973.

Nor should this account imply that major redistributive programmes are necessarily to be instituted by military regimes or popular revolutions. India (1955–65), Chile (1967–72), and Sri Lanka (1972 and 1975) implemented their partial land reforms by democratic processes. By its nature, this democratic process requires prolonged political manoeuvring with pressure groups and negotiations with landlords on size-ceilings, terms of expropriation and payment of compensation. It took Chile nearly two years (November 1965 to August 1967) to get the parliament to pass (with several compromises) the land reform of President Frei. Sixteen years passed in Sri Lanka, between 1956 when approval of a manifesto pledging land reform was attained, and the issue of Land Reform Act One in 1972. Contrast this with the revolutionary council of Nasser in Egypt, which took one single day to issue the land reform in September 1952.[6]

This point can be elaborated upon. In Chile, a country with a long history of democracy, the election promise of President Frei's government was to redistribute to 100,000 landless families, part of those large farms exceeding the generously prescribed size-ceiling. The result of the two years of parliamentary deliberations was a law, the first article of which states, 'farm property exceeding an area of 80 hectares of irrigated land *may* be expropriated'. Maximum holding for non-irrigated land was not defined. It is this kind of ambiguity which leads to legal loopholes and political compromise which limits the scope of land reform in the democratic approach. In the long process of political manoeuvring and compromise, already frustrated peasants with no direct weight in politics, wait for an uncertain outcome.

The Chilean experience with the democratic approach is relevant to the current dilemma facing Presidents Sarney of Brazil, and Aquino of the Philippines. Both came to power after long military and authoritarian regimes, respectively. The election promise in both countries was to institute land reform. By virtue of her constitutional power, President Aquino could have instituted and initiated the implementation of the promised programme prior to the convening of the Congress. Instead, she issued an ambiguous proclamation in July 1987 in which she left the crucial provision of ceilings on private land ownership and the payment of compensation to be decided by the Congress after the election. With the interests of big land-owners and the interests of multinational corporations well represented in the Congress, a long process of political bargaining and compromise is expected during which social unrest and dissatisfaction of the Philippines Peasants Movement and allied non-government organisations will likely grow.

In Brazil, and since President Sarney signed the 'National Plan for Agrarian Reform' in October 1985, nothing has happened with respect of the implementation of Article II, section 1.5 of the Plan's first part, pertaining to expropriation of private ownership of cultivable but unutilised land estimated at 80 million hectares. Thus, those expectant beneficiaries amounting to 1.4 million agricultural landless households supposed to become new owners of the estimated, but undefined 40 million ha between 1985 and 1989, continue to await political decision, cadastral survey, and the definition of properties not meeting the requirements for 'social function of property'. Without this, the slowly executed settlement schemes on public lands would be their only hope left. In the meantime, Mr Nelson Ribeiro, the Minister of Agrarian Development and Reform (MIRAD) has resigned, and hundreds of agricultural workers have been killed. Their crime was the occupation of the would-be expropriated areas in anticipation of ownership, as promised by the 'Alianca Democratica' during the election campaign.

It is fascinating to follow the progress in these two large countries.

What in fact was accomplished by December 1987, was not the redistribution of land, but the redistribution of words, responsibility and blame for not acting swiftly and for prolonging the state of uncertainty in rural areas. The dilemma is compounded by the widening gap between the high sophistication of the legal profession in formulating loophole ridden laws, and the political will to implement them. The millions of landless agricultural households still wait. Perhaps the prudent words of President Frei on 23 November 1965 contained in his address to Chilean landlords as he introduced his land reform Bill to Parliament may be useful today to many Latin American countries and in particular to Brazil:

> If we do not face the problem now, in a democratic way, I am sure that in the future whoever may assume the presidency would be forced to carry out an agrarian reform. But it is possible that then, after having prevented it being done under a democratic regime, it would be done in a very different way, and in conditions much more extremist and dangerous![7]

Hence, at the start of 1988, it seems that land reform has been on the wane since the end of the 1970s. By then, under different ideological contexts, about 27 developing countries had implemented redistributive land reforms along with the regulation or abolition of tenancy. Since 1980, and despite the prevailing and horrendous incidence of rural poverty, malnutrition and landlessness, the concern for land reform has declined. Yet, as noted by Alain de Janvry: 'it remains an important political issue in most countries of the World. . . . It is abundantly clear that the crises of food production and rural poverty, if anything, are worsening under the current development model' (de Janvry, 1981: 384 and 392 respectively). It is ironic that concern has declined so soon after virtually all developing countries had officially committed themselves, in July 1979 at the World Conference on Agrarian Reform and Rural Development, to take action for the realisation of an 'equitable distribution of land'. At that conference, their governments adopted a Declaration of Principles, a Programme of Action and a Resolution in which they agreed at paragraph 8 of the Declaration that, 'the sustained improvement of rural areas requires fuller and more equitable access to land, water and other natural resources; widespread sharing of economic and political power'. They also agreed to

> impose ceilings on the size of private holdings . . . implement redistribution with speed and determination . . . fix specific targets for the 1980s and 1990s for the reduction of rural poverty . . . concentrate on eliminating conditions of under-nutrition in the quickest possible time and certainly *before* the end of the century. (FAO, 1979: paragraphs I, A (iii) and (vi) and II, A(i) and (iv))

Having participated in the work of that conference, and having also visited several poor countries since 1979, I feel quite perplexed. My experience of countries with high degrees of land concentration, malnutrition and poverty suggests a widening discrepancy between empirical evidence and the rhetoric exhibited at the conference in Rome by several Ministers of Agriculture and Rural Development.[8] They were faced with a dilemma. Had they the courage to abstain from or reject the bold call for action, these Ministers were likely to be condemned by the press, liberal intellectuals and agricultural trade unions (where they existed). They also were likely to be denied the promised foreign aid linked with domestic action on land reform. Had they the conviction of land reform as a policy issue, their government's lack of *political* commitment combined with the absence of a lobby for poor peasants, meant that they would opt to maintain the status quo, merely providing a few services to rural women, and some improvement of agricultural credit in order to receive foreign aid. It is no wonder that a thoroughly-prepared report on the progress made since 1980 says:

> no significant policy or programmes fixing ceilings on the size distribution of private land have taken place since 1980, only a tightening of the implementation of pre-1980 legislation. . . . Even the distribution of public lands [settlement schemes] has slackened due to severe [budgetary] cut-backs. (FAO, 1986c: 48–50)

In sum, it appears that the problem of policy-makers in many developing countries tends to lie, at least in the short term, in the absence of one or more of the three 'Cs': commitment, courage and conviction.

The dilemmas in choosing IMF-induced adjustment policies affecting poverty and malnutrition

Policy-makers in developing countries which have experienced the impact of world economic recession in differing ways, must choose adjustment policies. They either respond on their own initiative, or are influenced by external agents *viz.*, foreign creditors via the IMF's stabilisation programme and the World Bank structural adjustment lending, depending on which of the two agencies takes the lead. The influence is particularly great on the Central Banks and Ministers of the government concerned who decide about the size and components of public expenditure to cut back, for which crops the prices should be raised or reduced, the extent of resources to transfer from one sector of the economy to another. The influence is manifested in how much to devalue the domestic currency, how far to reduce subsidies and whether to cut allocations to health and education, food, and fertiliser subsidies. It is assumed that the policy-makers and their technocrats realise, at least in broad terms, the expected distributional and production effects of such adjustment policies on agriculture relative to other sectors of the economy. In choosing policy instruments for adjustments and the sequence of their implementation they are expected to assess how their policies will affect domestic food production, real wages, food prices, and the poor's levels of consumption.

In the process of accepting these adjustment measures, the policy makers are bound to face dilemmas. By accepting the financial stabilisation and production adjustment package of the IMF and World Bank, the imbalance in the structure of the domestic economy may be slowly corrected and the balance of payments may begin to improve enough to attract the needed foreign exchange. However, they may simultaneously be condemned by certain sections of their society for submitting to foreign pressures, labelled in some countries as 'imperialist agents'. The political stability may be threatened by riots of the urban working class. On the other hand, to exhibit their nationalistic attitude by rejecting the externally proposed set of measures, policy makers may prolong the imbalances, losing their ability to repay foreign debts in the short term, while the burden for their servicing increases. The longer government action is postponed, the narrower their options become. If their short-term policies raise the prices of exportable crops, the volume of agricultural exports and foreign exchange earnings increase, provided that the supply of required inputs does not decline and the world market demand for these crops does not deteriorate in quantity or price levels. Yet, the increased reliance of the entire economy on the export of one or two crops increases vulnerability to external changes. Employment of landless labourers in agriculture may also decline following the cash crops producers' tendency to use more capital-intensive techniques and their inducement to shift resources away from labour-intensive food crops. In turn, there can be a further deterioration of the peasant sector and a fall in food production. Furthermore, this policy choice implies a redistribution of income away from food producers and landless agricultural workers to benefit producers of exportable cash crops.

Another dilemma arises from deciding on major cuts in food subsidies. Although these may improve budget deficits, they are, nevertheless, likely to worsen income distribution, raise food prices and aggravate the already high incidence of malnutrition among the poor in the absence of instituted food distribution programmes. A worsening of the already inferior quality of life is likely to occur in rural areas by substantial cuts in the capital and recurrent public expenditure on health, education, social security and the supply of safe drinking water.

Empirical evidence suggests that policy choice is not quite so neat. In the methodological domain, there are at least two problems. The first is the limitation of data on the likely effects on income transfer between wage earners and profit makers, on food consumption, real wages and incomes of the different categories of the poor. The second is the time-lag between changes arising from adjustment measures with respect to employment opportunities and price levels on the one hand, and the actual response of the farmers as producers, consumers and accumulators of material capital, on the other. For instance, the supply response to trade liberalisation – by farmers who have secure holding of land and who shift resources to increase the production of exportable cash crops – experiences a time-lag between cuts in production inputs subsidies, rise in exportable crops prices and changes in wage levels. Furthermore, immediate effects of adjustment policies are difficult to separate from the medium-term effects of development programmes already in operation for agriculture and which started before 1980. These distributional effects are among the many changes documented from the experience of ten developing countries in the significant study by UNICEF, *Adjustment with a Human Face* (Cornia *et al.*, 1987 and 1988).

In the domain of ideology and policy formulation, countries' experience indicates that policy makers are faced with problems that are inherent in the countries' development strategies which they themselves designed. For example, Brazil's development strategy is that of a market/export-led economic growth within a private property characterised by high concentration. During the recession, its economy was tied to variations in the international market forces; its balance of payment deficits rose sharply; and its agricultural exports' terms of trade fell by 12 per cent in 1982 as the prices of major agricultural exports (coffee, sugar and cocoa) fell substantially. As the impact of the recession deepened, GDP per head fell between 1981 and 1985; inequality in the distribution of income widened; annual growth of agricultural production fell sharply from 3.4 per cent in the 1970s to 2 per cent, and *per capita* food production from 1.6 to 1.2 per cent during 1981–5; food prices rose more rapidly than the cost of living index; food subsidies were cut by 80 per cent (from 5.6 per cent of government expenditure in 1980 to 1.6 per cent in 1985); the health care programme was cut and infant mortality rates rose for Brazil as a whole.

> From a social point of view, the adjustment experience can be considered a failure as macro-economic policies were formulated without any consideration for their human impact and as the social measures implemented to mitigate the impact of such policies were limited in scope, poorly administered, and to a large extent distributionally regressive. (Cornia *et al.*, 1987: 109)

Compare the Brazilian experience with that of China and India, the two most populated countries in the world with very low income per head, and one is convinced of the extent of the preferential importance which policy makers attach to the growth of agriculture, food production and to the welfare of the rural poor. In both countries, policy makers designing their respective development strategies within different ideological frameworks, stressed, self-reliance based on inward-looking development, small-scale foreign borrowing, and high rates of domestic saving to finance expansion in their development programmes. In 1985 the share of domestic saving in GDP was 34 per cent in China and 21 per cent in India. China, with its egalitarian agrarian structure, was virtually insulated from external shocks of the world economic recession, as agricultural exports represent only 20 per cent of the total. Between 1980 and 1985, the Chinese agricultural output grew annually by 9.4 per cent, the highest among developing countries as a whole. This high level is appreciably higher than the 1970s output growth of 3 per cent. Food production per head grew annually by 4.7 per cent during the world recession, while it was 1.3 per cent in the 1970s.

The minimal cost of recession in India was not translated into social costs, since policy makers maintained food subsidies at 0.4 per cent of the country's GDP. Every effort has also been made to support food production, which has led to its three-fold increase per head in 1980–5 as compared to previous levels in the 1970s. The total food supply did not deteriorate. On the contrary, the average calorie supply per head grew annually at 0.4 per cent (FAO, 1985b). This does not mean that the number of the rural poor in India actually declined during the recession, but it does mean that the poor are not worse off.

Implications for food productivity

Because domestic food production is important to the total availability of food in developing countries, we need to examine it in those countries with IMF support for stabilisation programmes which are usually allied with the World Bank adjustment loans. Average calorie supply per head (as a crude approximation of nutrition) is also a related factor, since domestic food production is the main source of total calorie supplies, the balance being met by food imports including food aid.

By 1987, policy makers in 71 countries introduced adjustment policies induced by the IMF and WB. Excluding South Africa and the European countries (Yugoslavia, Hungary, Romania, Portugal and Cyprus), and excepting Belize and Samoa (for which no information on the above measures is available) this leaves 63 countries that are regionally distributed as: 26 in Africa, 5 in the Middle East, 20 in Latin America and 12 in Asia. The countries are classified in Table 2.2 according to changes in food production per head (FPH) in 1980–5 compared to the 1970s, and in average calorie supply per head (CSH) in 1979–81 compared to 1970–1.

The declining changes were mostly in African and Latin American

Table 2.2 **Changes in food production and nutrition per head in 63 LDCs which introduced the IMF/WB adjustment policies, 1970–1 and 1979–85**

	Food production per head (FPH)	Average calorie supply per head (CSH)
Declining	44	21
Increasing	17	31
Constant or no significant change	2	11
Total	63	63

Source: FPH, FAO *Production Year Book*, 1985 and *Country Tables* 1987; CSH, *The Fifth World Food Survey*, 1985, FAO, Rome.

Countries (22 in Africa and 15 in Latin America for changes in FPH, and 13 and 4 countries respectively for CSH). The decline represents a high percentage indeed in both regions, despite a very wide variation in income (GNP) per head and natural endowment. It is true that some of the 22 African countries had frequent drought in 1980–5. Although CSH refers to all food supply (domestic production + imports + accumulated stocks) and to an overall average for the whole population, it does not indicate the actual acquisition of food-intake by individuals and is still meaningful. The adjustment policies of the governments in the 21 countries (with decline in CSH) representing 33 per cent of the total, failed to match the growth of their population with growth in the total food supply produced either domestically or imported. The decline in domestic food production per head (FPH) which is reflected in CSH suggests a neglect of agriculture's food sector, and its peasant producers, both in selection and enforcement of adjustment policies.

Whatever the political and economic circumstances in each country might be, the fact remains that 70 per cent of the 63 developing countries included in Table 2.2 and which introduced financial and production structural policies towards adjustment since 1980, have failed to maintain their 1970s level of food production per head. The likely implications can be explained in the following terms:

1. A fall in employment in the food sector of agriculture and a corresponding fall in productivity and the peasants' earnings and consumption levels.
2. Widening inequality in incomes between food producers on the one hand and export crops producers and agricultural inputs importers on the other.
3. An increasing share of imported food in total calorie supplies (this increased between the average of 1970s and 1980–4 from 6 per cent

to 13 per cent in Africa and from 8 per cent to 15 per cent in Latin America (FAO, 1985c: 15).
4. A greater demand on their scarce foreign exchange to import food (usually paid by earning from agricultural exports).[9]

Our simplified account of the response of policy makers to the impact of the post-1979 world economic recession does *not* suggest that *all* IMF-induced adjustment measures are unfavourable to domestic food production, the quality of human life and income distribution. The consequences of adjustment depend on the countries' initial conditions, development strategies, and on the content as well as the pace, sequence, and method of their enforcement. We have already discussed these variations in the cases of China, Brazil and India; all heavily populated with large size economies. Country experiences also suggest that policy makers in the relatively egalitarian agrarian economies receiving IMF/WB adjustment programmes have deliberately ensured that the growth of agriculture and food production is sustained and that the welfare of the poor is protected. Egypt, for example, which has a *per capita* GNP nearly one third that of Brazil, reduced food subsidies by only 0.8 per cent of total government expenditure from 16.4 per cent to 15.6 per cent between 1980 and 1984, whereas the reduction was ten times as much in Brazil. In their careful empirical examination, Cornia *et al.* (1987) and Singh (1985, 1986) showed how China, Botswana, Egypt, South Korea, and Zimbabwe have successfully coped with the impact of the post-1979 turbulence in the world economy. These countries with relatively egalitarian agrarian structures, were able to maintain a good record of economic growth, domestic savings, food production, and public expenditure on food subsidies, as well as on health and education. In the meantime, they have managed to bring proportionately greater benefits to the rural poor. The fairly good record of Zimbabwe was achieved despite the severe drought during 1981–4.

Table 2.3 lists 11 countries, many of which have been referred to in the above discussion. They are categorised into two groups. Countries in Group I have relatively egalitarian agrarian structures resulting from earlier major land redistribution programmes combined with the restructuring of land-based power. Such reforms in the institutional structure are reflected in post-1980 policy choice with regard to IMF – induced adjustment programmes. Group II, on the other hand, contains countries with a high concentration of land, incomes, and power, which in turn influences the choice of the mode of adjustment and how it affects the different socio-economic groups. The distinction of the initial position is considered significant for understanding the variation in the extent and direction of changes before and after the 1979 economic recession. During the recession, Group 1 was able to sustain and accelerate growth,

Table 2.3 Performance of 11 countries with IMF programme according to their concentration of land distribution, 1970–85

Country group	Annual growth rate % Total GDP		Annual growth rate % Agric. GDP		Gross domestic saving as percentage of GDP		Food production per head % annual rate of change		Government expenditure on health and education as percentage of total	
	1970–79	1980–85	1970–79	1980–85	1979	1985	1971–80	1981–85	1972	1985
Group I										
China	5.8	9.8	3.2	9.4	30	34	1.3	4.7	n.a.	n.a.
Egypt	7.6	5.2	2.2	1.9	16	16	−1.0	1.0	12*	13
South Korea	10.3	7.9	4.8	6.3	28	31	3.0	2.1	17	20
Thailand	7.7	5.1	5.4	3.4	21	21	2.2	1.7	24	25.2
Zimbabwe	1.6	2.5	−0.5	3.7	23	23	n.a.	−3.4†	n.a.	27
Group II										
Argentina	2.5	−1.4	2.5	2.8	35	16	1.8	−0.9	20	11
Brazil	8.7	1.3	5.0	3.0	21	22	1.5	1.2	15	10.8
Chile	1.9	1.9	3.5	2.1	15	16	0.6	−1.4	30	19.3
Costa Rica	6.0	0.5	2.6	2.1	13	22	1.6	−1.9	32	41
Kenya	6.5	3.1	5.4	2.8	15	16	−1.9	−5.3	30	26.5
Philippines	6.2	−0.5	4.9	1.7	24	13	2.4	−1.9	20	26

n.a. – information not available

* – for 1977

† – resulting from severe drought in 1981–4

Source: World Development Reports 1981 and 1987 except data on food production; FAO Production Yearbook 1985 and Country Tables, 1987

and further, to increase national savings to finance their development programmes. Equally important was their success in raising food production to match population growth and their refusal to reduce government expenditure on social services.

The performance of this group of five countries in agriculture and food productivity is in sharp contrast to that of the Argentine, Brazil, Chile, Costa Rica, Kenya and the Philippines. With the exception of the Philippines, the Gini coefficient of land concentration is over 0.7, which is quite high. Poverty has increased in Costa Rica for example, 'where poverty incidence increased between 1979 and 1982 from 17 to 29 per cent following the introduction of severe adjustment policies' (Altimir, 1984). For the same reason, poverty and income distribution have worsened in Brazil, where food subsidies were drastically cut and expenditure on health and education reduced by 30 per cent.

In most of the countries in Group II, the emphasis is on fiscal adjustment, *viz.*, improving the balance of payments, reforming the exchange rate, and reducing government expenditure. Their poor performance in food production tends to constrain rural development and to domestic food security at a high political and social cost.

On the basis of the scattered facts and their interpretation in the preceding section, it appears that the more egalitarian the agrarian structure, the greater the likelihood that policy makers will manage to avoid unfavourable impacts of the world economic recession on food production and the poor. The greater the concentration of land and powers of landlords, the greater the likelihood of neglecting food production, and ignoring distributional effects on the poor. Yet, this is too neat an antithesis, since we dealt with short-term effects of a complex problem impossible to separate from the chronic problems and issues raised throughout Chapter 1.

This complexity also necessitates conceptual clarification of ambiguities supported by empirical analysis. The rest of this book attempts to take up this challenge.

Notes

1   The limitations of conventional economic theory for an adequate understanding of the problems of developing countries were argued for a long time by Gunnar Myrdal (1968), who appealed for realism in theorising and formulating his alternative approach. There are many other economists, some of them already mentioned in the text, who stressed the irrelevant features of the neo-classical approach. The following works are suggested: Stewart (1971 and 1985); Seers (1969); Hirschman (1981); Sen (1983); Parsons (1984); Hirschleifer (1985); and Toye (1987).

2   In his Richard T. Ely Lecture at the annual meeting of the American Economic Association (28–30 December 1981), Professor George

Stigler (1982: 4–6) examined the causes for the changes of the economists' opinion about monopoly. He suggested a number of explanations. Relevant to our discussion are: the ideological bias of economists' support of anti-trust policy because of their 'traditional praise of competitive organization of markets and industries'; and that 'anti-trust testimony is probably one of the three or four major sources of income of economists'.

3   This quotation is from President Kennedy's speech at the 'Alliance for Progress' Conference in Punta del Este, Uruguay in 1961. Mexico did not join the 'Alliance' because of its disagreement that the ideas behind the Cuban land reform represent a beginning of a communist infiltration in Latin America, which require a formal international mechanism, backed by the USA, to guide land reform programmes. At that time according to Gary Olson, the American private capital invested in the countries of the region amounted to 75 per cent of total foreign direct investment and about 60 per cent of all American private investment in the world. Professor Montgomery reported that the USA initiated the Alliance also in response to pressure from Colombia, Venezuela, Brazil and Chile 'to mount in the Western Hemisphere something approaching the Marshall Plan in Europe' (Montgomery, 1984: 122).

4   In its *Focus on Poverty* (1983) the World Bank admits that rural development projects did not reach all poor and that they have provided few direct benefits for the landless, for tenants unable to offer collateral for loans and for the near-landless farmers who find it hard to borrow and acquire inputs. In fact some projects which financed the purchase of heavy farm machinery such as combine harvesters, tractors and modern rice mills have made the landless worse off by reducing their employment opportunities. In its macro-economic policy dialogue with policy-makers in LDCs, the Bank also did not use its considerable prestige and influence with respect to land reform. Being an international organisation, we do not expect the World Bank to force unwilling governments to implement land reform. One would expect the Bank to challenge existing gross inequalities and not to lend for projects if land tenure arrangements are so defective that they frustrate the achievement of the Bank's objectives laid down in its *Land Reform Policy Paper, 1975* and *Rural Development Policy Paper, 1974*. Even as John W. Lowe reports, the affiliate of the World Bank called the International Finance Corporation financed many multinationals operating in agriculture in developing countries and against the interest of the rural poor (see the list of countries and multinationals in Lowe (1977).

5   For instance the Labour government 1965–70 created the Ministry of Overseas Development to implement a new concept of aid as a tool for development in LDCs. World poverty and World Food Plan were clear concerns formulated in the White Paper on Development Aid for LDCs issued in August 1965. British government aid increased four times as much (from £55 million in the 1950s under a Conservative government to £214 million in 1970, or 0.5 per cent of GNP). Eighty per cent of development aid to LDCs was interest free. It should be recalled that

the first Minister Barbara Castle appointed a group of eminent development economists, including Dudley Seers and Paul Streeten as economic advisors, Thomas Balogh was advisor to the Prime Minister, Harold Wilson. For an understanding of the political philosophy of the Labour party behind development aid, see Chapter 15 'Overseas development policies under the Labour government' in Streeten (1972).

6   At the start of his professional career (1946–50) in Egypt, the author was selected by the then Director General of the Fellah Department the late Dr Ahmed Hussein, to serve in a technical unit entrusted to undertake field studies to be used for the preparation of draft legislation on minimum wages for hired agricultural workers, tenancy regulations and redistribution of large estates beyond a certain size ceiling. The studies and the proposed legislation were submitted to a parliamentary committee by Dr Hussein who became a Cabinet Member. It took five years of deliberations, submission of further empirical evidence and manoeuvrings by several parliamentary agricultural committees before they agreed on a drastically compromised programme which was presented to the parliament in 1951. Big landlords and their allies from businessmen and industrialists objected, in principle, to any government intervention in the existing land tenure system, called Dr Hussein 'the Red Minister' and forced him to resign. Instead they agreed: to a rapid reclamation of the state-owned land (amlak amireya) for distribution to the landless (mo'dameen); to require large estate owners to provide social amenities to their peasants living in 'esba'; and to increase public expenditure on health and social centres in rural Egypt. The view of these vocal opponents was that any intervention would disturb the existing equilibrium of social system in rural areas and disrupt agricultural production. This position was not a surprise since the landlords were expressing the views of King Farouk, himself the biggest landlord, to preserve the status quo. But their vision was so shortsighted, that a major land reform programme came into force only one year later and the King was ousted.

7   Quoted from Doreen Warriner's account of the political background of the land reform law of 1967. She explains the extent of uncertainty and ambiguity expressed by President Frei's senior officials with respect to the expropriation of private farms, and the payment of compensations. She comments:

> The difficulty for the Christian Democratic Party [of President Frei] is that facing both ways means bribing both sides, buying off the landowners by purchasing at high prices [at full market values] and allowing wide exemption from compulsory purchase, while winning support among farm workers by offering higher wages [on expropriated land]. (Warriner, 1969: 344)

8   Several years after the Conference, and during my meetings with the Ministers in their countries, I found it hard to remind them of their commitment at the Conference in Rome. One Minister could only recall the Conference work by remembering the audience with the Pope

granted to all delegates on that occasion. My impression was that: Ministers of Agriculture who, in general, are politically weak in their countries, did not grasp the dimensions of development issues related to employment, income distribution and agricultural growth arising from amending the defective land tenure system: and that their primary interest is to receive assistance in the form of projects to be financed from funds made available to FAO by the governments of Sweden, Norway and the Netherlands. Some Ministers refused to include leaders of non-governmental organisations on the meetings where issues were discussed and suggestions for action were made.

9   But, the value of these earnings has declined in early 1986, by 22.5 per cent compared to price levels in 1980 because of continued weak demand by the major importers of agricultural raw materials. For developing countries as a whole, the net result is a decline in agricultural terms of trade estimated at 8–9 per cent since the value of their imports of manufactured goods and crude oil fell by only 13 per cent (IMF: *International Financial Statistics*, May 1986).

Part 2

The analytical issues of land reform and rural poverty

Chapter three

Accessible opportunities: the meaning of land reform

This chapter presents the study's conception of land reform, and sets the frame of reference for the analysis of various countries' experience in the following chapters. The discussion consists of four major sections. The relevant principles of the theory of the State are discussed in respect to government intervention for adjusting property rights. In this first section, land reform is defined and the principal determinants of its effectiveness are suggested irrespective of its scale and ideological variation. The second section explores the dynamic links between restructuring the institutions of land tenure and power and the pace of poverty reduction. It views poverty as a structural phenomenon. The third section sets a framework for the study of the redistributive consequences of land reform. In doing so, the determinants of gains and losses, as well as the measurement problems of these consequences are examined. The fourth section explains the importance of the command over food via legally-secured access to land. Command over food is viewed not in terms of temporary public programmes for distribution, but through an intensive mixing of hitherto under-utilised labour with legally secured land holding.

Issues in land tenure

To understand the meaning of land reform, we need to understand the links among the institutions of property rights in land, power, and the authority of the State. To appreciate the role of land reform in alleviating rural poverty, the characteristics of land tenure which are likely to generate rural under-development need first to be identified. Only then are we able to understand the need for their amendment and to define the characteristics of land tenure which can enhance rural development.

The State and the institution of property: the controversy

In this study, the term 'land tenure' embraces institutional arrangements pertaining to property rights and duties. It also refers to the division of decision making among tenure groups, as owners and users of land combined with other means of production. These institutional arrangements may be legally established, customary, or enforced by a combination of both. They define the rights of property owners and users. For instance, under land-owner absenteeism, the separation of land *ownership* from its actual cultivation usually increases the number of operating units or *holdings*, through rental to several tenants. It is necessary, therefore, to examine the implications of separating the operational rights and responsibilities from ownership rights, and owning or operating land from labour use in the analysis of resource use in agriculture.[1] This examination includes property rights and use of water for irrigated land. The often neglected institutional arrangements in water transaction are critical in determining the productivity and income of small farmers.[2] Therefore, it is the operation unit (holding) and production relations which matter when studying the output and employment effects of land tenure as well as the distribution of the shares in product value.

The institution of property rights is the heart of any land tenure system. In the Western system of thought and historical tradition, the institution of *private* property rights is a foundation of capitalism, and is considered to be essential to democracy.[3] In pure socialism, the abolition of private property is an integral part of the entire economic system for attaining rural development via central planning and collective management. But, we suppose that whatever the political philosophy underlying the institution of property, there is no reason why a privately owned family farm, or a *communally* owned collective farm cannot enhance rural development. Under both arrangements, the State adjusts, in varying degrees, the institution of property rights in land by assigning property rights according to public interest.

In 1890, Alfred Marshall, the founder of modern economic theory, wrote: 'Taking it for granted that a more equal distribution of wealth is to be desired, how far would this justify changes in the institution of property, or limitation of free enterprise?'[4] The institution of property in the sense used by Marshall is taken to mean the intangible or the exchangeable rights in ownership and use of property as determined by law or custom. This content of property is distinct from physical or corporeal property (to use the terminology of MacLeod (1867) and Commons (1923 and 1934). It denotes leasing, sharing arrangements, indebtedness and mortgage, security of tenure and property-based power. This content determines both the flow of accrued income and its distribution among the participants. It also induces or inhibits investment in improving the productivity of the physical content of property (e.g., irrigation and soil improvement by applying fertiliser).

If our interpretation of Marshall's notion is correct, the question is: should these rights in private property be preserved on the grounds that property and economic freedom are sacrosanct irrespective of their distributional effect and class conflicts, or should they be conditioned by the state power? As Galbraith remarks:

For socialists, property was and in some measure remains not only the decisive but the sole source of power. . . . As long as it remains in private hands no others can possess power. . . . In non-socialist doctrine, by contrast, private property is so important as a source of private power that it cannot be concentrated in the hands of the government, yet it should enjoy the general protection of the State. There remains the question of 'how extensively the state should intervene to get a wider distribution of property (and associated income) and thus of the power emanating therefrom'. (1984: 47 and 87)[5]

This question has engaged the interest of many philosophers and analysts from different strands of economics since the work of John Locke on property rights (discussed later in Chapter 5). The prudent Adam Smith conceived a principle governing the role of the State 'Protecting, as far as possible, every member of the society from the injustice or oppression of every other member of it' (Book IV, Chapter IX: 651). This principle implies that the State exercises its political power to restrain the economic freedom of individuals or corporations who abuse such freedom for attaining private gains at the expense of others and social gains as in the case of violating property rights by monopolists. Fredrick List (1885) in his attack on *laissez-faire* policy distinguished between the rationality in private economy of the *individual* and the rationality in the *national* economy and asked: 'Can the individual in the conduct of his private affairs take acount of the conditions of land [property]? Does not the nation require that the freedom of the individual be restricted?' (in Baumol, 1965: 192).

These issues of social gains and losses arising from distributional effects of government intervention have been analysed with intellectual sophistication by welfare economists. This work was reviewed by William Baumol in relation to the theory of the State. He concluded:

Having done this, can we say, in any given case, that the government should, or should not, intervene? Further if we could give a verdict in favour of intervention, are we able to recommend the type and extent of the intervention? Here, I have serious doubts. . . . In this way we have not begun to investigate what may be the most significant part of our problem . . . I believe that the politician is, in many cases, justified in taking, and indeed forced to take, action on many (practical) problems; perfect analysis or no. (Baumol, 1965, Part II: 204, 206, 207)

In fact, this is what governments are doing. The very problem of the distribution of social benefits from regulating property rights is involved in policy action by government, even in a democratic and capitalist society.

Private property being the central bond of capitalism aroused public concern over the consequences of concentrated land ownership combined with power. Growing landlessness, chronic indebtedness of the peasants and eviction of tenants can threaten political stability. When the balance of power swings towards the interests of the poor peasants and the landless workers, the State intervenes to condition the institution of property and, in varying degrees, to limit the economic freedom of entrepreneurs in agriculture. In this quest for justice, the State in a capitalist system does not abolish private property in land, but instead, it regulates ownership rights and rectifies factor-makers in the rural economy. The extent of the State intervention in private property-market economies as expressed by Friedrich Von Hayek's remark, '. . . that all governments affect the relative position of different people and, that there is under any system scarcely an aspect of our lives which might not be affected by government action' (Von Hayek, 1980: 81), certainly is true. Insofar as government does anything at all, 'its action will always have some effect on who gets what; when and how'.[6]

In socialist economies, on the other hand, the nationalisation of landed property and other means of production in agriculture is combined with central planning. This combination severely diminishes the role of the market in determining the distribution of income in the entire economy. The alternative to the market is distribution of wealth and income by a highly statist control of production, exchange and distribution through a comprehensive planning system. This coherent system does not provide absolute equality, but it does attempt to ensure minimum inequality. As an ideological preference, historical experience shows that this approach was a radical response to long established feudal or colonial systems in agriculture. In contemporary socialist countries (Yugoslavia, Hungary and China, and currently, the Soviet Union), after an assessment of experiences, a wide ranging debate has arisen over the experience with common property, and the implications for peasants' incentives, motivations and rewards.

It is logical to conclude that where the institution of property – private or communal – inhibits motivation and access to opportunities, changes by the State must be introduced in different ways. Recently formulated theories, however, disagree with this reasoning. Instead, priority is assigned to the freedom of choice of everyone concerned (irrespective of conflicting interest and consequent inequality) regarding the institution of property. In his theory of entitlement, Nozick (1976) views no place for a central mechanism of the State in bringing about a redistribution of land holdings. According to Nozick, any such changes (such as land reform) are unnecessary because property is justly and legitimately possessed if acquired by means of voluntary exchange (purchase, sale, and inheritance) within the rules of legal procedures. By considering the legal aspects and the free market order as superior determinants in the acquisition of land, the theory overlooks whatever consequences the legally legitimate holding might lead to in terms of extreme inequalities of income distribution, poverty of the propertyless and exploitation arising out of institutional monopoly in the ownership of land and other means of production. It also overlooks whether the large holdings acquired in the past by means of grants (by colonial rulers for political convenience and in contingent circumstances), were *ethically* unjust, though they happened to be legally legitimate. It is, therefore, important to trace the origin of large holdings, *viz.*, how they were originally acquired prior to their legitimisation by State institutions. We may find that a large part was grabbed, or granted by virtue of status and that they were not acquired or purchased in the open market as earned wealth (by means of savings and the investment of labour and skills). Combined with Nozick's theory, such a discovery would have startling implications.

Just as the Norman Conquest of Britain in 1066 originated the granting of land by the Sovereign and the feudal system which was gradually reformed between 1286 and 1700, the pre-land reform concentration of large properties in Latin-America, many south-east Asian and Middle East countries were a function of colonial rule. History tells us that British Viceroys, the Spanish Crown and Ottoman Sultans granted large estates to holders of certain offices and influential families on whose support the colonial rulers were dependent. These estates were legally legitimised and became hereditary possessions. Many of these lucky holders of land dispossessed the powerless small-holders and exercised land-grabbing. At a later stage, large holdings from both origins were converted to freehold private ownership.[7] If the balance of power were to change in favour of instituting land reforms, would it not be legitimate for the State institutions to confiscate or expropriate this category of property as well as other forms of grabbed land? Would it not be just to restitute property rights to the currently landless households whose forefathers had lost them? The moral question is: if such historical transfer was ethically unjust, as proved by records, would the rectification of past injustices be justifiable under Nozick's theory of entitlement?

There is a mode outside State intervention by which inequalities are lessened; voluntary co-operation. Can powerless, landless farmers and influential landlords, having strikingly divergent interest, agree to reform the institutions of property and tenancy if such institutions prove to be unjust? This arrangement is suggested by Rawls (1973) in his theory of justice.

In his utopia of justice, he sets the foundation of the 'original position' in which everyone as a rational person (landless peasant, tenant, landlord, money-lender, trader, etc.) co-operates for the welfare of all, and freely chooses the institutions, including property. The inexplicable assumption is that the desires of all these groups of people are conflict-free. The plausible aspect of Rawls' theory is in giving priority to the disadvantaged groups. According to his scheme, agreed institutions are just *only* if they result in compensating benefits for everyone, and in particular for the least advantaged members of society (Rawls, 1973: 15). Unfortunately, he stops there, and does not develop procedural rules to guarantee these benefits. Furthermore, there is an inconsistency between this principle and his 'Difference principle' which seems to defend inequality for being a real and legitimate feature of societies. If the 'Difference principle' serves as a breeding ground of inequality in property and income, then the other principles of justice are also violated. Redistributive intervention by the State is unnecessary because, according to Rawls (1973: 176), 'everyone can rely on one another to adhere to the principles adopted' in the original position. This utopian theory has an ideological bias in its construction, which is that it is based upon free competition and the private ownership of the means of production without any active role by the State. The principles of any theory should apply to all systems of economic organisation.

Institutions and rural under-development

In agrarian economies with private property, when the holding of land, water for irrigation, and credit become monopolised, and the use of labour becomes monopsonistic, the landless peasants and wage-dependent workers are likely to live in conditions of poverty. Under such conditions, the opportunities for the fast growing number of unskilled agricultural workers to improve their socio-economic position are very limited. If the slow evolutionary process of tenure status improvement is left to the *laissez-faire* market mechanism, a poor agricultural worker in a less developed country (LDC) wishing to purchase one acre of farmland might require a lifetime of saving at a subsistence wage. In the face of strict rationing in credit markets, and scarcity of non-farm jobs for unskilled labour, the poor agricultural workers and share-croppers have no choice but to accept living in poverty. In such a situation the higher the degree of land-ownership concentration, the greater the incidence of poverty and inequality in income distribution. Consequently, land tenure differentiates between those who wield political and market power and those who submit and are subordinated.

It follows that in a private property market economy, land tenure can generate under-development in rural areas where the following conditions prevail:

1. Institutional monopoly in land and labour markets resulting in low productivity from under-utilisation of both principal resources and a loss of potential gains (to peasants) in total agricultural output (see Chapter 5 for the meaning of institutional monopoly).
2. Capitalists bidding higher prices for, and transferring title of, land property and its rent, resulting in inflationary prices without increased real output.
3. Barriers to entry into land and credit markets which inhibit agriculturally wage-based workers from purchasing farmland, and small farmers from gaining property title.
4. A social structure characterised by a minority of privileged powerful upper-class and a large section of inferior class of powerless, poor and disadvantaged rural population, with a wide social gulf in between.

It is obvious that these attributes of rural under-development cannot be explained in economic terms alone. Understanding popular participation or exclusion, social values and customs, attitudes of bureaucracy towards the peasants, inter-class relationships (power, social respect, prestige, subservience, servility) associated with land tenure systems is outside the domain of conventional economics. We have to benefit from the body of knowledge and methodologies developed in other branches of social science particularly sociology, anthropology and political science.[8] Unlike economic relationships, social characteristics do not change in the short term. They bear the marks of long-established class formation and once they have come into being, perpetuate themselves.

There are structural factors outside land tenure systems which determine the supply of agricultural land, the demand for its ownership and its products, and the rates of real wages. They include the natural endowment of land and water for irrigation, rates of agricultural population growth (and the scale of its pressure on land), pricing policy, rationing of capital and inadequate private and public investment in irrigation and soil conservation. The relative position of agriculture in the national economy is also important. Late development of non-agricultural sectors combined with slow demand for the increasing agricultural labour force is likely to lead to an increase in landlessness. This is true particularly in agriculturally over-populated countries with concentrated private property rights in land. Under the circumstances the expanding link between domestic agriculture with international markets is likely to promote the cultivation of cash crops for export at the expense of food crops. Most importantly, emphasis on high value export crops linked with mechanisation can lead to increasing the concentration of land ownership (see Chapter 5).

The preceding discussion raises a fundamental policy issue in tackling the problem of rural under-development. Can all these institutional obstacles be removed by State intervention to reform the land tenure system? In other words, can poverty be rapidly reduced if a substantial section of the agricultural population holds land as a food producing, stable income earning and labour-using asset? This brings us to the concept of land reform.

On land reform and agrarian reform

In general terms, land reform is a public action assigning a specific role to land tenure to amended what are considered by the State to be iniquitous practices against the public interest – practices which create conditions inhibiting rural development. In concrete terms, land reform is conceived in this study as a redistribution of private land property rights and use under different institutional arrangements enforceable by law. The aim is to remove barriers to entry into the factor markets and to provide peasants with command over food thereby rapidly reducing poverty and inequalities. However, this does not mean that *any* land reform can rapidly realise these changes, particularly where land is of low quality or not productive. Nor does it mean that land redistribution *alone* can achieve these results and sustain them over time. Though land reform is a strong demonstration of political commitment directed to abolish exploitation and to attack rural poverty, various land reforms differ in aims, pace and scale of implementation, as do results. The principal determinants of these differences are as follows:

1. Political commitment.
2. Scope of change – the scale and terms of redistribution, particularly the levels of size ceiling on ownership of land and the minimum size of distributed units in relation to the extent of landless peasants.
3. Implementation capability of state institutions including administrative enforcement of legal provisions and whether these provisions contain loopholes and ambiguous rules.
4. Complementarity of other public actions and institutional arrangements particularly the timely supply of complementary inputs.
5. Pace of implementation without uncertainty

Irrespective of ideological differences, the performance of land reform programmes is differentiated by a chain of these five elements. Without exception, the effects are functionally dependent upon each of them, *viz.* they form links in the composite function of land reform. In some literature, particularly that concerning the Latin-American region, the term 'agrarian reform' is used instead of 'land reform'. The term embraces a wide range of public institutional changes in agriculture which may but do not necessarily – include the redistribution of private landed property. Agrarian reform usually refers to: land settlement schemes in publicly-owned land, land registration, rental control, lending institutional credit to tenants to purchase land in the open market, consolidation of fragmented holdings, regulation of tenancy arrangements, etc. If government intervention leaves existing skewed distribution of land and rural power unchanged, these institutional measures cannot be considered land reform under our definition. This is because:

(a) they represent an evasion of the central issue in tackling rural under-development problems;
(b) in the face of existing political power of landlords, such changes, particularly the tenancy regulations cannot be effectively enforced and can even disrupt social relations in agriculture; and
(c) with tenancy regulation, as with scattered settlement schemes, social injustice, exploitative relationships and the incidence of rural poverty are not likely to be significantly reduced in the *national* context where the concentration of land-ownership is high and where the pattern of growth perpetuates inequality.

According to our definition, land reform could be termed agrarian reform but the converse need not be true. The term 'agrarian reform' has been expanded to an extent rightly noted by three seasoned scholars: Kenneth Parsons as 'reformation of the structure of the agricultural economy', and by Doreen Warriner (1969), 'its use in this wide sense blurs the real issue. The net is spread wide, the catch is miscellaneous.' Michael Lipton asserts that

> It is absurd to exclude major methods of land redistribution, whether distributivist or collectivist, from the definition of genuine land reform, for both involve radical equalizing changes in the land-based structure of rural power. Not only is such redefinition poor logic; the attitude behind it makes the best the enemy of the good, and plays into the hands of landlord-politicians. Perhaps the most common of all these over-rigorous evasions is, '. . .don't do anything till you can do everything, so do nothing . . .'. This broad definition lets 'the rich farmers keep their land, fertilized with the crocodile tears of frustrated reformers'. (Lipton, 1974: 274–5)[9]

The importance of sustaining gains

With land reform, as with agrarian reform, the reallocation of property rights along with accruing income and power is not sufficient to attain potential gains. Nor does it guarantee a continuation of the beneficiaries' incremental income in real terms, or their command over food. Other complementary inputs and measures are a prerequisite for sustaining initial gains over a long period and reinforcing their linkage with the process of rural development.

The speed in replacing the production and marketing functions of former landlords is crucial whether in private property (with farmers' co-operatives or associations) or in common property (collective farming, communes etc.). These arrangements are instrumental in ensuring the supply of production inputs such as water, seeds, fertilisers, and the sale of marketed surplus. Furthermore, investment in improving irrigation particularly in arid and semi-arid areas is crucial. The shorter the lapse of time between abolishing the old institutions and their replacement by relevant new order without uncertainty, the less the risk of diminishing the level of production and destabilising the flow of income to the beneficiaries and marketed surplus to urban centres. Any weakness or delay in these logistic operations is bound to lead to a short-term fluctuation which is usually used by opponents of land reform to strengthen their arguments against it.

For instance, when a considerable rearrangement of the irrigation system or the rehabilitation of the soil is required, the productive benefits from subdivided units is bound to be delayed. In such situations the expected gain to both the land reform beneficiaries, and the agricultural economy is dependent upon investment in improving the productiveness of land. Gains in the economy as a whole are dependent upon the scope of land reform and its impact on agricultural growth. Since development records of the non-oil producing developing countries show a positive relation between agricultural and national GDP rates of growth, sustained agricultural growth after large scale land reform is essential.

It follows that raising output in the reformed sector requires more than the celebrated remark by Arthur Young, 'the magic of property turns sand into gold'. This 'magic' works only with the motivation and energy invested by the beneficiaries combined with an adequate public investment and supply of complementary inputs. The motivation and incentive to intensively cultivate their plots of land, and to save depend upon the degree of decentralisation in decision making with regard to resource use, and the pricing policy, combined with the extent of the role of state institutions in the accumulation of marketed surplus at pre-determined low prices.

As taxpayers and food consumers, the rest of the nation cannot help but be interested in what happens in the countryside. The urban sector desires a stable flow of agricultural products, particularly food-crops and animal products. As land reform is not cost-free, there are financial considerations as well. Speedy implementation and complementary inputs to sustain its benefits incur expenditures from the national budget (and in turn the taxpayers). The scale of the burden on the national budget depends upon the extent of land redistribution, the investment requirements, the terms of compensation to be paid for expropriated property (particularly if it was owned by foreigners), and whether external resources are provided to implement land reform.

Focus on absolute poverty

Conventionally, rural development has a somewhat ambiguous and broader connotation than does land reform. It is a long-term process which can take generations to realise rather than decades. But the length of time could be considerably shortened if rural development started with a more equitable distribution of productive assets, notably land. By rural development we mean the dynamic process of combined government action with the participation of low income groups to realise a rapid and sustained reduction in absolute poverty (we stress the decline in the number of individuals living in *absolute*, not relative, poverty). Absolute poverty refers to living below a cut-off level of an estimated income or consumption satisfying the person's minimum necessities (notably food as the biological necessity for survival).

The distinction between rural betterment and rural development

Poverty is reduced in proportionate and absolute terms. 'Proportionate poverty' is the *percentage* of rural population (individuals or households) whose income/consumption falls below a poverty line identified and established by each country. Absolute terms refers to the *number* of the identified rural poor. In both cases the reduction of poverty is measured by the same criteria (income or nutritional standard) between two or more points of time (t_1, t_2, . . . , t_n) when n denotes the number of years. If the percentage has declined but the number has increased, we call this change 'rural *betterment* in a transitional stage towards rural *development*'. During each phase some poor individuals or households have become better off, rising above the poverty line. But for several reasons connected with the way inequality or poverty is generated, many others remain poor. Some, who were already above the poverty line, become poorer, eventually dropping below it. The balance and the exact composition of the poor and their ranking as poorer and poorest varies from one community to another within a country and between countries.

In order to direct programmes and public resources for a speedy reduction in poverty, it is necessary to categorise the rural population by occupation and identify the poor. As an anti-poverty policy, land reform focuses on two occupational sub-groups of the rural poor: the poorest farmers (small tenants, share-croppers and owners of tiny plots)

91

and the wage-based landless agricultural workers. in LDCs these sub-groups seem to constitute the majority of the rural poor (though the sex and age composition of the sub-group varies).

For a complementary measurement of changes in poverty incidence, the use of the Sen index is more meaningful though its data requirements are demanding. This is because it combines the proportionate poverty incidence with the ratio of the mean income or consumption of all the poor to the poverty line income or consumption. The combination also includes the measurement of inequality in income distribution among the poor (Sen, 1981: Appendix C). The Sen Index is an adjustment to, or weighting of, the simple measure of poverty incidence; the proportion of the poor falling below the poverty line to the total rural population.

The distinction between rural betterment and development may be more clear with a hypothetical illustration. Imagine two developing countries X and Y with an equal number of rural population and high degree of concentration of land ownership at an initial point of time, t_1. Suppose also that the statisticians in both countries agree to use the same criteria for measuring absolute poverty at t_1 and t_2. Let us suppose that the leadership in country X instituted and effectively implemented substantial land reform to spearhead rural development immediately after t_1, whereas in country Y the leadership did not because of a lack of political will. What follows is a hypothetical illustration of the relevant indicators, as shown in Table 3.1.

Table 3.1 **A hypothetical index of land and income distribution for countries X and Y**

	Percentage of rural poor	No. of poor (millions)	Inequality index (0–1) Index of land distribution	Index of income distribution
Country X t_1	0	10	0.7	0.5
t_2	20	8	0.3	0.2
Country Y t_1	40	10	0.7	0.5
t_2	33	13	0.8	0.5

The variations over time between the two imaginary cases is clear. Country X realised rural development, so defined; reduced both proportionate poverty and number of the poor and at the same time it reduced, through land reform, both indices of inequality. But despite its land reform, 20 per cent of Country X's rural population are still poor because the eradication of absolute poverty is a long-term process, and must address causes other than land concentration. Country Y has attained rural betterment, but not development, *viz.* the number of poor increased despite the proportionate reduction. Inequality is still high, as the distribution of land ownership has actually worsened through a process of land accumulation by the landowners. In both countries the battle against the twin problems of poverty and inequality is far from over.

If we accept the thesis that changes in the number of the poor and associated poverty characteristics are overall indicators of rural development, our distinction between 'betterment' and 'development' is not merely an academic one. By clarifying the meaning of rural development, we can further clarify its dynamic linkages with structural parameters in the national economy (see Figure 3.1). They suggest that rural poverty is a structural phenomenon and the variation in its incidence over time is determined by forces outside the orbit of land reform. The links illustrated by arrows suggest that for a large section of the agricultural labour force, increased productive capacity, earnings, and effective demand for food and non-agricultural commodities and services are determined not only by redistribution of land and power but also by other structural forces operating in the national economy. But a large scale of land reform enhances opportunities for the realisation of potential growth in productivity of land and labour. Hence, there is a feedback between the distribution of land/income/consumption/power and rates of economic growth *per head* over time.[10] The order of magnitude of these changes depends on the scale of land reform and the rate of absorption of agricultural labour within rural areas and in the rest of the national economy. Fertility reduction, migration from rural to urban areas and the rates of growth in the agricultural labour force have a substantial effect on the trend in differential rates of growth in *per capita* income between rural and urban sectors, and in the variations in the number of rural poor. The overriding objective of land redistribution in its dynamic sense should not be limited to providing current landless poor immediate benefits from redistribution of wealth, but to provide an escape from poverty for immediate descendants. Accordingly, policy makers should look forward to preventing an increase in *future* inequality in rural income distribution and concentration of power. Irrespective of diverse instituted arrangements, peasants who benefited from reform should not experience a relative decline in economic position when the real income of other socio-economic groups grows at a faster rate. Whilst absolute poverty is reduced, relative inequality in income distribution can increase over time. This is because the scale of the land reform sector and agriculture as a whole are not isolated from changes in the rest of a growing economy.

Population growth adds to the number of rural poor, who tend to have larger and younger (more children under the age of five) families than

Figure 3.1 Linkages among the structural determinants of rural poverty. Solid lines represent direct effect and dotted lines represent feedback effects

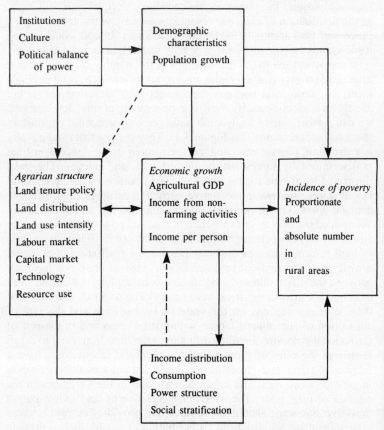

do rich farmers.[11] Lacking social and economic security, these large, poor families need children to care for their elderly. They also hire out child labour to supplement their income. With the notable decline in child and infant mortality, high fertility rates of rural population delay a reduction in the number of rural poor.

Issues in the consequences of redistribution

To study the distributional effects of land reform is to confront difficult measurement problems and to use ethical and moral judgements. This is unavoidable in a study of a policy which is essentially designed to solve a distribution problem and to confront moral issues of liberty and justice.

Empirical questions concerning the comparison of redistributive gains and losses, and changes in social status, power relations and participation are analytically difficult but nevertheless, they must be faced. Attempts must be made to analyse the consequences of redistributing land and opportunities. Because we cannot disregard the important considerations of ethics, social values and power in a political context, a realistic approach should combine qualitative judgement with quantitative analysis in a specific period of time. Such a pragmatic approach is justified in the absence of a coherent, formal theory of income distribution which would explain dynamic relationships. With the exception of Engels' law on human consumption behaviour, in relation to changing income levels, existing hypotheses are essentially idealised constructions. Their empirical test has proved their inconclusiveness.[12]

The determinants of gains and losses

In order to simplify our understanding of the consequences or re-distribution, we assume that those who are affected by land reform constitute two sub-groups; gainers (or beneficiaries), and losers. The gains include expected increase in the income/consumption of the poorer classes; expanded opportunities for the acquisition of command over food and self-respect resulting from the removal of institutional barriers. Expected losses are incurred by landlords through the transfer of their property rights and from the partial or complete suppression of their rights to receive rent. Subject to each country's conditions, other losers are likely to include money lenders, labour contractors and traders in irrigation water and farming machinery. All these capitalists are likely to be affected by partial or complete suppression of 'unearned' income from monopoly power in the factor markets. The entire society also gains through realising potential economic benefits from increasing the effective purchasing power of the beneficiaries. There are other possible gains including social stability in rural localities and the realisation of political stability.

To identify the determinants of gains and losses, our inquiry is guided by an *a priori* knowledge of the declared aims of land reform in many countries and of their pre-reform distribution of land and conditions of poverty. Publicly declared aims are usually in stock phrases such as the abolition of feudalism, exploitation, injustice, absentee landlordism, under-utilization of land, and of the arbitrary market power of landlords, water lords and moneylenders. These aims entail the transfer of income and corresponding redistribution of opportunities to enhance the abilities of the beneficiaries.

Having said this, the *initial* scale of income transfer by land reform in a given country is a cumulative result of a number of factors:

The analytical issues

1. The manner by which land and other physical assets are appropriated for redistribution, through confiscation, nationalisation or expropriation with or without compensation payment. The source and scale of compensation payment, from government bonds, public revenue, or foreign aid. Whether beneficiaries themselves pay for acquired land and other physical assets. Whether there will be possible outlets for the compensation paid within domestic economic activities or whether it will be exported for investment abroad.
2. The extent of redistribution of privately owned land. Whether it is full (complete egalitarian holdings) or partial, (leaving a substantial sub-sector un-reformed).
3. The scale and proportionate distribution of *publicly* owned land, either accompanying or following the redistribution of *privately* owned land.
4. Where land property is *not* nationalised, the redistributive consequences depend upon:
   (a) the level of the maximum ceiling on private land ownership;
   (b) the productive quality and average size of beneficiary holdings;
   (c) the gap or ratio between the average size of beneficiary holdings and the prescribed ceiling;
   (d) whether land is allotted per householder or *per capita* members of households;
   (e) the relative proportion of the sum of distributed land to total agricultural land; and
   (f) whether exemptions from the fixed ceiling are made, its total area and the identity of exempted land owners.
5. The proportional size of the beneficiaries to the total number of agricultural households. The composition of the beneficiaries' sub-groups according to their pre-reform tenure status (tenants, share-croppers and landless agricultural workers) and whether female heads of households are included or excluded.
6. Whether share-cropping and tenancy (renting-in and out) is abolished or maintained with regulations. If maintained, the effect varies according to the proportionate reduction in rent below market value and the share of landowners. Are there 'shadow' rental values higher than the instituted levels?
7. Freedom of, or restrictions imposed on, transfer and ownership of distributed lands, and changes in prices of land where land is not taken out of the market by nationalisation.
8. Changes introduced to regulate water tenure rights and the terms of its use for irrigation.
9. The degree of regulating the labour market is determined by:
   (a) changes in the terms of hiring labour (fixing minimum wages, or prohibiting the hiring of labour);
   (b) changes in custom-determined arrangements for the provision

of non-wage services (e.g. food, housing);

    (c) whether agricultural workers are allowed to unionise, or freely exercise rights of trade unions; and

    (d) whether the reform programme combines farming with non-farm employment activities, and the share of the beneficiaries' income from these sources.

10. The system followed in the accumulation of a marketed surplus produced by the beneficiaries; the ratio of the freely-marketed surplus to that compulsorily delivered to state organisations at a fixed price.

11. Institutional arrangements made in order to guard against:

    (a) The emergence of exploitative relationships between the beneficiaries as a group and the rest of agricultural households, (particularly agricultural workers); and against

    (b) the revival of different types of pre-reform exploitative relationships between the former money lenders, landlords, and the beneficiaries.

These determinants of the range of income transfer do not include the variant organisational forms of resource use in production and the channels of marketing. Examples of such forms are: individual family holdings with voluntary or compulsory co-operative association; collective or communal holdings and joint farming with co-operative organisations having different responsibilities. Any generalisation of categories under indiscriminate terms is misleading, as each country has its own vocabulary to describe its institutional organisation of farming responsibilities. The basis of such categorisation is made up of the proportional responsibilities of the beneficiaries as producers and savers, in relation to those held by the state institutions (or the ruling party representatives).

But gains are not only materialistic. There are other gains in the psychological and social terrain. Examples are:

(a) bases for social uplift, self-respect and dignity;

(b) liberation from oppression, coercion and subservience;

(c) freedom from absolute dependency for survival upon the monopoly power of landlords, moneylenders and contractors of hired labour; and,

(d) equal rights in participating in political activities and in rural organisations (through representatives) in developing rural communities.

Any observer of the pre-land reform oppression exercised by the cotton Pashas and royal estate managers of Egypt, the Zamindari of India, the tribal Sheikhs of Iraq and the owners of haciendas in the altiplano of

Bolivia would appreciate these intangible social gains. An incident which occurred in the 1930s in the author's village in Egypt left a powerful impression on him during his childhood. A landlord hit a peasant 'fellah' with a stick in front of his fellow villagers for what he considered a crime: the fellah did not dismount from his donkey when he passed the landlord who was sitting on his house porch. During the author's work in Latin American countries, in the 1960s it became obvious to him that the 'fellah' in Egypt was treated by his landlord no differently than the 'inquilinos' and 'campesinados' in Colombia, Peru and Paraguay.

Methodological problems in measurement

The foregoing sections suggest a number of difficulties in measuring the redistributive consequences of land reform. This is partly due to the multidimensional changes brought about within the dynamic forces of a changing economy and partly to the inevitable use of value judgements in the interpretation of justice and injustice, liberty and coercion, participation and exclusion, and welfare considerations. Many of these difficulties are not only to be found in quantification but also in finding consistent baseline data needed for temporal comparison (before and after implementing land reform).

In this section we discuss measurements of welfare and utility: changes in inequality in the distribution of land and income (or consumption); changes in motivation and participation; and issues in measuring the effect of income on food consumption and investment.

Welfare and utility

We begin with considering questions on welfare in relation to land reform's consequential gains and losses. Recently, Bigsten (1983: 49) concluded that welfare economics and the theory of utility were not applicable to the analysis of income distribution in developing countries. The same conclusion was reached earlier by many other scholars.[13] What of the usefulness of these theories in measuring the welfare impact of land reform?

Without entering into conflicting arguments on utilitarianism and welfarism, consider this simple example. In agricultural society, X, the aggregate amount of farm land is fixed and the individual households are supposed to choose freely between three statuses of land tenure: to be a landless worker (L); to be an unsecured tenant (T); or to own land (O). Assume that:

(a) the society prefers less inequality of income distribution than at present, based on its ethical and value systems;

(b) L has a lower level of welfare (income and social respect) than does

T who, in turn, has a lower level than O; and that

(c) if L and T's incomes increase, so do their welfare and satisfaction from meeting their needs.

If the individual preferences are in the order of: O is preferred to T, and T is preferred to L, the optimum state of welfare can accordingly be attained by re-distributing the limited aggregate level of land (not necessarily to be equally distributed), provided that O is compensated for the loss incurred from transfer of land ownership, that all landless workers and tenants are included in the redistribution, and that such transfer of property rights and income does not reduce total output.

Imagine three farmers; a landless worker who is illiterate, unhealthy, malnourished and who has a large number of children; a tenant, who is illiterate (but healthy and not at risk of malnutrition) owning two oxen and a plough; and an educated, healthy and well-fed landowner of 50 acres of productive land, 5 acres of which is rented out to the tenant-farmer. Both the tenant and the labourer have different sizes of households. Hence, the three have different economic and non-economic characteristics. Each has a unique utility function in response to their different tastes, abilities and incomes. As is to be expected, there is a conflict of interests among the three people, *viz.* with reference to the worker's terms of his labour utilisation, the tenant's leasing-in arrangements and the landowner's rational entrepreneurial motives for making the maximum profit out of his transactions with the two peasants.

In response to the preference of the society indicated earlier, and in order to attain a high level of potential total welfare, the society leadership decides to take 10 acres from the landowner out of his total area of 50 acres and transfer its ownership equally to the two peasants who do not have their plots free of charge. The re-distributive agency of the society serves as a broker and pays the affected landowner the price of the 10 acres on long-term instalments. Being a shrewd entrepreneur, he works harder on his remaining 40 acres to raise its output. The two jubilant peasants use their formerly un-utilised family labour and newly acquired access to complementary inputs and also raise the productivity of their holdings. They now enjoy a higher income and social status than before. The sum of the three individuals' benefits is likely to be higher than before the redistribution. Other things being equal, if the benefits derived from this limited example are extended to a larger number of households or to the entire agricultural community, (through an egalitarian system of complete redistribution of fixed aggregate land), the sum of the individual household's benefits is likely to be higher. The welfare of those who are now better off is higher than the dissatisfaction experienced by the ex-landlords, and total output is higher than before.

This over-simplified reasoning is based on a number of assumptions

99

about society X, and three individuals, and upon a moral judgement. Claims have been made without quantification of different inter-personal utilities of those whose social welfare has uniformly increased, and their needs met. Nor did we offer a calculus of the decline in the utility of those whose social status and property were diminished. Conventional utilitarianism and utility-based welfarism cannot help us either. As we understand this system of thought, it is concerned only with the sum of individual utilities (social welfare) and not its equitable distribution among individuals. The theory assumes that all losers (landlords) are homogeneous and all gainers (peasants) are also homogeneous. It considers that members of each sub-group have a similar utility function, and that their interests are identical. It ignores their differences in initial inequalities in the ownership of assets, and in human quality. Equally, it ignores non-utility considerations of liberty, power, self-respect, exploitation and coercive relationships which were stressed earlier as notions of special concern to land reform.

Land and income distribution

The measurement difficulties of welfare and utility do not exist in measuring changes in the distribution of land (ownership and operational holdings). Agricultural censuses provide data on the number and area of holdings by class size and tenure status (owners, tenants, labourers, managers of large farms with absentee owners). The change in the degree of concentration may be statistically measured by the Gini coefficient and ratio of the average (mean or medium) size of holdings in the highest to the lowest sized category of holdings. Land *ownership* distribution is usually more unequal than the distribution of *holdings* because some of the owned land is rented out to be operated by several tenants.

But land is only a means for securing the household income or consumption. Identifying inequality in income distribution as well as differences in the composition of income and the size of sources of non-land income is, therefore, necessary. To analyse inequality and compare incomes, we need to recognise differences in the composition of income and the size of households. *Per capita* income is, therefore, preferable to total household income. Current gross income is preferable to current cash income because of the need to include remittances, and self-grown food. (It usually does not, however, include government subsidised services and other benefits from public expenditure.) Total consumption is preferable to income because it indicates the components (food, clothes, transport, fuel, education, health etc.), the shares of which are important indicators of changes in living standard. From carefully conducted household expenditure surveys, we have data on 'what' and 'how' much individuals consume. In this study of income distribution in Malaysia,

Sudhir Anand (1983) has demonstrated how inequality is higher among individuals than households.

Gini and Theil indices of inequality in income distribution are powerful tools in judging changes in inequality in the income (or consumption) shares of groups and inequality among each group.[14] Provided that such data on income distribution is available and comparable (which is not easy), we can judge the extent of changes in the consumption pattern and in inequality before and after land reform. But how long after?

Time frame for comparison

The reduction in the concentration of *land ownership* is easily measurable soon after the completion of the redistribution procedures. But to measure the decline in inequality in the distribution of income or expenditure is more problematical, and requires observations over a longer period of time. Another consideration is the interaction between land reform and market forces in addition to the effects of population growth and complementary measures taken by governments to improve living standards in rural areas. Completing land redistribution, enforcing tenancy regulations, and arranging for irrigation, drainage, supply of complementary inputs and marketing of beneficiaries' produce takes, on average, 5–8 years. A further 8–10 years should be allowed for changes in the pattern of income-consumption distribution to stabilise. It appears that a total period of 15 years should provide enough time for:

(a) the stabilisation of the relative economic position of losers and gainers from land reform;
(b) the beneficiaries to experience their new responsibilities in production, marketing, capital formation and participation in the development of their communities; and
(c) the manifestation of improved abilities in beneficiaries as a consequence of new motivations, better nutritional standards and developed skills.

In his pioneering work, Soleiman Cohen (1978) recommends consideration of a 20 year period. His conclusion is based on a comprehensive simulation analysis of a considerable amount of data from two countries (Chile and India) with different political systems and agrarian structures. He shows how such a period is adequate to judge changes in income distribution, employment, agricultural growth, non-agricultural output and even more demandingly, the country's balance of trade and payments.[15]

Allocation between consumption and saving

The economic behaviour of the beneficiaries as consumers and potential

101

savers depends upon the extent of their pre-reform deprivation and of the control exercised over the beneficiaries by the reforming state institution. This control is particularly influential with respect to cropping patterns and to pricing and procurement of the marketed surplus. The beneficiaries who were poor, under-employed, malnourished and deprived of a minimum living standard are likely to eat more and better. With the expected rise in their income, the allocation for the two necessities (food and fuel) is likely to remain proportionately constant during the initial phase of the reform (the food share is likely to remain at about 70 per cent of total household expenditure because of the expected high elasticity of demand for food – around 0.8).

We know from the ideas behind Engels' law (1856) and Keynes' marginal propensity to consume (1936), that a rise in the beneficiaries' income leads to a steady fall in their income elasticity of demand for food, and a reciprocal rise in the demand for non-food items.[16] As noted earlier, this relationship is not expected to hold at an early stage of land reform. This has been substantiated by empirical research since the original work of Clark (1964), on the consumption behaviour of the poor.

Given that 70–75 per cent of beneficiaries' total income is spent on food, the balance of their total outlay will be allocated to the purchase of non-food items (clothes, furniture, bicycles . . . etc.) which are normally *domestic* products. There is no reason to believe that they would sacrifice their own present consumption for a consequent investment to increase future income. They are rational and consistent in improving their present households' nutritional standard and for meeting their immediate needs. Increased consumption is a logical prerequisite to reducing the poverty endured before land reform. At a later stage, when their needs are met, the balance for non-food expenditure and savings is expected to rise. The higher the aggregate demand (purchase) of locally produced non-food items, the greater is the employment of labour in the corresponding industries and services in the domestic economy.[17] This may be illustrated by the following hypothetical example:

	Before land reform	After period I	period II
Value of output/income	100	130	150
Consumption – Food	75	95	100
Non-food	25	30	40
Saving (investment)	0	5	10

The illustration shows that depending on their extent, the beneficiaries are contributing to the productive capacity of the national economy via their consumption of non-food items and their saving for adding new non-land assets or investment goods (e.g. purchase of livestock, irrigation pumps or shares in their co-operatives). The realised saving in excess of their current consumption can contribute to increased output levels. The order of magnitude of these income effects depends primarily on the scale of land redistribution and the enforcement of rental control.

For ex-landlords, the redistributive consequences depend on many factors: Is land reform complete or partial? How much was their pre-reform saving capacity? Are they compensated or not for the expropriated land and other farming assets? Is compensation an outright payment in cash or in government bonds? What is the rate of inflation in the post-reform period?

In countries where they are compensated, it would be highly unlikely for them to invest extensively in agriculture for fear of future expropriation. If compensation was in cash, it would be sensible for the government to prevent its flight abroad, and ensure its injection into the domestic economy through a number of outlets: savings in financial institutions and investment in industry, trade, services and housing construction in urban areas. Being experienced entrepreneurs, the ex-landlords are likely to increase productivity from the retained advantageously situated and higher quality land than that of the beneficiaries after expropriation. The affected landlords are also likely to continue saving and investing in activities which yield high return. Such activities, however, depend on the political environment, i.e. whether the authorities and the post-reform political mechanism continue to be hostile to them, even if they wish to invest outside agriculture.

Motivation and participation

A study of the redistributive consequences of land reform should include the ambiguous but developmentally significant motivation of the beneficiaries to participate directly and through their own representatives. There are different ways of looking at participation.[18] Participation can refer to sharing in economic power through enhanced abilities and production motivation induced by holding land and secure access to credit and technical knowledge. In an operative sense, participation means that beneficiaries share in local community decision making through expressing their needs, interests and priorities in developing their own communities. The term can also refer to active roles in the newly-created political structure through organisations and representatives of choice, thereby influencing programming and policy formulation to serve their interests.

These are hard issues for the analyst who is particularly dependent upon quantitative measurement. Perhaps we should be satisfied with qualitative statements based on field observations made according to

103

well-defined criteria for measuring the changes brought about by land reform. But the difficulty is not merely the methodology used. My experience has led me to believe that it lies chiefly in separating the operative ideology of the reformers from the perceptions of the beneficiaries. This is manifested in institutional organisations patronised or imposed by official authorities under an *a priori* assumption that they are good enough to meet the needs and interests of the beneficiaries. When farmers in land reform areas of several countries were asked about the choice of cropping patterns, marketing procedures and the initiative behind newly introduced programmes, their usual answer was 'ask the government or the local office of the ruling political party'. This illustrates the real dichotomy in the perceptions of those who are expected to participate, and the reformers' tendency to control. From the point of view of the State institutions, it seems that participation is a management tool used to achieve a pre-determined end; an end in which the beneficiaries had no say, and over which they wield no control.

With this paradox in mind, the analyst can study the set of attitudes and motivations of the beneficiaries, as well as the manifestation of power relations induced by land reform. Percentages or scores of field observations classified by income class and land tenure status may help in understanding changes in the following areas:

1. Motivations for better production and pattern of consumption.
2. Grass roots leadership and patterns of electoral participation.
3. The accountability of local organisations and their officials to the beneficiaries.
4. The responsiveness of the local network of government machinery to the needs of the beneficiaries.
5. The role of beneficiaries' organisations in
   (a) influencing programmes and policy priorities; and in
   (b) jeopardising the market power of established traders.

The creation of a widespread network of peasant organisations in rural areas whose members are *homogeneous* in economic and social status and have less conflicting interests can incite participation to satisfy the needs of peasants. However, there is a risk of continued paternalism and increased control by State appointed land reform officials. The political officials may use the beneficiaries' organisations to serve the government's political motives.

Though these participatory elements might appear to be difficult to quantify, efforts made so far by some scholars are indeed encouraging. Based on his field observations in Taiwan, the Philippines, Mexico and Colombia, Hung-Chao Tai (1975) established meaningful indicators of political participation as a consequence of land reforms. Another contribution to empirical analysis is made by Esman and Uphoff (1984) in their comprehensive study of action of local organisations as intermediaries in rural development. Even changes in power relations could be measured by indices. Hopkins and Van der Hoeven (1981) made such an attempt in their modelling work on economic and social factor in development, which they then applied to four countries.[19]

Command over food and access to land

In this last section we focus on a major consequence of land reform: the command over food, and how it is associated with developing human abilities. First, we need to clarify:

(a) the meaning of command over food via access to land as an insurance against risks of malnutrition and poverty;
(b) the nutritional effect of land redistribution through the expected rise in the beneficiaries' income;
(c) the multidimensional aspects of acquiring command over food-intake within the context of investment in human capital; and
(d) the association between malnutrition and the agriculturally wage-based landless workers who rely heavily on the market mechanism for their food-intake.

It must be noted that the term malnutrition is broader than under-nutrition. According to FAO Fifth World Food Survey (1985), the former refers to any physical condition implying ill-health that can be brought about by inadequate diet and thus includes under-nutrition which is primarily caused by an inadequate calorie intake. A person suffering from under-nutrition may not be suffering from the effects of deficiencies in protein, vitamin or other specific nutrients. In practice, both terms are used synonymously. The most reliable measure of malnutrition is based on the growth of the children and changes in the body weight of adults. Once the undernourished children are sorted out from the rest by means of anthropometric surveys, their parents' occupational identity and size of holdings may be established. Empirical research shows that information on rural households' food-intake and the distribution of food consumption can also be obtained through this method.[20]

The meaning of command over food

From the dawn of human history, command over food has been accounted as a major source of power and security. In *Power – A New Social Analysis*, Bertrand Russell (1940: 35) says, 'Power may be defined as the production of intended effects.' He also says, 'The impulse of

105

submission, which is just as real and just as common as the impulse to command, has its roots in fear' (1940: 18).

In situations where industry is in its infancy and agriculture is the main source of employment, a landless worker faces two types of fear and uncertainties in acquiring food. One is the unstable flow of income from hiring out his or her labour and the other is his or her dependency on the power of grain traders in an imperfect market mechanism. In both cases, he or she is subordinated by fear and indignation. But the peasant who owns or controls a small piece of productive land has, on the other hand, a higher degree of certainty and independence in acquiring most of the household's food from his or her holding. Thus, the latter has more power in commanding food than the former. International relations seem to resemble this notion of power. A rich country donating food to a low-income country commands a political power over, and imposes stringent regulations on the latter, which submits and is subordinated.

Commanding food can be viewed as a product of three interrelated elements: security in acquiring the household's entire dietary needs; a higher degree of independence from the imperfect market mechanism; and escaping the risk of malnutrition. The acquisition of food is *not* to be by means of its distribution by government institutions. Rather, it is through an intensive mixing of the hitherto under-utilised labour with legally-secured access to productive farmland. Certainly, *if* food-for-work and school feeding programmes, food subsidies and so forth are effectively executed in a stable manner and provided they are sustained over a long period of time, they can achieve good results. Nutritional benefits may reach the rural poor, *not* necessarily the poorest, either directly or via temporary employment. Experience tells us that this conditional 'if' or 'provided that' is subject to a number of uncertainties and programme vulnerabilities such as: a changing political environment, shifts in domestic policy priorities, leakages in execution, weakness in administration, the class-biased bureaucratic institutions and their collusion with traders, and, as we have seen in Chapter 2, there is the risk of budgetry cuts by internationally indebted governments in their response to the IMF-induced package of adjustments.[21]

It is indeed deplorable if food aid to developing countries does not reach the malnourished poor. In their careful assessment of aid, including food programmes and projects, Robert Cassen and his associates remarked that aid has been ill-directed to the poor: 'very little of it, has been directed at, or has had any impact, positive or negative, on the poorest (the 10 per cent at the bottom of the income distribution' (Cassen *et al.*, 1986: 110). They report a number of conflicting views revealed by an evaluation made of programmes of food aid (e.g. food supplied is allegedly sold off or taken by the army and civil servants) (1986: 161).

An authority on food aid states that 'Absence of [an employment-oriented] environment can reduce to little more than *temporary* relief even the most direct approach for aiding the poor'.[22]

It is necessary to clarify the association of command over food with secured access to land. Security in the peasants' acquisition of food should not be taken to mean a pronounced preference for a low risk subsistence agriculture with a mono-cropping system of cereals, root and tuber crops.[23] Nor does it mean a rejection of peasants' cultivation of high risk export crops with the consequential vulnerability to market forces over which the peasants have no control. We are aware of many developing countries' desperate need for foreign exchange from increased export crops to accumulate surplus and to industrialise. We know also that mono-industrial crops for export (tea, palm-oil, rubber, coffee) require a long period before harvest, during which the peasants' daily food needs must be satisfied. Furthermore, mono-cropping is vulnerable to crop failure which leads to unstable income flow through wide fluctuations in the level and price of food acquisition.[24]

There is no reason why a conducive price policy and access to technical knowledge combined with secured landholding rights should not lead to the beneficiaries from land reform increasing food and non-food crops production beyond their necessities. If left free to choose their cropping pattern, the beneficiaries are also expected to grow more food crops, mainly grains, root and tuber crops. (We have seen in Chapter 1 that small-holders of land in LDCs grow most of these countries' food grain.)

Satisfied food intake, combined with better access to health, sanitation and education, are converted into human capital accumulation, which in turn, raises their productivity and their abilities. Michael Lipton (1985) suggests a significant relationship through his use of the multiplier effect and adders' (accumulation) effect. A landholder's household converts calorie intake *via* labour into an income level sufficient to satisfy the household's dietary needs and to leave a surplus for accumulating new assets that 'can reduce future risks of poverty'.[25]

The conversion efficiency is determined by the owned or operated assets (including land, human skills, financial and real capital). According to Lipton's proposition, peasants who neither own nor operate land, nor do they own real capital (oxen, plough), experience fluctuating income and calorie-intake. These fluctuations diminish their chances of acquiring the necessary economic surplus to ensure against poverty. As Lipton rightly says: 'productive land turns out to be a much more life-cyclic asset than income' (Lipton, 1985: 4) Based on his review of the experience in a few countries, he concludes that land is still overwhelmingly the main productive asset by value for securing calorie intake. Skills and education further enhance the abilities which have benefited from the higher level of nutrition provided.

The important implications for nutrition and employment of land owner-ship distribution has recently been theoretically formulated by Dasgupta and Ray (1986, 1987). In a competitive market economy, malnutrition could be eradicated in time by *full* land redistribution and through full employment.[26] According to their model, *partial* redistribution of land to some involuntarily unemployed, as well as to those 'on the margin of being

Figure 3.2 Linkages among access to land, command over food and rural development

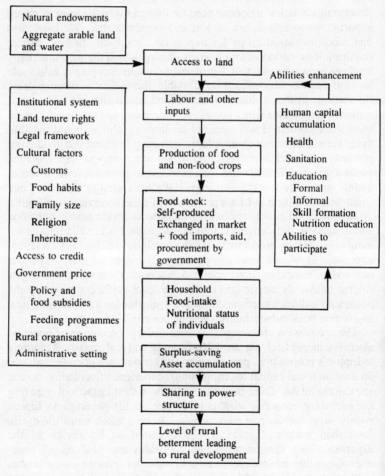

The arrows indicate direct effects. Effects of international trade, prices, and domestic storage of food are not included.

unemployed', may, in some cases, leave the risk of unemployment and under-nutrition unmitigated, particularly in economies with fixed aggregate land. Their conclusion is simple: 'inequality of asset ownership can be pinpointed as the *basic* cause of involuntary unemployment and malnourishment' (p. 25).

The dynamic interplay of the elements which contribute to the meaning of command over food are summarised in the simple diagram of Figure 3.2.

Food-intake and human abilities

There are conceptual and methodological difficulties in relating the quality of human life via enhanced abilities with access to land. These difficulties raise the following kinds of question: do qualities such as nourishment, health, skills and education have economic value? Are they capital assets which yield income over time, or do they represent current consumption, thereby reducing savings? Can we measure their effect on productivity, the rates of agricultural growth, as well as on performing participatory functions? Is the prevalence of malnutrition, high mortality rates, low life expectancy and illiteracy in rural areas associated with landlessness and highly unequal distribution of land? To what extent is the landless peasants' heavy reliance on the food-grain market responsible for their malnutrition and low chance of surviving famine? This section makes a brief attempt to explore these controversial questions.

Investment in human capital is viewed here as the provision of adequate opportunities to develop income-yielding abilities in the expectation that future benefits will exceed the costs incurred. By abilities we mean the enhanced capacity of the peasants to perform functions. This enhancement results from improved health, literacy and skills. The link is shown in the right hand box of Figure 3.2, as interacting with access to land and raising productivity. These are considered *created* capital assets which yield income over a person's lifespan. These human (non-material) assets give him or her the capacity to choose from *accessible* opportunities. The substance of our argument is that a landless peasant who is malnourished, illiterate and unhealthy is unable to act on his or her own will, simply because opportunities to escape from the poverty trap are restricted. As Commons remarked, it is absurd to talk about opportunities because 'we do not choose inaccessible alternatives' (Commons, 1934: 318).

The extent of malnutrition and illiteracy represents high current consumption of human capital stock and its depletion over time. A developing country which keeps a large section of the rural population in poverty, also denies them adequate opportunities for improving their abilities. In turn, it stunts the opportunities of the country as a whole to increase its wealth. As Marshall succinctly remarked in 1890: 'they go to the grave carrying with them undeveloped abilities and faculties;

wealth of the country – to say nothing of higher considerations – many times as much as would have covered the expense of providing adequate opportunities for their development' (Marshall, 1952, Book VI, Chapter IV: 467–8). The expected benefits from developing human assets of the rural poor (via accessible opportunities to hold land) should be an inducement for governments to redirect public resources in favour of the poorest among peasants.

Adam Smith, Von Thunen and Karl Marx ranked human abilities as valuable components of capital. Yet it was only recently and since the original work of Myrdal (1944, 1968), Schultz (1960, 1971) and Usher, (1978) that empirical evidence has been assembled from developing countries.[27] Hicks (1980) and Wheeler (1980) attempted to quantitatively measure not merely how these human qualities increase human productivity and economic growth, but also their interrelated effects, *viz.*, how nutrition and education affect each other and how both affect longevity and the productivity of the workers.[28] However, most of the studies have turned a blind eye to the relationship between access to land, nutritional standards, and survival changes. Similarly, in the theoretical domain of human capital, the emphasis has been on education as an important determinant of income differences.

Over the last two decades development economists, nutritionists, anthropologists, the medical profession and statisticians have conceptualised and conducted empirical reseach on aspects of investment in human capital.[29] However, like multidisciplinary treatments of development, (discussed in Chapter 2), comprehensive understanding of nutrition or malnutrition has been inhibited by its segmentation into narrow areas of concern sponsored by specialised professions. Considered a medical phenomenon by the medical profession, nutrition has consequently fallen under the auspices of the Ministry of Health in most developing countries. Consequently, and unfortunately, nutrition has become only a distant concern of many Ministries of Agriculture, where policies on food crops are formulated and technically supported. The same is true with regard to State institutions implementing land reform and settlement programmes.

Diminishing the reliance on the market for food

In private property-market economies, the primary function of the market order is to equilibrate the increasing demand for food through prices and wages' adjustments *without* government intervention. The bitter lessons learnt in these economies do not show the benefits of such a mechanism to those landless peasants who are net buyers of their entire food-intake. They rely for their current consumption on the current food prices. Such people are typically a high proportion of the undernourished and the victims of famine.

and on causes of famines is unequivocal in its suggestion that there is a strong association between access to productive land and the incidence of both under-nutrition and famine.[30] Those who have starved to death in most famines of the present century have been landless agricultural workers, paddy huskers, small tenants, pastoral nomads and rural women in service occupations. Alamgir (1977, 1981) showed that after the 1974 famine in Bangladesh, the number of the landless workers and the incidence of absolute poverty increased, whereas the economic position of the landlords and grain traders was strengthened.

In normal times of relative plenty, landless agricultural workers not receiving the wage-equivalent in grain are most vulnerable to suffering from malnutrition under the following conditions:

1. They have to rely on the labour market to exchange their labour for wages and on the grain market to exchange their wages for household food requirements (Sen, 1981).
2. They are vulnerable to displacement by capital intensive technology in production (e.g. mechanisation).
3. The seasonality in food production leads to involuntary unemployment and low calorie-intake before harvest time when food reserves are low and prices are high (Longhurst, 1983).
4. The type of labour in farming is physically demanding. These demands on their physical energy may be in addition to the calorie-loss incurred by walking the long distances to work (Lipton, 1983). This is also true for the distance travelled by many women to fetch water, and by many children to school. These three types of compulsory physical efforts require calories from an already deficient supply. (This is in sharp contrast to the urban elite, who try hard to lose their excessive calorie-intake by jogging or playing squash-rackets.)
5. In the absence of remittances, receipts and social security schemes, the subsistence level wages of the landless peasants leave no balance for social needs. This throws them into debt. The nutritional effect of such distress is more serious in living conditions in cold climates where the demand for clothing competes with demand for food.

On the basis of his research on the possible causes of poverty and famine Amartya Sen (1981, 1985) suggests an entitlement approach to commanding food by the legal means available to the society. He views starvation and famine as a manifestation of the failure of entitlement relations on the part of the poor. A person starves either because he does not have the ability to command enough food or he does not use this ability to avoid starvation. Ownership entitlement is in terms of land and labour power. If food is acquired by an agricultural worker through the market, his or her entitlement is violated by the collusion of traders as well as by landlords by means of a fall in wages, involuntary unemployment and artificial shortage of foodcrops. This results in a sharp rise in their prices. The exchange entitlement of other groups of the peasantry (small owners, small tenants, share-croppers, pastoral nomads) is violated by means of high prices of inputs and other goods. Because of cheap sale under distress and indebtedness, cattle and land are also lost.

How exchange entitlement fails under the market power of grain traders is the main thrust of Martin Ravallon's thesis (1987). He explores the links between the market mechanism and survival chances. On the basis of his careful investigation of two famines in south India in 1977 and in Bangladesh in 1974, Ravallion identified high food-grain prices as an important cause of starvation and deaths (1987: Figures 2.6 and 2.7). In examining the relationship between *aggregate* food availability and individual survival chance, he finds that the high food grain prices combined with a fall in employment determine the agricultural workers' survival chance irrespective of high food grain stocks in the country. His econometric investigation indicates that during the Bangladesh famine (1974), a 10 per cent drop in employment, resulted in a 21 per cent fall in the *individual's* consumption of rice (Ravallion, 1987: Table 1.2).

Thus peasants who have no accessible opportunities to hold productive land and consequently fail to establish command of their food needs, are the most likely candidates for high risk of hunger and severe ill-health leading to death. Climatic conditions cannot be held entirely responsible. Rather the oligopoly of traders controlling the food grains market and the non-neutral role of the state institutions are to blame.

At this stage our analytical framework of the meaning of land reform and accessible opportunities has been primarily hypothetical. Without empirical evidence from the experience of LDCs (which we shall present in the rest of this study), the discussion could continue only on hypothetical grounds, and would, of course, have less persuasive strength. It could end as Bernard de Mandeville ended his poem, 'The Fables of the Bees' in 1729:

> To such a height, the very poor
> Lived better than the rich before;
> And nothing could be added more.

Notes

1 Currie (1981) – see Chapter 10.
2 For a concise statement on the operational significance of land tenure in its relationships with income distribution and productivity in agriculture,

see Dorner (1964). On land tenure and stages of development in a historical context see Parsons (1962).

Whereas water rights for irrigation is a crucial determinant of productivity and income for small farmers in arid and semi-arid areas, it has, nevertheless, received little analytical attention by either economists or technicians concerned with irrigation problems. Implications of institutional arrangements constitute the subject of a study prepared by Daniel W. Bromley for the World Bank (1982). It presents examples from Mexico, Gezira Scheme in the Sudan, Pakistan, the Philippines and Taiwan. For examples in other countries see his Bibliography.

3   Dan Usher says (1981: 85, 89):

> There is no capitalist equity without security of property . . . an economy cannot be said to be capitalist at all, if property is insecure, for the squabble over the assignment of property is every bit as corrosive to democracy as the squabble over the assignment of income. It makes no difference whether people fight over the fruit of the tree. With property, as with income, a degree of feasibility may be traded off for efficiency or for a greater acceptability of the system as a whole. But there are limits beyond which the security and rights of property cannot be attenuated. . . . The legislature (by majority vote) has to specify the rules . . . and the line between the rights of property and the right each man enjoys by virtue of his status as a citizen.
>
> Economic freedom is not only of value in itself but is necessary as a prerequisite to democracy. . . . Not only is economic freedom required for political freedom, but they are two sides of the same coin, bound together because they are made of the same stuff.

4   Marshall (1952: 41) made this statement as part of his proposed questions with which economic science has to deal.

5   See Galbraith (1984).

6   Von Hayek develops a similar thesis as that of Usher with respect to the system of private property as the best guarantee of freedom.

7   As an example, the land granted to the Sheikhs in Iraq by the Ottoman Sultan was converted into freehold private property under British rule through the land settlement Act of 1932. The average area of each Sheikh reached 50,000 acres. Their total area was 68 per cent of the total arable land in Iraq at the time of the land reform in 1958, whereas their holdings represented only one-tenth of one per cent of the total number of land holdings. Other examples from Kenya and Egypt are presented in Chapter 5.

Amartya Sen discussed the issue of legitimacy raised in Nozick's book:

> The question I am asking is this: if results such as starvation and famines were to occur, would the distribution of holdings still be morally acceptable despite their desastrous consequences? . . . Why should it be the case that the rules of ownership, etc., should have such absolute priority over life – and death – questions? . . . I have

presented evidence to indicate that in many large famines in the recent past, in which millions of people (mostly rural landless workers) have died, there was no overall decline in food availability at all, and the famines occurred precisely because of shifts in entitlements resulting from exercises of rights that are perfectly legitimate. (Nozick, 1984: 311–12)

8 See, for example, Smith (1974) Chapter 15, Duncan and Artis (1951) and Kaufman (1953). These sociologists agree that income distribution in rural areas is the best indicator of social stratification. The significance of this criterion lies in its two-fold purpose – it shows explicitly material aspects of stratification and implies non-material aspects such as rights, authority, privileges and prestige. It helps the analyst in delineating the class structure of a rural community and placing individuals within it.

9 Parsons (1962: 17); Warriner (1969: xv see especially the section on Integral reform: 59–65); and Lipton (1974: chapter 9).

10 For a comprehensive analysis of the effects of changing distribution on growth see (a) Chenery (1979: Chapter 11). Figure 3.1 in the text is an adaptation of Chenery's Figure 11.3 in order to indicate institutional and agrarian structure; (b) Chenery *et al.* (1981: Chapters 1 and 11); and (c) Fields (1980). For an understanding of the role of rural labour market in generating poverty, see Collier and Lal (1986), Chapter 5 'The functioning of the labour market: agriculture' and Chapter 8 'Poverty and growth'.

11 On the demographic characteristics of the rural poor see Visaria (1981), Lipton (1983) and FAO (1986: Chapter 2).

12 For a careful review of the existing hypotheses on income distribution see, for example, Ranadive (1978) and Frank and Webb (1979) – Chapter 2 'Causes of income distribution and growth in LDCs: some reflections on the relation between theory and policy.

13 For a detailed discussion and critical review of the debate on welfare and utility theories see Parts III and IV in Sen (1982). For a brief discussion and relevance to measuring inequality see the section 'Welfare economics and distribution' in Bigsten (1983: 46–50).

14 The two measurements concern the comparison of changes in the degree of inequality. In this case, it is the share of size groups of landowners or holders in the total area (e.g. 70 per cent of the owners own 20 per cent of the cultivated land). A Lorenz diagram is obtained by plotting the cumulative numbers. The extent of the inequality is indicated by the area between the diagonal (absolute equality) and the actual curve; the greater this area the greater the inequality. The measure (Gini coefficient must lie between 0 and 1. For example, an index of 0.876 is an indication of higher inequality of distribution than 0.543). Gini coefficient is a simple and direct measure of ranking inequality. Theil index gives the same ranking as Gini index when the curves do *not* intersect. The advantage of Theil index is in measuring inequality *between* size categories and *within* each category of land-owners or income groups. For a detailed comparison of these two and

other measures of inequality see Chapter 4 'The measurement of inequality and poverty' in Bigsten (1983).

15 The simulations carried out for Chile and India over a period of 20 years suggest that a direct redistribution of land is essential if the poor peasant population is not to experience a deterioration in its relative income. Complementing the redistribution measures with credit advances and increases in productivity, taxes and wages would also benefit the non-agricultural sector. Rich farmers affected by the redistribution are projected to benefit after ten years when they can resume increasing their savings and build up their financial assets again: Cohen (1978).

16 These principles are concerned with: how food demand depends on the size of income and food share in total expenditure. Keynes' marginal propensity to consume is the ratio of a small change in consumption to a small change in income $\frac{\Delta C}{\Delta Y}$. The short-run increase in the income of a poor man will not change his propensity to consume (average). Colin Clark collected data from previous research on food consumption at different levels of real income. The best measure is by converting the monetary terms into kg. grain equivalent/person/year. He found that at the lowest level of income, elasticity of demand for food appears to be fairly constant over the range of real income observed. Elasticity of demand for food measures the percentage change in food consumption in respect of a percentage change in income. Marginal propensity to consume on the other hand, measures the *slope* of the demand line drawn through the points observed, see Clark and Haswell (1964), Chapter VIII – 'Consumption', (Chart XI and Table XXVII).

17 Mellor and Johnston (1984) report the results of country studies showing that in India, the rural consumption of manufactured consumer goods is two-and-half times that of the urban consumption of those goods. . . . In Asia, peasant farmers typically spend some 40 per cent of increments to income on locally produced non-agricultural goods and services. The income multipliers are substantial – in the order of 0.7, and the employment multipliers are probably larger.

18 There is an extensive literature on the meaning of participation in development. Examples are: Uphoff et al. (1979); Cohen and Uphoff (1980); Bhaduri and Anisur-Rahman (1982); El-Ghonemy (1984); Esman and Uphoff (1984); and Oakley and Marsden (1984).

19 Hung Chao Tai (1975); Hopkins and Van der Hoeven (1981); and Esman and Uphoff (1984). An index of power is formulated in Van der Hoeven (1981) which consists of a number of groups of people and number of people in each group; their mean income; their mean education level, and their proportion to the number of people organised in total. Hence the power function for a particular group represents both the size and its socio-economic characteristics. The index is used also to judge the sensitivity of a policy to power change and the groups' articulation of their demands.

20 Anthropometric Surveys on the nutritional status of children indicate

that malnutrition is higher in rural than in urban areas among children under five years of age. These studies have been carried out in Brazil (1975), Cameroon (1978), Egypt (1978), Haiti (1978), Lesotho (1977), Liberia (1976), Somalia (1983), Sierra Leone (1978), Togo (1977), Tunisia (1978–80) ahd Yemen Arab Republic (1978). The characteristics of rural households and the land tenure status of their heads could be identified. Sources of these studies are listed in FAO – The Fifth World Food Survey, 1985, p. 44. For Somalia see Tyler (1983).

21 Sri Lanka is an example of the effects of changing government policy on food subsidies. See Samaranayaka (1982) and Gooneratne and Gunawardena (1984). On the impact of the IMF's adjustment programme see the cases of Tanzania and Mexico in *Labour and Society*, International Institute of Labour Studies, Vol. II no. 3, September 1986. For an overall assessment see Ajit Singh (1986) in the preceding journal, and UNICEF Special Study *The Impact of World Recession on Children – 1984*. On the example of an evaluation of Food For Work programme, see BIDS/IFPRI Report on Bangladesh, 1983.

22 Cassen adds to the statement quoted from p. 110: 'At the same time, even though the poorest may not gain much from many projects in terms of income and productive assets, they do appear to have gained indirectly, from those projects which have cheapened their food' (Cassen *et al.*, 1986). The authority refers to W. Tims (Netherlands) and his statement was cited on p. 168 in Cassen's book.

23 Some professionals still refer to present-day subsistence and shifting agriculture in Africa as 'primitive' for its dependence on the use of the hoe, discontinuous labour and the restoration of soil fertility by resting unused land-practices conditioned by agro-climatic factors. Robert Chambers (1985: 86 and 101) remarked:

> In most of Africa, expatriates conducting agricultural research suffered from cultural conditioning which made it difficult for them to see indigenous farming as anything but backward.

> One first step is for outsider professionals, the bearers of modern scientific knowledge, to step down off their pedestals, and sit down, listen, and learn.

24 For a detailed discussion on the seasonality factor, see Longhurst (1983). On the impact of cropping patterns on nutrition via fluctuations in prices, income and employment, see Pinstrup-Andersen (1983). On nutritional implications of economic and technical change in agriculture, see Taylor (1977).

25 See Lipton (1985). The concept is explained on pp. 1–4 and in a diagram on p. 46.

26 Dasgupta and Ray (1986, 1987).

27 (a) In his *An American Dilemma – the Negro Problem* (1944) and *Asian Drama* (1968), Gunnar Myrdal analysed the cumulative causation of poverty particularly the interdependence of economic factors and health,

education and social discrimination in employment. See in particular Vol. III, chapter 29 'Investment in man' in *Asian Drama*. (b) T.W. Schultz stressed the importance of the subject in his Presidential address at the 73rd Annual Meeting of the American Economic Association, St. Louis, Missouri, USA, December 1960. His relevant work is listed in the Bibliography. (c) On the same subject of human capital approach see Becker (1970a, b).

28 (a) See Usher (1978). (b) Part II of *World Development 1980* analyses the findings of research on human resources development. Page 38 presents the methodological problems in relating the contribution of human resources to economic growth. They draw on the studies prepared by World Bank and analysed in: Hicks (1980), King (1980) and Wheeler (1980).

29 (a) The concepts of entitlement and capabilities are developed in Sen (1981, 1985). On nutrition in rural development programmes see Lunven and Sabry (1981). (b) On human metabolic efficiency at different economic levels see Sukhatme (1978). (c) For the identification of the contribution of women to agricultural production see 'Women in Developing Agriculture' *The State of Food and Agriculture*, FAO, Rome (1983) Chap. 2, and *Women in Food Production*, FAO, Rome (1983). (d) On basic needs approach, see Streeten *et al.* (1981).

30 Sen (1981, 1985), Alamgir *et al.* (1977, 1980), and Ravallion (1987). *FAO Study on Haiti* is an example of food consumption surveys which include data on landholdings by size groups and nutritional status. It covers a sample of 261 households surveyed during January–April 1980. The results show that landless and holders of less than 0.5 hectares are the worst-off in nutrition, mortality and weight-for-age of the children. With increased holdings, there is a trend towards a rise in nutritional status and a decline in mortality rates. This group of poor farmers represent 44 per cent of the sample. Farmers growing food crops are better off than those growing coffee in the same size group. The study was carried out by I. Shorr, T. Ahlers and J. Manson in collaboration with Organisme de Developpement du Nord (ODN). Findings from field studies in seven LDCs on access to land and nutritional standard are summarised in Melville (1988).

Chapter four

Large estates: issues in efficiency and employment

Would the break-up of large privately owned estates, as usually demanded by many land reformers and peasant movements, raise land productivity and increase employment? What are the resulting economic functions of holding wealth in the form of large estates? Can we judge efficiency and social gains in large-sized farms both in capitalist and socialist agriculture solely in economic terms? These practical but ideologically controversial questions have been central to the concern of land reformers in many developing countries, and have received the analytical interest of many economists.

The purpose of this chapter is to examine these questions. It also attempts to crystallise the range of economic arguments emerging from empirical experience. Problems of the definition and measurement of efficiency in land, credit and labour utilisation under different production relations, and with different combinations of means of production will be discussed. It seems that the problems lie chiefly in the indiscriminate use of these terms of measurement, regardless of different social and political contexts. According to Myrdal:

> The very concepts designed to fit the special conditions of the Western World – and thus containing the implicit assumptions about social reality by which this fitting was accomplished – are used in the study of under-developed countries. Where they do not fit, the consequences are serious. (Myrdal, 1968: 16–17)

Before we discuss why these standardised measures do not fit, we need to keep in mind the premiss that the empirical evidence reviewed reflects each country's peculiar experience, its endowment with productive assets, institutions, and its structure of political power.

Issues in economic arguments

We may say that there is general agreement about the productive use of land and labour to accelerate economic growth in different sizes of holdings. What is at issue and has given rise to controversy is the criteria used in assessing and comparing the relative productiveness of resource utilisation between large and small land holdings under different economic systems and with different social arrangements. The controversy also arises over policy issues concerning the realisation of potential output and employment gains from the redistribution of under-utilised land and labour. This is particularly true as regards large-sized farms or where the holding of land is highly concentrated and the owners are absentee.

In respect of the criteria used to assess efficiency in the allocation of the means of production there is not much merit in an abstract discussion of the theoretical frame as related to large- and small-sized farms. This has been well presented elsewhere.[1] Instead, we shall use empirical evidence to identify questions of efficiency, accessible opportunities to credit and technology, economies of scale, and employment as they have been addressed in practice and how the conclusions were founded within the experience of specific countries. A distinction will be made between large-sized farms with privately owned land in capitalist agriculture and State-owned and managed farms in socialist agriculture. The issues to be examined and indices to be used concern the following criteria:

1. The bases for calculating factor prices of the means of production especially in respect of the choice of shadow prices (opportunity costs) of family labour.
2. Output per unit of land and per unit of labour power.
3. Intensity of the use of means of production and their factor combination (land, labour, capital and intermediate inputs such as seeds, manure, fertiliser, etc.).
4. Employment per unit of land in terms of the number of days per year and the number of workers utilised per unit of output produced.
5. The degree of responsiveness to technical change or innovations in agriculture.
6. The unified management with family labour in the person of the resident farm operator as compared to absentee owners and insecure tenancy.
7. The basis for calculating the costs of production in socialist agriculture and the reward to workers in large State-owned farms.
8. Questions of motivations, incentives and social consciousness.

Capitalist efficiency criteria: the Western bias

Let us first consider the experience of the Anglo-Saxon countries from which most of the criteria and indices have been abstracted. Internationally, these technologically advanced countries have achieved considerably high output per person in agriculture. In the USA, Canada, New Zealand and Australia typical farms managed by one resident family range in size between 500 and 2,000 acres. The high level *per capita* productivity is due partly to efficient management and skilled manpower of the owner-operator, and partly to the use of a high rate of capital and accumulated technical knowledge on land which is abundant relative to labour power. In these countries, the greater amount of capital invested in farms, the greater the need for management ability and public investment in agricultural research. (This is combined with high quality of extension service to the farmers who typically have a good standard of education.) All of these advantages contribute to higher productivity *per person* in agriculture. Intensive and competitive use of capital, in the form of large-scale mechanisation, is thus economically justified in these countries' factor-combination in agriculture.

Bachman and Christensen (1967) reported that farm sizes doubled in the USA between 1940 and 1965 while the number of adult workers per farm averaged the same (about three). They remarked that this average is the same for Indian family farms, while the size of individual farms in the USA was abut 100 times higher than in India.[2] Considering the average farm size in India was 6 acres (and very large farms 50 acres), and that the labour force in agriculture relative to the total is only four per cent in the USA (about 5 per cent in advanced Anglo-Saxon countries) while it is 70 per cent in India, the problems in universal applicability of criteria for efficiency and scale of production become evident. The efficiency of large-sized farms in advanced countries' agriculture refers to a higher return on capital and manpower (management and family labour) and it is measured in terms of output per man-hour. The unity of management and family labour is an essential feature because of the inherent inefficiency of absenteeism in private land ownership.[3] This point is worth remembering when we examine the prevalence of absentee owners of large estates in developing countries.

Expanding the example of the USA and India, consider the data given in Table 4.1. These data show some fundamental variation in natural endowment and factor-combinations in a selection of five developed and eight developing countries. In the former, productive land is not scarce and does not constitute a limiting factor in production. The ratio of agricultural population per hectare of arable land is very low, ranging between 0.02 to 0.7 persons per hectare, while the median size of holding is large, ranging from 147 hectares in the UK to 1,307 in New Zealand. In addition to the advanced skills and capabilities of farmers, this

Table 4.1 Labour, Land and Capital in Agriculture Variations in Samples from Developed and Developing Countries

Countries	Labour	Land			Capital	
	Agricultural labour force as percentage of total (1)	Agric. population per ha arable land (2)	Median size of holding per ha (3)		Number of tractors per 1,000 ha arable land (4)	Use of fertiliser kilogram per ha (5)
Developed						
Australia	7	0.02	1,993		8	26
Canada	5	0.05	359		14	51
New Zealand	11	0.7	1,307		204	1,025
United Kingdom	3	0.2	147		77	370
USA	4	0.1	526		25	113
Developing						
Bangladesh	75	7.8	0.9*		1	65
Egypt	46	8.1	0.9*		17	344
India	70	2.9	5.5		3	47
Indonesia	57	4.0	2.3		1	90
Kenya	81	6.0	11.7*		3	34
Mexico	37	1.1	9.8*		6	67
Pakistan	55	2.7	8.5		7	61
Philippines	52	3.3	5.4		2	33

*Average size of holding in hectares

Source: Column: 1 World Development Report – Indicators, 1986 – The data refer to 1980
2, 4, and 5 FAO *Country Tables*, 1987 – The data refer to 1984 or 1985
3 1970 World Census of Agriculture – analysis of results FAO, Rome, 1981 and 1984.
Bangladesh average size of holding refers to 1983/84

combination of low agricultural population per hectare, and high median size of holding helps to explain the relatively high number of units of capital used. The opposite is generally true in developing countries whose share of agricultural labour force to total labour force is seven to ten times larger than those of advanced countries. Although these data do not show the quality of land and its cropping pattern, the relative price of factors of production is indicative of their relative scarcity. For instance, in 1970 the average price of one hectare in the USA was US$ 800 and the daily agricultural wage rate was approximately US$ 12. Contrast these rates with Egypt's price of land and labour at US$ 1,500 per ha and $0.5 per daily worker in the same year. There is an exceedingly wide variation in the ratios of factor prices: land is 66.6 times that of wage rates in the USA, while it is 3,000 times that of wage rates in Egypt.

This variation cannot be explained solely in economic terms. We cannot ignore the institutional framework of property rights, the degree of imperfection in factor-markets and custom-determined production relations within which resources are allocated and their economic returns determined. As will be discussed in the next chapter, institutions, customs and economic response interact and shape each other. Because cultivable land is scarce and expensive in many developing countries we have selected, the economic response of their farmers is to maximise the return on output per unit of land. Thus, the intensity of land use is very high, particularly in irrigated areas (three crops a year are produced from one feddan (acre) in Egypt). Yield increasing and (therefore, labour-using) fertiliser is adequately applied, while labour-saving capital equipment, such as tractors, cannot be justified in economic or welfare terms, and so are much less used (as seen in Table 4.1). With the exception of Egypt (which experiences temporary migration of farm labour to neighbouring oil-rich Arab countries and because of heavily subsidised tractors), other LDCs in our sample use on average three tractors per thousand hectares. These are mostly concentrated on large farms and highly commercialised plantations. The use of traditional farm tools by small farmers (hoes, hand sickles, buffalo or ox-driven ploughs and threshers) instead of heavy tractors and combine harvesters is not a manifestation of irrational economics or primitive methods. Faced with institutional constraints in the credit market and the low demand for labour by non-agricultural sectors, these striving, hard working peasants are indeed rational. 'Rational' and 'irrational' styles of work will be considered in light of the empirical evidence which follows.

It is important to point out that if social environment, intra-family relations, and institutional barriers are ignored, the habitual use of criteria for measuring efficiency under perfect competition assumptions of production is of little economic meaning. Equally unsound is judging whether, and how, micro-production relations can maximise profits using aggregate production functions based on insecure data. We are also deluded by the consequential prediction of outputs under conditions of certainty (in the classical sense of a farm operating with complete technical knowledge and unlimited capital).

Judgements cannot be based on the premise that what is good for one system of economy is good for all others, or that the 'interest of all is the interest of each', as Edgeworth (1881) asserted in his model of change in competitive markets and what, in modern economic terms, remains 'the core' of the economy (Sen, 1982: 86).

It is this set of Western-biased criteria of economic relations that is still used by some economists and business agents in agriculture to advocate large farms and commercial plantations in developing countries. The advantages of large estates, according to this view, are as follows: they use technical knowledge, competent management and skilled manpower as in modern industry; the level of education among the landlords provides them with entrepreneurial skills; and large estates increase the marketable surplus, domestic saving and capital formation. In addition, large estates are considered to be pioneers in applying technology which they diffuse among small farmers; they release agricultural labour power for urban and industrial development; they overcome the problems of fragmentation of holdings; and they provide efficient marketing services and high quality of agricultural products, etc.

Based on this reasoning those in favour of large estates call for an agricultural development strategy which achieves high growth rates of agricultural output and concentrates scarce resources in highly commercialised and profit-motivated large-sized farms regardless of the consequential problems of inequity, poverty and under-employment in agriculture. Different adjectives were given to this pattern of agricultural growth such as 'modern', 'dynamic', 'progressive', 'capitalist' and 'Bimodal' (in the case of dualised agrarian structure).

Socialist efficiency criteria: State farms

The Anglo-Saxon doctrine that, 'to be efficient one must be very large and intensive in capital investment', has also been a major feature of State-owned and managed farms in socialist countries, since their beginnings in the Soviet Union in the 1920s. These large farms have to be seen as an integral part of the economic structure, centralised authority of the State and nationalised land property. They also have to be studied within moral and material objectives, and the incentive systems of specific countries over specific periods of time.

The meanings of 'employment', 'profit', and 'incentive' vary greatly, not only among socialist (more commonly referred to as Communist countries), but within countries during periods of time. For instance, concepts in China under Mao Tse-Tung (1949–76) differed from those of Zhao Ziyan Deng, initiating readjustment and management of the agricultural economy in 1979 as part of national economic reform. Management of State farms in Cuba, which are the most extensive in relative terms in all socialist countries, varies from the 1960s to the 1970s and the 1980s though the Cuban leadership of Fidel Castro Ruiz has not changed. State farms also exist in countries with private property market economies such as Egypt, Tunisia, Ghana and Iraq, but they are not dominant in their agrarian structure.

In socialist countries and those which consider themselves socialist it is difficult, if not impossible, to generalise on their performance and efficiency. They are diverse in organisation and role not only between countries but also between one State farm and another in the same country. There are still, however, some basic principles and common features which could be broadly outlined. They are centrally planned and in many countries co-exist with collectives and tiny individual plots for household private use. They are giants in size and in their share in capital stock and many of them form large agro-industrial complexes. In addition, many specialise in the production of one commodity, and have widespread use of technology. They provide the State with command over the production and marketing of essential food and cash crops for export thereby ensuring the supply of food to the urban population (including armed forces and civil servants). Their generation of employment is considerably expanded when the production of raw material is integrated with processing in a complex of agro-industry. Finally, though centrally managed by skilled staff they suffer from heavy bureaucracy. In issues of equality for women, large State farms made progress with entitlements and employment, significantly improving their women's status even in South Yemen, a Muslim and traditionally rural society.

In order to appreciate the large scale of operations of State farms, a few examples may help. In the Soviet Union the area of State farms accounted for 106 million hectares, representing 66.4 per cent of total agricultural land in 1978. They employed 11.3 million employees. Their proportion in China is much smaller, only 4.3 per cent to total agricultural land in 1982 but they employed 4.8 million – almost half the number of employees in the Soviet Union. Nevertheless, the area of the State farms in China was substantial – 4.4 million hectares. The proportion of State farms acreage to total agricultural land varies in other countries; 85 per cent in Cuba, 5 per cent in Vietnam and Ethiopia, and 4 per cent in Mozambique. On average the size of each State farm is considerable, ranging from 2,000 to 16,000 hectares.[4]

The role of these institutions in the national economy has to be seen against the historical background of long colonial history (e.g. Cuba, South Yemen, Mozambique and Vietnam), or semi-feudal agrarian economies (e.g. China, Ethiopia, and Russia). Large farms previously owned by absentee landlords or foreign owned plantations were converted to State-owned and managed farms. With the exception of Stalinist Russia, agriculture has been given absolute priority in development strategy. The priority was expressed by Mao in the 1950s, 'Agriculture is the foundation of National development from 1960 onwards' (White *et al.*, 1983: 12). However, since 1980 there have been such dramatic shifts, and rethinking of the economic management within agriculture in many countries, that it is difficult to catch up with these changes.

Measuring efficiency of resource use in State farms in economic terms is difficult for a foreign analyst because of the difference in cost accounting procedures. The difficulty also rests on whether the State farm is an autonomous enterprise or just an integral unit of a wider structure. Procedures also vary according to the relation of the central plan to the 'market'. Wages, salaries, bonuses and prices of the means of production and output are administratively and politically determined in many socialist countries. It is not an uncommon practice for the large number of employees and workers to have guaranteed salaries and wages regardless of the actual level of productivity. In cases where the State farms fulfil the established target of gross output, all staff and workers are usually paid bonuses. While employment of the large number of management staff and workers is guaranteed by the State, the lack of clearly defined material incentives to work harder still presents problems.

In Cuba, for example, reliance on consciousness combined with ambiguous material incentives had disastrous consequences for the newly established State sugar cane farms in the 1960s. However, when the macro-indicators of performance in the agricultural sector as a whole are used, the performance of the socialist countries appears to be as good as those with market economies and private property. In fact, some socialist countries (e.g. China, Cuba and North Korea) performed even better. Two such overall indicators were used by Keith Griffin: the annual growth rates of agricultural production and of labour productivity during 1970–80. In his words 'Hence there is nothing in these data to suggest that the performance of countries with communal tenure systems is inferior to those with individual tenure systems.'[5]

Perhaps these macro-indicators of performance can serve as an approximation of the performance of State farms in countries where they are the major source of agricultural GDP, such as in the case of Cuba where the share is 80 per cent. Although much of the rest of socialist agriculture (collectives or communes) were well studied, particularly in China, micro-studies at a State farm level are very scarce. Such studies are inhibited by a multitude of factors, some of which were already mentioned, such as material and non-material incentives, centralisation and decentralisation of management, and strict hierarchical chains of command. To these we can add politicisation of institutions and State farms, bureaucratisation of agriculture and labour utilisation, linking or de-linking the planned economic activities from or with the market, and the different definitions used by State farms with regard to 'productive' and 'non-productive' services.

But terms such as centralisation or decentralisation of management are ambiguous and require clarification from empirical studies. A recent study on Cuban rural economy by an international team of experts in 1985 bring some of these factors to light. It favourably judges the performance of State farms based on official figures of crop yields which show an increase of about 4 per cent per annum between 1975 and 1983. According to the findings of this study, the objective of the management system since about the mid-1970s has been to promote economic efficiency. Key features include economic accounting at the enterprise level, prices based on cost of production, decentralized decision-making and material incentives to boost productivity, efficiency and equality of output. However, the Cuban economy being centrally planned has naturally determined the limits of decentralisation and devolution of decision-making. Input and output prices are fixed by the State, the wage rates and the payment systems are also laid down by the State (Ghai *et al.*, 1988: Chapter 7).

This good record of State farms in Cuba is not matched by their performance in Mozambique, according to a study by the author during April–May 1984 (FAO, 1985d). Three State farm areas were visited: Capo Delgado in the North, Zonas Verdes in the South, and Chekoe in the West. Though representing 4 per cent of agricultural land, State farms cover 150,000 hectares of the best, mostly irrigated land. They produce strategic crops for export, food consumption in urban areas, and for agro-industries (cashew nuts, maize, rice, cotton, tea, sunflowers, and cocoa). Following independence from five centuries of Portuguese rule, (Mozambique gained independence in 1975), the country leadership assigned State farms high priority in investment of a large share of two scarce resources: foreign exchange and technically qualified staff. Nevertheless, expectations were not met. The visited farms experienced the serious problem of inadequate technical personnel, a lack of experienced managers, and a high degree of politicisation of management. Product prices or daily wages were, instead, centrally determined, and supplies of agricultural equipment and spare parts for crop processing factories were inadequate. These constraints are manifested in the steady decline in the volume of agricultural exports by 8 per cent per annum during the period 1976–83. Cotton and cocoa oil exports fell by 26 per cent during the same period. As shown in Table

4.2, the marketed sunflower and cocoa fell sharply between 1981 and 1983 and cotton output dropped by 12 per cent during the period 1977–84. Compared with the communally cultivated land (co-operatives known as the peasant sector), there is a light variation as suggested by data on Zonas Verdes in Table 4.2. This was also noticed in Chekoe State farms growing maize and rice. Productivity per hectare in their State farms was 2.5 tons of maize and 3 tons of rice compared to 1.5 and 2.5 tons on average respectively in the co-operative/peasant sector.

Table 4.2 **Mozambique State Farms' Marketed Crops in Two Zones 1981–3**

Crops and years		Zonas Verdes				Capo Delgado*	
		State Farms		Co-operatives			
		Tons	Indice	Tons	Indice	Tons	Indice
Maize	1981	33789	100	1704	100	3541	100
	1982	47477	141	1458	86	8036	226
	1983	27232	81	785	46	5026	142
Rice	1981	25594	100	1407	100	377	100
	1982	38677	151	979	70	527	139
	1983	15022	59	546	39	1139	302
Sunflower	1981	3285	100	509	100	934	100
	1982	933	28	245	48	577	62
	1983	602	18	152	30	383	41
Cocoa							
Copra	1981	15000	100				
	1982	12710	85				
	1983	9796	86				

Source: Compiled from data given by the State Marketing Organization, AGRICOM E.E. in Maputo. *No disaggregated data for State farms and Co-operatives (collectives in Aldeas Comunales). Data before 1981 were not given because AGRICOM was established in that year. Zonas Verdes in the South, and Capo Delgado in the North are the two areas visited in addition to Chekoe State farms referred to in the text. For detailed information on rural development and agrarian institutions see, WCARRD Mission Report No. 13, April–May 1984, FAO, Rome

Considering the proportionately high resources allocated to State farms, their performance is far below expectations. Although workers share in management, receive high wages, and free education and health (in addition to some meals), they were unable to exchange their wages for scarce goods, such as clothes, matches, beer, transistor radios, and glass. To obtain these goods, some workers either walked long distances to cross the border to buy in Malawi, Zimbabwe and Swaziland, or they paid exorbitant prices on the black market.

Empirical examination of efficiency on capitalist large estates in developing countries

Questions of the advantages, merits, and economic performance of large estates in developing countries with private property-market economies are fundamental. They should, therefore, be left to empirical evidence. We shall use for this purpose, two sets of evidence: a cross-sectional analysis, and case studies of farms or households in certain countries. Under the former, a review of the findings of four studies can be briefly presented.

1. A joint study by Peter Dorner and Don Kenel (1971) in which the findings of studies of seven countries are analysed (India 1955–60, Japan 1960, Mexico 1960, Brazil 1963, Philippines 1963/64, Taiwan 1965 and Colombia 1966).
2. A study of seven Latin American Countries (Argentina, Brazil, Chile, Colombia, Ecuador, Guatemala and Peru) carried out in 1963–6) by CIDA.[6]
3. Berry and Cline's (1974) cross-country comparison with the use of regresson analysis of data set from 30 countries.[7]
4. Giovanni Cornia's (1985) comprehensive analysis of data taken from 15 countries collected by the Food and Agriculture Organization of the United Nations (FAO).[8]

Productivity of land and labour

The wide range of findings brought by these penetrating studies confirm that, with slight variations, output per unit of land in all countries declines systematically with the rise in farm size. Physical output and value of gross output per unit of land is consistently much lower in large farms than in small farms. The range of variation is very large in land-abundant and sparsely populated countries (South America) compared to land-scarce countries with population pressure on land (e.g. Egypt, India and Pakistan). Large estates (haciendas) in Latin America which constitute 50 per cent of total farm land in the seven countries studied by CIDA are characterised by under-utilisation of land, widespread absenteeism and a shift towards pasture for raising livestock. The study asserts that this manifestation of inefficient use of resources of large estates was inconsistent with their high management capacity and their advantageous position in access to credit, technical assistance and in water supply for irrigation.

There is a consensus among the studies in their cross-sectional analysis, that labour utilisation per unit of land (measured in terms of man-days per year and number of workers per unit of output) is considerably lower in large estates than in small-holdings. This was especially apparent in countries with a high degree of unequal distribution of land. The studies clearly show that labour intensity per unit of land is positively correlated with land use intensity and negatively correlated with farm size. This relationship provides part of the explanation of the inverse relationship between output and the size of land holding. CIDA's and Cornia's cross-section analysis found out that there is an excessive amount of labour crowded in small farms, implying a wasteful use of labour power and a declining marginal productivity of labour input. This situation co-exists with under-utilised land in large estates in the same country, suggesting that the peasants are trapped in their small farm sector. The four studies have shown that the imperfection of capital markets has aggravated rural under-employment. As large estates have preferential access to cheap credit (low interest rates and subsidised machinery), they substitute machinery for labour. They deliberately choose lower labour to land ratios than would result from an imperfect labour market alone.

Undoubtedly this series of cross-section analyses provides us with interesting broad indicators of resource use and output related to the size of land holdings. Still, the authors face data limitations inherent in all comparative analyses of the situation in a large number of countries. Important among these are:

(a)   the type of soil and productive capacity of land area (which differs from farm to farm and from one country to another);
(b)   the costing of family labour inputs;
(c)   the choice of shadow prices (opportunity cost) of the means of production in judging total social productivity and potential gains;
(d)   capturing the effects of absenteeism among land owners on the application of technology and on current operating decisions; and
(e)   the differences in the institutional contexts of production relations.

It is because of these limitations and diversity of situations that case studies of specific countries are more meaningful, especially when they are based on large samples of agricultural households. They usually accommodate the above-mentioned variations across a range of farm sizes. The sets of data they provide, when combined with the production function for a specific situation, make their findings on factor proportions and production relations more relevant than a cross-sectional analysis.

We are fortunate to have a number of such studies in a large number of developing countries. They examined in depth the fundamental issues of the relative technical and economic efficiency of large- and small-holdings under different conditions of natural endowments and social

129

systems. Some of them examined these issues in the same country within a three to ten year interval to find out whether there was any change in the pattern of relations. Examples of such studies are: Sarjit Bhalla's analysis of data on 1,772 agricultural households collected three times over the period 1968–71 by India's National Council of Applied Economic Research; William Cline's analysis of data collected in 1973 on Brazil which he compared with his earlier 1963 survey of seven major districts; Hayami and Kukuchi's surveys of two villages in the Philippines carried out in 1966 and 1976/77; Michael Henry's case study of the economies of scale in rice production in Guyana in 1974 and 1984, and Paul Collier and Deepak Lal's analysis of Kenya's Integrated Rural Surveys 1974–9 and the 1978 Labour Force Survey.[9] There are other country studies including Keith Griffin's examination of the situation in Ecuador and Morocco, Doreen Warriner's 1969 field findings in Brazil, Chile, Venezuela and pre-land reform Iraq,[10] as well as my own study of resource use and income in pre-land reform Egyptian agriculture (1935–51). In addition, studies on the labour market and technology in Egyptian agriculture were completed by Commander and Hadhoud in 1984.

Though the chief concern of these comprehensive studies varies, all examined the pattern of production relations between large and small farms and the implications for agricultural/rural development. They also provided explanations of the economic, and technical causes and the institutional barriers inhibiting the access to credit, technical knowledge and water rights for irrigation for small farmers. In addition, Bhalla, Hayami-Kikuchi, and Henry investigated the question of whether the pattern of factor-combination established in their previous studies continues after the introduction of high-yielding varieties in the 1960s and early 1970s and the associated investment activities required by technical change. Henry went on to consider the effects of a continuing pattern on production, employment and land tenure relations.

The findings of these case studies confirmed the conclusions reached by the cross-sectional studies in respect to lower output and labour input per unit of land among large farms compared to small-holdings. In his analysis of the set of data on India, Bhalla ascertains that these relationships remain significant even after differences in land quality are allowed for (in Berry and Cline, 1979: 154). He remarks that though imperfection in all factor markets is responsible for these relationships, imperfection in the labour market is the most important factor (in Berry and Cline, 1979: 172). The studies on the Philippines and Kenya (Central Province) showed an association between absentee landlords and land concentration.

In the former, more than 70 per cent of 'South Village' land in 1977 was owned by five large landlords who lived in Manila (Hayami and

Kikuchi, 1985: 135). In Kenya, 'a considerable amount of land purchase has been undertaken by absentee urban high-income groups'. This has increased land concentration and worsened the imbalance in factor proportions between large and small holdings (Collier and Lal, 1986: 132).

A pre-land reform study on resource use in Egyptian agriculture (El-Ghonemy, 1953) shows that small farms of less than 5 acres representing 81 per cent of total holdings met 95 per cent of their total labour requirement from their family labour, thus using only 3 per cent of total tractors, 2 per cent of threshing machines, and 6 per cent of irrigation pumps (which were shared among co-operatives). At the other extreme were large landholders of 100 acres and over who represented less than one per cent of total landholders. These landholders had access to credit, technical knowledge, and who often employed hired qualified managers. They often relied on hired labour and less intensive land use, as they owned 80 per cent of the tractors, 83 per cent of total threshing machines, and 35 per cent of irrigation pumps (most with high horsepower). A recent study conducted in three Egyptian villages during 1984 (Commander and Hadhoud, 1986) shows that small-holdings of less than one acre had higher productivity (yield per acre) than larger areas. (It should be noted that maximum ownership of land prescribed by land reform is 100 acres per household.) This association was clear *only* for wheat and maize, but not for cotton and rice. When value of land productivity was computed using regression analysis, the results show that productivity rises for farms up to 10 feddans (acres) but falls off for the larger farms. The resource allocation among the crop-rotational combination in small farms is believed to be responsible for this variation. (Commander and Hadhoud, 1986: Chapter 8, Table 8.E). Calculated average productivity per labour hour (physical units in kilograms), for wheat and cotton is higher for small farm size below 10 acres than above that size (Table 8.5). As all farms are irrigated and material inputs such as fertilisers and insecticides are accessible to all size farms at a heavily subsidised price, the difference in productivity can be attributed to intensive family labour on small farms.

Economies of scale

When factor prices are included in calculating the ratio between the value of total output to the value of all factor inputs, the economic efficiency of large farms appears to be lower than small farms in the case studies on India, Brazil, Guyana and the Philippines. This is an important indicator of the economic performance of large estates and it rejects the claim of their dynamic superiority in production and employment. As Professor Cline states in his study of Brazil, 'the large farm sector uses its available land inefficiently from the standpoint of the economy as a whole' (Berry and Cline, 1979: 58). The study of the Philippines concludes that 'there are no significant differences in the economic efficiency of large and small farms – overall, there is no evidence that large farms were most efficient technically than the small' (Hayami and Kikuchi, 1985: 144). Henry in his sample survey of rice production by size of holding in Guyana found out, through a rigorous analysis of the data, that the large farms were economically inefficient beyond 15–20 hectares under certain assumptions of economies of scale. Referring to his country Guyana he says, 'In this case the price we pay for efficiency is a preponderance of large farms along with the attendant problems of socio-economic development' (Henry, 1986: 11).

Technical change

We next turn to the responsiveness of farmers to technical change. The widely held view that large estates are superior over small farms in technical change has proved to be generally false. This was clear from the hard evidence brought by the studies cited above and many others on the adoption of high yielding varieties (HYV) and related technology. They show clearly that small farms are at least as innovative as large estates in their responsiveness to technological change. Their response in adopting new processes of production has occurred despite their disadvantageously low initial endowment of land and capital, and the high cost they must pay for credit. This response by small and large farms to technological change has been documented in many field studies: Azam and Khan on Pakistan, Bardhan and Sen on India, Taussig on the South of the Cauca Valley in Colombia, etc.[11] Consider one example. In his study on India, Bhalla indicates that the percentage of HYV area of rice and wheat was higher in farm size below 5 acres than in farms above 25 acres in 1968 (14.6 per cent compared to 11.1 per cent respectively). But large farms expanded their area faster than small farms by 1971 because the latter suffered from credit constraints, particularly for irrigation capital, which is essential for this type of technical change (Berry and Cline, 1979: Tables A–16 and A–17). In terms of the proportionate number of people adopting technology, the difference was slight.

Moreover, similarly hard evidence was brought by the case studies of Guyana and the Philippines in respect of changes in the production process resulting from the adoption of new rice technology (seed, fertilisers and weeding). There was no difference between large and small farms. The only difference, as expected, was in mechanisation (harvesting and threshing) introduced by large farms. Despite the high quality of management in large farms, the Philippines' study states clearly, 'With *similar* input use, there was little difference in paddy yield per hectare on large and small farms' (Hayami and Kikuchi, 1985: 144). Collier and Lal indicate that Kenyan small farmers, despite severe credit rationing by commercial banks and marketing co-operatives, grow modern hybrid maize in addition to pyrethrum, coffee and tea as in large farms (Collier and Lal, 1986: Table 5.4).

There is no merit in continuing with other examples of empirical evidence on this issue of responsiveness to technological change. It is clear that in risk bearing, in their responsiveness to technological change and in economic efficiency of resource use generally, large farms are not superior over small farms despite the latter's formidable institutional obstacles.

Policy issues

After this review of empirical evidence, the question is whether contemporary arguments in judging the differential effects of large estates and small-holdings on production, investment and employment, are more convincing than the succinct words of Adam Smith. In his *Wealth of Nations*, the fountainhead of economic thought, he remarked in 1776:

> Compare the present condition of these (great or large) estates with the possession of the small proprietors in their neighbourhood, and you will require no other argument to convince you how unfavourable such extensive property is to improvement.[12]

Perhaps one may say that economic analysis has advanced in the use of econometric methods and computer techniques in measuring or judging statistically the same phenomenon. We are now more able than before to measure statistically the degree of association between size of holdings and productivity, employment, economies of scale, investment, growth and technical change. But the conclusion reached by the many scholars' analysis shown in our discussion does not fundamentally differ from that of Adam Smith.

The other difference since Adam Smith's time, is the emergence of the functioning of socialist ideology in agriculture which has recently spread in Africa. This socialist ideology was mixed with pure nationalism after a long colonial structure of capitalism. Within this ideology is a rising controversy over remuneration, productive motivations and material versus non-material incentives in respect to State farms, and to the State nationalisation of private ownership of land intended to achieve egalitarianism and social gains.

Historical experience of current socialist agriculture suggest that no national government starting out with the inherited colonial structures could have taken a path other than conversion of large foreign-owned estates into State farms. Such institutions represent a mixture of socialism and nationalism. Within their specific circumstances, each developing country had to establish its indigenous system of State farms: setting objectives and improvising criteria to attain their economic efficiency linked to a national system of economic planning and management. These objectives and the criteria used differ from Western capitalist criteria of resource efficiency in large privately owned farms. In socialist agriculture, State farm production functions are linked with wider objectives of social transformation of the rural system ambiguously known in literature as 'integrated rural development'. State farms are assigned the role of spearheading social objectives of alleviating illiteracy and gender inequality, and providing health and recreational services.

Together with guaranteed employment and payment of bonuses over and above cash wages, these free services constitute an integral system of incentives to boost productivity. Concrete concepts of labour remuneration, efficiency earnings, investment in human resources, costs of production and the pursuit of social utility, therefore, differ fundamentally from those of economic efficiency applied to the analysis of capitalist agriculture. The real difference seems to lie in the objectives set, and their different interpretations formed under particular ideologies. The tendency to generalise about *all* State farms and *all* socialist agriculture compounds the confusion. Differences are bound to continue. The functional unity of 'State-Party-Planning-Marxism' makes the role of the State (or government or party central committee) internal to the behaviour of producers and consumers in the market. Though an inseparable complex, Anglo-American systems of economics habitually consider the role of the State as an externality.

Our discussion about State farms is handicapped by the lack of an objective examination based on rigorous empirical evidence. Nevertheless, from what we do know of State farms and from observations in Hungary, Romania and Mozambique, we would be wrong to dismiss such important institutions on the basis of *a priori* ideological bias as inefficient under a system of command and government monopoly. There are, however, broad and common problems facing large estates in both capitalist and socialist systems in LDCs. The first is the distortion of factor and product prices by different mechanisms.

The second is exploitation taking different forms in both systems. Agricultural workers are exploited in capitalist large estates when their remuneration is less than the value of their service (their average and marginal productivity). In socialist State farms they are exploited by differential remuneration to status, and privileges by virtue of official hierarchy in the Communist party, the managers' self-interest in over-investment and the degree of association with the political organs.

Which form of the two evils is better or worse is an ideological question.

The third common welfare issue relates to potential social gains. In judging efficiency considerations, the question is not a capitalist large landowner versus the State as the landlord. It is 'whether' and 'how' the resources owned by each of these two categories of owners are efficiently utilised for the interest of the nation as a whole. We should, therefore, be concerned with the potential gains in agriculture and to society from the allocative efficiency of its two most important resources, *viz.*, land combined with water and labour power. This has policy implications.

A major policy implication for private property-market economies concerns the potential gains from redistribution of large farms. This chapter has presented sufficient and reliable evidence to question the loudly voiced and fossilised impression that large estates *per se* are superior in allocative efficiency and that they are necessary farm institutions conducive to the dynamic development of productive forces in underdeveloped countries. The sets of empirical evidence brought by a number of scholars reveal that large estates, in general, are inefficient in: resource utilisation, total social productivity of factor combinations, and intensity of land use under different qualities of land, cropping system and different degrees of population pressure on land.[13] They also show the negative effects of absentee owners of land on discouraging investment in improving land productivity and on renting out land under insecure tenure arrangements. The evidence presented clearly shows that small farmers are innovative and respond rapidly to technical change despite the institutional barriers placed before them.

Can we then conclude that the economic arguments and conceptual reasoning throughout the previous and present chapters justify, in principle, the breaking-up of 'inefficient' large estates? The evidence suggests that the restructuring of resource use and ownership would bring high proportional income gains to the landless workers, and indebted tenants with negative income. In fact, all studies cited in our discussion are either suggestive of land reform or specifically recommend it.[14] They based the potential gains on rigorous economic arguments. But alas, economic considerations are, in reality, of secondary importance to the government's political commitment.

Notes

1 See, for example: Bachman and Christensen, 1967 with comments by Heady in Chapter 7; Sen, 1984: 37–72; Berry and Cline, 1979: Chapter 2; Currie, 1981; and Dandekar, 1962.
2 Bachman and Christensen, 1967: 242.

3　In 1964, Prof. Theodore W. Schultz examined the status of the operators of US farms between 1930 and 1960. The operators were classified as owner-operators, tenants and hired managers. He found out that there was a positive correlation between owner-operatorship and the rise in farm output per man-hour i.e. the higher the percentage of owner-operators the higher the output. Conversely the higher the percentage of tenants and hired managers the lower the output. He concluded that 'Absentee arrangements are in general inefficient'. He added that when the market approach is adopted, 'The difference in the efficiency of absentee and resident production decisions in farming becomes relevant'. See Schultz, 1964: 120, 118 and 104 respectively.

　　The results of 1970–4 World Census of Agriculture in 49 countries show that the holdings actually operated by land-owners amounted to 61 per cent of the total. In seven Latin American countries an area of 109.2 million hectares were operated by hired managers appointed by the absentee owners. In Brazil 4 per cent of the total number of holdings accounting for 30 per cent of the total land area fall under this category. Out of the total holdings, 14,000 were operated by hired managers and were in the range of over 1,000 hectares each (Tables 5.1 and 5.16 of the *1970 World Census of Agriculture*, FAO, Rome, 1981). Most of the absentee owners are civil servants, urban professionals and business-men, members of the armed forces and politicians who hold their farms for prestige, power, speculation and profit making from renting-out arrangements.

4　With the exception of Mozambique and Cuba the data are taken from Kifle, 1983. The data on Mozambique are based on my field visit in May 1984, see *Report of the WCARRD Follow-up Mission to Mozambique*, FAO, Rome, 1985. The data on Cuba are from an ILO's paper by Peter Peek (1984: Table 6). The share of other farm institutions in agricultural land is 8 per cent for collective farming and 7 per cent for private farms. Most of the private farms are in the range of 2 caballerias (28 ha). Between 1963 and 1983 the percentage of private farms to total agricultural land declined from 38 per cent to 7 per cent whereas that of State farms increased from 61 per cent to 85 per cent (see Cuba in Chapter 6).

5　This quotation should be seen against the background material on which it was based. Griffin admits that these measures are crude and should be regarded as rough approximations only. See Griffin, 1986: 173, Tables 11.1 and 11.3.

6　Barraclough (ed), 1973. Chapter Two presents the overall framework of the study. This volume was edited jointly with Juan Carlos Collarte.

7　Berry and Cline, 1979. The questions addressed in this comprehensive and penetrating study are in Chapter 1. Chapter 5 presents the conclusion and policy implications.

8　Cornia, 1985: 513–34. The analysis is based on data collected by FAO Farm Management and Production Service between 1973 and 1979. For comparability purpose, all value figures were transformed into 1970 US dollars, and the area was converted into hectares. The countries covered by the analysis are: Sudan, Syria, Ethiopia, Nigeria, Tanzania, Uganda, Barbados, Mexico, Peru, Bangladesh, Burma, India, Nepal, South Korea and Thailand.

9 The following studies are listed in the same order as they appeared in the discussion:

(a) Bhalla, Surjit S. 'Farm Size, Productivity and Technical Change in Indian Agriculture', Appendix A in Berry and Cline, 1979: 141–86. The sample consisted of some 3,000 cultivating households who were interviewed in each of the three years 1968/9, 1969/70 and 1970/1. Out of this sample, 1,772 were selected for analysis. The author states that the oversampling of high-income households allows the data to be used for the study of the production behaviour of large (over 25 or 30 acres) farmers – a procedure not possible with most previous data sources in India. Also its extensive coverage means that all of the major crops grown in all regions of India can be analysed, and the different stages of adoption of the new technology meaningfully studied.

(b) Berry and Cline, 1979. The Study of Brazil appears on pp. 44–58.

(c) Hayami and Kikuchi, 1985. This is based on case studies of two villages in the province of Laguna: East Village and the South Village, both are in a rice area. The two villages were surveyed in 1976 and 1977 and the analyses used earlier survey of 1966 as benchmark.

(d) Henry, 1986: 72–9.

(e) Collier and Lall, 1986.

10 (a) Griffin, 1976. The case study on Morocco was prepared in 1973 and appears as Chapter 2. The Ecuador study is contained as Chapter 5 and it focuses on labour markets and the rural poor's labour.

(b) Warriner, 1969. Her penetrating observations and analysis of these countries' agrarian structure and the factors affecting productivity and investment in large estates are in Part Two.

11 There are many studies on technical change and size of farms. Examples are: Sen, 1966; Azam, 1973, Bardhan, 1973; and Taussig, 1982: 195. In his section on 'the green revolution in peasant agriculture 1970–72' Taussig describes, from his field survey in 1970, 1972 and 1976 how all farmers adopted new varieties and inputs for growing soya and corn regardless of the size of holdings. The yields per unit of land were around no more than 60 per cent of those obtained on the large farms in the same area over two years 1970–2.

12 Under the heading, 'Great proprietors are seldom great improvers' Adam Smith explains how the large landed estates' proprietors in the United Kingdom 'had no leisure to attend to the cultivation and improvement of land'. Their style of life (dresses, staff, house, etc.) constituted a state of mind and habit that led to the neglect of their vast estates. He adds that 'if little improvement was to be expected from such great proprietors, still less was to be hoped for from those who occupied the land under them' – (*The Wealth of Nations*, Book III, Chapter II – 'Of the Discouragement of Agriculture in the ancient

state of Europe after the Fall of the Roman Empire'. The quotations in the text and above are on page 364.

13 This does not imply, of course, that large estates including commercial plantations are inefficient everywhere in developing countries. In fact, Collier and Lal (1986: 139–40) found out that the plantations in Kenya are some 30 per cent more labour-intensive than the average small holding which uses predominantly hired labour. They also enjoy economies of scale in enforcing hired labour contracts.

14 Cline, Griffin and Henry recommend in their studies specific actions for land redistribution in Brazil, Morocco, Ecuador and Guyana respectively. A World Bank's study states 'The extent and gravity of the employment problems and income disparities in LDC's (Least Developed Countries) have caused a new concern over land reform from an equity as well as a productivity stand point' . . . 'This report concludes that land reform is consistent with the development objectives of increasing output, improving income distribution, and expanding employment, and that the Bank Group should support reforms that are consistent with these goals' World Bank – *Land Reform Policy Paper*: 8). See also the section on Major Policy Options (p. 39) of the same report. Cornia's cross-sectional study concludes 'If the joint targets of increasing food output, yields and labour absorption are to be achieved, a few policy interventions should be recommended . . . Land reform giving the rural poor direct access to productive assets . . . Because of the demonstrated superiority of small *vis-à-vis* large farming, land redistribution would have, if thoroughly implemented, immediate beneficial effects in terms of output growth, enhanced income distribution and, as a result, of alleviation of rural poverty' Cornia, 1985: 532.

Part 3

The obstacles and realities in reducing poverty

Chapter five

Institutional monopoly and rural poverty

Having examined the economic arguments about large farms in both capitalist and socialist agriculture, we proceed in this chapter to explain the institutional arrangements by which land and other means of production are monopolised. To explore this process of monopolisation and its implications for shaping the rural economy and for generating poverty in LDCs, the discussion is guided by three related hypotheses:

1. In less developed countries, land ownership is more commonly secured by institutional means than by the market mechanism.
2. The lower the concentration of land ownership/operation (LC), the lower the level of absolute poverty in rural areas, (irrespective of the level of a country's income per head).
3. Realizing high rates of agricultural growth is not conditional upon the combination of LC and the dominance of large estates.

Before exploring these ideas, it is useful to explain just what 'institutional modes' of owning land denote, as identifying them helps to explain how the current concentration was created in the first place. In broad terms, they are the non-market arrangements such as inheritance, inter-family marriage, regulatory legislation for land redistribution, grants by the State or its sovereign, land-grabbing by virtue of social power and official status, and other concessional arrangements between the State and plantation holders.

The chapter is organised in four sections. First, a *conceptual* explanation of why it is important to focus on institutions is presented, followed by a proposed framework for identifying elements of institutional monopoly in the agrarian economies of LDCs. In the third section we employ the tools of this framework to analyse the *empirical* experience at two levels. The first is a detailed examination of how land and related factor-product markets were monopolised within the historical experiences of Egypt and Kenya, the two selected case studies. The second level is an inter-country analysis of the quantitative relation between LC and growth in agricultural output and the incidence of both absolute poverty and landlessness in a sample of 20 LDCs.

Why focus on institutions?

The institutional determinants of controlling productive assets in the agrarian economies of LDCs have, to date, received less attention than they deserve. Little is known about how the monopoly powers of existing large estates and multinationals (MNCs) operating in agriculture have come about, how the barriers to entry of small farmers and wage-dependent landless workers differ from those of the manufacturing industry or what institutional arrangements create barriers to entry.

To understand the generation of monopoly/monopsony power in agrarian economies it is therefore incumbent upon us to combine the study of institutions with relevant principles of economics. In his presidential address to the Royal Economic Society in 1986, Professor Matthews succinctly summed up the role of institutions in economic systems: 'Institutions do matter, and the determinants of institutions are susceptible to analysis by the tools of economic theory' (Matthews, 1986: 903).

In many agrarian economies, transactions are usually enforced more by customs of society and personal relationships than by law. This distinction was empirically illustrated by Pranab Bardhan (1984: Chapter 12) in his comprehensive study of the interlocking factor-markets prevailing in local communities of rural India. After examining the concepts of market and non-market transactions he concluded:

> In a given historical and institutional context, whether or not the transactional modes through which resource allocation, work organiza-tion, and product disposition are arranged resemble those of the market is clearly a matter of empirical judgement. (Bardhan, 1984: 157–8).

In fact, Alfred Marshall realised a century ago that '. . . the chief fault in English economists at the beginning of the [nineteenth] century . . . was that they did not see how liable to change are the habits and institu-tions' (in Matthews, 1986: 903). Marshall's Principles proposed that the study of changes in land tenure and the institution of property were among the questions to be investigated by economists.[1]

The neglect of institutional determinants of concentrated asset owner-ship and market powers extends to the study of multinational corporations (MNCs) operating in developing countries' agriculture. In literature, the focus remains on MNCs' foreign capital investment-cum-technology in import-substitution manufacturing, processing of agricultural products and manufacturing of farm equipment and agricultural chemicals. Little or no attention is given to the influence of MNCs on shaping income distribution, access to land and labour utilisation in agriculture. Bain

(1956), Hymer (1960, 1971, and 1976), Streeten (1972, 1981), Singer (1982), Dunning (1981) and Todaro (1981) have enlightened us with their intellectual constructions of the international oligopolistic power of MNCs. Such a role is primarily abstracted from the theory of industrial organisation and LDCs' experience with MNCs in industry and trade.

To understand poverty implications of monopoly in market structures of LDCs' agriculture, we first suggest how institutional arrangements create barriers to entry into the land, credit, and product markets; how monopolisers restrict or forbid trade unions of agricultural workers; how they control factor/product-markets in the monopolists' location; and finally, how these monopolisers through institutional arrangements effectively manipulate the government's rules of procedures, enabling higher rates of profits relative to others.

The conception of institutional monopoly in agrarian economies

In Arabic culture, there is a widely held belief that 'perfection and full knowledge are solely for God (Allah)'. Perfection in economic competition, however, exists only in abstract theory and in textbook graphs. During the early part of the 1930s, a lively debate surrounded Edward Chamberlin's theory on monopolistic competition and Joan Robinson's published work entitled *The Economics of Imperfect Competition*. Part of the debate focused on the comments made by Nicholas Kaldor (1935) as to whether these two theories took into account the presence of institutional monopoly. These referred not to agriculture, but to the manufacturing industry, where institutional barriers to entry of new firms are exercised through pricing of product differentiation, advertising, licensing, and the persistent higher profit rates of some industries over others resulting from registered trademarks and patents. The same reference pertains to William Nicholls' (1941) analysis of large American industries which processed agricultural products. We suggest that in agrarian economies, barriers to entry are different and therefore they need to be identified and extracted from empirical situations in developing countries.

Combining economics and institutions in an historical context

The combination of relevant principles of economics with institutions enables us to study the elements of monopoly in the agrarian market structure in specific geographical areas and in a particular period of history. This approach offers a number of advantages:

1. It helps to explain the erroneous view created when institutional components of the market structure in agriculture are separated or

ignored during consideration of market imperfections and disequilibrium.

2. It provides an understanding of the institutional content of the market power in terms of the procedural rules applied to setting prices for land lease, labour, water use for irrigation; lending credit and linking loans with labour or purchase of crops; and influencing prices of agricultural products.

3. It identifies the unique market power and economic advantages enjoyed by a few monopolists over other farming entrepreneurs. Among these advantages are: the size of asset ownership and its share in the total; a large share in the market structure (inputs controlled, products sold, and primary agricultural commodities exported); the ability to block the poor from owning lands; the actual location of economic activities; and the ability to build coalitions among monopolists and between them and the State organs.

In addition, our approach stresses the need to trace the origin of land accumulation and the dynamics of corresponding market power, while avoiding a static view of the concentration ratio at a single point in time. It also helps to identify the institutional arrangements used to establish barriers to entry. Finally the approach helps to explain the coalition of monopolists (irrespective of the nationality of asset ownership) to seek high economic rent at low cost with minimal risk. Among the means to be explained, is how the monopolists manipulate public policy for legal protection, and government administrative machinery for serving their own collective interests.

This approach is followed in the study of the historical experience of Egypt and Kenya. A major element, LC is used in the inter-country analysis in order to understand its relation to the incidence of rural poverty and landlessness.

Elements of institutional monopoly

The few entrepreneurs in agriculture who enjoy monopoly (or monopsony) advantages usually exercise a combination of practices in the market structure. While keeping this combination in mind, individual elements of these practices can also be considered separately as follows.

Concentration of land

As productive land is the crucial income-yielding and labour-using asset in agriculture, the concentration of its ownership is the principal determinant of other monopoly elements. It leads to the control of the terms set for renting it out to peasants, determination of wage levels, the number of workers hired, the share in purchased inputs and in the sale of farm output.

The extent of such monopoly power depends on the size and locality of the large farm and plantation. It is also determined by the demand for renting the land, and the supply elasticity of labour. If, for example, the landlord or plantation manager is the sole rentier of land and buyer of hired landless workers in his locality (due to the substantial size of his farm), he can gain supernormal profit from charging high rent, and simultaneously paying wage rates lower than those which would apply under a competitive labour market. Thus, the combination of the farm size, the continuity of its holding over a substantial period of time, and its specific location are significant characteristics of market power in agrarian economies. It is therefore necessary to study the stability of the share of large landowners (or holders) in total number and total area over a substantial period of time (say, three or four decades) in a given country or locality. This is illustrated later by data from Kenya and six Latin American countries

To understand the relation between concentration and poverty we need to analyse how LC limits the options of the poor to raise their earnings and nutritional standards above the poverty line. These option limitations are manifested in seriously restricted access to purchase of land, in chronic indebtedness to landowners, and in the very low return on labour. This low level of earning (and its corresponding low level of consumption) combine to form a major determinant of poverty.

Barriers to entry in agrarian economies

In the defective land tenure systems of agrarian economies characterised by LC, insidious conduct by entrepreneurs differs from that practised in manufacturing. Practices such as commercial advertising, licensing, trademarks and patents as property rights, differentiation of products, price slashing by new entrants, or merges designed to expand output and reduce cost are not applicable to agrarian entrepreneurs (see Demsetz, 1982). Nor are anti-trust or monopolies and restrictive trade legislation applied to land tenure and the related market power in agriculture. In the absence of enforced regulatory legislation on tenancy arrangements or restrictions of property rights in land, landlords, plantation managers, sellers of pump-irrigation water (water lords), farm equipment dealers and moneylenders practise malicious monopoly powers without fear of legal penalisation.

There are five dominant practices barring entry. The first is eviction of tenants by landowners without compensation payment. The second is the auctioneering of land, with tenancy middlemen, who can meet financial requirements which serve as an insurance against risk. These middlemen further sub-divide the land into smaller units, subleasing them to small tenants at rates higher than those paid to the absentee landlord or his agent, providing a high profit margin. The third practice is the hierarchical system of contractual and sub-contractual hiring of large numbers of landless workers. These workers are paid wages far below their average and marginal productivity in order to provide a profit for each level of the hierarchy.

The fourth dominant practice is in rationing credit by barring tenants, small owners and landless workers from entering the institutional credit market. By restricting access to credit a large section of the peasants are denied investment and pay the opportunity cost of possible increases in their earnings. The results are a higher cost borne by peasants than that of farmers having easy access to credit. The peasants' added costs take the form of higher interest rates paid to moneylenders, usually linked with the commitment of the borrowers to sell their crops at reduced prices.

The fifth barrier to entry is in denying agricultural workers their right to organise trade unions, and in restricting activities such as the right to strike. It is, therefore, important to identify the attitudes of governments, landlords, plantation managers and MNCs towards the steps taken by agricultural workers which would enhance their bargaining power. For instance, it is important to know if governments permit free election of trade unions' leaders, or, contrarily, if they exercise their authority to remove leaders from office and prohibit their re-election. Still another aspect to consider is whether or not agricultural workers are allowed affiliation with industrial workers to enjoy better terms of real wages, social amenities and compensation payment. Understanding these institutional questions helps to identify the barriers blocking poor peasants from increasing their earnings through gaining collective power and voicing their opinions about their working conditions and needs.

A sixth possible form of barring entry is the monopolist's specialisation in producing high value cash crops – crops which other farmers are banned from growing. This rationing deprives peasants of opportunities to diversify production to seek higher earnings, while simultaneously granting stronger market power to influential landowners or plantation managers.

The multiple functions of large farm owners give them exclusive and special monopoly powers. Imagine a rural locality, in which a big landowner is the mayor of the village, a trader, a moneylender, an owner of water-pumps for irrigation where water is scarce, and in addition, he may be an influential politician. If he is the sole rentier of land, as well as the sole employer of landless workers, he is a capitalist with absolute monopolistic-monopsonistic power in his locality. This exclusive economic control is usually practised within the legal and institutional framework sanctioned by the State under the prevailing legal system and structure of power. This legal protection of monopoly profit seekers is inimical to a large section of the agricultural population, and represents a localised poverty trap.

Special monopoly advantages of multinationals operating in agriculture

Our discussion so far has not made the important distinction between the role of domestic and foreign asset ownership in market power. As powerful institutions in international production and trade of high value crops, MNCs demand special emphasis. They have an increasingly important influence on shaping the agricultural economy of many developing countries via private foreign capital investment, transfer of technology and management skills, net capital outflow, and controlling some economically strategic export crops. Naturally this influence depends upon: each country's development strategy; the nature of its agrarian structure *before* involvement of MNCs; the rate of its domestic saving required for achieving the targeted rate of agricultural growth; the type of MNC operation (direct investment, contract farming, joint venture with domestic partners); the financial and legal terms of operation as negotiated with the government of the host country; the host country's ability to effectively screen the contractual arrangement, control and evaluate the benefits from MNCs' operations without regard to vested personal interests of officials; and the extent of the host country's openness to international capital movement and trade.

Our concern is limited to the influence of MNCs' operations in agriculture on the pattern of distribution of land, income, consumption and power, labour utilisation and the reallocation of scarce resources between food and non-food crops. Yet another related area of concern is identifying the MNCs' elements of oligopolist market power, including the collusive alliance with national agents in LDCs. All are questions which suffer from a scarcity of hard evidence. More difficulties lie in the scarcity of data on the net social cost and gains within agriculture, including the split of gains between MNCs and the domestic economy, particularly the distribution of fair share to local workers. (We single out the workers because they are the resource which provides LDCs with a comparative advantage.)

By virtue of their very nature of seeking high profit, their substantial size and mode of negotiating contracts with LDCs, multinationals are quite able to surmount barriers to entry into holding land for production, processing and export of economically strategic crops. They also appear to be quite capable of securing high rates of monopoly profit (setting prices above marginal and average cost) and to secure generous concessions and preferential treatment in taxation, in pricing, and in repatriating their high monopoly profit (usually tax free) to parent firms in their home countries. The special advantages of MNCs lie in their monopolistic package which includes: the integrated system of research

147

capabilities, crops and technology choice, timely input supply, processing, sophisticated marketing techniques, transport, export and high level of skills in supervision, management and organisation within a gigantic operation.[2]

To maximise the economic reward of high profits from these monopolistic/oligopolistic advantages, while minimising the risk, MNCs use their *own* government's political facilities, obtaining sufficient support for being part of their government's foreign investment policy. To obtain the necessary political lobby and social cover as an insurance policy against potential risk, MNCs seek alliance with influential landlords, businessmen, senior officials and politicians of host countries. To further reduce risk, MNCs investing capital in LDCs' agriculture develop safeguards against possible future nationalisation, or procure guarantees for full compensation payment. Towards this end, they gradually switch from direct investment in plantations to joint ventures, contract farming, processing agricultural raw materials, marketing and management of public corporations producing high value crops.[3] MNCs also use their influence on governments intending to issue land reforms. In this case, MNCs strive to exempt their plantations from application of the size ceiling on private land property, or to receive a guarantee for absolute exemption (as occurred in the Philippines' Land Reform Decree No. 27 of 1972).

Why do most LDCs encourage and welcome foreign capital investment? Because LDCs usually need capital flow to agriculture which is starved of its capital needs, as shown in Chapter 1. Nor can they resist the prospects of higher agricultural growth, advances in technology and management for the modernisation of the export crop sector, and a higher volume of exports to earn foreign exchange. With this goal in mind it is not surprising that LDCs provide MNCs with generous incentives and preferential treatment. This LDCs' governments usually do from a disadvantageous bargaining position. In many cases, LDCs are unfamiliar with the internal structures of MNCs, the methods employed to calculate profits and manipulate prices (transfer-pricing) of imported capital goods and exported products between the MNCs' own subsidiaries and firms located in other countries. Nor can they interpret the twisted accounting systems of MNCs sufficiently to estimate the exceedingly difficult but highly important distribution of gains in terms of net flow of capital, net contribution to export earnings, public revenue, and the volume and share of labour benefits.

Fair distribution of gains is particularly important with regard to rural development, as multinationals operating in LDCs' agriculture are not welfare orientated institutions (*viz.*, concerned with equitable distribution of income and consumption in rural areas). Questions about distribution of gains which should be raised include: the ownership of the land which will benefit from producing exported crops; the terms of labour utilization and the share of wage bills in total gains; the identity of the local and national partners of MNCs who reap the rewards resulting from foreign investment in agriculture; what happens to the food producing sector and to the income gap between subsistence peasants and the 'modern' sector; and how the food consumption pattern changes. *Cui bono*?

All of these issues revolve around the question: Do the special monopoly advantages of MNCs provide a net social gain to developing countries? An answer to this controversial question is suggested by Paul Streeten:

> While such [MNCs] investment has attractions for some countries faced with labour surpluses and foreign exchange shortages and poorly endowed with natural resources, the potential gains may not be considered worth the social risks and social costs, including a form of dependence and dualistic development of a new kind, different from that of the colonial plantations economy, but similar in its distributional impact. (Streeten, 1981b: 278)

Exploitation as an element of institutional monopoly

Governments instituting land reforms assign high priority to abolishing the exploitative elements of institutional monopoly in their agrarian economies, although they seldom use this terminology. Instead, they express the idea in terms of prevailing unsatisfactory economic and social relationships arising from *laissez-faire* policy in capitalist land tenure systems. Or, they view institutional monopoly as 'feudalism', the term borrowed from pre-seventeenth century Europe. Feudalism in its *real* sense (with coercion and military service to landlords), however, did not exist in the pre-reform situations of contemporary developing countries. Country experiences suggest that governments carrying out land reform express the presence of exploitation in terms of its combined institutional forms:

1. Landownership concentration.
2. Serfdom in terms of bonded labour and landlords exacting illegal levies and services from their peasants.
3. The dominance of foreign-owned assets in agriculture (particularly land) and the owners' collusion with the former government administration to depress the earnings of tenants and landless workers.
4. Widespread absenteeism among private owners of large farms associated with
   (a) renting-out land under insecure tenancy, high rents, and without compensation payment for eviction or improvements;

    (b) detrimental effects of inadequate or non-investment of accumulated profits on land productivity; and

    (c) persistent accumulation of wealth and privileges manifested in an affluent lifestyle enjoyed by the absentee landlords contrasted with the wretched life of the peasantry and their persistent impoverishment.

5. The heavy burden of the peasants' indebtedness.

6. Illegal land grabbing.

Exploitation, though a familiar expression widely used by countries justifying land reforms is nevertheless ambiguous, and so, more questions must be raised. For example, what is the mode of market power relations in the use and exchange of resources which could be legitimately viewed as exploitation? What criteria can we use for the identification of the exploiters and the exploited?

Based on his compiled data from Irish and English agriculture during the period 1851–71, Karl Marx conceived exploitation in terms of the capitalist extraction and accumulation of 'surplus value', particularly from displacing labour by newly invented machinery of his time, and from setting wages at socially determined subsistence. He considered the rate of surplus value as a measure of exploitation. From the class conflicts within capitalist agriculture, he identified the capital owners as the exploiters (e.g. landlords and the spinners of cotton and wool), and the wage-earners (labourers), as the exploited living in 'increasing misery'. The prevailing exploitative relations in production, in his words, '. . . have sprung up historically and stamp the labourer as the direct means of creating surplus-value' (*Capital*, Part V 1906: 558).

Another group of exploiters was added by Lenin in his study of late 19th century Russian rural economy. In that work, *The Development of Capitalism in Russia* (1899), Lenin considered the middle farmers with a commercial orientation of their means of production as exploiters of the poor peasants who own only their labour power and working animals. But his generality lacked the identification of the exploitation criteria in production and exchange. This was first attempted during the 1920s by field research conducted by two groups of Russian scholars led by Chayanov and Kritsman. In his comprehensive review of their work, Terry Cox (1986) reported a number of indices which were used as criteria in the identification of exploitation relations.[4] The focus was on detecting certain capitalist elements which, for obvious ideological reasons, overlooked the reinvestment of the 'exploiters' surplus both in and outside agriculture.

Another explanation of exploitation comes from two American Scholars, Nozick (1974) and Roemer (1982). They go beyond the Marxian hypothesis, both attacking his explanation. From their point of view, exploitation is seen as a violation of property rights and entitlements. This view is, in a sense, an expansion of the ideas founded by John Locke in the 17th century with regard to private property rights, including free labour and its products. To Nozick and Roemer, exploitation is not the rate of appropriation of surplus value, which they consider applicable to feudal conditions. Each places different emphasis. Nozick argues that the exploited do not possess the scarce entrepreneurial abilities and marketing skills to innovate and to bear market risks and uncertainties in free market transactions based on voluntary exchange. Thus, his argument is extracted from a competitive market mechanism which does not characterise the rural economy in many LDCs, where customary obligations and traditional transactions are dominant and the peasant's options are restricted.

For Roemer, the key to exploitation lay in the availability of alternatives and freedom of choice. Workers are exploited when they cannot form a coalition (such as a trade union) in order to withdraw freely from the exploiter, taking with them their private endowments, in order to become better off, whereas their exploiter becomes worse off. Another criterion is the equality in access to tangible means of production (other than labour) because of imperfect functioning of the competitive market. Under socialism, on the other hand, where access to the means of production including land is, in principle, secured to all farmers, exploitation takes the form of limited freedom of choice of alternatives and inequalities due to relationships of dominance in the centrally controlled economy.

All of these contributions to the meaning of exploitation are formed by individual scholars with varying backgrounds, and within each author's unique system of analysis. Abstracted from different institutional conditions, the analytical reasoning behind each interpretation seems to be consistent with each conclusion reached. For example, John Locke, the founder of the concept of property relations, was arguing against the absolute power of arbitrary 'divine rights' of the King of Britain in the 17th century. Under his rule, a large section of the farming population were effectively deprived of their property rights through the King's granting of absolute monopoly rights in land to a few noblemen who were entitled to subdue their landless workers and peasants. On moral grounds, Locke argued that, in a world of non-scarcity of land, nothing was made by God to be monopolised.[5]

Despite the unique analytical reasoning behind each interpretation of exploitation, we do find a number of common elements. Locke's notion of exploited property rights in granting and inheriting land are narrowly conceived by Marx, corresponding only to labour and what it produces as the substance of its value. Marx's appropriated surplus value corresponds, in part, to the classical economic rent or monopoly

151

profit resulting from the monopolist's deliberate wage-setting below the value of the worker's marginal product in an imperfect competitive market. Appropriation of monopoly profit is also an approximation of Roemer's notion of 'some are benefiting at the expense of others'.

Similarities and differences taken into account, our discussion suggests that despite its ambiguity, exploitation is an intrinsic component of institutional monopoly. The following section attempts to clarify the practical meaning of this concept through examples of empirical situations.

Empirical evidence

We turn now to apply the institutional monopoly elements already discussed, and to test the three hypotheses stated at the start of the chapter. Our discussion is on two levels: the first explains the overall process of monopolisation of factor and product markets under several institutional arrangements of land property rights within an historical context. It then identifies the implications this has for inequalities, agricultural growth, and conditions of poverty in Egypt (before the 1952 land reform) and Kenya. Both countries have three central characteristics: a long colonial rule, a scarcity of productive land, and private property-market economies. On the second level, we focus on an inter-country analysis of the quantitative relation between the concentration of land as the principal element of institutional monopoly and the incidence of rural poverty and landlessness in 20 LDCs. This quantitative analysis also estimates the extent to which land concentration determines the rates of agricultural growth.

Historical experience of Egypt and Kenya

Egypt

The historical experience of Egypt from the second half of last century until the Gamal Abdul-Nasser revolution in July 1952 (which instituted land reform) represents what seems to be a classic example of a coalition between domestic and foreign capitalists in the monopolisation of asset ownership and use in the rural economy. During that period there was a sequence of institutional changes and historical contingencies which cumulatively accentuated the control of privately-owned land by a few Egyptian and Egypto-Turkish landlords, together with a dozen British, French and Belgian multinational enterprises.

The landlords constituted two groups: first, the members of the ruling royal family and, second, the holders of high office, military officers, religious leaders and favoured Egyptian families. From 1812–40 the ruler Mohammed Ali (commissioned by the Ottoman Sultan to oust Napoleon's troops, breaking away from the Ottoman Empire in 1805) granted each member of the first group vast tracts of land (10,000–20,000 'feddans' or acres) tax free. By 1870 the ruling royal family owned 664,000 acres and controlled 426,000 acres of State-owned land, Daira-Al-Saniya (Baer, 1962). Together these accounted for 25 per cent of the country's total agricultural land. The second group was granted land ranging from 500 to 6,000 acres – each against payment of differential rates of land tax with entitlement to unpaid forced labour (uhdah). Between 1855 and 1870 these landed grants were converted to full ownership rights.[6] In addition to these grants, these big owners practised land-grabbing and some had as much as 20,000 acres in their possession.

Since the eighteenth century the peasants (fellaheen) have continued to cultivate small units under usufruct rights (2–5 acres each) against payment of land tax (one-third of total harvest raised to half in 1864). This was a heavy burden which forced some of them to forfeit their holdings. They provided forced labour (corvee) for public works (e.g. the construction of canals and the strengthening of the Nile dykes during the flood season).

Multinational enterprises and other foreign capitalists entered the Egyptian agricultural sector in the last quarter of the nineteenth century via the ownership of newly reclaimed large plantations (sugar, cotton). For the first time in Egypt, they established a foundation for linking credit to land mortgage. The Khedive (ruler) granted these foreign enterprises the right to own land, combined with an exemption from taxes on accumulated profits. He also granted them political capitulations according to which they could not be penalised by Egyptian authorities for violating laws and customary rules. The estates owned by these multinational enterprises reached a peak after the British occupation of Egypt in 1882 and just before the First World War when ownership amounted to as much as 0.7 million acres, or 13 per cent of Egypt's privately-owned land.[7] In the author's province of Bohera, foreign corporations owned 24 per cent of the total of privately-owned land. This was, indeed, a high degree of concentration in land ownership in an agriculturally over-populated country with scarce cultivable land.

In addition to land, capital market in agriculture was already highly controlled by two foreign enterprises (duopoly) which provided credit for the purchase of land and which mortgaged about 10 per cent of total agricultural land. The coalition of a relatively small group of domestic and foreign capitalists exercised a high degree of control in all spheres of economic and political activities in the first half of this century. A few influential landed families, including some members of the royal family, were dominant in all these economic organisations, forming a coherent system of control. This control is apparent through the multiple roles which they maintained, membership in Parliament and on the boards of directors of foreign companies, sugar and cotton industries, trade and financing companies.[8]

Table 5.1 **The Average annual cash rent per Feddan (acre) and the rate of increase, 1928–51 as compared with cost of living index**

	Average cash rent		Percentage of increase	Annual rent index	Cost of living index
	£E	US$[d]	(1930–31 = 100)[e]	(1939 = 100)	(1939 = 100)
1928–9[a]	11.0	55.00	157		
1930–1[b]	7.1	35.50	100		
1932–3[a]	5.1	25.50	72		
1937–8[a]	6.5	26.78	91		
1938–9[c]	7.2	29.66	101	100	100
1942–3	15.2	62.62	214	211	242
1943–4	18.0	74.16	253	250	279
1944–5	19.0	78.28	268	264	293
1945–6	19.4	79.93	273	269	287
1946–7	22.0	90.64	310	305	279
1947–8	23.3	96.00	328	324	281
1950–1	34.0	97.58	479	472	293

Sources:

a. Lambert, *Divers Modes de Faire Valoir les Terres en Egypte* (Cairo, Egypte Contempraine, 1938).
b. Department of Agricultural Economics and Statistics – Egypt's Ministry of Agriculture, Cairo. Study made in 1931.
c. Fellah Department, Ministry of Social Affairs. Unpublished studies, Division of Research and Statistics (years 1938–9, till 1950–1).
d. £E = $2.87 since September 1949; $4.12 (1933–49); $5.00 prior to 1933.
e. Index number refers to the Egyptian currency
f. Compiled from *Annuaire statistique*, 1946–7, p. 693 and Annual Statistics, Pocket Edition, 1950, p. 167

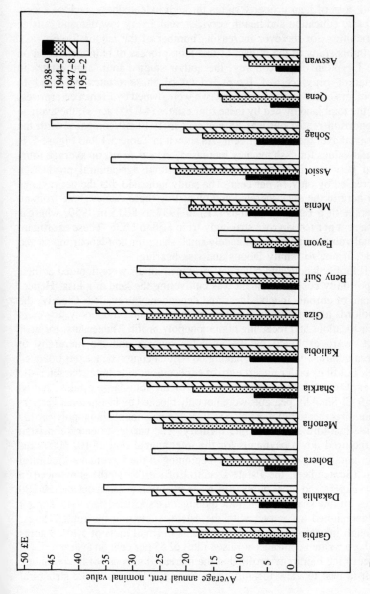

Figure 5.1 Average rent per Feddan (acre) in Egyptian provinces, 1938–52

Peasants in the districts of the large estates (some were as large as 70,000 acres, e.g. Kom Ombo plantation) were subjected to monopsonistic power and lived in conditions of poverty rooted in depressed earnings; low wages, forced labour, high rents, easy eviction from rented land, loss of land property rights through indebtedness, lack of access to basic education and health services, and a very low demand outside agriculture for the ever increasing number of the labour force.

In his study of the impact of this long process of monopolisation on the Egyptian rural economy, the author studied four large estates in different provinces of Egypt.[9] Two of these estates belonged to members of the royal family, and two were owned by French enterprises. Of the total land owned by these four estates (44,100 acres), the average proportion rented out was 86 per cent in 1949–50 compared with the national average of 60 per cent. As shown in Table 5.1 and Figure 5.1, rental values for cash tenancy increased, in *real terms*, on average four-fold between 1931 and 1951 whereas total agricultural production increased by only 14 per cent. The study indicated that the net revenue per acre in the area operated and owned by these estates, rose from an average of 5 Egyptian pounds (£E) in 1937 to £E15 in 1950, whereas cash rent per feddan rose strikingly from £E8 to £E36. These exorbitant rental values left a proportionately small share for non-labour inputs and little, if any to family labour and risk-bearing.

If family labour and other self-provided inputs were imputed at their opportunity costs, the tenant was cultivating the land at a loss. Hence, a state of chronic indebtedness and dependency prevailed. Clearly, the landlords and foreign enterprises were exercising monopoly power in their locations and receiving high monopoly profit. The tenants, for their part, were exploited by the absentee owners and the hierarchy of intermediaries. In addition, having no written contracts, tenants operated their holdings under uncertainty of expectation; a definite characteristic of exploitation. For example, in one of the four large estates studied (Kafr El-Sheikh), peasants were not only blocked by institutional barriers from direct lease but were also required to pay double monopoly profits to the landlord and to an intermediary. The barrier to entry consisted of required down payments for the total annual rent of 10, 500 acres after auctioning the lease. At the beginning of the Egyptian agricultural year (September), the Estate's central office (Tafteesh) announced in newspapers and local public places its intention to lease out the 10,500 acres for one year and called for bidding on a specified date. The highest bidder signed a contract with the estate, subletting the rented acres, through intermediaries, to 735 peasants in small plots of 5 to 20 acres with *no* written contracts at raised rates of 55 per cent on average. Each level of the hierarchy profited at the increased expense of the peasants.

It is best to view institutional monopoly elements in the structural context of persistent demand for the limited stock of cultivated land owing to increasing population pressure. On the one hand, the agricultural population doubled between the time when the first population census was made in 1897 and 1950 prior to the institution of land reform. On the other hand, the acreage of cultivated land increased by 20 per cent and cropping area by 34 per cent. Accordingly, the ratio of cultivated land to *per capita* agricultural population declined from 0.78 to 0.44 acre per person. A typical Malthusian situation emerged. Productivity per working person in agriculture declined steadily to two-thirds of its base in the year 1913.[10] Real wages in agriculture, already low, declined between 1934 and 1944, and then stagnated until 1949. Landlessness, seasonal unemployment and child labour utilisation (about 40 per cent of total hired labour in agriculture was below 15 years of age) increased steadily. The Gini Coefficient of the distribution of land ownership increased from 0.688 in 1896 to 0.758 in 1950.

Apart from the unabated population growth, there are two possible explanations for this state of rural under-development. The first possibility is low capital investment and reduction in the use of fertiliser. But while the supply of major inputs fluctuated during this period due to two World Wars and the depression of 1929–30, official data shows that the supply of fertiliser, machinery and irrigation water was in an upward trend between 1913 and 1950.[11] Nevertheless, productivity per acre (Feddan) of the main crops manifested an overall decline over the period 1935–51. The decline was more substantial in the food crops: maize, millet, beans, sugar and rice, than in cotton (see Figure 5.2). The second possible explanation lies in the significant influence exerted by institutional forces, especially the contractual arrangements in the land tenure system leading to disincentive to invest in land improvement and the rationing of the credit market already outlined. Both explanations are connected and converged in the high degree of imperfect functioning of all factor markets in a capitalist agriculture characterised by a *laissez-faire* policy.

Absenteeism among owners of land and the higher marginal profitability of renting out land (as compared to that operated by owners) increased the area under tenancy arrangements (including share-cropping), to 55–60 per cent on average between 1930 and 1950. This large-scale separation of land-ownership from production responsibilities deprived the tenants from institutional credit which requires land as collateral. Furthermore, the Five Feddans (acre) law of 1912 prohibited the seizure of land in this size range against debt. Accordingly 78 per cent of land-holders operating 23 per cent of agricultural land in 1950 suffered from capital rationing. Hence, another institutional barrier was established.

Within the structure of the economy in 1947, employment in industry (9 per cent) construction, trade and services accounted for 30.5 per cent

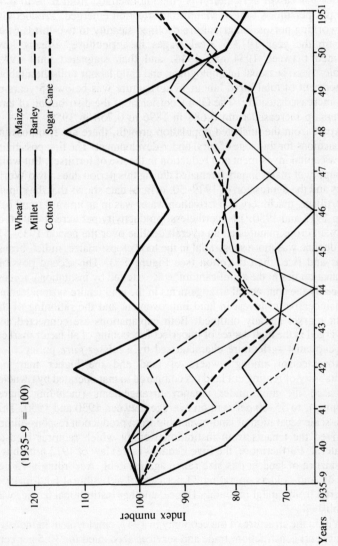

Figure 5.2 The trend in crop productivity per Feddan in 1935–51, Egypt

Source: Calculated from data given in *The Agricultural Economic Bulletins*, 1949, 51, Ministry of Agriculture, Cairo, Egypt

of the total labour force. Hence, the bulk had to be contained in the crippled agriculture whose assets ownership was concentrated. Landless workers (neither owning nor renting-in land) increased in absolute number and in proportion to total agricultural households. Although it is difficult to find firm data on this large group, Radwan and Abdul-Fadil made estimates ranging from 37 per cent in 1929 to 44 and 60 per cent in 1950s[12] Most of the landless workers were casual (*taraheel*), not permanent. They were hired by the landlords' contractors (*moqawil anfar*) especially in provinces where the concentration of land holdings was higher than elsewhere. The contractors exercised monopsonistic power in the rural labour market, tying the workers to them by paying part of their wages in advance for their consumption requirements, demanding extra unpaid days of work and deducting about 15–20 per cent of their wages for transport costs and profit.

Thus, exploitation and monopsony power in the rural labour market depressed the earnings of the 3 million landless households to the extent that their wage share in total agricultural income was only 5.3 per cent in 1950. Their average *per capita* income was only 16.4 Egyptian Pounds per annum, or the equivalent of 0.18 per cent of the *per capita* income of the rich landowners (with more than 50 acres).[13] Another factor which helped to depress the earnings of landless labour was cheap child labour at some 40 per cent of the wage rates of adult males. Many children were forced to substitute hard work for education. Education and health conditions of the landless youth were so bad that in 1939 the army found that only 4 per cent of their recruits could be enrolled without first receiving medical treatment.[14] Under such conditions of rural under-development, the author estimated the incidence of rural poverty at 56.1 per cent in 1949/50 (see Chapter 6, Egypt).

But under such complex elements of institutional monopoly, which options were there for landless peasants to purchase land? Prices of land were very high in terms of both sale price and rental values.[15] The annual average cash rental per acre in Egypt exceeded the price of land and farm buildings per acre in the USA between 1930 and 1947. The land price in Egypt was 25 to 30 times as high as in the USA and so clearly both tenants and hired agricultural workers were unable to purchase land as they were not able to obtain loans from banks. In fact, between 1925 and 1948 mortgage credit was advanced almost exclusively to those with large estates who owned on average 100 acres (Baer, 1962: 101). The possibility of hired, landless workers buying a piece of land was therefore very remote. The price of land with average soil fertility was US$ 1,500 (425 Egyptian Pounds) per acre during 1945–50. In the meantime, the average daily wage for a hired adult worker in agriculture was only US 42 cents (95 milliems) and the average number of salaried working days per annum was 200. A hired adult agricultural worker had

159

to accumulate *all* his wage earnings without spending anything on living costs for a period of 14–17 years to purchase one acre, based on these figures. If he spent half of his wages and, assuming a constant ratio of wage-land price, this period would double – a very unrealistic proposition.

Two other possibilities were left for the small tenant and the hired agricultural worker to own land, neither of which provided much hope. They might be lucky enough to obtain land through the government programme of selling State-reclaimed land on easy terms, or he might receive an intra-family inheritance. An official report on the sale of state-owned reclaimed land during the period 1935–49 from the Egyptian Ministry of Finance indicated that out of the total 182,623 Feddans sold, only 1.7 per cent went to tenants and permanent hired agricultural workers (modameen), whereas 90.7 per cent was sold to big landlords and land companies.[16] As for the possibility of inheriting a piece of land, again the opportunities were very limited as shown by Radwan and Lee (1986). The families of these peasants had very limited landed assets if any at all.[17]

Thus, it was no wonder that the Revolution of July 1952 had the immediate objective of abolishing most of the elements of institutional monopoly in rural Egypt. The content, scale and impact of the 1952 and 1961 land reforms will be examined in the next chapter.

Kenya

Institutional monopoly in Kenya's agriculture began in the first decade of the current century under the British colonial administration. The control of the institutions of land property, of authority and power, and of transaction in contractual arrangements of labour use, was rooted in the Crown Lands' Ordinance of 1902 issued by the British Governor, Sir Charles Elliot. Approximately 5 million acres (a substantial area of the good arable land) with high rainfall in the highlands were allocated to British settlers and the British multinationals (Brooke Bond and James Findlay). In most of this reserved area, the land was given on a 999-year lease under a freehold title. This large area was the homeland of the Kikuyu and Masai tribes who had occupancy rights for land use, but were driven away to native reserves on the slopes and lowlands where they continued to pursue their traditional cultivation and livestock herding. Each settler of the newly procured land in the highlands acquired on *average* about 2,500 acres under concessions that made the land almost free (Lugogo, 1986). The area was then developed into plantations of high value crops for export (coffee, tea, sisal and pyrethrum) in addition to wheat, maize and livestock for domestic consumption.

Consequently, the owners of these plantations enjoyed exclusive advantages of institutional monopoly until the independence of Kenya in 1963. With their grip on the best cultivable land, and their collusion with the government of their time, the plantation owners had both market and non-market powers in the following ways:

1. They were able to dominate the institutional support and technical agricultural services required for commercial farming.
2. They could command policy-making via the legislative council (which they had dominated since the early 1920s (Fage, 1978)), and the influential Kenya Farmers Association.
3. They were able to capture a disproportionate share of public expenditure in the form of infrastructural facilities (e.g., road construction and marketing facilities), and social services (health and education). This occurred despite the fact that nearly 70 per cent of the tax burden was borne by native Africans in the 1920s (Brett, 1973, cited in Collier and Lal, 1986: 30).
4. They could establish entry barriers to the highly commercialised plantation sector which dominated the market power in agriculture. They were able to ban native African farmers from growing high value crops (tea, sugar-cane and pyrethrum), hence controlling the production, pricing and export of these crops. Diana Hunt (1984: 12) explains the purpose of this malicious practice as a safeguard against a reduction in the supply of cheap labour utilised in the plantations and to maintain control over the market. Although this export enclave prevailed for a long time, the barriers were gradually lifted during 1940–50 under the growing political pressure and violence which led Kenya to independence in 1963.
5. They were able to exercise a monopsony power by:
    (a) influencing the passage of several laws in 1919 and the 1920s which required the district officer in labour-supplying areas to coerce African labourers to work for them; and
    (b) being exempted from the application of minimum wage laws, which resulted in enforcement restricted to urban areas.
   In fact, wage rates and terms of employment were controlled by the alliance of plantation owners and other foreign owned enterprises throughout the economy under the powerful Federation of Kenya Employers.

The Colonial administration responded to the rising number of landless workers and discontented African peasants and their tribal leaders by expanding opportunities for land property. A few years prior to independence, programmes for individual rights to freehold title of land and consolidation of fragmented holdings were initiated, and later expanded. These institutional arrangements were considered essential for the adaptation of tribal land rights to the requirements of agricultural

161

credit supply and other lending schemes. Another programme, the Million Acre Scheme, sub-divided part of the White highland plantations to Kenyans in small plots through a substantial settlement scheme externally financed by the British government, Commonwealth Development Corporation and the World Bank. In this programme, the land was purchased from plantation owners at full market value with their right to transfer the sale value abroad. Leys (1975) estimates the area transferred to small-holders at 1.2 million acres out of a total of about 5 million acres owned by European plantation owners.

After independence, a new class of Kenyan large landowner emerged by means of free market purchase and government lending arrangements. Many of them were members of Parliament, Cabinet Ministers, senior civil servants, and urban businessmen. Nevertheless, despite the efforts made to establish and expand the individual property system of small-holders, the overall pattern has continued; land distribution within a capitalist system of heavy control of asset ownership in agriculture retains its high degree of land concentration. According to the results of the 1981 census of agriculture the Gini Coefficient of land concentration was 0.77, (slightly higher than 1971 (0.74)). Of the total number of 2,112,000 holdings in the small farm sector, 83 per cent are less than 2 hectares. To the other extreme, the large farm sector has 2,192 farms, with a total area of 2.6 million hectares; 81 per cent of the farms are over 200 ha each, 930 of which are each 500 ha and over. During the period 1970–81, the pattern of land concentration was virtually stable, as shown in Table 5.2. This is probably why Colin Leys says, 'Not surprisingly, the general result [of Africanization of the farm structure] was that the protected position of the large-farm sector was left substantially intact' (Leys, 1975: 105).

Table 5.2 **Change in size distribution of land holdings in the large farms sector, Kenya 1973–81**

		100–199	*200–499*	*500–999*	*1,000 and over*	*Total*
1973/4	Number	392	810	498	436	2,136
	Area (Hectares)	57,000	269,000	345,000	1,865,000	2,636,000
1981	Number	419	843	479	451	2,192
	Area (Hectares)	59,441	275,471	342,032	1,945,394	2,619,338
Changes in						
1973/4–1981	Number	+27	+33	−19	+15	+56
	Area (Hectares)	+2,441	+6,471	−2,968	−19,606	−13,662

Note: percentage of each size group to total number and area cannot be calculated because the 1981 census changed the classification to include small, intermediate and large farms sectors which overlap in the size groups between 10 and 50 hectares

Source: 1973/4–World Census of Agriculture
1981 – FAO Statistics Division, Rome

It appears, however, that the market power of the pre-independence plantation sector has declined in relative terms, because of the lifting of barriers for the small farm sector to cultivate tea, coffee, pyrethrum and sugar-cane, and the increasing intensity of land use in that sector. But these two favourable developments do not seem to have diminished the influence of large farms and multinationals on the aggregate market structure.

Old MNCs carried on, and new ones entered the market structure. Private foreign capital vigorously responded to government encouragement following independence. Investment in agriculture offered attractive incentives and concessions, particularly in Kenya, with its political stability, high expectation of no expropriation or size-ceiling on landed property and the availability of cheap labour. Furthermore, privileges were granted to MNCs investment activities such as capital transfer, taxation, remittance of profits, export privileges, importation advantages, full compensation in case of nationalisation, hiring foreign personnel, etc. These transactions were institutionally regulated by the Foreign Investment Protection Act 1964. Nevertheless, as reported by ILO Mission (1972) and Leys (1975), many MNCs abused their privileges.

Some changes in the operation of MNCs were evident after independence. With the rising nationalistic movement, some MNCs adapted their operations to fit into the government's development strategy as followers or partners, instead of as leaders with colonial perceptions. While some have become partners in joint ventures with public agencies, (e.g. sugar cane), others like Del Monte have fully monopolised the production in contract farming, processing and export of pineapples. To a lesser extent, some MNCs, like Unilever, have maintained a high market share in the control of poultry production, vegetable fat and edible oil, dairy products, tobacco and medicinal plants. Whereas the production of tea, coffee, and sisal has expanded in the small-holder and Kenyan large farms sectors, the supply of technology and the marketing of these crops are still substantially controlled by MNCs. This is unquestionably a high degree of market power in the Kenyan agricultural economy.

The accumulated land and the utilisation of capital and labour for the production of these high-value crops for export represent special advantages of economies of scale, and the ability to accumulate high rates of monopoly profits. Of equal importance is the resulting shift in resources away from food production. Whereas the areas of cash crops (tea, coffee and tobacco) have been rocketing by 300 and 400 per cent, those of food crops plunged with the exception of maize and potatoes as shown in Table 5.3. The acreage of millet, sorghum and sweet potatoes fell both in absolute and relative terms by 40 per cent, and cassava by 45 per cent. There has, however, been a remarkable expansion of maize. Yet, domestic food productivity *per capita* declined, with a 'growth' rate

Table 5.3 Changes in land use among food, and cash crops in Kenya, 1960–86

Crops	Area in 1,000 Hectares				Change between 1960–5 and 1986	
	1960–5	Percentage of total cropping area	1986	Percentage of total cropping area	Percentage change in absolute area	Change in percentage cropping area
Food crops						
Maize	1,020	61	1,360	57	+33	−4
Millet and sorghum	350	20	210	9	−40	−11
Potatoes	53	5	80	3	+51	−2
Sweet potatoes	50	3	30	1	−40	−2
Cassava	90	5	50	2	−45	−3
Cash crops						
Tea	21	1	81	4	+290	+3
Coffee	55	3	150	6.3	+173	+3.3
Tobacco	1	0.06	5	0.2	+400	+0.14
Other crops*	30	1.8	404	17	+844	+15.2
Total cropping area	1,670	100	2,370	100		

Other crops are pulses, sisal, wheat, vegetables, pineapple, sugar cane and cotton, for which no complete data are available for 1960–5.
Note: percentages of crops to total area are rounded, and so do not necessarily add up to exactly 100.
Source: FAO Production Yearbook 1970, Vol. 24, and Yearbook 1986, Vol. 40.

of (-0.8) during the period 1970–84, signalling the inability of food production to keep pace with the rising demand for food resulting from the high rates of population growth (4.1 per cent). Consequently, imports of cereals has substantially increased (World Development Report, 1987 (indicators) and FAO Production Year Book, 1985).

In the rural labour market, the exemption of farming from the application of minimum wage rates has led to a loss in equity gains to hired workers in large farms and plantations. The same applies to the lost gains to casual workers on plantations due to the ineffective enforcement of the Regulation of Wages Order (1980 amendments). The bargaining power of the agricultural workers to improve their terms of employment has been constrained by two institutional measures: the restrictions imposed on trade unions by the government and the powerful institution of the Federation of Kenyan Farmers, dominated by the vested interests of owners of large farms and plantations. Collier and Lal (1986) consider that the degree of monopsony power exercised in the plantation labour market has recently declined, despite the fact that the plantations set wages collectively, and collectively employ a significant proportion of the rural landless wage labour force. This decline is primarily due to the high cropping intensity in the small-holders' sector. However, the unique advantage of the plantations in adopting labour-saving technology and economies of scale in farm management has enabled them to reduce the percentage of hiring-in labour from 50 per cent in the early 1960s to about 30 per cent in the late 1970s. They also use casual labour under contractual arrangements by which they are employed at piece-rate wages instead of daily rates, and are closely supervised.[18] These advantages over small-holders resulted in the segmentation of the labour market in agriculture.

The interlocking combination of concentration of land and segmented labour market in the Kenyan economy has had a discernible effect when considered alongside the high rates of average annual growth in population and that of entrants in the agricultural workforce (4.1 per cent and 3 per cent respectively between 1975 and 1985). The absolute numbers and percentage of landless agricultural workers rose over the past two decades from 10 per cent to nearly 15 per cent, and even 17 per cent of total agricultural *households* (depending upon the definitions used by estimators). The extent of the landlessness appears even higher if squatters on large mixed farms and some of the nomadic population are included. These people are trapped in conditions of rural poverty, the scale of which ranges between 40 and 50 per cent of total rural households at the end of the 1970s.

If opportunities to generate employment for the increasing agricultural labour force appear to be quite limited, the landless workers' chances of purchasing land on the open market are equally remote. There is a high degree of institutional credit rationing – commercial banks and marketing co-operatives preclude any possibility for lending credit to a landless agricultural worker. The banks require land title as security and the co-operatives favour growers of cash-crops and not subsistence food producers. The landless farmer's hope of purchasing one acre of land at the average price of 10,000–15,000 shillings per acre is an unrealisable dream. The annual income per household of the rural poor was about 1,700 shillings in 1977 (IRSI, 1977; Hunt, 1984; Livingston, 1986). In his survey on the origin of land acquisition among the small-holders in the Kisii district of Nyanza Province, Bager found that only 3 per cent of total area had been purchased by a few owners of larger holdings. The rest was acquired mostly by inter-family inheritance and marriage, and some had to rely on squatting on the white estates.[19] Like their fellow Egyptian landless farmers in the 1940s, the present Kenyan landless households depending on agriculture have to wait for land reform. This seems to be unattainable under the present political balance of power, despite the strong arguments for a major land re-distribution advanced by several international missions and knowledgeable economists.[20]

All elements of institutional monopoly based on ownership of assets and vested interests function in agriculture in a coherent system of in-fluences upon policy makers. The coalition of vested interests of Kenyan large farm owners, plantations and MNCs exercises a substantial influence on the apparatus of policy formulation through their powerful institutions. The power structure can frustrate efforts towards land reform, and also dominates the pricing mechanism. Some examples of the means of dominance which harm the landless workers and consumers' interests include: the Marketing Boards which control prices and marketing of many agricultural crops; and the commodity focused bodies, such as the Coffee Producers Union, Maize Board, Meat Commission and Creamery Co-operative which control milk and dairy products. Leys lists several examples of the multiple-roles of many large farmers who, at the same time, are holders of leading positions in government administration, political machinery, public corporations and urban economic institutions (Leys, 1975: 103–4).

Given the institutional obstacles confronting rural development and given the present structural characteristics of the Kenyan economy, the prospects of rapid alleviation of rural poverty and gross inequalities in the distribution of income and opportuities are gloomy. It is true that official development plans since 1979 express an increasing concern for rural poverty. However, the macro-indicators of the performance of both agriculture and the total economy show an overall low level of produc-tivity. Due to the design of its development strategy, the performance of Kenya's economy has been adversely affected by the world economic instability since 1980. Average annual growth rates of the total GDP and agricultural output fell over the period 1965–85, the former from 6.4 per cent to 3.1 per cent and the latter from 4.9 per cent to 2.8 per cent. At the same time, growth rates of food production *per capita* declined and did not keep pace with population growth and the total external debts reached US$4.5 billion in 1986. These disappointing indicators have occurred following over 70 years of substantial influx of private foreign capital and technology in Kenyan agriculture.

Cross-section analysis of twenty developing countries

So far we have relied on a qualitative analysis of our conception of institutional monopoly in agrarian economies and of the historical experience of Egypt and Kenya. The empirical evidence gathered from these two case studies has implied the relationship between land concentration (LC), poverty (P), landlessness (LNS) and the direction of agricultural growth (AGR). We need to ascertain the validity of the relationship between these four variables in a set of data for 20 LDCs (including Egypt and Kenya) through simple statistical methods (correlation and regression). This test attempts to make the formulated concepts measurable. In doing so, it is recognised that these variables act and interact on each other in different strengths within a complex agrarian system. We also need to keep in mind that the degree of association between these variables (as measured by these simple statistical methods) varies according to the set of data used.

Methodology

The functional structure of this inquiry can be expressed as:

$$P = f(LC)$$
$$LNS = f(LC)$$
$$AGR = F(LC)$$

This is a simplified aggregate structure of pre-determined variables in which LC is central (as suggested earlier in our theoretical framework on institutional monopoly). There are, of course, several variables affecting the incidence of poverty, landlessness and rates of agricultural growth other than the degree of land concentration. Examples are: density of population on agricultural land and the intensity of its use; weather; real wage rates and the demand for agricultural labour; pricing policy; investment in agriculture; technological change; non-farming sources of the rural poor's incomes; population growth; social habits and customs affecting the pattern of consumption and attitude to work, etc. The influence of population growth is implied in the use of annual rates of

167

Table 5.4 **Relationship between rural poverty, land concentration, agricultural growth and landlessness in 20 developing countries**

Countries in ascending order by value of agricultural GDP	Agricultural GDP 1973–83			Gini Coefficient of concentration of land holdings' distribution and year of estimate	Estimated landless households as % of total agricultural households	Estimated % of rural population in absolute poverty and reference year
	Per head 1982 US $	Annual rate of growth				
		Total	Per head agricultural population			
Bangladesh	64	3.2	0.7	0.549 (1984)	31 (c)	78 (1982)
Kenya	107	3.4	−0.1	0.770 (1981)	15 (c)	45 (1978)
India	114	2.2	1.0	0.621 (1977)	30 (a)	51 (1979)
Nepal	114	1.0	−1.3	0.602 1980)	10 (a)	61 (1978)
Sri Lanka	139	4.1	2.8	0.619 (1982)	19 (a)	26 (1981)
Madagascar	182	−0.2	−2.0	0.800 (1984)	n.a	50 (1978)
Pakistan	190	3.4	1.4	0.539 (1980)	31 (c)	39 (1980)
Thailand	213	3.4	1.8	0.460 (1978)	10 (a)	34 (1978)
Indonesia	254	3.7	2.7	0.620 (1973)	36 Java (a)	44 (1980)
Jordan	261	4.3	4.6	0.690 (1983)	7 (c)	17 (1979)
Egypt	282	2.5	0.8	0.430 (1984)	24 (c)	18 (1982)
Honduras	283	3.3	0.4	0.780 (1974)	33 (c)	58 (1980)
Philippines	413	4.3	3.2	0.530 (1981)	37 (a)	42 (1982)
Turkey	440	3.4	3.6	0.580 (1980)	28 (a)	20 (1986)

Jamaica	546	−0.2	1.8	0.815 (1979)	41 (b)	51 (1981)
Panama	564	1.4	0.6	0.840 (1981)	20 (c)	30 (1978)
Brazil	658	4.2	3.7	0.859 (1980)	39 (a)	67 (1980)
Korea, South	806	1.5	3.0	0.301 (1980)	4 (c)	10 (1980)
Paraguay	1,161	6.0	3.4	0.939 (1981)	27 (c)	63 (1980)
Venezuela	1,553	2.6	2.7	0.920 (1973)	27 (b)	56 (1980)

Sources:

Column 1. The State of Food and Agriculture 1985 – Annex table 13; Values in US Dollars are based on World Bank Atlas method.

" 2. World Development Report 1985 – Table 2 Basic Indicators.

" 3. Calculated on the bases of growth rates of agricultural population for each country in FAO Country Tables, 1985.

" 4. FAO Statistics Division, except Bangladesh and Egypt, which are calculated by the author, see Table 1.5.

" 5. (a) FAO – C87/19 – August 1987 Table 5 (b) ILO publication ACRD IX /197/11 (c) Kenya: Collier and Lal *op cit.*, Egypt and Pakistan: El Ghonemy, *Economic Growth, Income Distribution and Poverty in the Near East*, Table 20, FAO, Rome, 1984. Honduras: Peek *Agrarian Structure and Rural Poverty – The Case of Honduras*, ILO, Sept. 1984. Jordan: *Statistical Yearbook 1983*, Table 68 (only Jordanian landless). The rest of countries are estimates of agricultural workers in several editions of Yearbook of Labour Statistics, ILO, Geneva.

" 6. Compiled by the author from several sources (see Table 1.1, 'The dynamics of rural poverty', and Table 2, p. 103 of c87/19, both published by FAO, Rome 1986 and 1987 respectively, except Egypt: Adams, 'Development and structural change in rural Egypt, 1952–1982' *World Development*, Vol. 13, No. 6, June 1985, Table 1. p. 707 and Turkey estimated from *The Socio Economic Situation and Outlook of the Turkish household* in 1986, unpublished study prepared by Esmer, Fisek and Kalaycioglu and sent to the author by TUSIAD, Ankara.

n.a. not available

growth of agricultural GDP per head, the incidence of poverty and of landlessness as a percentage of total rural and agricultural households respectively. The time factor is another important variable, and is also implied in the use of a ten year period for calculating the rate of AGR. The ten year period 1973–83 is chosen because it corresponds to the years of reference of the other data on poverty, landlessness and land concentration. The land concentration index is stable in terms of the share of holders in total number and areas of holding (at least in the short term), unless a major land redistribution programme is suddenly instituted.

Granted that other variables are important, the pair of variables in each of the three equations is chosen to serve the analysis within the context of our inquiry on institutional monopoly. Accordingly, the statistical observations from the sample of 20 LDCs given in Table 5.4 are plotted in three diagrams (Figures 5.3, 5.4 and 5.5). P, LNS and AGR are dependent variables (Y) and LC is the common independent variable (X). The purpose is to see how the scatters of observations of each pair of variables behave. The correlation and regression coefficients are quantitative measurements of how closely they relate and the extent to which P, LNS and AGR are dependent upon LC. In the graphs, we have added four countries (China, Colombia, Mexico and Morocco) which are neither given in Table 5.4, nor included in the analysis. Because of their data limitations, inclusion could have influenced the result of the analysis.[21] We included them in the scatter diagrams *solely* to show how additional observations from other countries would behave among the 20 countries in the sample.

Ordinary least square method for estimating the regression ($Y = a + bX$) is used, where Y denotes the dependent variable (P or LNS or AGR), a is the intercept of the regression line with the vertical axis Y, b denotes the slope of the regression line and X is the independent variable (land concentration index). In addition to the variation in Y explained by this relation, there is unexplained variation due to other omitted effects and errors in measurement. To find out the relationship between Y, the dependent variable and land concentration index, the unknowns a and b have to be estimated, and the unexplained portion of variation in Y among the countries in our sample has to be calculated.[22]

Before we present the results of our cross-section analysis of data given in Table 5.4, we should indicate the statistical limitations of the data in terms of: (a) different years of estimation; (b) the lack of a uniform measurement of rural poverty incidence and landlessness among LDCs which was noted earlier in Chapters 1 and 3; and (c) the high level of aggregation of these estimates. The Gini Coefficient of land distribution, which measures concentration, also has limitations. First, it refers to land holdings (farm size) irrespective of their tenure status as provided by the available agricultural censuses. Second, it measures the inequality in the distribution of holdings which is usually less unequal than the distribution of landownership because of renting out part of owned land to be operated by several tenants. Finally, it conceals the differences in land quality i.e. yields by variations in soil fertiity, location and whether the land is irrigated or rain-dependent. It is useful, however, as a measure of the degree of controlling land. This degree of control is the core of our conception of institutional monopoly in agrarian economies.

The results of analysis

Keeping in mind the limitations of data used, the results are briefly presented leaving the details in Appendix B.

Rural poverty The scatter diagram (Figure 5.3) shows how plotted observations move together. In most cases the high incidence of poverty is accompanied by a high degree of land concentration. This association is obvious in the behaviour of data on Gini index of land distribution and levels of rural poverty in the Latin American countries on the one hand, and in China, Egypt and South Korea on the other.

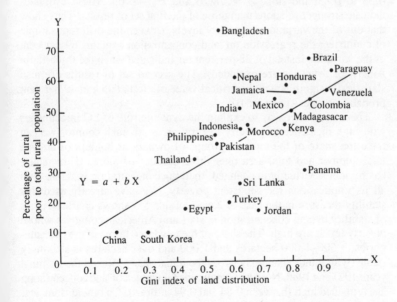

Figure 5.3 Relationship between rural poverty and land concentration ratios

Source: Based on data in Table 5.4 Colombia, Mexico, China and Morocco are not included in the calculations (see text).

The cross-sectional analysis of data given in Table 5.4 indicate a positive coefficient of the correlation between P and LC being 0.53. This means that in most cases the higher the LC, the higher the incidence of P and vice versa. The regression coefficient of poverty (Y) on land concentration index (X) indicates a highly significant level of relation at a probability of 99 per cent and 95 per cent as tested by both the t and F methods respectively. The slope of the regression line ($b = 57$) intercepts the poverty axis Y at a low point (5.5). Furthermore, the co-eficient of determination of the effect of LC on P is 0.28 which means that out of the total variation in the levels of rural poverty incidence, the regression on LC explains 28 per cent. The unexplained portion of variation (the residual) is due partly to measurement error and partly to the effect of the omitted factors other than LC.

These low coefficients of correlation and regression are likely due to the exclusion of Morocco and the three Latin American countries, (Colombia, Mexico and Peru). We excluded them for reasons explained earlier, in order to have a more representative sample whose results are not influenced by an over-representation of the Latin American coun-tries. In fact, when these countries are included in the' analysis, the coefficients are substantially greater. The positive correlation rises from 0.53 to 0.83, the slope $b = 78.26$ and $r^2 = 0.69$. These estimates indicate stronger relations than those of the first set of results. They show that out of the variation in poverty levels between the different sample of countries, the regression on land concentration explains 69 per cent of the variation instead of 28 per cent (as indicated when the three Latin American countries are excluded). The second set of results are also statistically significant at the critical value of t test at 95 and 99 per cent probability (see Appendix B).

There is another way to explain the dynamic role of LC in countries with high incidence of poverty in rural areas. In each country we can trace the share of the top size groups of owners or holders of land in total number and total area over three decades or more. If this share has remained virtually unchanged, then the concentration is stable with all its implications for persistent poverty. We have already used this stability measure in the case of Kenya. Table 5.5 shows characteristics of stability in land concentration in six Latin American countries whose poverty levels are high. The share of the few large farms in the two cate-gories of 500–1,000 hectares and 1,000 and over hectares is strikingly stable (with minor change) between the initial year 1950 and the terminal years 1971 and 1980. Not surprisingly, the Gini index of land concentration has remained high (between 0.84 and 0.94 in Brazil, Colombia, Jamaica, Paraguay and Venezuela and between 0.73 and 0.78 in Honduras and Panama). With the exception of Panama, the poverty levels in this group of countries ranges between 42 and 67 per cent of total rural population.

Table 5.5 **Stability of land concentration among top size groups of large holdings in six Latin American countries 1950–80**

Country and year of agricultural census		Share in total number of holdings %		Share in total area of holdings %		Gini index of land concentration (all holdings)
		500–1,000 ha	1,000 and over	500–1,000 ha	1,000 and over	
Brazil	1950	1.8	1.5	10.4	50.8	0.83
	1960	1.2	1.1	11.4	44.2	0.84
	1970	1.0	0.8	11.3	39.5	0.84
	1980	1.1	0.6	11.1	44.7	0.86
Colombia	1954	0.6	0.3	13.5	26.7	0.85
	1960	0.3	0.2	10.0	30.4	0.86
	1971	0.4	0.3	10.4	30.4	0.86
Honduras	1952	0.2	0.1	7.7	20.6	0.73
	1971	0.2	0.1	7.0	15.5	0.78
Panama	1950	0.1	0.1	5.3	12.7	0.72
	1960	0.1	0.1	5.0	15.7	0.74
	1971	0.2	0.1	6.6	16.3	0.78
Venezuela	1961	1.0	1.3	7.1	71.7	0.94
	1971	1.4	1.7	9.6	66.7	0.92

		Share in total Number %	200 Hectares and Over	Share in total Area %		Gini index
Jamaica	1960	0.2		45.2		0.80
	1969	0.1		45.3		0.80
	1980	0.2		44.3		0.85

Source: Calculated from Agricultural Censuses data on 1950, 1960, 1970, in the 1970 World Census of Agriculture, Analysis and International Comparisons of Results, FAO, 1981, and from the results of 1980 Agricultural Census of Brazil and Jamaica obtained by the author from Statistics Division of FAO, Rome, Italy.

We have not yet examined the part of our hypotheses referring to the relation between poverty and land concentration as independent of the country's average level of income. Using per head agricultural income, the first column in Table 5.4 shows that this relationship does not follow the per head agricultural income. This is why the countries have been listed in descending order. Latin American countries have very high average income levels and high poverty, compared to the much lower incomes and poverty levels of Egypt and Thailand, (whose Gini index is relatively low). The absent positive relationship also applies to average per head gross national income (GNP) in 1983. Low income countries like India, Pakistan and Sri Lanka, whose GNP *per capita* is in the range of US$260 to $390 have lower ratios of LC and P relative to those of the Latin American countries whose GNP *per capita* ranges between US$ 1,500 and US$ 1,800 in 1985.

Landlessness The correlation between LNS and LC, though positive at 0.36, is much lower than that between P and LC. This is due partly to the variation in the occupational classification of agricultural households as many landless workers have also non-farming jobs, and partly to a lack

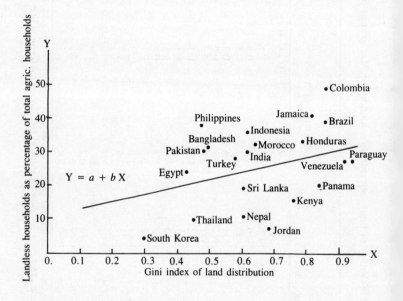

Figure 5.4 Relationship between landlessness and concentration of land holdings
Source: Based on data in Table 4.3. Colombia, Mexico, China and Morocco are not included in the calculations (see text).

174

of a uniform definition of a landless agricultural household who is neither owning nor renting land. Some countries with high LC have rapid urbanization and increasing non-farming jobs whether urban- or rural-based (e.g. Jordan, Kenya, and Panama). Nevertheless, landlessness remains positively correlated with the degree of concentration of land holding.

Agricultural growth This inquiry has addressed the question: to what extent is the degree of LC in private property-market economies (covered in our sample of 20 LDCs) related to the dynamic growth of agriculture? Here again an inter-country analysis limited to a single independent variable (LC) cannot give an adequate answer because it omits several geographical and structural variables such as erratic rainfall, percentage of irrigated area, technology, variation in production of food and export crops, incentives system and pricing policy, pattern and rates of investment in agriculture, etc. Nevertheless, it is worth attempting to explain the relationship because of the widely held opinion of some politicians, neoclassical economists and business agents, that large farming enterprises in LDCs are necessary for the realisation of a dynamic agricultural growth.

The analysis is based on two levels and uses the total annual growth rates of agricultural GDP and the rates per head of agricultural population during the period 1973–83 (a period which corresponds to data on land concentration in the countries of our sample). A simple regression analysis of *total* agricultural GDP growth rates (dependent variable) on the degree of land concentration shows a very low but positive regression coefficient. It is, however, statistically insignificant. Its coefficient of determination being 0.04 indicates that only 4 per cent of the variation in total agricultural GDP growth rates of our sample of 20 countries during the period 1973–83 is explained by the degree of land concentration. Their weak association is shown by their correlation coefficient $r = 0.091$. Though positive, this is very close to zero, *viz.* the two variables are weakly related, do not move together, and have no observed linear relation. This insignificant relation suggests that the predominance of large estates and multinationals' plantations controlling a large proportion of land tends not to be associated with higher growth rates. This form of association was supported by the regression analysis results by Berry and Cline (1979, Tables 3.3 and 3.4) and the World Bank Study (1974, Table 2.1).

The second level of analysis is conducted using average growth rates *per head* of agricultural population during the same period. This is more relevant to our concern about poverty. The statistical observations for the sample of 20 countries are plotted in the scatter diagram (Figure 5.5). Their behaviour shows that agricultural production per head does not move together with the index of land concentration. On measuring this form of relationship, the correlation is very low and *negative* ($r = -0.03$). Similarly, the regression of agricultural growth per head on

175

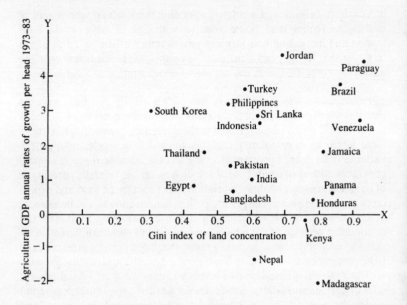

Figure 5.5 Agricultural production per head and land concentration index

Gini index of LC is low, negative (−0.354) and statistically insignificant at 90 and 95 per cent confidence intervals testing by both *t* and *F* methods. (see Appendix B) The intercept of the line determining the relation with Y (agricultural growth per head) is high at 1.97, and has a negative slope.

These results can easily be inferred from the wide scatter of the sample of observations Y and X in Figure 5.5. The scatter diagram shows no obvious linear relation as both the rates of growth and LC do not go together in most of the observations plotted. As we see from the diagram, whereas countries with high concentration of land (e.g. Colombia, Brazil and Paraguay) realised high rates of agricultural growth, others like China and South Korea, with egalitarian distribution of land, also realised high growth rates. At the same time, the two groups have opposite extremes in levels of poverty. This tenuous relationship supports our hypothesis about the relationship between agricultural growth and the character of equity in land distribution. Thus, there is too much unexplained diversity. On the face of it, it might seem that the question of combining agricultural growth with social gains from greater equity is not a matter of cut-and-dried generalisation. It cannot be universalised, so we must approach the subject more empirically in certain defined conditions. This requires

176

understanding the circumstances of changes in land distribution and agricultural growth in the specific setting of each country's policy aims in development. This chapter was only a beginning towards this empirical approach, which is pursued on a country by country basis in the next chapter.

Concluding remarks

Our historical review of country experience (Egypt and Kenya) and the statistical analysis of data available from 20 developing countries confirm the three hypotheses stated at the beginning of the chapter, *viz.*: land ownership is more commonly secured by institutional means than by open market mechanism; the lower the concentration of land distribution, the lower the incidence of absolute poverty in rural areas and vice versa; and dynamic growth of agricultural output is not conditional upon the degree of land concentration. Hence, the predominance of private large estates and multinationals' plantations in agriculture is *not* necessarily associated with higher rates of *per capita* and total agricultural GDP growth. Due consideration should be given to variables other than LC, including weather, technology, incentives and pricing systems, density of agricultural population on arable land, and pattern and rate of investment in agriculture.

Our discussion also suggests that for the study of monopoly elements in the agrarian economy of agriculture it is necessary to identify the institutional arrangements which create barriers to entry and restrict the options of the poor to raise their earnings. To understand the linkages, our approach suggests the appropriate combination of the relevant principles of economics with institutions and custom-determined production relations in each country's own historical context. The historical approach followed in the study of Egypt and Kenya helps explain how contemporary land concentration and shaping of the market structure originated during colonial rule. The type of analysis presented shows the erroneous view created when customary and institutional determinants of the interlinked factor markets in agriculture are separated or ignored while considering market imperfections.

The case studies of Egypt and Kenya suggests that concentration of productive land is the major mechanism of exercising institutional monopoly in agriculturally-based economies characterised by no government intervention in the private property markets. The relationship of land tenure to development suggests that the assumptions made in the literature on perfect competition in the land market is highly questionable. Evidence from the historical experience of the two countries shows that although the land market provided for tenancy arrangements, it did not provide for purchase of land. Non-market means of transaction are the

177

common source of the persistent accumulation of wealth and power, particularly land grants during the colonial period. Institutional barriers inhibit the landless peasant from purchasing land in the open market. Furthermore, the formation of large estates under historical and political contingencies created wealth by status and not by skills and entrepreneurial abilities. This institutional conditioning has resulted in the descendants of large estates' owners inheriting the consequential privileges in the society. Accordingly, such privileges as power and educational opportunities have been denied the children of the poor peasants.

Throughout the chapter we stressed barriers to entry as a significant feature of institutional monopoly. Though differing from barriers identified in industry, the identified types of barriers in the agrarian market structure characterised by private property and concentration of land, do share two common characteristics with industry. The first is the large scale of operations. The other, is the restriction of opportunities for those seeking entry, as outlined above, and abstracted from Egyptian and Kenyan experiences. This restriction leads to increased costs borne by the peasants seeking entry into the credit market and land transactions. The increased costs of the poor are an approximation of the high monopoly profits gained by large farmers, middlemen, MNCs and money-lenders. We know from Chapter 1 that the characteristics of poverty include low labour capability resulting from malnutrition and illiteracy. This characterisation tends to reduce the opportunities for the poor to compete in remunerative rural- and urban-based activities to seek higher return on their labour. This sequential chain of restricted options imposed on the poor perpetuates their conditions of poverty.

However, the definition of barriers to entry in both agricultural and industrial activities remains ambiguous, with different researchers using different criteria. The same applies to the term 'exploitation'. Unlike agriculture, however, the actions of those 'inside' and those 'outside' the barriers are legally regulated in industry. How the institutional barriers in agrarian systems are removed by land reform programmes is the subject of the next chapter.

Notes

1   In his *Principles of Economics*, (1890), Alfred Marshall in Chapter IV of Book One outlined 'Questions investigated by the Economist'. It includes the institution of property about which he asked 'Does economic freedom tend of its own action to build up combinations and monopolies, and what are their effects?' ' . . . Economics is thus taken to mean a study of the economic aspects and conditions of man's

political, social and private life; but more especially of his social life'
(Marshall, 1952: 34, 35). In Chapter X of Book VI on Land Tenure,
Marshall called our attention to 'custom and tradition rather than
conscious contracts' (Marshall, 1952: 530) that prevail in the traditonal
land market.

2 More than half of MNCs operating in the food processing sector are
based in the USA with aggregate sales of US\$ 103 billion about 16 per
cent of which was produced in developing countries. This is followed
by the UK with total sales of \$38 billion; 30 per cent produced in
LDCs. But the three large Swiss MNCs produced 90 per cent of their
total sales in LDCs. Nearly 30 per cent of all MNCs' food processing
is controlled by two (Unilever and Nestlé). Three multinationals control
70–90 per cent of the marketing of wheat, cotton, tobacco, coffee,
natural rubber and bananas. One MNC, (Pioneer Hi-Bred) controls 40
per cent of the world seed market (see *Transnational Corporations in
World Development* (1983; 4–5), UN Centre on Transactional
Corporations, UN, New York. In Brazil, 17 per cent of assets in
food processing are owned by foreign MNCs. About 50 per cent of
total food processed in developing countries is controlled by MNCs;
the average revenue of each amounts to US\$ 300. Paul Streeten
(1982: 314) reports that at the global level, foreign production
of the MNCs accounts for as much as 20 per cent of the world
output.

3 Hans Singer and Javeed Ansari relate the pattern of foreign investment
in LDCs during colonial rule and after independence. Under the
former, the foreign investment had the overriding objective of
contributing to the maintenance of the stability of the imperial system.
This led to a sharp division of the colony's economy into the advanced
sector, which increased exports and used cheap labour from the
backward or traditional sector. This system was built into the agrarian
structure of most developing countries after their independence. Hence,
it became necessary for MNCs to orient their business in ways
acceptable to the governments of LDCs. The authors commented that
the MNC proved to be 'the only world organization that has to date
demonstrated its ability to integrate vertically entire industries and to
integrate horizontally economic activities over a very widely spread
area' (Singer and Ansari, 1982: Chapter 10 – 'The multinational
corporation in developing countries').

4 Terry Cox presents in Chapters 4, 5, and 6 the detailed research
carried out by Kritsman and his team during the period 1927 and 1930.
Cox states that the research, ' . . . represents the peak of remarkable
flowering of Marxist empirical social research in Russia in the 1920s',
'It is still relevant more generally to sociological research today', (Cox,
1986: 247).

5 These different concepts illustrate how circumstances in specific periods
of history are behind the analytical reasoning in their formulation. John
Locke was reacting against Sir Thomas Filmer's writings in 1689 in
which Filmer supported the Divine Right of British Kings as a natural

right to dominate the liberty and property of their people 'answerable only to God from whom Kings derived the right'. Accordingly, Locke formulated his principle of 'natural right of life, liberty and property' derived from the right of labour to its *own* product which aggregately constitute the wealth of the nation. Locke viewed private property to precede sovereignty. Thus private property, when *not* monopolised, was conceptualised against the arbitrary rights of the King and it was later written into law by the Act of Settlement in 1700 (see Commons, 1923: 222; and 1934: 25–9).

6 Based on the account made by the Egyptian historian Ali Pasha Mubarak (1887), Baer recorded some contemporary family names and described how each of them obtained, during the 19th century, its extensive areas of land from successive rulers; mostly through grants and land grabbing. Detailed records of these large estates were known at the time when the land reform of July 1952 was implemented.

7 Considering that only 21 foreign corporations were engaged in agriculture, they owned 55 per cent of total private land according to the 1939 Census of Agriculture. Most of these lands were acquired by seizures against mortgage and by purchase of public land controlled by the Khedive (Daira Al-Saneya), who was forced to sell most of it to pay the accumulated debt which was overdue to three British and French banks. The financial bankruptcy led to the British occupation of Egypt in 1882; an important factor in the expansion of the henceforth foreign private investment in agriculture during 1890–1910.

8 A strong coalition between influential landed families of Egyptian and Egypto-Turkish origin and the foreign corporations operating in Egypt was revealed by the Stock Exchange Year Books in the 1940s, and later when large private enterprises were nationalised between 1956 and 1961. In these records a handful of names appeared in most of the lists of the boards of directors of large corporations in industry, agriculture, and trade, as well as land mortgage banks. For an enlightening discussion of this interwoven fabric of power structure and a classical oligopoly see Baer (1962: 128–9) and Issawi (1947).

9 This study was carried out by the author in 1951, one year before the July 1952 revolution. It is analysed in El-Ghonemy (1953: 57–9.

10 Productivity per worker in agriculture is an important indicator of income and standard of living. Mahmoud El-Imam calculated agricultural production from 1913 to 1950, which he represented by an index for major field crops (see El-Imam, 1962).

11 Other factors not inherent in land tenure system and imperfect functioning of factor-markets in Egyptian agriculture are the supply of fertiliser and water for irrigation. As to the latter, Egypt's perennial irrigation system from the State-controlled network of canals and barrages was not changed and its improvement continued. With regard to the *total* supply of fertilisers, the monthly Bulletin No. 7 of the Egyptian Ministry of Agriculture states on page 11 that imported fertiliser was:

```
average 1935-39  552,300 tons
        1945      260,125 tons
        1947      457,755 tons
        1949      621,148 tons
        1950      683,506 tons
```

Thus, a sharp decline occurred during the Second World War but was surpassed in 1947 and the level in 1950 exceeded that of pre-war level. Furthermore, Egypt started producing nitrates and phosphates on a larger scale during and after the Second World War, and thus added her own production of fertilizer to the imported stock.

12 The reason for this variation in the estimate of landless households is the difference in the assumptions about the percentage of rural households engaged in non-agricultural activities. Radwan's was 15 per cent and Abdul Fadil's was 19 per cent. Also, Abdul Fadil used a higher figure for rural households (2,700,000) while Radwan used 2,400,000 based on a different calculation of the family size in rural areas. (See Radwan 1977: Table 1.2; and Abdul-Fadil, 1975: Table 2.12.)

13 The proportional relation between annual *per capita* income of hired agricultural workers and landowners in the size group of 50 feddan and over is based on a study by the Department of Agricultural Economics of the Egyptian Ministry of Agriculture published in 1948. According to this study, 'National Income from Agriculture 1945-1947', Table 11 – Government Press, the average annual *net* income from owned and operated farms was as follows:

200 feddans and over 15,026 Egyptian Pounds
50-200 1,926 Egyptian Pounds

My study (note 9 above) estimated the average annual cash income of an adult hired labourer in agriculture during 1947 and working for 200 days a year at 14.0 to 16.4 Egyptian Pounds.

14 Medical reports showed that about 75 per cent of agricultural workers were infected by Bilharzia due to being deprived from purified drinking water and many of them also suffered from another parasite (Ankylostoma). This affected their mental and physical inertia and in turn their productivity estimated to be approximately 30-35 per cent less than the non-infected workers. Professor Cleland's study shows that there was only one qualified medical doctor for 13,000 rural people in 1939. His inquiry shows that the results of the Army's medical examinations of the recruits rejected 80 per cent, accepted 20 per cent including 16 per cent who 'are usable after medical treatment, i.e., only 4 per cent were found fit (Cleland, 1939: 465).

15 The price of land was not determined only by its productivity and location. It was primarily determined by family heritage and social prestige as well as speculation in land by landowners, urban professionals (lawyers, medical doctors, civil servants and businessmen) who placed a premium on the purchase of land as means of safe

investment. The market value of one feddan in 1947 was £E430.6, while its valuation according to its productivity and the market interest rate should have been £E194. The data on land prices in the USA are taken from USA Dept. of Agriculture, 1940 and 1950 Census of Agriculture, Washington D.C. For a detailed discussion on investment in holding land in Egypt, see El-Ghonemy (1955).

16 Public Domain Department (Amlak Amireya), Ministry of Finance, (1949) 'The Department's Work Since its Establishment', Cairo, Table 3: 47 (Arabic).

17 In their sample survey conducted in 1977, Radwan and Lee examined the history of land ownership among 1,000 households from different income classes in 18 villages. The findings show that 'of all households which reported some loss of land, 43 per cent are now completely landless (they were in the size group of less than one acre)'; that 12.1 per cent owned their land by land reform law and that only 14.6 per cent of total households had ever purchased land in their lifetime. As much as 45 per cent of the total areas purchased went to those with large land ownershp. The study states that inheritance is the major dominant way of current land ownership' 'land purchases have thus contributed to a greater concentration of land ownership' (Radwan and Lee, 1986: 72, 75). Interestingly, I found that the ratio of landless workers' wages to the price of land in Yemen Arab Republic during a field study in September-October 1986 was close to that of Egypt as stated in the text. Collier and Lal (1986) found a situation in Kenya resembling that of Egypt and Yemen Arab Republic in respect of the landless workers' extremely limited opportunities to purchase land. As for marriage, customs and social values in Egypt give preference to the number of acres owned by the groom or his father. Even among the owners, a landlord of 100 acres would likely lower his status if his daughter was to marry the son of an owner of, say, five acres. It was observed that landlords' class, especially of Turkish origin, refused to marry anyone from outside their own rank.

18 The rate of labour employment in agriculture is determined by seasonality and location of cash crops demanding large amounts of labour during a short period. Livingstone (1986) explains the unique conditions of the supply of labour in each of the tea, coffee, and sizal estates and sugar plantations (Chapter 3). For instance, he reports that not only is coffee-picking highly labour intensive, but it is concentrated within a very short period of time (November and December), during which labour requirements increase to 115 times those of April. Most of the labour used (80 per cent) is casual (seasonal). In the tea estates, 75 per cent of labour comes from outside tea producing areas. In sugar cane areas, plantations also use a high proportion of labour on casual terms. Subcontractors are made responsible for the supervision of 50 to 100 workers (all recruits from the subcontractors respective area) during all operations. 'Labour finds itself in the hands of subcontractors applying all the ruthlessness of informal sector' (Livingstone, 1986: 31).

19 Cited in Collier and Lal (1986: 129). According to the national

integrated Rural Survey IV of 1978/9, only 5 per cent of rural households were found to be renting-in any land and their rented area was only 0.9 per cent of the total area of small-holders' land.

20 The international team of experts was headed by Professor Hans Singer and the mission was organised by ILO of the UN in 1972. The mission recommended 'the redistribution of land towards the smaller and more labour-intensive farm units. Far from leading to a sacrifice of output for the sake of more employment and better income distribution, evidence suggests that this is likely to lead to higher total output and incomes' (Singer, 1972: 165). Furthermore, Livingstone (1981) and Hunt (1984) argued the case for land reform based on the expected continuing growth of new entrants to agricultural labour force at the annual rate of about 3 per cent while employment in agriculture declined during 1972–80 at the rate of −1.7 and the employment in modern non-agricultural activities combined with multinationals and Kenyan large farms was as low as 14 per cent. By the year 2000, Hunt estimates that 4.5 million *new* entrants to agriculture would likely be poor. Hunt remarked that present rural development programmes reached only 15 per cent of the rural poor. She asserts that: 'There can be no doubt that land reform represents the single most effective means available to Kenya for expanding productive employment above poverty level in agriculture between now and year 2000' (Hunt, 1984: 278). The suggested ceiling on private land ownership ranges between 3 and 10 hectares. See also Hunt (1984), pp. 219–26 for a summary of her recommended strategy and that by Livingstone.

In her *The Impending Crisis in Kenya*, (1984) Hunt indicates how 15 senior government officials, 6 members of Parliament and 14 traders, each owning over 500 acres, dominated the power structure in Nakura District. Three of them were also shareholders of corporations owning land. A similar situation existed in Kiambu District. This dominance of powerful landlords-cum-senior government officials influenced the President of Kenya not to institute a land redistribution programme which he promised when he came to power in 1978. Hunt remarked, 'considered in this light, the prospects for radical land reform look bleak. . . . Now there is no colonial authority and the African leadership own much of the land' (Hunt, 1984: 288, 289).

21 These countries have been excluded from the Table and analysis primarily due to data limitation; China does not have census on landholdings. I estimated roughly the land distribution at *circa* 0.19 based on the Gini index of income distribution in agriculture being 0.211 given in the World Bank publication (*Rural Development in China*, 1984) and on the assumption that the allocation of land under the Household production responsibility system follows income per adult members of the agricultural households. The data for Colombia and Mexico refer to 1970 and Morocco for 1960. These limitations may influence the arithmetical mean of data for the other 20 countries. Furthermore, the inclusion of two more Latin American countries would increase the weight of that

region in proportion to other regions of developing countries.

22 The reader who is not familiar with the meaning of equation, correlation and regression may read their simple explanation in textbooks on econometric methods. For example to know about the meaning of functions and variables, it is suggested to see Chapter 2 of *Fundamental Methods of Mathematical Economics* by Alpha C. Chiang, McGraw-Hill, (International Student Edition). For an understanding of the elementary basis of correlation and regression and their analytical application in economics, see Chapter 2 in *Econometric Methods* by J. Johnson, McGraw-Hill, (International Student Edition), or Chapters 2 and 5 in *Econometrics* by Ronald H. Wonnacott and Thomas H. Wonnacott, published by John Wiley and Sons.

Chapter six

Case studies of complete and partial land reform

In this chapter we advance the empirical discussion on the extent to which changes in the degree of land concentration affect the pace and scope of rural development as defined in Chapter 3. The experience of a selected sample of five developing countries is reviewed on a country-by country basis. This review is presented in the context of an explanatory framework for grouping countries into categories. The case studies are presented with two chief aims in mind. The first is to understand how the varied agrarian systems which existed before land reform explain the policy choice. The second is to explore how the policy choice of different arrangements of the institution of property rights in land under different ideological preferences determines the accessibility of peasants to opportunities for benefiting from the process of rural development. In the context of each country's ideological choice, this accessibility is studied within the created system of incentives and the different types of agricultural production organisation.

The chapter reviews policies implemented in China, South Korea, Iraq, Cuba and Egypt. These countries have been selected for having different natural endowments, density of agricultural population relative to cultivated land, political ideologies, social structure and historical contexts. To capture the dynamic changes with respect to growth, equity and poverty, the review covers a post-reform period of 30–40 years.

Guiding principles

For the purposes of both this review and the inter-country comparison which follows in the next chapter, countries are grouped into broad and homogeneous categories according to the scope of change in the pattern of land distribution. This is despite the existence of a variety of forms of agricultural production organisation associated with property rights in land. Based on *a priori* knowledge of changes in the degree of land concentration, the countries are classified as having:

(a) a complete land reform policy;
(b) a partial policy, dividing the agrarian system into reform and non-reform sectors; and
(c) no policy intervention in the status quo of the distribution of privately-owned land, leaving the structure of power unaltered.[1]

A land reform policy is complete if it meets the following conditions following implementation:

1. The beneficiaries have direct access to individual or collective land ownership representing at least two thirds of total agricultural households.
2. All or at least two-thirds of landless peasants are absorbed, leaving none or a small fraction as landless workers.
3. The redistributed cultivable land amounts to over half the total.
4. *Per capita* food production is consistently rising.

With regard to partial land reform policy, redistributive requirements are relative to the above listed five conditions. This implies a lower scale of the percentage of new landowners to total agricultural households and a correspondingly smaller proportion of redistributed cultivable land. Differences in the scale of reform are traced to the level of size ceiling on individual land ownership relative to the average size of redistributed units. Consequently, partial policy is likely to leave a substantial section of landless peasants who remain as either tenants or wage-based workers. Furthermore, a higher degree of inequality than that of complete reform is expected.

At the other extreme, the third category is broadly characterised by a *laissez-faire* policy towards the land tenure system which results in a continued constraint on rural development. The characteristics of this category have already been described and analysed in Chapter 5. These characteristics and their implications were illustrated by the pre-reform conditions in Egypt and the agrarian system in contemporary Kenya. They are also briefly outlined in the review of agrarian conditions existing *before* land reform in three countries having complete land reform policy.

In operational terms the review considers the four determinants of land reform performance in the rural economy (suggested in Chapter 3: 87) as experienced in different phases of implementation by the selected countries. Briefly, these determinants are: the scope of change in the policy choice; consistent political commitment in the enforcement of land reform policy; the implementation capability of the State institutions; the complementarity of other public actions to sustain the initial gains; and the pace of implementation with clear policy objectives.

In this empirical review, no preference is implied for one approach over the other. Rather, the intention is to show, as objectively as the data permit, how the scope of land reform policy influences the distribution of income or consumption, productivity per agricultural worker and the incidence of rural poverty. We also attempt to identify the dynamic forces operating in the national economy exogenous to the institution of property rights in land (private or social ownership) that tend to stabilise or disequalise the pattern of rural income distribution over time following land reform implementation.[2] The sustainability of the initial redistributive gains depends on the sequential provision of complements of inputs and institutional arrangements for credit and marketing to replace those abolished. These are matters of empirical evidence to be judged from the review.

As paramount aims in development, improvement of nutritional standards, life expectancy and educational levels are given special emphasis in the review. The study also explores whether countries realising egalitarian land distribution and fast improvement in quality of rural life have been able to maintain a steady growth rate in food production and an adequate share of national savings and investment in GDP. Because the distribution of land, other assets, and income is closely associated with power, the characteristics of the structure of power are explored as far as they seem to obstruct or induce land reform policies.

China, South Korea, Iraq and Cuba are the countries selected for review under the category of complete land reform policy. China, the most populated country in the world, chose a policy of social ownership of productive assets within a unique structure of incentives and production organisation. This structure has been subjected to a series of adjustments and institutional innovations at different phases of implementation. In contrast, the experiences of South Korea and Iraq represent egalitarian land reform policies based on private property-market economies. In both cases, rapidly growing non-agricultural sectors, though derived differently, result in positive policies for rural migration. Wide differences in natural endowment, the agricultural land-based density of population, and sources of financing land reform implementation give each policy unique features. Due to data limitations, the review of Cuban experience will be brief in comparison to the three other countries. Its policy choice for State farms has already been discussed in Chapter 4.

Egypt is chosen to represent the many developing countries which adopted a partial land reform policy. The changes introduced by a series of land reforms between 1952 and 1969 are analysed, continuing the discussion of pre-reform conditions presented in the previous chapter. Whereas the land reform and the rural economy are private property-based, the supply of most working capital, the sale of marketed surplus and the allocation of land and the Nile water for the cropping pattern are mostly State-controlled. Had the space permitted, it would have been desirable to include other countries in our detailed review of partial land reform, such as Morocco, Mexico, India, Bolivia, Peru, Sri Lanka and Pakistan. Some of them are included in the inter-country comparison which follows the country-by-country review.

China

The rapid transformation of the Chinese agrarian economy over the last 40 years has been of great interest to development analysts, practitioners and international organisations. According to their field visits, and with data released by the Chinese authorities, several scholars have documented and analysed the Chinese experience from their own perspectives. Our concern is to probe the extent to which the institution of property rights in land, together with other means of production, have shaped agricultural growth and equity thereby affecting the incidence of rural poverty.

The fundamental changes initiated during the series of reforms (1948–79) are best viewed against the characteristics of the preceding agrarian structure.

Pre-1948 agrarian conditions

Our assessment of the prevailing agrarian conditions prior to 1948 land reform is based on Buck's survey of farms in North and East-Central China during 1921–4; the results of the Land Commission survey in 22 provinces during 1934–5; and the selected materials from Chinese scholars written during the period 1920–36, compiled and translated by the Institute of Pacific Relations.[3] These classic studies of Chinese rural society and its agricultural economy reveal the following broad characteristics:

1. Land ownership was concentrated, varying in degree from one region to another. But the scale of large private farms was far below that of today's Latin American countries, Pakistan, or even that of Egypt prior to 1952 land reform. The size of large Chinese farms ranged from 20 to 1,380 hectares, with the average size 2,000 *mu* (335 acres or 139 hectares). The cultivators of dominant small and fragmented holdings represented about 70 per cent of total landholders, yet their actual area represented only 20–25 per cent of the total holdings. Each owned and/or rented a farm of 15 *mu* (2.5 acres) on average, many of which were fragmented in six to nine scattered plots. Productive assets were primarily those of labour power. According to a comprehensive farm management survey of 4,312 farms in

Kashing during 1935, 59 per cent of the farm had no working animal stock (see Tables 12 and 13 in *Agrarian China*, Institute of Pacific Relations, 1939). In four provinces for which data on size distribution is available, the Gini Coefficients are high, ranging from 0.540 to 0.735 (see Table 6.1).

2. The scale of tenancy including sharecropping ranged from 30 to 50 per cent. Rental levels were high, ranging from 50 to 70 per cent of the harvest. Payment was made as a cash advance thus assuring the landlords income in case of crop failure.

Table 6.1 **Gini Coefficient of land concentration in four Chinese regions 1929–36**

District and province	Year	Gini Coefficient
Wusih near Shanghai[1]	1929	0.666
Chitung, Northern Kiangsu[2]	1933	0.735
Chekiang, South China[3]	1936	0.674
Henan, North China[3]	1936	0.540

Note: The Gini Coefficient is calculated from data given in *Agrarian China*: Selected Source Materials from Chinese Authors, Institute of Pacific Relations, George Allen and Unwin, London 1939, Tables 1, 2, 3 and 4.

Sources: 1 Wong Ying-Seng, Chien Tsen-jui and others 'The Land Distribution and the Future of Capital', unpublished M.Sc., 1932.

2 Survey by the National Rehabilitation Commission, 1933, Chang I-pu *Land Distribution and Tenancy in Kiangsu, Chung-Kuo Nang Ts'un*, vol. 1, no. 8, May 1935, Shanghai.

3 Sun Shao-Tsun 'The Land Problem of Modern China', *Education and Mass*, vol. VIII, no. 3, 28 November 1936, Wusih.

3. Pure landlessness was not high, with the proportion of landless to total agricultural households ranging between 20 and 30 per cent (as estimated by the studies cited). As the average number of working days per year was only 130–60, average annual earnings for workers was correspondingly low.

4. Among peasants, heavy indebtedness and land mortgages prevailed. Part of this indebtedness rested with the above-mentioned demand for advance cash payment. Furthermore, peasants were heavily taxed, both formally, and through informal levies in the form of land taxation and unpaid military service. Local officials, landlords and grain dealers acting as middlemen abused the power of tax collection and military requisition.

5. The consumption of poppy-opium damaged the health and economic position of the peasants. Approximately 40 per cent of the total adult male population were addicted to the narcotic. Addiction was particularly high in Szechuan, Fow-Chou and Yunnan.

6. The monopoly powers of multinationals combined with the coalition

Table 6.2 **Selected indicators of agrarian change in China, 1930–85**

	1930–40 average	1952	1960	1979	1980	1985
1. Income *per capita* agricultural population. Distributed collective income, yuan current prices		43.1 (1957)		62.8 (1976)	85.9	
Total income, yuan, at constant 1957 prices		73.0 (1957)		113.0 (1976)	170.0	
2. Average food grain consumption Kg. *per capita*		197.5	163.5	188.0	212.5	
3. Daily calorie supply *per capita*	1,993 (1933)		1,942 (1961–3)	2,222	2,526	2,602
Daily calorie supply as percentage of requirement	90		82	97	107	119
4. Infant mortality per 1,000	200		90	68	39	35
5. Life expectancy at birth	29	36 (1950)	51	63 (1975)	67	69
6. Adult illiteracy Rate %	78	60		34	30	
7. Index of State investment in agriculture, 1952 = 100		100	264	479 (1965)	993 (1979)	
8. Irrigated land as percentage of arable land		19.7	29	37		44
9. Fertiliser use kg per hectare arable land	2 (1949)	2	5	41	150	195
10. *Per capita* food grain production, kg		285	215	291	326	350

11. Crop yield of cultivated land tonne/hectare		*1965*	*1975*			
wheat	1.0	0.9	1.4	2.0	2.9	
rice (paddy)	2.5	2.7	3.0	4.2	5.2	
cotton	0.5	0.5	1.5	1.6	2.2	

		1960–70 average	1971–80 average	1981–5 average
12. Population annual rate of growth %	2.0	2.3	1.8	1.2
13. Agricultural labour force rate of growth %		1.6	1.9	1.5
14. Agricultural production rate of growth %		6.2	3.8 (2.8)	6.5 (7.9)
15. *Per capita* agricultural labour productivity rate of growth %		4.6	1.1	5.0

Notes: Yuan exchange rate was US$1 = 2.50 yuan in 1950, 1.54 yuan in 1979 and 1.71 yuan in 1981.
Collective income is income, in cash or kind, distributed to production team members out of the net income realised by the team.
Figures in parentheses refer to corresponding year.

Sources: In the order of indicators as numbered:

1, 2. N.R. Lardy, *Agriculture in China's Modern Economic Development*, Cambridge University Press, England, 1983, Table 4.6 for item 1, and Table 4.3 for item 2.

3. For 1933 Lardy *Ibid*., Table 4.1 (Weins' estimate). For the rest, *Fourth World Food Survey*, FAO, Rome, 1977, Appendix C, and FAO *Production Yearbook*, Vol. 3 and Vol. 39.

4, 5. For period 1930–40, D. Perkins and S. Yusuf, *Rural Development In China*, a World Bank Publication, Johns Hopkins University Press, Baltimore, USA, 1984: 133–7. The rest from World Bank Development Indicators, and *China Socialist Economic Development*, Country Study, 1983, Volume III.

6. As in (5) except Perkins, 1984: 171–2.

7. Calculated from Perkins, *Ibid*. Table 2.6.

8. For the year 1952, K.C. Yeh in *China, a Handbook*, edited by Yuan-lium, Newton Abbot, Devon, UK, 1973. Table 20.2. The rest from *Country Tables*, FAO, Rome.

9. For 1949 and 1952 Sartaj Aziz, *Rural Development – Learning From China*, Macmillan, London, 1978 Table 3.2. The rest from FAO, *Ibid*.,

10. Lardy, *Ibid*. Table 4.2 except 1985 calculated from data in FAO Country Tables 1987.

11. *FAO Production Yearbook*, several volumes.

12. World Bank, *World Development Report* Indicators, several issues.

13, 14, Calculated from data on total agricultural production in physical terms and
15. average annual rates of growth of agricultural labour force, FAO *Country Tables*, *Ibid*. Figures in parentheses refer to agricultural GDP as reported in World Bank Development Indicators for periods 1970–80 and 1980–6.

of local traders and collectors effectively depressed the earnings of small tobacco farmers.

The agrarian system features outlined in these six points had serious consequences for agriculture, and accordingly, for rural poverty. Investment in labour-using and yield-increasing technology was negligible. This type of investment can hardly be expected in conditions where 10 per cent of total landholders as absentee owners and rentiers controlled 70 per cent of total cultivated land. Nor could insecure and indebted tenants or other poor peasants afford technological change despite their long tradition of good farming which included organic manure application, terraced planting and transplanting of rice, irrigation, and pig, fish and silkworm raising. Without the necessary investment by landlords and state institutions, the proportion of irrigated land remained at a low 16 per cent around 1947. Yields of the main food and non-food crops were also low (see Table 6.2). According to Ramon Myers, food grain outputs for the period 1930–7 'show an index of virtually no growth (average level was 1–2 tonnes per hectare). The cropping index rose slightly, but scarcely any new technical advances were introduced. Therefore, total factor productivity probably became negative during the 1930s (Myers, 1982: 43).

Low productivity was not the only feature of pre-1949 Chinese rural society. Illiteracy, particularly among women, was high at 80 per cent, as was the incidence of ill-health, (widespread tuberculosis, malaria, cholera, smallpox, and leprosy). Infant mortality was high at nearly 200 per thousand, while average longevity, 29 years, was extremely low. Scattered data suggest a rough estimate of absolute poverty of 60–65 per cent in the rural areas.

Together, these interlocking institutional, economic and social factors led the British economic historian R.H. Tawney to write in 1939:

> Land tenure will require to be reformed and the stranglehold of the moneylenders and middlemen to be broken before much can be expected in the way of technical progress. Both China's economic prosperity and her political stability depend on the standard of life of this great army of cultivators. (Institute of Pacific Relations, 1939: xvii, xviii)

According to a Chinese scholar who analysed the Nanking University's field investigation in rural areas: 'While the general phenomenon among the rural rich is a trinity of landlord, merchant and moneylender, that among the rural poor is another trinity of poor tenant, hired farm labourer and coolies.'

Thus, in 1948–9, Mao Tse-Tung rapidly instituted a series of land reforms designed to tap the productive power and latent abilities of about 250 million poor peasants and farm workers.

The transformation of the agrarian economy 1948–78

The role of land reform in enhancing the process of rural development in China, the most heavily populated country in the world, cannot be underestimated. Dynamic and comprehensive, the programme held broad objectives and worked through several stages of implementation, beginning in 1948 amidst the devastation of the war with Japan which began in 1937. In rural areas, its success or failure would directly affect nearly 400 million persons, 88 per cent of the total population. Led by a large-scale land reform programme, the chief elements of the process of rural development are outlined in broad terms as follows:

1. Elimination of the power of landlords, moneylenders and traders, in rural areas. To do so, land was expropriated without payment of compensation. It was then redistributed to the mass of peasants, tenants and landless workers on an egalitarian basis, thus ensuring greater equality.

2. According priority to agriculture as the foundation of national development. Emphasis was placed on the sustenance of high rates of growth in the production of food grains, based on labour-intensive technology (guided by the National Programme for Agricultural Development formulated in 1955). This called for modernising agriculture with a blend of modern technology and traditional methods. In order to minimise the impact of flood or drought on production, emphasis was placed on expanding irrigation, drainage and land development. Self-reliance in development and self-sufficiency in supplying food grains (as far as possible) at local, provincial and national levels was a goal.

3. Mobilization of the agricultural labour force. This required enhancing their abilities, and converting their productive capacity into capital. Harnessing this enormous power for rural development was central to the formation of co-operatives and communes. These institutions encouraged self-reliance in development and decentralisation of decision making to the local level. Management of economic functions and administrative units of the government were combined.

4. Developing skills by establishing small-scale, labour-intensive industries, spatially scattered in rural areas. Lesser developed areas were given priority for such industries, thus evening out inter-regional imbalances in incomes. Accordingly, the costs of transport and production inputs (chemical fertilisers, iron tools, farm machinery, cement and energy) were reduced.

5. Balancing the demand for food with its supply. This required restricting both population growth, and migration of the rural population between and within regions.

6. Finally, at the heart of the process for transformation, development of human resources. Towards this goal improvements aimed at: universal literacy; pragmatic, simple and accessible health and sanitation services, combining modern medicine with traditional methods (including barefoot doctors); equality between men and women; payment of welfare subsidies to the poorest, old, weak and disabled; and motivating the peasants towards hard work and earned rewards with collective goals superior to individual gain.

Distilling the Chinese rural development strategy into these few elements is fraught with difficulties, chief among them identification of the links between political ideology and economic organisation of resources. The point to bear in mind is that the elements outlined above were rooted in complete land reform, and nourished with Chinese ideological thinking. Adjustments continued over a period of three decades from 1949 to 1978 through a pragmatic approach relevant to Chinese rural conditions.

The initial stage was the redistribution of land by 1952. Based on individual ownership of land, producers' co-operatives provided the necessary means of production. The extremely limited supply of water for irrigation, particularly in the northern regions where annual rainfall was less than 250 millimetres, meant that total cultivable land was only 98 million hectares. According to Kenneth Walker (1965: 5) and Sartaj Aziz (1978: 10), about 47 million hectares of cultivable land were equally distributed 'among 300 million landless and land-poor peasants each receiving an average of 0.15 hectares (0.4 acres)'. An additional 4.2 million hectares (4.3 per cent) were converted into state farms.

An indication of 'a return to capitalism' in production relations, however, moved the government to take further steps toward collectivisation. It was claimed that some post land-reform owners were unco-operative, and others sold their land to other peasants and worked as wage-based labourers. Accordingly, the country leadership moved quickly to collectivise all individual holdings and transfer their ownership rights to collective co-operatives. This was accomplished *nationwide* with dramatic speed, but at the expense of a short-term decline in grain and sugar cane output (1958–62). Strong technical support to the co-operatives was provided by the government, and in 1958, local administrative units (hsiangs) were amalgamated with the co-operatives to form communes. Small private plots for the use of peasants were individually allocated (as kitchen gardens and for raising chickens and pigs for family use or sale) in order to supplement individual food consumption and income from the collective share. All means of production were collectively owned by the communes, their production brigades and teams. Peasants were rewarded for their farm labour and commune-run non-farming enterprises on a work-points basis. The communes also appeared to represent decentralisation, constituting the lowest level of production unit and the lowest unit of local government in charge of economic functions, education, health, sanitation and infrastructural facilities.

Post-1978 changes in production incentives and rewards

With some minor variations between regions, the system described above continued until 1977, one year after Mao's death. Then, ideological struggles too complex to be outlined here erupted among the new leadership (White, 1983; and Khan and Lee, 1983). Since 1978, institutional changes have been introduced to improve the peasants' production incentives and incomes. These changes may be classified into five interdependent subsets of arrangements: material incentives through household production responsibilities, redefinition of the communes' functions, expansion of private plots, State assistance to the poor, and strict birth control.

First, there were arrangements to promote the individual producer's material incentives and to motivate his or her production and exchange activities. These arrangements are an integral part of a nationwide reform of the pre-1978 system of economic management. Their aim is to shift primary consideration from production alone to increased consumption and trade services. No longer is household income determined entirely by the distribution of collective income at the commune/team level (based on working points earned). Instead, incomes are gradually to be linked with household production and the volume of sale of marketed surplus in the free market. Under the new institutional arrangements, an autonomous entity called a production team (consisting of 30–40 households) delegates production responsibilities to either an individual, or a group of households. The production team represents the State as the owner of communal land and major capital equipment. The arrangements vary according to cropping pattern (irrigated land, grain versus cash crops, degree of mechanisation, etc.).

The account given in Khan and Lee (1983); Perkins and Yusuf (1984); and Griffin (1984), shows the prevalence of one arrangement. An individual household is contracted for a specified period of time to have the right to use a plot of land, equally allocated to men and women on either a *per capita* or per worker (adult) basis (average about one acre per family). The household has the legal obligation to pay a share in land taxatioin as well as in welfare funds for health and education services. He or she must deliver a fixed quota from the total produce at a price fixed by the State (the level of which was increased by 36 per cent between 1978 and 1982). The balance of goods may be retained for sale at the 'free' market price. Income differentiation may arise from variations in the quality of land, the portion of non-collective income relative to total income accrued to each household, the pattern of investing individual households' savings, and the variation of capital equipment and livestock owned privately by each household.

Such contracting arrangements resemble tenancy arrangements in many developing countries which have private property-market economies. In the case of China, the powerful incentives lie primarily in the following:

1. The intensification of land use to maximise the size and value of the balance which remains after delivery of the prescribed quota.
2. The new freedom to finance capital equipment (e.g. tractor) with State Bank Loans, and then to either use, or rent the equipment.
3. The enjoyment of security of tenure for the duration of the contract.

The second post-1978 institutional innovation is the separation of functions and responsibilities of the production teams from those of local government administration in the commune. Both, in turn, are separate from the formal political organs. This separation was formally instituted in the new Chinese constitution of September 1982.

The third institutional innovation lies in the revival and expansion of households' private (personal) plots of land which lie outside communally controlled land. The ceiling imposed on its area was raised from up to 6 per cent to up to 15 per cent of total cultivated land in each rural community. These plots are not subject to either the controlled cropping pattern or to the delivery of a prescribed quota of produce. Although variable, plot size may reach 600 square metres (one *mu* or 0.16 acre). Still another incentive is granted to households who can develop barren land (e.g. planting fruit trees). In such a case, security of tenure is granted, as well as exemption from delivery quotas. This new incentive has raised the portion of personal cash income from plots, and has provided households with an increased security of food intake.

The fourth innovation targets State assistance to poor peasants who have *per capita* annual incomes below 50 *yuan* (about US$30). The assistance takes different forms, including exemption from delivery quotas, receipt of welfare benefits (relief), heavily subsidised chemical fertilisers and free education, and health services, etc.

Finally, in order to match food demand to supply, post-1978 policies strictly control births. The preferred number of children for each married couple is one, and births are restricted to two. Rural migration to urban areas is also restricted. These restrictive measures are complementary to the first four institutional changes listed, and intend to:

(a) realise an ambitious plan to raise *per capita* income from its average $US 300 in 1981 to US $1,000 by the year 2000;
(b) limit government expenditure on public services and food subsidies;
(c) reduce the rate of growth in food grain consumption.[4]

The innovations set forth above seem to shift greater responsibilities towards the peasantry in the spheres of production, savings and investment. Though limited, this economic freedom provides material incentives to strengthen private consumption, and to increase household savings and capital accumulation within an emerging market mechanism.

Emerging redistributive consequences

Unique characteristics have emerged from this continuous transformation of the agrarian economy which began with a substantial redistribution of material assets and incomes. The first is that the benefits from all the continuing dynamic phases were achieved by relying on Chinese resources and by pursuing approaches to social change relevant to the country's conditions of poverty; changes within a chosen ideological path.

They tend to be supported by the peasantry's inspired traditional Confucian values of discipline, obedience, patience and co-operation. The second characteristic is the speed and high implementation capability with which institutional, technical, and social transformations of the agrarian economy were realised. The third is the magnitude of the reduction in poverty within rural areas where the confined population was not permitted to migrate to the cities. The fourth is that despite the substantial public expenditure on the improvement of the quality of life, the low income Chinese economy was able to achieve a high share of gross domestic savings and investment in GDP. In 1965 and 1985 the share of the former amounted to 25 per cent and 84 per cent and the latter was 25 per cent and 38 per cent respectively. Gross domestic investment grew during the period at an average annual rate of 13 per cent, nearly four times the rate of other low income countries (World Development Report, 1987, Tables 4 and 5, Indicators).

Perhaps the most remarkable change in the countryside since 1949 has been the fast reduction in income-based absolute poverty from roughly 60 per cent before the 1949 reforms to a range of approximately 6–11 per cent in 1979 to 1981. At the same time, there has been a sustained reduction in the number of poor from about 240 million to approximately 50–80 million over this period. According to official studies, the poor in 1981 are concentrated in 87 counties in four provinces.[5] This achievement is attributable to persistent commitment on the part of the country leadership to provide the mass peasantry with accessible opportunities for secured and equal access to land; a guaranteed minimum level of food grain consumption (150 kg of wheat or 200 kg of rice *per capita* per year); and rapid and significant reduction in illiteracy and infant mortality. All of these have contributed to a substantial 130 per cent rise in life expectancy at birth from about 30 years in the 1930s, to nearly 70 years in 1985 (see Table 6.2). Along with these human gains, there have been sustained high rates of agricultural growth, crop yields and *per capita* food grain productivity.

Obviously, the complete land reform had the greatest effect in rapidly reducing gross inequalities in land distribution (and hence income), from a Gini index of land concentration of 0.7 in the 1930s to very equal distribution of land. Income distribution in rural areas was 0.211 in the 1970s according to Perkins and Yusuf (1984).No recent and complete set of data on the distribution of total income (collective and private) is available. This equality in the distribution of productive assets has enabled widespread benefits from the realised agricultural growth.[6] However, there have been, and will continue to be, marked regional differences in *per capita* income and consumption. An influential source is the marked variation in natural endowment; amount and quality of agricultural land and climatic conditions. The threefold expansion in the irrigated area since 1949 from 16 to 45 per cent in 1985 is a crucial public investment towards reducing these differences.

The effects of the post-1978 institutional adjustment and economic reforms on the distribution of households' income/consumption between regions cannot be left to arguments in the abstract. From the experience gained during the initial period 1978–83, Keith Griffin and his five associates concluded from the empirical field studies:

> We have seen that, in practice, rural China remains remarkably equal society and no statistically reliable evidence exists to show that the degree of equality has diminished since the post-1978 reforms were introduced. Those who believe the contrary have had to rely on anecdotal evidence. . . . If in fact, income inequality and social stratification do become serious problems in the years ahead, the explanation probably will lie with changes in the relations of production. (Griffin, 1986: 310)

After examining evidence collected during 1982 and 1983 about ownership and use of means of production (in Fing Guo, and Liquan communes in Shaanxi province and Jiou Long, Ge Le, Chongqing in Sizhuan province), they added;

> changes in the relations of production do contain a latent possibility of greater income inequality and social stratification. The potential is, nevertheless, *only latent* and as we have seen, there is *no* evidence yet of increased inequality [my emphasis]. Moreover, the rules governing access to land, the hiring of labour and ownership of the means of production are not immutable. Hence, it is best, perhaps, to continue to regard the current period as one of experimentation, albeit on a national scale. (Griffin, 1986: 315)

In this long dynamic process of adjusting the institution of property rights and the structure of incentives and rewards, we must not overlook the fact that the Chinese agrarian economy has been fundamentally characterised by social ownership of major productive assets. In this national context, planning and the market mechanism are considered complementary and not as alternatives. But will it work? Can the Chinese economy realise greater economic growth, private consumption, savings and investment, and, at the same time, maintain the high degree of equality in income distribution achieved up to 1978? We share Gordon White's curiosity about how the 'market' can be utilized to serve socialist aims' (White, 1983: 1972).

South Korea

Like China, rural development in South Korea was based on egalitarian distribution of assets and income at an early stage of national development. So too did South Korea institute a complete land reform with centralised planning and labour-intensive agriculture which would employ abundant labour and scarce land. But here, the similarities end because the ideological base and the structural characteristics for South Korea differ. South Korea has a relatively small rural population, and, unlike China, the movement of the rural labour force towards urban centres was free and fast. Policy choice was based upon *private property* within a market economy which is fundamentally capitalist but controlled by the State. Whereas China had based its land reform policy on nationalising land (with distribution free of payment), South Korea chose regulated contractual transactions with payment of compensation by beneficiaries to affected landlords. Finally, South Korea's reform was initially induced by an external agent, the United States Liberation Forces, after the defeat of Japan in the Second World War. Nevertheless, like China, the experience of South Korea in rural development offers innovative ideas.

The pre-1945 agrarian system

The discussion that follows of the pre-1945 agrarian system draws upon the following sources: Hoon Lee, 1936, The United States Agency for International Development Spring Review, 1970; Sung-huan Ban *et al.*, 1980; Keidel, 1981 and my own discussion with Dr Clyde Mitchell, who was the American economist in the US Administration of South Korea (1947–50) and Dr Hyuk Pak in 1968 when he was in charge of land economics research.

Two major surveys recorded the land tenure systems and production relations in South Korean agriculture for the decades immediately preceding 1945. One, a cadastral survey by the Japanese colonial administration, was carried out during the period 1910 to 1918 for land taxation purposes and for establishing Japanese ownership of a large portion of agricultural land. The other identified the nationality of landowners (Japanese, Korean, Chinese and other foreigners) in 1927. Together, these surveys were useful bases for formulating and implementing the land reforms of 1945 and 1950. They illustrated the high inequalty of existing land ownership. According to the surveys, Japanese settlers representing 1.3 per cent of total landowners possessed almost 55 per cent of total South Korean irrigated land in 1930, with an average ownership of 100 *cho* (240 acres) each (Hoon Lee 1936: 149). Compared with the already high Gini Coefficient of 0.624 for all Korea this index for irrigated areas was even higher at 0.823 (see Table 6.3).

Table 6.3 **Distribution of land ownership – Korea 1927 and 1930**

Size classes in Cho	1927 (all ownerships)		1930 (irrigated)	
	Number of owners %	Area %	Number %	Area %
Less than 0.1	18.00	1.30	27.0	0.7
0.1 – 0.5	32.00	6.40		
0.5 – 1	19.40	10.10	16.0	1.2
1 – 5	26.00	42.70		
5 – 10	3.00	15.27	45.5	15.5
10 – 20	0.90	8.95		
20 – 50	0.54	9.63	8.5	18.3
50 – 100	0.14	2.90	1.5	10.1
100 and over	0.02	2.75	1.5	54.2
	100.00	100.00	100.00	100.00
Gini Coefficient	0.646		0.823	

Note: One Cho is little less than one hectare = 2.4 acres
Source: Calculated from data given in Hoon K. Lee, 1936, *Land Utilization and Rural Economy in Korea*, Table 61 for 1927, and data on p. 149 for 1930

In addition to the high degree of land concentration, absentee ownership was widespread. The extent of tenancy in the provinces of South Korea, quickly rose from 40 per cent in 1920 to 56 per cent of total landholders in 1938 falling to 49 per cent in 1945. Based on his field survey of a sample of 1,249 farming units in 1931, Hoon Lee reported that most tenants were burdened with indebtedness through high rent (50–70 per cent of harvest) and lacked access to institutional credit. Forced to rely heavily on landlords and moneylenders, the tenants were charged interest rates ranging from 40 to 70 per cent per year. (Simultaneously, landlords were able to acquire institutional credit at 5 per cent.) According to Hoon Lee, landlords ' . . . live in towns and large cities without knowing where their lands are located' (Lee, 1936: 157).

Landless agricultural workers accounted for 30 per cent of total agricultural households in all Korea. Calculations of size income distribution in 1925 by Keidel (1981) show that landlords representing 4.5 per cent of total landholders received a share of 52 per cent of total farm net income. Based on his calculations of gross and net income of agricultural households by tenure status, he roughly estimated the poverty incidence (landless and small owners and tenants) at 60 per cent of total agricultural households in South Korea in 1925 (Keidel, 1981: 45 and Table III-9). This state of poverty was dramatically described by Hoon Lee:

> They survived (outside the working seasons) by eating millet bran, legume pods, tree bracken, grass roots. They live because they cannot die. . . . When sickness and disease befall them, their fate is doomed.

Health services and administration of hygiene in these rural sections are far behind the times. (Hoon Lee, 1936: 171, 172)

Incentives to invest in improving land productivity were lacking among the peasants and absentee landlords. Such investment was fundamentally important in South Korea where arable land, irrigation and chemical fertilisers were scarce.[7] Yet the opportunities to raise productivity and earnings were denied many. Investment in irrigation was limited, and existed primarily in areas that were dominated by Japanese settlers (e.g. the Province of Chulla). Although Korean farmers, like their fellow Chinese, were traditionally skilled in using green, animal and human waste for manuring field crops, average yield per hectare (1933 to 1938) was low; rice 2.0 tons, wheat 0.8 tons, barley 0.9 tons, and cotton 0.4 tons (FAO Production Yearbook, 1953, Vol. VII, part I). Consequently, agricultural output grew slowly at the average annual rate of 1.6 per cent during the period 1920 to 1939, only half the growth rate of the 1950s.

The 1945–50 land reforms

The United States Military Forces administered South Korea for three years, from 1945 to 1948. But they did not enforce redistribution of Korean privately owned land as they did in Japan. Instead, the US administration chose to: substantially reduce rents; secure tenancy rights; take over the 324,464 hectares formerly owned by Japanese settlers for redistribution among actual tillers; and play a key role in the land reforms of 1949 and 1950 following the establishment of the Republic of Korea in 1948. The 1949 law, and its 1950 amendment were implemented in the turmoil of the 1950 to 1953 war between North and South Korea, which devastated agriculture and took 1.3 million lives.

Despite the internal political conflicts over expropriation of land and compensation payments, fundamental changes in the institution of property rights in land were effectively introduced during the period 1945 to 1953. These changes included the following:

1. The outright transfer of income in real terms from landlords to tenants by the substantial reduction in rent from 50 to 70 per cent of the harvest to a maximum of 33 per cent. This was accompanied by provision of a higher degree of security of farmland tenancy.
2. The direct sale of 573,000 hectares (28 per cent of total cultivated area) from Korean landlords to their tenants. (This occurred as a direct result of the landlords' anticipation of forced distribution, and their desire to avoid transaction complications of receiving bonds for compensation.)
3. The redistribution of 245,554 hectares, formerly held by Japanese

owners, to the tenants who were cultivating the land.

4. The Korean government's purchase of 332,000 hectares from landlords whose land holdings exceeded the prescribed size ceiling of 3 Chungbo (a little less than 3 ha or 7 acres) per owner. Purchase price was paid in government bonds (at 150 per cent of the average output of the main crop expressed in terms of rice in order to maintain its value in real terms). Former landlords were encouraged to invest the value of compensation in industry. The new owners, on the other hand, paid the government the full value in addition to land taxes. Both transactions were efficiently implemented within five years.

5. A programme for investment in agriculture and for loans to farmers begun in 1954, despite the enormous public expenditure for military purposes arising from conflicts with North Korea. With substantial aid from the United States, the Agricultural Credit Bank was established for lending to rural areas.

6. Distribution of the total area amounting to 1,150,554 hectares (listed in 2, 3 and 4 above) in plots averaging 0.9 ha.

The dynamics of accessible opportunities, 1955–85

The large scale land redistribution had four primary consequences. The first was income transfer resulting from combined rent reduction (most in kind) and freeing tenants from their accumulated debt. This transfer resulted in their increased income in real terms. Total area under tenancy was dramatically reduced from 49 per cent to about 4 per cent of total agricultural households (and, in fact, was 'officially' considered illegal by land reform legislation). Second, the number of owner-operators (mostly former tenants and landless workers) increased from 14 per cent, to nearly 75 per cent (with the balance of land held by public institutions such as schools, communal clans, churches and agricultural research farms). With about 79 per cent of agricultural households (75 per cent owners and 4 per cent tenants) directly reaping benefits from the institutional changes, the number of hired landless workers was reduced from 30 per cent of total agricultural households to about 3 per cent (the latter were gradually absorbed into non-farming activities). With the very low ceiling prescribed for expropriation, about 60 per cent of the total area of cultivated land was redistributed. The third major effect was a rapid reduction in land concentration with a corresponding reduction in inequality in income distribution. Table 6.4 shows the sharp decline in the Gini Coefficient of land concentration between 1945 and 1965 from 0.729 to 0.384.[8]

Finally, we should not understate the intangible and unquantifiable improvement in the peasants' sense of dignity, self-respect and production incentives provided by individual land ownership.

Table 6.4 Stability in the size distribution of land holdings after land reform in South Korea 1960 to 1980

Size in hectares	Before land reform 1945 N %	1945 A %	1960 N %	1960 A %	1965 N %	1965 A %	After land reform 1970 N %	1970 A %	1980 N %	1980 A %
Under 0.5	33.7	11.3	⎱ 71.0	53.1	33.93	12.44 ⎱	66.9	38.4	64.00	36.98
0.5 – 1.0	33.4	12.3	⎰		31.76	26.68 ⎰	26.4	40.5	29.56	43.15
1.0 – 2.0	22.9	14.1	24.1	33.4	25.66	40.49			5.05	12.76
2.0 – 3.0	⎱				5.57	15.31 ⎱	⎱ 6.7	21.1	⎱ 1.48	7.11
Over 3	⎰ 10.0	62.3	4.9	13.5	1.17	5.08 ⎰	⎰		⎰	
	100	100	100	100	100	100	100	100	100	100
* Gini Coefficient	0.729		0.388		0.384		0.314		0.303	

Note: *The different size class intervals over the period 1960 to 1980 affect this index. (The use of less number of classes in 1960 and 1970 by the World Census of Agriculture for a uniform classification and the use of more class intervals in the surveys of 1945 and 1965.)

N = Number of Land Holdings   A = Areas of Land Holdings

Sources: 1945, United States Agency of International Development Spring Review, *Land Reform in South Korea*, prepared by Robert B. Morrow and Kenneth H. Sherper, June 1970, Table 3.

1960, 1970, and 1980, Agricultural Census results, tabulated by Statistics Division, FAO, Rome.

1965, Eddy Lee, 'Egalitarian Peasant Farming and Rural Development: The Case of South Korea' in *Agrarian Systems and Rural Development*, edited by Dharam Ghai *et al.*, Macmillan, London, 1979, Table 2.14.

Having redistributed the scarce productive assets and removed the institutional barriers to participation in an egalitarian system of private property, land reform set the stage for dynamic rural development. To gauge its interaction with the rest of the economy, it is important to consider a perspective longer than the first 1945–55 phase. Changes since 1955 have to be seen against a background of 35 years of Japanese Colonial rule (1910–45) disruption in commercial and government services resulting in the 1945 partition, and finally the war between North and South Korea from 1950 to 1953. Irma Adelman summed up this background:

> The Korean fortunes in the South in 1945 were rapidly eroded by the economic chaos caused by the partition; . . . the loss to the North of all heavy industry, major coal deposits, and almost all electric power generating capacity . . . and the flood of over 1.5 million refugees from the North . . . property damage resulting from the fighting has been estimated at US $2 billion. Agricultural output dropped by 27 percent between 1949 and 1952 and real GNP by 12 percent. Prices rose by 600 percent between 1949 and 1952. (Adelman 1974: 281)

Under such circumstances, and having become owner-operators of their holdings, the beneficiaries faced practical constraints during 1950–4: limited access to credit and inputs to substitute for that provided by landlords; limited access to technical and social services from the disorganised institutions of the State operating in local rural areas, etc. The period of 1955 to 1960 was, therefore, a period of reconstruction. But to understand the implications of land reform for rural development, we should consider a further 10 year period (see p. 101).

There are problems in identifying the effects of the Korean land reform. Because it was complete in scope, there are no non-reform sectors to serve as comparisons (as we see later, for example, in Egypt). For an inter-temporal comparison before and after 1945, two problems arise. One is the change in the country boundaries after 1945. The other refers to income comparability, and pertains to the choice of price index for deflation. For example, there are two sets of data on the annual rates of growth of agricultural production during the period 1935 to 1945, and 1945 to 1953. Sung-huan Ban's estimate covers crops and livestock output using the 1934 price index. Keidel, on the other hand, included only crops and used 1970 prices for deflation to compare the values in constant prices (Keidel, 1981: Table III–2). The following table illustrates the different findings for annual rates of growth for the value of agricultural output in South Korea.

	1930–9 %	1939–45 %	1945–53 %	1953–61 %	1961–9 %
Ban	2.9	−3.5	2.1	3.6	5.1
Keidel	–	0.0	0.9	4.0	4.5

Despite these measurement problems, the data show an upward trend after the *full* implementation of land reform in the late 1950s. The growth rates reached an impressive level in the 1960s by any international standard. With the agricultural labour force growing at the low rate of 0.9 per cent during the period 1960 to 1970, labour productivity grew at the rate of 3.6 per cent (a much higher rate than the average of all developing countries at 0.6 per cent). So too, did the average annual rate of food production increase, at the rate of 4 per cent, again higher than the average of all developing countries at 2.6 per cent (Korea Year-book of Agriculture and FAO Country Tables, 1987).

Crop yield per hectare, another indicator of the performance of the restructured agrarian system, is free of valuation problems. By 1965 the yield (tonnes per hectare) of paddy rice, barley and wheat had more than doubled and the cotton yield grew to four times that of the average during the period 1933 to 1940. Contributing to this rate of growth were three types of technical change: the sharp rise in the use of chemical fertiliser supplied by substantial US aid (PL 480) and the domestic fertiliser import-substitution industry; the fast expansion in public investment in irrigation, land reclamation and soil conservation; and the high cropping intensity and diversification in the cultivated area (the expansion in vegetable, fruit and livestock production). Consumption of chemical fertiliser rose on average from 22 kg per hectare in the 1930s to 92 in 1955, reaching 376 kg per ha in 1985. Irrigated area as a percentage of total arable land was expanded from 25 per cent in the 1940s to 39 per cent in the 1960s and 57 per cent in 1985. The index of land use intensity (frequency of cropping in the same area during one year) increased from 130 per cent in the 1930s to an average of 160 and 190 per cent between 1965 and 1970. The intensity was much higher in the size group of less than one hectare than the larger size groups of 1–2 and 2–3 ha (Dong-Wan and Yang-Boo, 1984: Table 24). Other institutions contributed to the change, including newly established co-operatives, agricultural credit facilities, health centres and the innovative Saemaul Undong movement that consolidated government services in villages and enlisted the effective participation of rural households in developing the social and production potentials of their communities.[9]

Although all growth cannot be exclusively attributed to land reform, we cannot ignore the important role that it did play. For the first time, peasants directly benefited from their efforts. The system of incentives and motivations provided for increasing land productivity via intensive family labour and favourable pricing policy for agriculture. The egalitarian base of the rural economy and the introduction of incentives have undoubtedly been primary ingredients in the process of rapid and sustained agricultural growth, and the consequential alleviation of rural poverty. Average farm income per household increased by 51.4 per cent in real terms between 1963 and 1975 (an annual growth rate of 4.3 per cent).[10] Rises in both *per capita* rural population and per agricultural household income have been reinforced by spectacular expansion of educational opportunities and rapid outmigration of the rural population at the annual rate of 1.5 per cent between 1960 and 1970. The allocation to education represented between 50 and 63 per cent of the central government expenditure on social services, and 2.5 to 3.5 per cent of GNP during the period 1961 to 1985 (IMF Government Finance Statistics Yearbook, various issues).

Irma Adelman attributes the stability in the improved income distribution in rural areas to increased levels of education as well as the growing rates of remunerative labour absorption in the fast growing labour-intensive industries for export (Adelman, 1974: 281–4). In fact, agricultural population declined during the 1960s at the negative annual rate of 1.4 per cent. The net rural migration to urban areas was estimated at 3.6 million; 65 per cent of whom were of working age, and 40 per cent of whom were female (Ban, 1980: Table 137).[11] The substantial falls in the agricultural labour force and rural population of working age have operated on the supply side of the rural labour market as a significant factor in raising real wages and *per capita* incomes of those who remained on the land. The improvement of human capital quality of labour via greater access to education has also contributed to productivity and to narrowing income differentials in the labour market.

The high implementation capability within a stable political climate made these achievements possible. Greater investments for employment creation and favourable terms of trade for agriculture were combined in consecutive five-year plans. These measures of government control of the reallocation of resources, along with preferential pricing and taxation policies contributed to the stability of the pattern of income distribution in rural areas. At a Gini Coefficient of 0.298 in 1963 to 1965, the low degree of inequality was stabilised – with slight variation – and the agricultural labour wages in real terms rose steadily (Lee, 1979: 36 and Table 2.7). This equality in rural areas is greater than the national Gini Coefficient at 0.344 in 1965. Significantly, the beneficiaries were motivated to increase their saving ratios (savings out of average household income). Lee indicates that the new owners of less than one hectare were able to raise their savings from 4 per cent in 1963 to 16 per cent in 1973 (Table 2.12). These savings were encouraged by the government by their exemption from taxes under the small savings promotion scheme. Emerging slight inequality in rural income distribution is explained by the advantageous position of owners of 2–3 hectares who reaped greater benefits from the price effect via greater marketed surplus.

We recall from earlier analysis (Chapters 3 and 5) that the stability in the pattern of land distribution contributes to stability in the distribution of income among agricultural households. The results of Korean agricultural censuses, along with other surveys given in Table 6.4 and Figure 6.1 indicate a generally stable pattern of landholdings between 1969 and 1980, despite a small variation. This variation is more noticeable between the size classes below one hectare, than those of 1–2 hectares. The decline in the share of the former class is more likely due to their sale and renting-out of land in favour of migrating to urban centres. Thus, the migration of members of small-holders' households to urban areas and abroad has worked as an equalising factor, with increasing remittances sent to remaining land holders, many of whom are increasing in age. Another equalising factor is the rapid expansion of non-agricultural employment *within* rural areas.

The shift in shares of size classes of land-holdings indicates how the Korean leaders allowed for adaptive changes in response to a new pattern of socio-economic behaviour in the rural economy. This has occurred despite the fact that the 1950 land reform law prohibited leasing-out of allotted plots to new owners, as well as the ownership of more than 3 hectares. However, the proportional rise in those holdings over 3 hectares is very small, suggesting that after 30 years, land reform has not lost its force in the Korean rural economy. To check further rises due to purchase of land by urban speculators, a progressive land taxation with higher effective rates on holdings above 2 hectares may guard against future land concentration.

The question now is: to what extent has Korean rural development reduced the incidence of absolute poverty in rural areas. Given the sustained rise in the average *per capita* income and wages in real terms, and given the political commitment to sustain an egalitarian rural economy with fast growth, a substantial reduction in rural poverty should follow. One way of identifying that reduction is to consider changes in the quality of life in rural areas. The 1979 nutritional survey of the Ministry of Health and Social Affairs shows that the average daily calorie intake *per capita* of the rural population was 2,707 or 22 per cent above the minimum requirement and that only 3 per cent of the rural children under the age of five were below the Korean standard for height-for-age. No deficiency in weight-for-age anthropometric measures was found (Dong-Wan and Yang Boo, 1984: Tables 61 and 63). These are marked improvements in food consumption and nutritional levels. This accomplishment was confirmed by the Fifth World Food Survey (FAO, 1985: Appendix 1c),

207

Figure 6.1 Lorenz curves for changes in the degree of inequality in land distribution in South Korea, 1930, 1945, 1970 and 1980

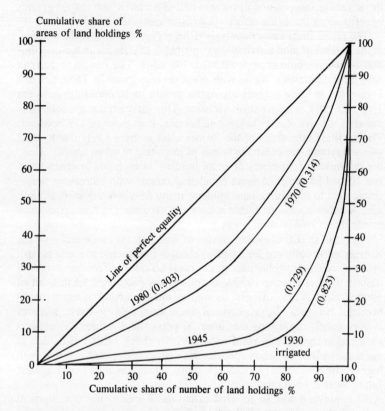

Source: Based on data in Tables 6.3 and 6.4. Figures in parentheses are Gini Coefficients.

indicating a rise of 39 per cent of average daily calorie supply per person between 1961 and 1963; and 1979 to 1981.

With regard to education, Adelman and Robinson (1978) report that the dramatic expansion in education noted earlier reduced the incidence of illiteracy from the high level of 80 per cent in 1940 to 20 per cent in 1965. By 1983, national illiteracy rates fell to 12 per cent among women and 4 per cent among men (UNICEF: 1984). According to the Ban study (1980: Table 135), similar progress was made in health. Infant mortality fell from 258 per thousand in 1945, to 42 per thousand in 1970, and to 34 per thousand in 1980. Accordingly, a most important achievement was realised; life expectancy at birth rose on average from 52 to

62 years for men, and 56 to 71 years for women between 1960 and 1980. These indicators of the quality and quantity of life manifest the real meaning of development. They also point to a dramatic improvement in the characteristics of poverty.

Using available estimates of rural poverty referring to different points in time, with different cut-off-points, and by different researchers is not entirely secure, yet, because of the clear trend shown, it is useful to consider them.

Reference Year	Estimated Incidence %	Approximate Number of Rural Poor (in millions)	Source
1925	60.0	9	Keidel, 1981 for provinces of South Korea
1965	40.9	4	Dong-Wan and Yang Boo, 1984
1978	11.0	2	World Bank, Social Indicators Data Sheets, June 1984
1980	9.8	1.6	Dong-Wan and Yang Boo, 1984

However approximate the estimates of the scale of rural poverty, they suggest a remarkably rapid reduction in both the proportion and the absolute number of the rural poor in a private property-market economy. We should not forget that since 1950 the land reform programme has laid a foundation for the realisation of rural development as defined in Chapter 3.

It is another question whether, in the face of current concentration of the supply side on export-led high growth strategies as opposed to social development, this commitment can be sustained.[12] Warning signs have emerged in the form of a tendency towards income disparities within rural areas, and between agriculture and other fast growing sectors of the economy. The importance of sustaining the gains from the spectacular rural achievements over the last 40 years cannot be over-emphasised, as Korea moves into the year 2000 as a new 'developed' country.

Iraq

This is the third selected case for examining characteristics and implications of the complete scope of land reform, but in this case, we focus on a country whose experience and economic structure are unlike China and South Korea. Iraq is endowed with rich natural resources: oil, abundant cultivable land, water provided by adequate rainfall in the

North, (300–600 mm per year), and her two big rivers, the Tigris and the Euphrates. Furthermore, she is not overpopulated: the density of her agricultural population being only one tenth that of China and South Korea, yet these resources were undeveloped. Prior to land reforms of 1958 and 1970, the Iraqi rural economy suffered from a high degree of land concentration, extensive land use operating within a tribal system, and exploitative tenancy arrangements. Agriculture, functioning at low productive capacity was stagnant. Thus, amidst an abundance of land and oil revenues a large section of Iraq's relatively small 3.9 million rural population in 1957 lived in poverty and lacked motivation. The long awaited land reform of 1958 was introduced by the July 1958 revolution which overthrew the Monarchy, abolished landlordism and attempted to diminish the extreme powers held by tribal chiefs (sheikhs).

The pre-1958 agrarian system

To understand the impact of land reform on rural development since 1958, consider the pre-existing land tenure system. Until the defeat of the Ottoman empire in the First World War (1919), Iraq was under Ottoman rule and its land property was officially (*miri*) owned by the Sultan in Istanbul who granted inherited rights of use to the occupiers against payment of tax. When the Ottoman Land code was issued in 1858 to register individual land for a full private ownership (*tapu*) most of it was registered as huge private properties of tribal chiefs, town notables and Kurdish Aghas (village heads in North East Iraq) over the heads of the peasants. Angered by this injustice, peasants began fighting tribal heads, the registration procedures were halted and, consequently, the State was made the landlord of all unregistered land (*miri sirf*). Later attempts (1910 to 1932) by the Mandate of British administration of Iraq to re-establish registration failed. Sir Ernest Dawson, who was managing this work wrote in 1932: '. . . today only a fraction of the cultivated land is somewhat uncertainly held on tapu tenure'. According to Saleh Haidar (1944) and Doreen Warriner (1948) by 1943, only 17 per cent of agricultural land was registered as private property (*tapu*), and most of this was in the name of the politically influential tribal chiefs and city merchants (with 5 per cent as religious endowment). The balance, 78 per cent was officially the property of the State (made up of 22 per cent 'lazma' land held communally by the tribes (Dirah) under lease from the State, and 56 per cent *miri sirf*, or pure property of the State). Charles Issawi gave this explanation: ' . . . under the Mandate, the British introduced minor improvements, but did not attempt to alter the system for fear of antagonizing the landlords and tribal chiefs, on whose support they were dependent' (Issawi, 1982: 147).

Following independence in 1932, the process of land accumulation by the sheikhs and their powers in shaping national policy were reinforced. Two laws issued in 1940 and 1945 for the sale of the State land, *miri sirf*, expanded the existing property of the sheikhs and city merchants, particularly in the southern provinces and the Sinjar region of Mosul province in the north (Hassan Ali, 1955). The sheikhs blocked legislation to raise land taxes, and silenced attempts to reform the land tenure system. Using increased proceeds of oil royalties in the early 1950s, attempts were made to redistribute a fraction of State land to landless agricultural households in the seven land settlement schemes. In addition, the Development Board (*Majlis Al-Imar*) allocated 40 per cent of its development funds in 1951–8 to flood control irrigation, land reclamation and settlement schemes. While some of these schemes were successful and benefited settlers, other schemes failed through defective planning, land salination from expanding irrigation without drainage, and the resulting abandonment of distributed units.[13] The effect of these schemes in the national context was negligible.

As an alternative to land reform, this slow and narrow approach was a short-sighted illusion, and manifests the policy makers' intention to by-pass the real issues in the agrarian system. It did, however, serve as a training ground for technocrats, many of whom, for the first time, came directly in touch with the realities of rural Iraq, recognising the aspirations of poor peasants to own land.

The realities were quantified by the 1958 census of agriculture. Six-tenths of one per cent of landholders held (ownership and lease from the State) 47 per cent of agricultural land in the size class over 1,000 hectares. In this category, five highly influential tribal sheikhs held 4 per cent of the total land, each of them owning (or holding under lazma tenure) more than 25,000 ha. At the other extreme, 58,000 peasant households (mostly tenants) in the size group of less than one hectare represented 34.4 per cent of total holders. Among them, they held only 0.3 per cent of total land.

The 1958 and 1970 land reforms: a formidable task

The implementation of the land reform of 30 September 1958 in Iraq began with a vigorous process of expropriation of the large, privately-owned and leased estates. Against the payment of compensation, those estates exceeding the prescribed limit of 2,000 donums (50 hectares) in rain-fed areas of the North and 1,000 donums (250 hectares) of irrigated land in Central and Southern Iraq were expropriated. Lands belonging to the royal family and to those families considered as the 'enemies of the revolution' were confiscated without compensation. The total area affected was roughly estimated in 1964 at 8–10 million donums, or 2–2.5 million hectares.[14] (A donum or Mishara is equal to 0.62 acres or 0.25 of a hectare.)

Implementation of the reform of 1958 suffered from several difficulties. Three factors emerged from the author's successive visits which offer some explanation.[15] The first is the political instability manifested in three *coup d'états* during the 1960s. Identified in Iraq as revolutions, each espoused a different ideological base for policy choice, and each generated turnover in the limited number of trained staff serving in the agricultural sector. Though strong commitment to land reform was clearly maintained, the political conflicts and different promises confused the peasants (see Gabbay, 1978). Conflicting questions of policy choice included whether to redistribute or to retain for the State the land in excess of the size ceiling; the form of property rights after redistribution; functions of co-operative organisations; the payment of compensation to former land owners and to water pump owners, as well as the question of payment for the allotted land by new owners and State tenants.

A second factor influencing the implementation of land reform in its initial phase, was the insufficient capacity of the State institutions who were unprepared for the speedy changes which would affect nearly two-thirds of the country's agricultural land, and a major sector of total agricultural households. Furthermore, the 1958 law stipulated that this formidable task be completed within five years. Politics aside, practice proved that redistribution was difficult in the absence of undisputed records of land title registration, adequate numbers of trained staff, and a network of institutional credit supply and marketing services to replace the functions of the ex-landlords. Most importantly, redistribution of land, particularly in the south would be useless, unless accompanied by secure access to irrigation water, treatment of soil salination, and by making arrangements with the former landowners, (mostly tribal chiefs, and their managers or '*sirkals*') who owned the water pumps. The public investment in technical changes was necessary to accompany institutional changes in the land cultivated under large estates (some 25,000 hectares each), half of which had been left fallow each year. Dividing these huge areas into small, individual farms of 7–10 hectares for irrigated land, and 15–30 hectares in rain-fed areas as stipulated by land reform law, required arrangements to raise the level of production, labour utilisation, and in turn, the income of new owners. Without meeting these requirements, land reform would remain a slogan to turn against the politicians.

The third factor observed by the author in 1964 which influenced implementation was the deeply rooted tribal affiliation of the peasants (fellaheen). Even in the face of eroding power of the tribal chiefs and their farm management agents, the affiliation of the peasants remained strong enough to frustrate ongoing government efforts to organise agricultural co-operatives and local associations. This was the case despite the fact that new ownership of land was conditional upon member-ship of such co-operatives.

At the village level, a number of practical problems encountered by the farmers emerged from the author's field study during 1964 in the Provinces of Amara and Hilla (renamed in 1971 as Maysan and Babylon respectively). From discussions with tribal sheikhs, sirkals owning water pumps, heads of local government offices and a jurist (El Sayed Jawad Al Awady) it was found that the following conditions existed:

1. Former holders of 3,000 to 5,000 donums under *miri lazma* for three decades were considered illegal holders and were left with 150 donums (later raised to 300 donums), instead of the 1,000 donums which they expected to retain from the land reform law.
2. New owners maintained their tenancy in the area left to former landlords who had no right to evict them as stipulated by the land reform law (one landlord had seven tenants cultivating 140 donums out of his 300 donums in addition to their allotted new units).
3. Whereas the sheikhs and sirkals had most of their assets expropriated and their official tribal power abolished, their influence remained intact because their production functions had never been replaced. This included supply of water from pumps, credit needs of beneficiaries, and marketing their produce.
4. Dispute prevailed over the payment of the 20 per cent of the harvest for use of the sheikhs' water pumps for irrigating the land allotted to new owners.
5. Basic data were absent in local offices.

In addition, there was an extreme shortage of staff whose time was spread thinly over the tasks of expropriation, redistribution, solving problems about land rights, and the management of the large areas temporarily kept for eventual redistribution.

Despite these problems, the author was informed by land reform authorities in 1964 that within four years 80 per cent (about 7 million donums) of land subject to expropriation was already requisitioned by the State institutions. Out of this area only one-fifth (1.5 million donums or 373,000 ha was redistributed to 45,000 peasant households. The remainder was kept under 'temporary administration by the Ministry of Agrarian Reform'. This large area was leased to the would-be owners numbering 250,000 families, each cultivating on average 25 donums.

By recognising emerging problems and latent defects in the design of 1958 land reform law, policy makers made adjustments which culminated in the May 1970 land reform law. This second legislation pooled all former pieces of legislation and lowered the size ceiling on private landownership in irrigated areas by 40 per cent. Collective farms were legally established by Article 38 according to the 'principles and rules of socialist co-operation'. Detailed entitlement and responsibilities of both the beneficiaries and losers were clearly defined, and the administrative overlapping was resolved by establishing a central body (the Supreme Agricultural Council) with extensive authority. In addition, the 1970 law allowed for variation in soil fertility, type of cropping and location of land in relation to market towns, and introduced flexibility about the minimum size of units to be redistributed in order to allow for a larger number of beneficiaries.

According to data obtained from the Central Statistics Office, the situation in early 1975 was as follows:

Land

Area distributed to new owners	5,862,765 donums (1.47 m ha)
Area leased to tenants under the Government Temporary Administration	4,331,405 donums (1.08 m ha)
Total affected area since October 1958	10,194,170 donums (2.55 m ha)

Beneficiaries

Number of new owners	157,862 households
Number of tenants on the temporarily administered land subject to distribution	100,425 households
Total Direct beneficiaries as percentage of total agricultural households	258,287 households about 40 in 1975

Despite the shaky database, the process of expropriation and redistribution was speeded up between 1975 and 1977 owing to the political settlement agreed between the central government and the leaders of the Kurdish populated provinces in the north. This ended the military confrontation, and granted an autonomous administration in the northern provinces. Accordingly, 0.45 million hectares were redistributed to nearly 60,000 families, making the total of new owners 218,000 households and the total redistributed area 1.92 million hectares by 1977.

The policy provided for the gradual allotment of the rented area under temporary administration as ownership units and collectives after the completion of drainage and irrigation work. The reclamation of State-owned land was also to be accelerated for its distribution or for establishing State farms. Three institutions are adopted in the new system of land tenure; private family farms constituting most of the distributed area; collective co-operative farms; and State farms. The first was backed by university trained graduates in agriculture. These state-patronised co-operatives were responsible for the supply of heavily subsidised means of production including farm machinery. We do not know the pre-1975 areas of collective co-operatives and State farms. What we do know is that they proved to be inefficient. In fact, by 1983 the response of the Iraqi peasants to collectives was so weak that their numbers rapidly fell from 77 in 1975 cultivating 120,830 hectares, to 10 in 1983, cultivating 7,543 hectares. According to Alwan (1985), many State farms were liquidated for inefficiency, with only 11 large farms operating 170 thousand hectares retained in 1983 for specialising in the production of cotton, sugar cane, sugar beet and sunflowers. The area covered by State farms and collective co-operatives combined represented only 3 per cent of total agricultural land in 1983. Thus, official statistics tell us that the reformed agrarian system is fundamentally private property-based and operated in the form of the institution of individual family farms by new owners. What they do not tell us is how many of them *actually remained* on land, or how much of their farms were actually cultivated. In the absence of micro-studies, it is difficult to judge these changes.

The impact of reforms on rural development

Thus, after 12 years of uncertainty starting in 1958, the stage was set for land reform to lead a process of rural development. This role was reinforced by according agriculture (including drainage and irrigation) and human resource development top priority in national development plans. The investment allocation for agriculture was substantially increased by 600 per cent between 1965 and 1978. For social services, including housing, health and free education and students' meals, the allocation rose from 115 to 1,081 million Dinars (US $3.5 billion), a sharp rise of 840 per cent. This dramatic increase was funded by the fast growing oil revenue which followed the nationalisation of the three foreign-owned oil companies in 1972, and the accompanying rise in world oil prices beginning in late 1973. As an oil based economy (55 per cent of GDP and 82 per cent of government revenue in 1977), public investment could be rapidly expanded without having to rely on external capital, foreign aid, domestic private savings, or enforced cuts in consumption. As a relatively small contributor to GDP, agriculture's importance is in providing employment to a large section of Iraq's labour force (50 per cent in 1965 and 30 per cent in 1980). It is also responsible for providing most of the country's food supply and raw material such as sugar-cane, dairy products, cotton, and sunflowers to domestic industry.

In sum, the scale of reforming the agrarian content of the economy was quite large. According to Iraq Official Statistical Abstract, by 1984 an area of 2.4 million hectares was distributed to 262 thousand agricultural households. If we add the areas of rented land (temporary administration), that of State-owned land under tenancy subject to distribution after completion of its development and the area under State farms, the total amounts to nearly 3 million hectares, representing about 60 per cent of total arable land. If we add to the above number of land recipients, those cultivating the balance of temporarily administered land expropriated and those tenants on the newly reclaimed State owned land estimated at 60 thousand agricultural households, the total reaches roughly 322 thousand or nearly 56 per cent of total agricultural households in 1980. (Arable cultivated area 5 million hectares, total agricultural population 4.04 million and average size of household 7 persons, see p. 223.)

Agricultural growth and productivity. The impact of this large scale of land reform on agricultural output has to be judged against the pre-1958 reform situation. The insecure tenure and exploitative relationships of the pre-reform agrarian system imply no, or very low, production incentives or motivations, and therefore, yields of main crops were very low during the period 1948–58 (see Table 6.5).

However, this low output per land unit continued during the early phase of land reform, from 1959 to 1964, due partly to the drought in 1959 and 1960 and partly to reasons already discussed. In 1964, during the author's study in Qalet Saleh, Nahr Sad, Abu Bishut in Amara province and Al-Shomaly in Hilla province, it became obvious that agriculture and the rural infrastructure needed everything to adjust the backwardness of production organisation to the rapid change in the institutional framework. The availability of oil money to the central authorities in Baghdad responded to demands for investment in small irrigation and drainage work, and improving livestock. According to the study, where expensive water pumps were installed (59 horsepower each), canals and drains constructed, the cultivation of land was neither intensified, nor diversified, as the peasant continued growing more barley than rice in only one third of their allotted holdings (10 of 32 donums on average). Nor were cropping patterns diversified by double cropping rice with legumes, sugar cane or cotton, all of which had expanding markets. Salinity continued to cause crop failure, and forced the would-be beneficiaries to migrate to nearby Basrah where demand for labour was growing quickly.

Discussing the economic considerations with authorities made it quite clear that the question of realising an economic return on investment of oil money in modernising agriculture was of little concern. Real output in agriculture did not seem to match the heavy public investment in irrigation and drainage, fertiliser consumption (seventeen times higher than its initial level of one kg per hectare), or rocketing number of government staff devoted to agriculture. Despite doubling the level of rice and cotton yields, and a slight improvement in those of wheat and barley, yields are still far below the Iraqi potential. Furthermore, the prolonged drought of 1973 to 1975 severely damaged the wheat and barley harvests, particularly in the northern region. This crop failure could have been averted by higher investment rates in irrigation. The sluggish growth in rates of food grain and meat production could not keep pace with faster rates of annual population growth from 3.2 per cent to 3.6 per cent between the 1960s and 1970s. Using FAO index numbers, average 1978–80 of *per capita* food production and *per capita* physical agricultural production were 85 per cent and 79 per cent of their levels in 1952–6 respectively. It is true that with her plentiful oil revenues, Iraq could afford to make up for the balance of increasing food imports. But this is inconsistent with the overriding proclaimed objective in the development plans, i.e. food security and self-sufficiency.

Still, there is great scope for gaining from the substantial investment in technological change if the farmers were motivated to work hard. Raising productivity of land and peasants is imperative to sustain the initial equity gains from land redistribution and rent control.

Equity and poverty. To what extent have land reforms since 1958 shaped the income distribution in rural areas, and affected nutritional levels, or reduced the incidence of poverty? The political leaders' proclaimed clear objective was a social reform.[16] The intangible social gain is the liberation of the peasants from their dependency for survival on the arbitrary powers of the tribal sheikhs, and the sirkals who had been classic institutional monopolists. The reforms have nearly eliminated such economic control.

A major effect has been the substantial and rapid reduction in the degree of inequality. Table 6.6 indicates that the share of land held by farmers holding less than 20 ha has sharply risen from less than 8.4 per cent in 1958 to almost 53.2 per cent of agricultural land in 1971. In addition, farmers in the size class of less than 30 ha in 1982 represented 95 per cent of the total number of landholders, and held 69.5 per cent of total land. Another significant effect of land reform is the corresponding sharp decline in the share of the area of holdings over 250 ha from 68.5 per cent in 1958 to 4.5 per cent in 1971. This change towards an egalitarian agrarian system is clear in the reduced Gini Coefficient of land concentration from the highly unequal index of 0.902 in 1958 to 0.394 in 1982 (see Figure 6.2).

Unfortunately, information about the distribution of income and consumption in rural areas prior to 1958 land reform is decidedly lacking. Therefore, we must rely upon the observations made by Warriner (1948),

Table 6.5 **Changes in conditions of agricultural income, and rural quality of life Iraq, 1948–80**

Indicators	1948–52 average	1958	1961–5 average	1969–71 average	1974–6 average	1980
1. Agricultural/rural *per capita* annual average income (exp. Dinars, current prices	3.5 a (1950)	26 b (1960)	42 b (1962)	69 cR (1972)	108 cR (1976)	1,58b
2. National (GDP) average income *per capita*, Dinars at current prices	32 (1950)	51 (1956)	82 (1961)	138	407 (1975)	
– at 1975 prices		110	134 (1961)	154	389 (1976)	
3. Daily average calorie supply per person	n.a.	1,856	2,012	2,678R (1972)	2,839R (1976)	2,840c
4. 3 as percentage of requirement	n.a.	77	85	102	116	118
5. Infant mortality per 1,000	cir. 350R	140 (1960)	121	100	111R	73
6. Life expectancy at birth, years	n.a.		n.a.		n.a.	
Male		47		53		57
Female		50		56		61
7. Illiteracy rate as percentage of adults	n.a.	84R	82	66	n.a.	32R
8. No. of water-pumps for irrigation per 1,000 ha arable land	n.a.	1.1	1.3	1.4	1.8	n.a.
9. Fertiliser use, Kg per ha	Less than one	1	1	3	6	17
10. Institutional agricultural credit Dinar per ha arable land	n.a.	0.98	11.12	409.76	490.71	n.a.
11. Yield, Tonne per hectare						
Wheat	0.48	0.4	0.53	0.88	0.77	0.72
Barley	0.77	0.5	0.75	1.19	0.93	0.72
Rice (Paddy)	1.16	1.12	1.42	1.95	2.73	2.75
Cotton (seed)	0.27	0.46	0.74	1.30	} 1.33	0.87
(lint)	0.14	0.18	0.24	0.40		0.57

Indicators	1953–61	1961–70	1971–80
12. Agricultural labour force productivity *per capita* average annual growth rate of agricultural production	0.3	3.3	1.2
13. Agricultural GDP average annual growth rate	1.5	5.7	−1.5 (1970–7)

14. Food Production Index:

1952–6	1958	1961	1968	1969–71	1973	1974/5	1979/80
100	106	123	167	119	104	94	150

Note: Data are until 1980 when the war with Iran started.
R refers to rural population or rural areas.
One Dinar = 3.2 US Dollars up to 1980.
Figures in parentheses refer to corresponding year.

Source: According to row numbers:

1.   Letter 'a' refers to tenants and share croppers only (see text), 'b' refers to *per capita* agricultural GDP calculated from FAO Country Tables and 'c' refers to *per capita* expenditure in rural areas taken from M. Bakir, 'The Development of Level of Living in Iraq', unpublished Ph.D Thesis, University of Leeds, 1979, Table C21. Material in this table and in the text are cited with permission from the Department of Economic Studies of the University.

2.   Current prices: 1950 and 1956 from Fenelon study in *National Income in Iraq*, Selected Studies, Central Statistical Organisation, Baghdad, 1970, Table 4. Other years are from World Bank Development Indicators. Constant at 1976 prices: Central Statistical Organization cited in Bakir, *Ibid*, Table C30.

3. and 4.   FAO Food Balance Sheets except 1972 and 1976 from Bakir, *Ibid*, Tables C12 and 13.

5.   For 1949–52, data taken from D. Adams, *Iraq's People and Resources*, University of California, 1958. For other years from UNICEF *Statistics on Children* May 1984.

6.   World Development Report – Development Indicators, World Bank, several issues.

7.   Data for rural areas from Bakir, *Ibid*. The rest from UNICEF, *Ibid*. Illiteracy rates in rural areas in 1970 were 68 among male and 96 among female adults.

8 and 10.   Calculated from the results of the 1958 Census of Agriculture and from several issues of the Iraqi Ministry of Planning, 'Statistical Abstract and Annual Abstract of Statistics'.

9.   *Country Tables 1987*, FAO, Rome

11, 12,   *Production Yearbook*, FAO, Rome data for 1948–52 and 1961–5 are
14.   calculated from Vol. 24, 1970; 1969–71 from Vol. 31, 1977; 1974–6 from Vol. 30, 1976 and data for 1980 from Vol. 34, 1980.

13.   Data for the period 1953–61 are from K. Hasseeb, *The National Income of Iraq, 1953–61*, Oxford University Press, 1964. The rest is taken from The World Bank Development Indicators, *Ibid*. On falling production 1970–77, see p. 217.

Table 6.6 **Changes in the distribution of land holdings in Iraq, 1952–82**

Size of holdings in hectares	1952* Number of holdings %	Cum	1958 Number of holdings %	Cum	1958 Area of holdings %	Cum	1971 Number of holdings %	Cum	1971 Area of holdings %	Cum
Less than one	19.2	19.2	34.4	34.4	0.3	0.3	12.5	12.5	0.6	0.6
1 – 5	20.8	40.0	27.1	61.5	1.7	2.0	32.2	44.7	8.0	8.6
5 – 10	12.8	52.8	11.2	72.7	2.2	4.2	23.6	68.3	16.9	25.5
10 – 20	15.2	68.0	10.4	83.1	4.2	8.4	20.3	88.6	27.7	53.2
20 – 50	19.2	87.2	9.7	92.8	8.6	17.0	9.8	98.4	29.0	82.2
50 – 100	6.4	93.6	3.2	96.0	6.3	23.3	1.2	99.6	7.3	89.5
100 – 150	1.8	95.4	1.0	97.0	3.4	26.7	0.2	99.8	3.0	92.5
150 – 250	1.6	96.9	0.9	97.9	4.8	31.5	0.1	99.9	3.0	95.5
250 – 1000	2.3	99.3	1.5	99.4	21.5	53.0	0.1	100.0	4.5	100.0
1,000 ha. and over	0.7	100.0	0.6	100.0	47.0	100.0		100.0		100.0
Total percentage	100		100		100		100		100	
Total number of holdings and area (hectares)	125,045		168,346		5,831,815		539,440		5,156,027	
Gini Coefficient			0.902				0.566			

1982

Size of holdings	Number %	Area %
Less than 2.5 ha	23.0	2.8
2.5 – 30	72.1	66.7
30–75	4.1	16.7
75 ha and over	0.8	18.8
Total percentage	100	100
Total number of holdings and area (hectares)	682,864	6,147,000
Gini Coefficient	0.394	

Note: *Size distribution of holdings by area, for obvious political reasons, is not given in the 1952 Census of Agriculture.

Cum = Cumulative share of number or area of each size class as shown by Lorenz curves in Figure 6.2.

Source: Calculated from data given in: 1952/53 Agricultural and Livestock Census results published in *Statistical Abstract*, 1956, Ministry of Economics, Government of Iraq: 82, Table 95. 1958 Census of Agriculture and Livestock results published in *Statistical Abstract*, 1960, Central Bureau of Statistics, Ministry of Planning, Republic of Iraq, Section VII, Table 90. In arabic the term 'ownership' was used, whereas in English, the results of the 1958 Census used 'holdings'. 1971 – Results of Census of Agriculture, Central Statistical Organization, Part II. In our calculations, categories of 'holders without land' and 'over 2,000 donums' are excluded, the latter is mostly government and collectively managed as shown in Tables 3 and 4 of the Census results. 1982 data are from a report to the ruling Baath Socialist Party held in Baghdad, January 1983 (p. 138) cited in: Abdul Sahib Alwan, *Agrarian Systems and the Alleviation of Poverty in Iraq*, a study published by the United Nations Economic and Social Commission for Western Asia, Table 1. We do not know how the data were calculated in this report which has less size classes than other years, making comparison difficult.

Cumulative share of
areas of land holdings %

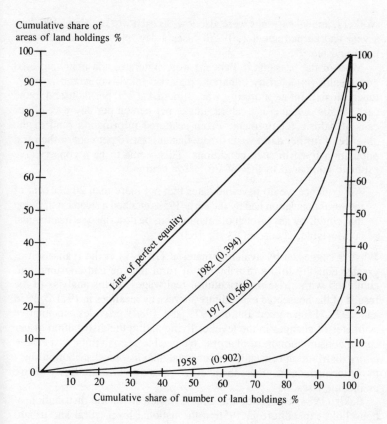

Figure 6.2 Lorenz curves for changes in the size distribution of land holdings
in Iraq, 1958, 1971, 1982
Source: Based on data in Table 6.5. Figures in parentheses are Gini Coefficients.

the World Bank Mission (1950), Adams (1958), and Alwan (1961).
Published material shares the view that prior to land reform the terms
of leasing land to the tenants, who were mostly sharecroppers were in
most cases exorbitant.[17] The annual income accrued to the tenant was
estimated at 20 Iraqi dinars in 1951, or approximately 3–4 dinars per
person. In that year, Fenelon, the Director of Statistics in the Iraqi
Ministry of Economy calculated the national average per capita income
at 31 dinars (Fenelon, 1956: Table 4). Depending on the variation in
household size, the average annual income per member of the tenant
household amounted to a very low ratio ranging between 8 and 12 per
cent of the national average at current prices. For the hired agricultural

221

workers, annual earnings were also low, as each worked about 100 days a year and earned about 150–250 filses a day, plus, in many cases, a meal and tea.[18]

Most of the peasants (fellaheen) were illiterate, and many suffered poor health (infected by bilharzia, malaria, ankylostoma and possibly tuberculosis). Infant mortality was estimated at 350 per thousand in the early 1950s. On average calorie-intake per person per day was 77 per cent of calorie requirement. From scattered information (and in the absence of further data) we estimate that at least 70 per cent of the rural population lived in such conditions. This seems to be a conservative estimate compared to that of Professor Penrose.

> All evidence we do have indicates that not more than 20 per cent of the rural population had by the early 1950s attained a standard of living that could, by any stretch of imagination, be described as healthy and comfortable. (Penrose, 1978: 163)

What is suggested by available material (1971–9) is the realisation of greater equality in the distribution of rural income and consumption, combined with a rise in agricultural real wages. In his analysis of the results of the household expenditure surveys by localities in 1971/2, 1976 and 1979, Mohammed Bakir (1979 and 1984) provides quantitative estimates of changes in the level of living and in the distribution of *per capita* consumption in rural areas. We need to keep in mind that *expenditure* distribution is usually less unequal than *income* distribution since the latter includes savings, the average rates of which are likely to rise as income rises.

Bakir (1984) calculated the Gini Coefficient for the distribution of household expenditure in 1956 at the national level (rural and urban) at 0.630 which dropped sharply to 0.241 in 1972 and 0.220 in 1979. For *rural* areas, the index shows a greater equality: 0.150 in 1971/2, and 0.173 in 1979.[19] These are very low estimates particularly if compared to those on China and South Korea, suggesting a possible abnormality in the data and requiring caution.

Nevertheless, the substantial and rapid reduction in the degree of inequality after land reform is a remarkable achievement. At the same time, the fast rural out-migration has contributed to an increased *per capita* income/consumption of those who remained on the land. In fact, the annual rate of change in the agricultural population has steadily fallen between 1960 and 1980 from 1.9 (1960–70) to −0.7 (1971–80), despite the increased rate of growth of the total population from 3.2 to 3.6 respectively.

But to what extent has rural development, spearheaded by land reform combined with the effects of the rapidly growing economy of Iraq, reduced the incidence of rural poverty? Unfortunately, neither the government statistical office nor the Iraqi scholars concerned with rural development have estimated poverty's incidence. This is probably for political reasons. No minimum level of *per capita* income or expenditure has ever been established as a poverty line. For our purposes, we must make such an attempt.

We consider the rural population whose average daily calorie intake is estimated at 90 per cent or less of daily requirements to be poor. According to FAO and WHO recommended criteria, this group are at high risk of malnutrition.[20] The analysts of the Iraqi household expenditure surveys used these criteria in calculating the nutrients of food consumption. The results show that a section of the surveyed rural population met only 78 per cent and 72 per cent of the mean requirements in 1972 and 1976 respectively. This group is prevalent in the overlapping socio-economic groups of 'low-income' and 'rural south' (Bakir, 1979: Tables 5.23, C.23 and C.28). The sampled rural *households* in 1976 have 28 per cent in the category of low-income group, based on an average sized rural household of 7.8 persons. Because of a wide variation in actual food-intake within and between members of households based on age, sex, health and working conditions, this does not mean that all individuals in these groups are undernourished. Considering the small size of the sub-sample surveyed in 1976 and allowing for errors in underestimating the non-cash expenditure on food from self-produced items (cereals, dates, milk and fish), we roughly estimate the order of magnitude of the rural poor at 15 to 20 per cent in 1976. They have living characteristics consistent with those of poverty.[21] The poor seem to be concentrated mostly in the south and the rest were living in isolated and remote areas in the rainfed land of the north. Statistical objections to this rough estimate could be made as regards the combination of calorie intake and income level, as well as to the inference to the entire rural population from a small sample survey. Still, our estimates point to substantial and rapid reduction in poverty incidence and improvements in the level of living between 1958 and 1976, the most important of which are:

(a) nutritional levels rose from 77 per cent of daily requirements in 1957 to 116 per cent in 1976;
(b) infant mortality was reduced by 70 per cent; and
(c) life expectancy increased by 60 per cent for males, and 22 per cent for females.

But social gains from the large-scale land reform programme cannot be sustained over time unless the productivity per person in agriculture is substantially raised. The signals of a slowly rising inequality in income as an impact of the dynamic changes in the oil-based economy should serve as a warning. They also underline the necessity for greater motivation among the new owners to raise their productive capabilities.

Cuba

It is useful to consider briefly the implications for rural development of the massive 30 year old land reform programme in Cuba. (The Cuban experience of complete land reform and its implications for rural development have been well documented in a recently conducted study by an ILO international team of experts. The study was completed in 1985, and released in 1986 (see Ghai *et al.*, 1988).)

In 1958, prior to land reform, 9 per cent of the landowners held 73 per cent of the land. American-owned sugar companies controlled 23 per cent of the total agricultural land. Sugar cane represented 53 per cent of the total crop area, with sugar and cattle combined amounting to 52 per cent of the total agricultural product. At the same time, food imports accounted for 23 per cent of the total imports (Gayoso, 1970: 19–22). In May 1959 with a clear economic objective of sharply reducing inequality, abolishing tenancy, diversifying and intensifying agricultural production, land reform was introduced. Productive assets and educational opportunities were also redistributed. To free dependency on sugar cane, and to increase food production, the institutions of private farms, production co-operatives and State farms were chosen, under a comprehensive planning system. This path was reinforced by according agriculture and expanded irrigation priority. Accordingly, irrigated land was expanded from 13 per cent in 1959 to 32 per cent of total arable land in 1984. Fertiliser consumption rose sharply from 63 kg per hectare in 1960 to 179 kg in 1984.

It was clear from the beginning that private farming and State farms constituted the major institutional framework of agriculture. Expropriated private land ownership in excess of 67 ha was redistributed to the peasants in units of 30 ha (on average) free of charge as private and individual farms. Large sugar cane plantations, cattle ranches and unused land were converted into State farms (people's estates), the area of which amounted to 60 per cent of total agricultural land in 1963. This policy choice, and the ability to implement it, were studied by the author in August 1959 when he examined the thinking behind it with Mr Antonio Jimenez, President of the Agrarian Reform Organization, and Dr Regino Boti, Minister of Economy, in August 1959.[27] Their view was that the reform aimed at liberating the tenants, sharecroppers and landless workers from exploitation by absentee large farmers and American monopolists in agriculture. Private property in land as family farms was granted (almost free) and State farms were considered as the engine of agricultural growth and the focus of socialist ideology. Production co-operatives (collectives) were considered unwarranted in the view of the two Cuban authorities because of the already large size of private farms (average 35 ha) after the 1959 land reform. Instead, these private farms were to be controlled by the State through such means as the supply of inputs, pricing and marketing procedures by service co-operatives. The situation changed substantially following the second reform in 1963 which lowered the size of distributed units to 16 ha on average, and expropriated an additional 25 per cent of private farms of over 67 ha. The expropriated land was taken over by the State to expand the dominant State farms. Furthermore, those who owned private farms were encouraged to affiliate with State farms. Production co-operatives (collectives) grew from less than 1 per cent of total agricultural land in 1963 to 5 or 6 per cent in 1985–6 and State farm areas increased from 60 per cent in 1963 to 83 per cent in 1985–6.

Since 1959, these continuing institutional changes have strengthened the command of the State in many aspects of managing the Cuban rural economy: organisation of agricultural production, supply of the means of production, marketing of the products and processing of agricultural raw material – all governed by a comprehensive planning system. Production of meat and other crops grew at a fast rate despite a number of problems: the drought of 1961, the hurricane of 1963, the emigration of many technical staff to the USA, and a series of ideological uncertainties during the 1960s with regard to material incentives which disrupted the output level of sugar cane until 1965.[23] The index of agricultural production (1974–6 = 100) grew at 3.9 per cent in the 1960s and 3.4 per cent in the 1970s. Notable was the fast growth in cereals by 12.3 per cent in 1970–80 (FAO Production Yearbook and Country Tables, 1985). There was also a rise in value productivity per agricultural worker in the State farm sector at constant prices between 1971 and 1983 from 1,430 to 2,180 *pesos* according to a recent study by ILO (Ghai *et al.*, 1988). Their study reports that total investment in agriculture increased between 1970 and 1983 by 130 per cent, fertiliser consumption by 34 per cent and irrigated areas by 73 per cent (Ghai *et al.*, 1988: Table 6.13). It states that while sugar retains its grip over the export sector, crop production for domestic consumption, particularly root crops, has consistently increased in relative share.

With the 1963 reform design of the ratio between maximum private landed property to distributed units at two to one (67 and 35 hectares on average) the provision of material incentives, food subsidies, rapid expansion of education free of charge and social benefits, greater equality in rural income distribution was realised. Measured by the Gini Coefficient, inequality declined from its post-land reforms low level of 0.35 in 1962 to 0.28 in 1973 and to 0.21 in 1978 (Ghai *et al.*, 1988: Table 6.7) Between 1960 and 1985 illiteracy rates declined by 89 per cent, infant mortality by 54 per cent and life expectancy reached 77 years for females, and 73 years for males; a level as high as the rich industrialised countries. With the drastic redistribution of productive assets and income, these characteristics of a highly egalitarian rural society suggest a minimal level of poverty, moving toward complete elimination.

Egypt

This is the selected case for examining the scope and implications of choosing a *partial* land reform policy. In Chapter 5, p. 152, the historical experience of Egypt since the early nineteenth century until the land reform of September 1952 was presented as a case of institutional monopoly in agriculture. (In order to maintain balance of presentation, a significant amount of background and supplementary information has been placed in the notes pertaining to this section.) The characteristics of the rural economy during the decades immediately preceding the implementation of land reform are briefly explained as follows:

1. There was a heavy concentration of landholdings and extensive absentee land-ownership. Thirty-five per cent of agricultural land was possessed by 94 per cent of total landowners, whereas one-tenth of one per cent of total owners controlled among themselves 20 per cent of the fertile land. A dual agrarian system prevailed and a process of polarisation rapidly developed. The percentage of the mini-owners of less than 2 hectares (55 feddans) increased, while the average size of their ownership decreased, from 0.42 ha to 0.3 ha between 1916 and 1950. Accordingly, income distribution became highly skewed. Average annual net farm income of the owners of less than one feddan (0.4 ha) was only 0.05 per cent of that of those rich landowners in the size group of 200 feddans (83.3 ha) and over in 1949/50. Measured in terms of the Gini index, this high inequality in income distribution was 0.858 (El-Ghonemy, 1953: Table 35).
2. About 60 per cent of cultivated land was operated under insecure tenancy arrangements. The percentage was even higher at 86 per cent in some provinces where large estates and foreign-owned plantations of sugar cane and cotton existed. Landlords and foreign enterprises exercised monopoly power in their locations and received high monopoly profit. They established institutional barriers for direct lease and also had the right to evict tenants without compensation payments. By leasing out land through auction, they forced small tenants to rent from a hierarchy of intermediaries resulting in payment of exorbitant rents. Consequently, rental values rose in real terms four-fold between 1931 and 1950. Combined with capital rationing in the institutionally-provided credit market (which was primarily

controlled by two foreign banks), these high rents resulted in both chronic indebtedness of the tenants, and very low incentives for improving land productivity.

3. Despite improvement in the irrigation system, the rural economy experienced a steady decline in productivity per agricultural worker due to the fast-growing agricultural population, slow growth of output, and the highly inelastic supply of cultivated land. Land concentration, combined with demographic pressure, led to a rise in landlessness. Nearly 45 per cent of agricultural households neither owned nor rented land. A Malthusian situation existed: food productivity *per capita* total population in 1949–52 was 70 per cent of its 1900–4 level; and population pressure on land increased resulting in a fall in the ratio of cultivated land per head of agricultural population from 0.78 in 1900 to 0.44 in 1952.

4. In the face of low wages, high rental values, rationing of the credit market, and inflationary land prices, the mass of hired farmworkers and small tenants did not have the earning capacity to purchase land. Nor were they likely for social reasons to obtain land through institutional means such as marriage, inheritance, or as gifts. The sale of reclaimed State-owned land was largely captured by the big landowners and foreign land companies (90.7 per cent during 1935–50).

5. Social unrest and discontent prevailed in the countryside among the indebted tenants and the unorganised poor farmworkers. Several proposals to improve the land tenure system (particularly after the Second World War), were repeatedly rejected by the government, and were silenced by the strong coalition of the dominant influential landlords, members of parliament and the former royal family who were themselves the largest landowners in the country.

Thus, the pre-1952 land-based power structure obstructed rural development and stratified the rural society into an upper class minority of rich landlords and cotton merchants and a mass of very low income and poor *fellaheen*. In between lay a wide social gulf. Importantly, the pattern of distribution of land, assets, educational opportunities and income led to widespread poverty, the magnitude of which is estimated at nearly 56.1 per cent of total rural population in 1950 based on annual income levels. Our estimate is a result of several studies carried out in villages during 1947–50.[24]

The contents of partial land reform of 1952 and 1961

Against this background, the September 1952 land reform was instituted by the revolution of July 1952 led by Gamal Abdul Nasser. The resulting change in power structure was a response to simultaneous calls for reform by a group of Egyptian intellectuals and an outbreak of rural unrest.[25] When the land reform was proclaimed, its overriding objectives were social and political:

A class of minority has directed the country's policy according to its own interest and in a manner inconsistent with the principles of democracy. The time has come to carry out land reform in Egypt as a basic step to build Egyptian Society on a new basis by providing free life and dignity to each peasant and by abolishing the wide gap between classes and by removing an important cause of social and political instability. (Translated explanatory note to Land Reform Act No. 178, 9 September 1952)

Economic goals were broadly expressed in terms of 'to pave the road for rapid economic development' and 'to check the rush of those rich possessing savings to purchase land and to direct every new investment into land reclamation, industrial and commercial activities'.

But these bold objectives and the pre-1952 aspirations of peasants and social reformers among the intelligentsia were only partially realised by the series of land reforms issued beween 1952 and 1964 (see Table 6.7). By 1980 (after the completion of their implementation), 847,887 feddans (356,112 hectares) or 13.9 per cent of total cultivated land was redistributed to 353,286 peasant families representing 9.6 per cent of total agricultural households. This redistributed area represented 87 per cent of total land acquired by the State through confiscation, expropriation against payment and purchases of foreign-owned land companies. The balance, mostly orchards and less productive land, was retained as the property of the Agrarian Reform Authority according to Law No. 52 of 1966. In addition, 214,166 feddans (89,949 ha) of State-owned reclaimed land using the High Dam water were distributed during the 1960s (Egypt: Statistical Yearbook, June 1986: Table 2–22).

Following completion of land reform implementation, between 30 and 38 per cent of total agricultural households remained landless workers (depending on the definition and classification used), and they suffered the consequences of being excluded from the reforms. The prescribed minimum daily wage rates in the 1952 Law remained ineffective until the labour market allowed their upward trend in late 1960s and 1970s. The demand for their labour also declined in the *initial* phase of the subdivision of labour-based large estates into small family farms. Furthermore, cultivated land under tenancy arrangements was marginally reduced from 60 per cent in 1951 to 50 per cent in 1965. Tenancy was regulated by fixing a ceiling on rental values at seven times the land taxes assessed in 1949 and at 50 per cent of harvest in the case of

Table 6.7 **Areas acquired for redistribution by Egyptian land reform laws 1952 to 1969**

	Area in feddans
Initial Land Reform Law No. 178 of 1952	
Law No. 598 of 1953 for confiscation of ex-Royal family estates	450,305
Law No. 152 of 1957 and Law No. 44 of 1962 for transfer to land reform of Wakf lands entrusted to charitable and public purposes	148,787
Second Land Reform Law No. 127 of 1961 for reducing maximum land ownership of individual household to 100 feddans	214,132
Purchases of lands sequestrated in 1956 including those of Kom Ombo Land Company	28,807
Law No. 15 of 1963 for the acquisition of foreigners' land ownerships	61,910
Law No. 150 of 1964 for the confiscation of land owned by Egyptians put under sequestration (Hirasah)	43,516
1969 law amending some of the above laws (estimate)	32,000
Total	979,457

Source: Compiled from records of the Agrarian Reform Authority, Ministry of Agriculture, Cairo

sharecropping, providing the tenants with security of tenure for a renewable period of three years under written contract. Auctioneering land for lease was prohibited, as was sub-leasing. The maximum area rented by any cultivator was limited to 50 feddans (20 ha).

Another feature which characterises this land reform as partial can be seen in varying size ceilings implemented at different times. The calculated percentage size distribution of land ownership before and after land reforms is given in Table 6.8. The initial land reform of 1952 fixed a size ceiling of 300 feddans, or 126 hectares on land privately owned by one household. The land reform of 1961 lowered this ceiling to 100 feddans or acres (42 ha). In 1969, a ceiling of 50 feddans was fixed for one person's ownership but its effect was minimal. Land acquired by the State was to be redistributed to tenants (already cultivating the land) in small units of individual ownership of 2–3 acres (about one hectare on average).

Throughout the reform process, the institution of *private* property rights in land has been maintained in practice and established in the New Constitution of 1956 and the Egyptian Charter of 1962 (Mithaq). With political will and high implementation capability, the programme of land distribution progressed on schedule.[26] Over a period of 40 years, State institutions were to compensate (in government bonds) affected owners whose land was expropriated against instalment payments by the new owners. In turn, new owners were charged 15 per cent of the land price for administrative costs (reduced later to 10 per cent). In 1964 a fraction of the political leadership (the Abul-Nour Group) provided pressure

Table 6.8 **Changes in the size distribution of landownership in Egypt, 1951–84**

Size of ownerships (feddans)	1951		1965		1984	
	%O	%A	O%	A%	O%	A%
Less than 5	94.3	35.4	95.0	57.1	95.2	53.0
5–10	2.8	8.8	2.5	9.5	2.5	10.4
10–20	1.7	10.7	1.3	8.2	1.3	10.9
20–50	0.8	10.9	0.9	12.6	0.7	11.9
50–100	0.2	7.2	0.2	6.1	0.2	7.5
100 and over	0.2	27.0	0.1	6.5	0.1	6.3
Gini Coefficient of Landownership	0.611		0.383		0.432	
Gini Coefficient of landholdings	0.715 (1950)		0.456 (1975)			

Note: %O – Number of ownerships, percentage.
%A – Area of ownership units, percentage.
One feddan equals 1.04 acre, or 0.42 hectares.
Inequality in the size distribution of landholdings is higher than ownership due to many owners leasing-in additional land (thereby increasing their areas of holding) and acquiring multiple holdings.These are then recorded by the census of agriculture as *one* holding belonging to one holder.

Source: Calculated from data published by the Department of Agricultural Economics, Egypt, Ministry of Agriculture and the *Statistical Yearbook*, 1952–85, General Agency for Public Mobilisation and Statistics, Cairo, June 1986.

to legally write off half the instalment payments and abolish charges for interest rate and government services. Land recipients were also exempted from the payment of land tax.

Egypt's partial land reform is manifested in the ratio of the fixed ceiling to the average size of the redistributed units to new owners. At a ratio 126:1 established by the 1952 land reform, the ratio dropped to 40:1 by the 1961 reform. Though the change is positive, it still contrasts sharply with the ratio achieved in complete land reform, for example, 3:1 in land-scarce South Korea, or 9:1 in the land-abundant Iraq. Another measure of partial scope is the changing share of size classes of land ownerships and the corresponding share in land. The size class of 200 feddans (80 ha) and over was eliminated, as were most of the individual household ownerships exceeding 100 feddans (40 ha). As presented in Table 6.8, the share in total land of 95 per cent of the small owners of less than 5 feddans (2.1 ha) increased from 35.4 per cent before the reforms to 57.1 per cent in 1965. But the shares of the size category of 10–50 feddans (4–20 ha) remained virtually stable, as did the upper class of 50–100 feddans (20–40 ha) their percentage remained unchanged at 0.2 while the corresponding share in land fell by only 0.9 per cent.[27] Thus, after a series of land reforms, while the degree of land concentration was improved substantially, the range between size classes remained wide.

Another feature of this wide range among size classes is the high inequality among the small-holders of less than 5 feddans. Out of a total number of landholders in this category, 31.4 per cent were in the class of less than one acre, and held 8.9 per cent of land. 7.2 per cent in the size class of 4–5 feddans held 18 per cent of the total land in the size group of less than 5 feddans in 1961. The number and area of the dwarf holdings of less than one acre doubled in one decade, between 1950 and 1961, suggesting a rapid process of fragmentation. Thus, polarisation of landholdings continued after land reform.

The implications for productivity and equity

Consider the impact of land reform in the context of a broad strategy to control resource use, income generating assets and trade in the Egyptian economy in general, and agriculture in particular. Consider, also, the impact of land reform on the remaining non-reform sector. The government has always been in full control of the management of the Nile water supply for irrigation, a policy reinforced with the huge public investment in the construction of the High Dam in the late 1950s and early 1960s. The State control of planning crop-rotation has been further extended from the reform to the non-reform sector. In addition, regulating prices, and marketing main crops are also now controlled throughout agriculture. These functions have been vertically integrated into the nationalised processing industries and subsidised consumer goods.[28]

These features of State control may explain the centrality of government's role in the management of agricultural co-operatives in the land reform sector, particularly with regard to the organisation of agricultural production and trade. New owners were obligated to join the co-operatives (*Gam'eya*) and to subscribe to its capital share (3–5 Egyptian pounds). Over-staffed by professionally trained personnel in agriculture and accounting, these institutions gradually became the local office of the Land Reform Authority, providing a wide range of managerial and technical services. As such, it is the sole supplier of subsidised chemical fertiliser, insecticides, seeds, and tractors, as well as advancing cash loans against the security of crops. (Prior to land reform, loans were made against the title of land.) The *Gam'eya* procures all harvest of cotton and sugar cane, and part of the rice, wheat and beans. Each year procurement prices are fixed by the government, at levels 20–50 per cent below world market prices (see Chapter 1: 38). Crop-rotation is also enforced by the *Gam'eya*.

Agricultural output and productivity. The organisation of production

231

within the crop rotation presents a special feature of Egyptian land reform. Redistributed units are divided into two or three separate pieces to match the planned crop-rotation in each co-operative's area. The amalgamated pieces constitute a large plot (hode) of 30–50 feddans (12–20 ha) planted in a single crop (crops are then rotated on a two or three-year cycle). Each owner has a distinct area registered in his or her name, cultivated individually and the produce of the land is so identified after harvesting. This innovative arrangement represents a mixture of individual but conditional ownership of land and collective farming, and joint management by the owners and government technocrats at the *Gam'eya*. It combines the advantages of both private property incentives and large scale production. Small units are consolidated to reap the benefits of the agronomic-technological advances and can be ploughed, irrigated and sprayed against insects at the same time. A significant impact of land reform on the large non-reform sector was the forceful and rapid extension of this system in 1964–6 from the land reform sector to the rest of the agricultural sector. In this case, farmers' membership of co-operatives was voluntary.

By 1966, Egyptian agricultural production and trade was controlled nationwide at the village level by a network of 4,358 co-operatives in the non-reform sector and 550 located in the reformed sector. In 1956 Professor Mario Bandini of Italy (on whose advice this system was initiated), expressed his view to the author that it represented a pragmatic solution to the distributed small units along with the availability of a large number of professionally trained university graduates in agriculture.

There is no scarcity of studies about the impact of land reform.[29] Because the institutional organisation as described above was confined to land reform areas until 1964 and only then extended to the rest of the farming areas, comparable data on average productivity per unit of land during 1952–64 is more relevant. The author compiled case studies carried out during this period by the Land Reform Authority (*Hai'at Islah Zira'i*) in three areas (El-Ghonemy, 1968) and they are reproduced in Table 6.9. The data indicate a slight variation despite the advantageous position accorded to the land reform sector where technical staff and technical inputs were concentrated. The yields of cotton, sugar cane and maize have clearly risen at faster rates in the land reform sector than in the national averages, while rice yield was uniformly high. Three technological changes throughout agriculture should be taken into account:

(a) the introduction of some high yielding varieties in *all* farming areas during this period;
(b) the consumption of subsidised chemical fertiliser per acre (feddan) which rose by 280 per cent; and

Table 6.9 **Average yields per feddan in three land reform districts, and national averages 1954-64**

District	Main crop	Unit	Average yield per feddan 1950/52		Average yield after the implementation of 1952 land reform											
					1953/54		1955/56		1957/58		1959/60		1962/63		1963/64	
			Local	N	LR	N	LR	N	LR	N	LR	N	LR	N	LR	N
El Manshia (cotton area)	Cotton[a]	Kintar[b]	3.5	4.2	4.1	3.9	3.6	3.5	4.7	4.7	6.0	4.2	6.8	5.4	7.1	8.0
	Wheat	Ardab[c]	4.1	5.1	4.3	6.4	5.7	6.6	4.8	6.6	5.7	6.9	8.0	7.3	6.3	7.7
	Maize	Ardab	4.7	6.3	4.7	6.5	6.6	6.4	6.9	6.4	8.9	6.3	8.9	6.9	10.6	7.8
	Cotton	Kintar	3.5	4.2	5.0	3.9	4.0	3.5	5.4	4.7	3.3	4.2	5.5	5.4	5.4	6.0
Demera (rice area)	Rice	Dariba[d]	1.7	1.4	2.7	1.9	3.0	2.3	3.0	2.1	2.7	2.2	3.2	2.6	3.2	2.3
	Maize	Ardab	4.5	6.3	6.5	6.5	7.0	6.4	8.5	6.4	10.5	6.3	11.0	6.9	—	—
El Mata'ana (sugar cane area)	Sugar Cane	Ton	37.0	39.0	45.5	41.7	52.0	41.4	57.5	41.5	51.3	45.5	51.2	44.1	52.0	36.5

Note: (a) Long staple cotton.
(b) Kintar = 157.7 Kgs.
(c) Ardab = 150 Kgs.
(d) Dariba = 954 Kgs; Ton = 1,000 Kgs.
LR = Average yield in area of land reform.
N = National average yield.
Data on national average yield, for cotton show the yield per same variety as in land reform areas.

Source: Based on data compiled from studies carried out by the Statistics and Research Office of the Land Reform Authority, Dokki, Giza. National averages are from *Bulletin of Agricultural Economy*, Ministry of Agriculture, Dokki, Giza (several issues).

(c) the share of agriculture (including land reclamation and irrigation in public investment which reached its highest point since 1952 at 23.4 per cent in 1960–5 because of construction of the Aswan High Dam combined with accelerated land reclamation. (The share declined sharply to 9.7 per cent in 1971–5 and further to 6.8 per cent in 1976–83.)

Accordingly, total food production grew in 1952–64 at the annual rate of 3.5 per cent and *per capita* at 1.1 per cent and annual growth of total agricultural production increased from 2.8 per cent in 1952–9 to 3 per cent in 1961–70. These steady growth indicators are reflected in the index of agricultural production (1952 to 1956 average 100).

	1956	1957	1958	1959	1960	1961	1962	1963	1964
All agricultural sectors including land reform areas	107	115	116	120	127	112*	135	136	141

*The sharp fall in production in 1961 is due to the disastrous cotton crop failure caused by a severe damage by cotton leaf worm; cotton accounted for one-fifth of total cropped area and 29 per cent of cultivated area.

Hansen and Marzouk (1965: 78) estimated that during the initial phase of land reform (1952–60), net value added productivity per feddan increased in real terms by 30 per cent and per unit of agricultural labour force by 21 per cent (consisting of 11 per cent value added productivity and 10 per cent accrued from the transfer of value added from absentee owners excluded from the labour force, to the active owners and tenants actually cultivating the land).

The variation between land productivity in the reformed and non-reformed sectors was confirmed in a sample survey conducted in 1973 by the author in three reformed areas located in two Provinces in the Delta.[30] The sample covered 611 households and compared their 1973 social conditions with the original data collected in 1953/4 at the time of land reform implementation. The average yield per feddan (acre) in the sampled areas and in the total agricultural sector in 1973 are as follows.

	Inshas	*Itay Al-barood*	*Gabaris*	*National average*
Cotton (Kintar)	5.5	6.0	6.8	4.6
Wheat (Ardab)	11.0	9.4	9.9	9.8
Maize (Ardab)	10.0	10.8	10.9	10.0
Rice (Ton)	2.4	2.2	2.5	2.3

Cotton yields per feddan were higher in these sampled areas, than the land productivity of other crops which were around the national mean. There was a rise (over 20 years) in household size of new owners from 6 to 8.9 persons, while their land remained constant. However, thanks to the rise in their livestock assets and in areas cultivated by vegetable, fruits and clover (*barseem*), *per capita* gross value of output has increased. We do not know how the household gross income was estimated in 1953/4, when the beneficiaries were allotted ownerships. However, the case of Gabaris is given in Table 6.10 to illustrate the profile of change between 1953 and 1973.

Table 6.10 **Changes in asset ownership and** *per capita* **income in a land reform area Gabaris, Egypt, 1953–73**

	1953/4	*1973*	*Change %*
Number of new owners' households sampled	110	110	—
Number of persons	690	981	+42
Average size of household	6.2	8.9	+44
Land per person (feddan)	0.45	0.31	−31
Livestock heads per household	1.0	2.6	+160
Estimated average gross income per household (pounds, current prices)	73	515*	+605
Per capita real gross income (adjusted by consumer price index for food 1953 = 100)	12.5	22.7†	+816.6

Note: * The share of value added by livestock products is 41 per cent.
        † The consumer price index was 244 in 1973.
Source: Calculated from a sample of 110 new owners (random at 5 per cent) conducted by the author in 1973 in collaboration with the Egyptian Land Reform Authority (see Note 30).

The significant share of livestock products in household aggregate income was also confirmed in the other two sampled areas. It was even higher (42–44 per cent) in Inshas (Al-gosak, Ghafaria and Beni-Saleh villages). Another non-crop source of income is from non-agricultural employment which contributed 20 per cent, 28 per cent, and 24 per cent in these three villages respectively. In fact, hiring-in labour was uniformly found in the sampled area for three possible reasons:

(a) the average age of heads of households has increased (over 60 years of age in 38.5 per cent of the sample households);
(b) substitution of family labour reduced by increasing recruitment of young men for armed service: and
(c) an increasing number of widowed female heads of household.

On average family labour accounts for 45 per cent of total labour inputs in cotton and 70 per cent in rice production, with hiring-in at its highest during the peak season of cotton picking and cutting, and rice planting and transplanting. (It was found that ploughing was fully mechanised. No hiring was recorded in the case of clover (*barseem*), maize and wheat.

In sum, the evidence presented suggests that:

(a) beneficiaries of land reform with small units of land (2.4–2.8 acres) all hire-in labour during the peak seasons;
(b) the share of crop value in gross household income is diminishing while that of livestock ownership and non-agricultural activities is significantly increasing; and
(c) sampled areas show that not every land reform area has higher yields than the rest of the agricultural sector.

Distribution of income and alleviation of poverty. Data given in Table 6.8 show a substantial reduction in land concentration in terms of ownership and holdings' distribution. This is reflected in the sharp fall in the Gini Coefficient between 1951 and 1965, a reduction primarily resulting from the set of land reform laws listed in Table 6.7. Greater equality in the distribution of rural income and consumption was associated with the re-distribution of land. Once enforced, instituted rent control had an even greater impact as it benefited all tenant cultivators who in the 1961 Census were estimated at nearly one million holders including sharecroppers. Costly and substantial food price subsidies providing an annual average gain of E£25 on average per person did, however, reinforce the effects on income.[31] The close association between redistribution of land and greater equality in the distribution of income and consumption is shown by the sharp decline in the Gini Coefficient from 0.858 in 1949/50 to 0.370 in 1958/9, and to 0.270 in 1964/5. (The first was our estimate and the latter is Adams' (1985).) But the official family income/ expenditure survey carried out in 1974/5, the ILO Rural Poverty Survey in 1977, and the IFPRI survey in 1982 show a rise in inequality since 1965. These different estimates are best shown together:

	1949/50	1958/9	1964/5	1974/5	1977	1981/2
Gini Coefficient of inequality in income/expenditure distribution in rural areas	0.858	0.370	0.270	0.348	0.393	0.337

The low degree of inequality realised by 1964/5, has, however, worsened particularly since 1975. This does not mean that the State and political leadership in Egypt have reversed their commitment to land reform or that the established size ceilings on private ownership are no longer enforced. Nor does it mean that government policy to control the organisation of agricultural production and the terms of trade has fundamentally changed. Some explanations can be offered in conjunction with the changes in the rural labour market and the composition of asset ownership since mid-1970.

Until Nasser's death in 1970, the land reform policy choice was accompanied by tight governmental control of the land market, agricultural prices, food subsidies and the planning of the entire economy. Around 1975, President Sadat's *Infitah* (opening or liberalisation of economic activities) policy relaxed this control and unintentionally brought into force a chain of 'disequalising' factors. Two forms of change can be cited. The first is the change in the profile of the rural labour market which arose from the pro-emigration policy and dramatic changes in the international labour market within the Middle East. These changes induced landless workers and many skilled members of rural households to seek higher earnings in the neighbouring Arab countries where the demand for labour was rapidly rising following the oil boom in 1973/4.[32] As observed by the author in his own village, and documented in the debate on the subject, some of the sizable remittances (reaching a total of US$3.9 billion in 1984) were chanelled into the land market. These combined with the quasi-investments in the purchase of land from domestic profits from non-agricultural activities, thus inflating the prices of the highly inelastic supply of land. Consequently, agricultural land prices rocketed, reaching about E£5,000 per feddan or US$6,000 per acre in 1984 (in contrast to E£800 for one feddan in 1975).

In addition, there has been a trend towards non-land asset ownership through the purchase of livestock and tractors for hiring out.[33] It is revealing to note from the field study of Hopkins *et al.* in 1982 that a few landless workers purchased tractors and irrigation pumps from their remittances as profitable investments through hiring-out (Hopkins *et al.*, 1982: 189). Commander reports from the findings of his 1984 survey of three villages that a household head owning less than one feddan purchased a tractor and a thresher largely through remittances:

> the hire charges amounted to around 15–20 Pounds *per day*. The result was not only a highly expanded aggregate gross income but also a drastically modified composition of household income. Hire income was around twelve times greater than the household income from non-agricultural wage work and livestock sales, the only other sources of income. (Commander and Hadhoud, 1986)

Ownership of non-land productive assets such as farm machinery (mainly tractors and irrigation pumps) has expanded on a large scale. Between 1973 and 1983, the tractor stock in farming doubled, while a rental market for leasing farm machinery flourished particularly for ploughing, irrigation and pest control. Government policy to expedite mechanisation of agriculture induced this new market. Another contributing factor was the sudden upward shift in agricultural wages since 1960 which increased labour costs by 58 per cent for cotton and 39 per cent for rice as a proportion of total costs of production (Commander and Hadhoud, 1986: Tables 8.14 and 9.3).

An important factor contributing to diminishing equality between 1965 and 1982 lies in the adverse effect of land transactions among landholding groups whereby owners in the size group of 5–20 acres (2–8 ha) purchased land from those owners of 5 acres and less. We have already noted this tendency in size distribution of land during the period 1964 to 1984 as shown in Table 6.8 (see Chapter 5, note 17). The studies of Zaytoun (1982) and Commander (1986: Table 8.24), showed that the holders in the size group of 5–10 feddans were the highest gainers in the shares of gross income between 1977 and 1984. The differential is attributed to investment in enterprises such as raising poultry, animal husbandry for meat production and growing higher value crops such as vegetables and fruit. These enterprises are not subject to the government-controlled pricing system. Consequently, evasion of planned and low-priced crop allocation increased and fines were relaxed. Government control over rent and land transaction also diminished.

Thus, factor markets and the structure of asset ownership have changed since 1974/5. The rise in agricultural wages in real terms in combination with non-land asset ownership by low-income groups have served as equalising factors. They may explain the decline in inequality from a Gini Coefficient of 0.393 in 1977 to 0.337 in 1982, still higher than the 1965 level of 0.270.

The alleviation of rural poverty 1950–82

The alleviation of poverty can be judged from the officially conducted Family Budget Surveys since 1958/9, ILO Survey of 1977 and the IFPRI Budget Survey of 1982. They all point in the positive direction of a substantial improvement in nutritional level and a reduction in the incidence of poverty. The results of the Fifth World Food Survey (FAO, 1985) confirm this positive change. Although the survey refers to the national level, its results are indicative. The average daily calorie supply per person grew by 2.2 per cent per annum from 2,561 in 1969–71 to 3,178 in 1979–81. These improvements are reflected in the 50 per cent increase in life expectancy between 1950 and 1980.

The estimates of the rural population falling below the poverty line corresponding to the successive years 1949/50 to 1982 show a proportionate decline from 56.1 per cent to 17.8 per cent during this period. The numbers of the poor have also diminished from 7.7 million to 4.2 million despite the rise in the average annual rate of population growth from 2.2 per cent to 2.8 per cent during this period. Although these are estimates based on arbitrarily fixed poverty lines and calculated average rural household size, they are presented together in Table 6.11.[34]

With the exception of 1974/5, the estimates show a downward trend in poverty incidence between 1950 and 1982. Sen's index is more sensitive to changes because it combines measurements of the percentage of people falling below poverty lines, the gap between their average income/expenditure and the poverty line, and the Gini Coefficient of the distribution of income (or expenditure) among the poor. The latter two measures may explain the rise in the index in 1964/5 and its sharp fall in 1982 when all three components seem to have improved. In fact, Adams (1985: Table 3) indicates a narrowing of the poverty gap in constant prices from 32.5 in 1963 to 23.4 Egyptian Pounds in 1982.

Table 6.11 **Incidence of poverty in rural Egypt, 1949/50–1982**

	1949/50	1958/9	1964/5	1974/5	1982
Rural population ('000s)	13,710	15,968	17,754	20,500	23,760
Percentage of rural poor	56.1	27.4	23.8	28.0	17.8
Number of rural poor ('000s)	7,691	4,468	4,225	5,740	4,229
Sen's Index of Poverty	—	0.079	0.178	—	0.061

Note: For the meaning of Sen's index, see Chapter 3, p. 92 and Amartya Sen, *Poverty and Famines, An Essay on Entitlement and Deprivation*, Clarendon Press, Oxford, 1981, Chapter 3 and Appendix C. The index for these years was calculated by Adams, see below.

Source: 1949/50, El-Ghonemy, see Note 17 of this chapter on the data base; 1958/9, 1964/5, and 1982, Richard Adams, JR., 'Development and structural change in rural Egypt 1952-1982', *World Development*, Vol. 13, No. 6, June 1985; 705-23, Table 1 for poverty estimates and Table 3 for Sen's index; 1974/75, Samir Radwan and Eddy Lee, 'The State and agrarian change: a case study of Egypt, 1952-1977', in *Agrarian Systems and Rural Development*, Dharam Gai *et al*, (ed) The Macmillan Press, London, 1979, Table 5.3

This fall in rural poverty presents a paradox in the face of:

(a) the limited scope of land reform in terms of the scale of the redistribution of land, other assets and incomes;
(b) the relative neglect of agriculture since 1965 in terms of its share in current public expenditure and investment as well as the unfavourable terms of trade indicated earlier in Chapter 1, p. 38;
(c) the slow growth of agricultural output at the average annual rate of 2.7 per cent and the fall of physical food production *per capita*

from 205.4 kg in 1948 to 1952, to 185.7 kg in 1978 to 1982; and, related to this,

(d) the failure of food production to match the population growth.

This failure resulted in a disturbing decline in food production per person which has led to a 120 per cent rise in food imports and reliance on substantial food aid between 1974 and 1984 (FAO Production Yearbook and World Bank, World Development Report, 1986, indicators).

Why then, has the incidence of poverty steadily declined? Apart from the initial but dramatic decline after land reform, there is a complex of dynamic factors lying outside the domain of land reform (outlined above). They are centred around:

(a) the externally induced change in the profile of the rural labour market and the consequential rises in real wages in agriculture and in the income share from non-land asset ownership (particularly livestock and farm machinery for hiring out);

(b) post-1973 food subsidies substantial in their levels, and in their coverage of consumer goods which provided the poor with access to cheap food, fuel and clothing; and

(c) free education leading to expanded access to employment opportunities outside agriculture.

Landless workers, excluded from receiving land under the orbit of land reform, were able to substantially improve their standard of living following the post-1975 construction boom in urban Egypt. This boom was accelerated by concessional capital inflows from oil rich Arab states, as was a rapidly expanding labour market. These factors, exogenous to the stagnating agriculture attracted landless workers with higher returns for their labour outside agriculture. However, post-1975 events suggest that these exogenous forces are volatile and uncertain. The sharp fall in oil revenue of Arab states has reduced the demand for unskilled labour from Egypt by about 30 per cent in 1985/6. It is hardly possible to forget that Libya already expelled Egyptian workers and many are expected to return from Iraq following the war with Iran. These experiences suggest that the policy to sustain poverty alleviation via reliance on exogenous sources for labour absorption is subject to the volatile economic and political environment in the labour importing Arab states. In this light, it seems that the policy to expedite mechanisation of agriculture on the assumption of permanent scarcity of labour is short-sighted.

Therefore, raising productivity in Egyptian agriculture, accelerating land reclamation for its distribution to the landless, and expanding the domestic labour market through structural changes in the economy are necessary. The post-land reform use of the land market for speculative profits leading to polarisation of the distribution of holdings should be restrained. Higher effective rates of progressive land tax and ownership over 20 feddans to check further rise in this category should be considered. Established ceilings on land rent should be enforced. Otherwise inequality in rural income distribution is likely to widen and the problems of the landless fallaheen shall become more pressing in the coming decade.

The discussion now turns to a comparison of rural development profiles of Egypt and the other four countries just studied, with those of a sample of LDCs which implemented partial land reforms. Having focused on five specific countries over a long time frame, we are able to understand the political economy of land reform under the immensely varying circumstances of each country. We now have a better idea of land reform's origin, and its relevance to pre-reform land tenure problems. We also understand its path in production organisation and how it has interacted with different characteristics of each economy in the process of poverty reduction. In the next chapter we compare the differing pace of poverty reduction under complete and partial land reforms.

Notes

1   Any attempt to make a typology of land reform policy is controversial and overly rigid. There have been several attempts. For instance, Voelkner and French (1970) developed an analytical model encompassing all factors of social, political and economic change and development They used 31 items for identifying the historical phases of implementation. Each phase is related to the development stage reached by the country concerned. But their definition of land reform is very broad, and fits into the ambiguous term 'agrarian reform' explained in Chapter Three. Their work is useful methodology for a system analysis of total agricultural development. On the other hand, de Janvry (1981) categorises land reform policies according to the degree of change made in production and class relations. His broad classification of initial land reforms falls under semi-feudal, capitalist and social modes of production. According to this typology, de Janvry classifies 33 land reforms in 20 countries.

2   We measure the characteristics of this tendency in terms of the inequality index of Gini Coefficient of land and income or expenditure distribution illustrated by the Lorenz Curve. If a tendency towards increased inequality in rural areas is evident, we attempt to identify the conditions which mark its turning point.

3   Most statistics used in the pre-reform period are taken from this comprehensive volume. It contains results of Chinese scholars' research work in different provinces on subjects concerning the distribution of landed property, farm management, agricultural marketing and credit,

and rural handicrafts supplementing the peasants' incomes from the land. The contents are reviewed in an introductory chapter by R.H. Towney, Professor of Economic History, London School of Economics, who underlined that any realistic study of modern China must start from the question of land tenure. Writing in 1938, he stated that the writing of the Chinese scholars points to the fact that 'rural society in China has reached a crisis' (Institute of Pacific Relations, 1939: xvii).

4 For a detailed study of why population growth is controlled, the Single Child Family Plan and its relation to food and social cost of raising children, see Saith (1984).

5 This was based on a study prepared for 1977, 1978, 1979, and 1981 by the Commune Management Bureau of the Chinese Ministry of Agriculture. Chronic poverty is defined as *per capita* distributed collective income averaging less than 50 *yuan* in each of the three years, 1977 to 1979. The results by localities are analysed by Lardy (1983: Chapter 4, 'Living standards and the distribution of income'). He indicated that poverty, for reasons explained, is concentrated in the provinces of Kansu, Henan, Yunnan and Kweichow. The number of counties with chronic poverty declined from 221 in 1979 to 87 counties in 1981. Lardy argues that the Ministry's study underestimates poverty among teams *within* counties. The estimate of 60 per cent poverty before the reforms in the late 1940s is calculated from data for 'poor peasants' in the Chinese studies in Institute of Pacific Relations (1939). All cited estimates on rural poverty incidence in China are approximate, showing only the order of magnitude.

6 An important source of widespread employment and earnings has been the expanded network of small-scale industries in all rural areas. In these enterprises, women, have the same entitlements as men, the equipment is simple, the level of technology is low and the intensity of labour is high. (The concern for maximum utilisation of labour has probably been behind the limited scale of the mechanisation-based State farms to only 4 per cent of total cultivated land).

7 Farmers relied on organic fertilisers of animal origin including dried fish and bone dust as well as fertilisers of plant origin such as bean cakes, oil cakes and rice bran. Green manures were also used: clover, alfalfa, vetch and beans. The use of chemical fertilisers which started in the 1920s reached only 20–30 kilogrammes per hectare in the 1930s and, according to Hoon Lee, were very costly to the tenants who had to get an advance loan from their landlords to be paid at harvest time but at the high interest rate of 50 per cent (Lee, 1936: 214–15).

8 The USAID data for 1945 cited in Table 6.4 refer to size distribution of units as 'management scale' which can be interpreted as operational holdings. Eddy Lee says, 'Thus the main thrust of the land reform was the replacement of tenancy by owner cultivator and not a radical shift in the size distribution of production units (holdings). 60% of all cultivated land was tenant farmed in 1945 and at least 50% of farm

households are pure tenants' (Lee, 1979: 25, 26), (see also Table 6.4).

9 Saemaul Undong meaning new community movement represents a significant feature of rural development in South Korea. It started in 1971, and is based on voluntary participation of local rural people to create small irrigation schemes for rice cultivation. It later developed into establishing small industries, rural electrification, spread of high yielding varieties, improvement of rural housing and providing safe drinking water. In addition, it trained young farmers, consolidated fragmented holdings, and constructed rural roads. This movement gained strength in the 1970s and was instrumental in the relocation of industries in rural areas. On average the funds used were made up of 70 per cent contributions from rural people, and 30 per cent from the central government.

10 The average income in monetary terms was deflated by using an income-group specific index based on consumption weights. Eddy Lee examined the data of the Farm Households Income Surveys conducted by the Korean Ministry of Agriculture and compared the differential changes by size of holding. Average income of holders in the size group of less than one hectare (where most land reform beneficiaries lie) rose between 1963 and 1975 by 54 per cent while that of more than 2 ha increased by 47 per cent. Agricultural wages in real terms rose from 167 *won* per day in 1963 to 237 *won* in 1975, a steady rise of 46 per cent in 12 years at an average annual rate of 4 per cent. (See Lee, 1979: Tables 2.4 and 2.6.)

11 Annual net outmigration from farm households rose from an average of 243,000 persons per year during 1960 to 1966, to 568,000 persons per year during 1966 to 1970. The rates of female migrants were higher than male migrants in 1966 to 1970. Over half of the total migrants were between age 15 and 30. This fast movement resulted in a decline in the farm working-age population in proportion and in absolute numbers. (See Chapter 12, 'Off-farm migration' in Ban *et al.*, 1980.)

12 See the interesting discussion on the implications of the fourth and fifth five-year development plans in the 1980s for income distribution and social development in: (a) Szal (1984: 361); Szal concluded that:'Income distribution appears to have deteriorated in the 1970s and there are indications that key factors may cause the deterioration to continue'; (b) Kim and Yun (1988: 80, 81). They state that: 'According to the 1986 Economic White Paper by the Economic Planning Board, the overall distribution of income improved during 1965 to 1970 due to the employment creation through labour-intensive projects for export-led growth, and deteriorated rapidly during 1970 to 1976 because of large capital-intensive projects and the impact of severe inflation'. With regard to the 1980s, they say: 'In the wake of Korea's export-led high-growth development strategy serious social problems including unfair economic opportunities, income disparities between regions and among sectors, and the lack of provisons for the basic needs of the poor have arisen.'

13 These projects were developed in State land in Dujaila, Sinjar, Hawija,

Latifiya, Mussayeb and Makhmur. The planned area for redistribution was 2,126,580 *donums* but the area *actually* distributed was 232,960 *donums* according to Hassan Mohamad Ali, the Chairman of Land Development Committee who accompanied the author for a study visit to Latifeya and Mussayeb during 1955/6. The author also visited the Dujaila scheme with Dr Burnell West who was working as the FAO soil expert in Iraq.. It was noted that: (a) salinity had increased due to over-irrigation without adequate drainage, and it had forced land out of production in many parts; (b) different specialised ministries and UN experts were involved in these projects but without co-ordination between the settlers' needs and the work of national and international technicians; (c) about one quarter of the settlers were former civil servants having no experience in farming; and (d) the approach in planning and implementation was an engineering and not a rural development approach. During his visit, the author was preparing a study on land tenure and settlement for FAO Regional Symposium on Land Problems in the Middle East, held in October-November, 1955 at Salahuddeen near Irbil north of Iraq.

14 During his 1964 visit, the author was given conflicting statistics on land already expropriated, and land subject to requisition by the Ministry of Agrarian Reform. The figures on the latter ranged from 6.3 to 10 million *donums*. It seems that the difference was due to whether the areas of land tenure categories of miri *lazma*, miri *sirf*, as well as the uncultivable land, were included or excluded. With regard to compensation payments, the land reform law of May 1970 specifies compensation payments in the case of requisitioned, but not confiscated, land. The affected owner is entitled to payments for the value of trees, installations, pumps and other agricultural machinery. The amount of accumulated debts against the owner is deducted from compensation payments. The rates of payments for the requisitioned land vary from 20 Iraqi *Dinars* per *donum* for irrigated land (rice), to 1.5 *Dinars* for low rainfall areas. The payment was to be made in government bonds under the 1958 law, and was changed to cash in the 1970 law. Even under the former, the government paid in 1964 and 1965 a lump sum not exceeding 10,000 *Dinars* to each affected owner as an indication of goodwill and in order to pacify the angry landlords who were not paid anything since their properties were requisitioned against compensation.

15 The author was invited twice by two Ministers of Agrarian Reform: Dr Abdul-Saheb Alwan in 1964, and Dr Ahmad Al-Dujaili in 1967 for advice on specific issues in the course of land reform implementation. He also visited Iraq in 1975 to study the implications of the second land reform law of 1970.

16 When Colonel Abdul Karim Al-Qassim, the leader of the July 1958 Revolution proclaimed land reform on 30 September 1958, he stated: 'We have found that agrarian reform is the foundation of social reform which our great nation is historically entitled to . . . the law will do away with feudalism forever and liberate the fellaheen.'

Similarly, in announcing the 1970 Law on 21 May 1979, Izzat Al-Douri member of the Central Committee of the Baath party and minister of Agrarian Reform stated the aim as follows: 'Liberating the hard toiling masses, notably the peasants and workers from all the forms of exploitation and oppression . . . exterminate the corrupt feudal system' (The Agrarian Reform Law, Ministry of Information, 1970: 4–6).

17 Some of these conditions have already been discussed, but it is useful, for the sake of comparison to consider more of the specifics: the sheikhs' share of the gross harvest ranged from 50 per cent in the northern rain-fed land, to two-thirds in flow-irrigated areas (five-sevenths if land was pump-irrigated). From their tiny share, the tenants paid about 25 per cent, some as the Istihqaq tax to government, and some levied for the upkeep of the canals and contribution towards the social obligations of the sheikhs. In her study of land tenure in Iraq in 1948, Warriner estimated that the 'sheikh' and the 'sirkal' together took up to 80 per cent of the crop, leaving the cultivator some 20–30 per cent (p.107). They were basically rentiers of land and sellers of pump-irrigation water in addition to being the suppliers of credit in a form of wheat and barley in advance of the harvest. 'The fellah is not as a rule able to repay the loans from the sale of produce, and so gets deeper and deeper into debt to the landowner and the sirkal. Thus the former tribesman of Iraq has been reduced to the position of a serf-tenant, who is entangled in crushing indebtedness, and so is tied to the holding which he cultivates' (Warriner, 1948: 115).

18 Landless and share-croppers are estimated at 73 per cent of total agricultural households in 1952 and 67 per cent in 1958 from results of the 1957 population census and agricultural censuses of 1952 and 1958.

19 This slight increase in inequality between 1971/2 and 1979 calls for some explanation. One is the rise in incomes of agricultural households whose holdings are adjacent to towns benefit directly from producing dairy products, vegetable and fruits with higher value than the traditional cereal crops grown by most of the farmers (Alwan, 1985: 57). This was evident from the 1971 census of agriculture data on land use in holding by localities where farmers near cities grow, on average, 30 per cent cereals and the rest is labour intensive fruits, vegetables and livestock production. The data analysed by Bakir (1984) provide another explanation: the rise in the share of the top 20 per cent in the size distribution of expenditure from 28.4 to 30.6 per cent of the total expenditure of rural households between 1971–2, and 1979. This is probably due to an increase in their incomes from expanded cultivation of high value cash crops. Another possible explanation is the unequal distribution of marketable surplus grain among farm households due to substantial improvement in the terms of trade for the agricultural sector by which the larger landowners benefited more.

20 See: 'Food Consumption Tables for Use in the Middle East', FAO, 1970: 'Recommendations of FAO/WHO *ad hoc* Expert Committee' 1973; and the *Fourth World Food Survey*, FAO, Rome 1977. In these

documents the conversion is made on the basis that 315 calories equal 100 grams of wheat.

21 The sub-sample data of the 1972 and 1976 household surveys analysed by Bakir (1979) include a 'low income' group in rural areas. Its average annual *per capita* expenditure in 1976 was 57.2 per cent Iraqi Dinar. Assuming that the expenditure of this group is almost equal to their incomes, their average expenditure amounts to only 15 per cent of the national average *income* (389 Dinars at 1975 prices estimated by the Ministry of Planning). The low income group is the only classification in rural areas which was at high risk of undernourishment. The nearest group is the rural south, and received on average exactly the required calorie-intake, which places them at risk of under-nutrition. The rural south was not categorised by income or expenditure level into low, medium or high. These two groups, low income and rural south were the only ones whose average, annual *per capita* expenditure fell in real terms between 1972 and 1976; the former by 4.6 per cent from 40.2 to 40.1 Dinars, and the latter by 8.7 per cent from 62.7 to 58.8 Dinars (calculated from Bakir, 1979: Tables C12, C23, C28, and 5.23). On the rural south, Bakir says: 'This region has been the most unfortunate region in Iraq as far as the level of living is concerned, hence it has been the prime source of rural migrants . . . this is the only regional group to show a decline in level of living' (p. 176). This decline is manifested in deterioration of 13 out of 24 indicators between 1972 and 1976. Other characteristics of the identified rural poor are: (a) low productivity reflected in their low *per capita* income and expenditure; (b) higher share of food expenditure (67 per cent) in total *per capita* expenditure; (c) higher illiteracy rate (86 per cent) than average rate; and (d) poor housing and sanitation conditions (75 per cent mud houses with only 2 per cent of them having safe drinking water in 1976).

22 The author in his capacity as land tenure specialist with the United Nations FAO was a participant and co-ordinator of an international team whose visit was requested by the Cuban Authority. The statement and observations made here were based on two months (July, August, 1959) survey of the agrarian system, providing advice on the economic basis for fixing the minimum units for allotment to the beneficiaries, and views on the implementation capability to the National Institute for Agrarian Reform (INRA). The team consisted of Professor V.M. Dandekar, Gokhale Institute of Politics and Economics, Poona, India; Prof. Marco Antonio Duran, Head of Agricultural Economics Department of the National Agricultural College at Chapingo, Mexico. See, *Report of the Regional Land Reform Team for Latin America*, FAO, Rome, 1961, Expanded Programme of Technical Assistance, No. 1388.

23 Sugar cane harvest declined in this early phase of Cuban reform primarily due to organisational and management shortcomings. It fell from 55.8 million tons in 1960/1 to 50.6 million tons in 1965. Since then it started rising and reached 82.9 million tons in 1970. The management shortcomings are frankly described by Ernesto Ché Guevara (1964). See also, Dumont, 1964; 42–59.

24 This estimate is based on a minimum household net income of 35 Egyptian
Pounds in 1949/50. A breakdown of the data base is as follows:

	No. of poor households
Hired agricultural workers over 15 years of age calculated from 1947 Population Census and 1949/50 Agricultural Census:	1,060,150

(Annual earning per working person was on average
13–15 Egyptian Pounds based on: (a) studies carried
out by the author during his work in the Fellah
Department, Ministry of Social Affairs; and (b) the
rural survey of 2,682 landless households. This latter
study was carried out by the field staff of the
Department in 1950 under the guidance of Dr Zelenka
and Dr Cassidy from ILO, Geneva. The author worked
as their research assistant. The purpose was to estimate
the households whose earnings were below the
established minimum income of 35 Egyptian Pounds for
social security purposes. See El-Ghonemy (1953: 72–3).)

Share Croppers (Agricultural Census of 1950):	26,900
Holders of less than one feddan (1950 Agricultural Census):	214,300

(Annual average net-value added per feddan was
between E£8 and E£15 based on a study by the
Ministry of Agriculture on *National Income from
Agriculture 1946–47*, Cairo, Table 11, p. 41 (Arabic).)

Pure tenant-cultivators of 1–2 feddans:	150,000

(Calculated from 1950 Agricultural Census. The
income of tenants in 1947–50 was estimated by the
author in El-Ghonemy (1953: 57–9).)

Family heads of nomadic population camping around villages estimated by the author based on observations in the Districts of Delingat, Abu-Hommos and Kom Hamada in Bohera Province in 1949:	30,000
Peddlers in villages, small towns and Ezbas (big farms):	25,000
Disabled heads of rural households 0.2% (a rate used in the population Census and was close to the rate found in the 1950 study cited above):	30,140
Total estimated heads of poor households:	1,537,090
Number of poor persons (using uniform average 5 per family):	7,685,450
Rural population in 1950 (based on 1947 Population Census and Average Annual rates of growth between 1947 and 1960 Censuses):	13,710,000
Estimated number of rural poor as percentage of rural population:	56.1

25 Several incidents of the peasants' unrest occurred during 1947–1951, including the following examples.

In 1946 about one thousand tenants and farm workers attacked and ruined the office of Kom Ombo, a Foreign-owned plantation in Asswan Province.

In 1947, the farmers in Behoot and Shoha, Dekahlia Province revolted against their absentee landlords as a complaint against raising the already high rents and the ill-treatment by the head manager. Similar outbreaks were reported in Shubra Ris, Gharbia Province and the Sheikh Fadl sugar cane plantation in Menya Province.

In all these instances, the peasants acted spontaneously and without instigation of an organised movement. As observed by the author in Sheikh Fadl uprising, the government authorities treated them as a case of civil disturbance, without giving any consideration to the social roots or the fellaheen's economic hardships.

A number of proposals were made by intellectuals and social reformers in an attempt to solve the problems. First there was a proposal by Gam'eyat Al-Nahda El-Qawmia for fixing a ceiling on rent, a floor on daily wages, and a size ceiling on private land ownership of 100 feddans (acres). The proposal was submitted in February 1948 to the Senate House of the Parliament (Maglis Al-Sheyoukh) with a note saying: 'There is an urgent need to ameliorate the living conditions of the Fellaheen by abolishing exploitative relationships before the conditions get worse and it will be inevitably dangerous and could not be avoided.' *A Proposed Agrarian Reform*, Misr Press, 1948: 13. Second, The Third Conference of the Agricultural Colleges' graduates held in Cairo, 1949 made this recommendation; 'The Conference recommends that the Government take measures to establish a maximum limit for individual land ownership and to prohibit the fragmentation of small holding into less than 3 feddans.' *The Proceedings of the 3rd Agricultural Conference*, Cairo, 20 March – 8 April 1949, recommendation No. 13, Madkoor Press, 1949: 314 (Arabic). Third, The First Annual Conference of the Egyptian Agricultural Economic Association held in Cairo in March 1952 (four months before the July 1952 Revolution) recommended 'the issuance of a law to regulate the landlord-tenant production relations and to restrict the land to those who cultivate it', 'The major socio-economic problems of rural Egypt', in *The Proceedings of the Conference*, El Illoom Press, 24–28 March 1952. Fourth, The Fellah Society (Gam'eyet Al Fallah) in its meeting of June 1952 (one month before the Army revolution) issued a statement which was presented to the Prime Minister by its President Dr Ahmad Hussein saying: 'Urgent measures need to be taken promptly. The economic conditions of the fellaheen are worsening. Being the major section of the population, their very low incomes have resulted in high poverty, low purchasing power, low taxing capacity and stagnant agriculture,' El Misry daily paper, 29 June 1952: 5 (Arabic). Dr Hussein, when he was a cabinet member in 1950, presented a draft legislation to secure the peasants' basic needs. But as he stated: 'I was fought in the Parliament until I was so disgusted that I resigned', an address delivered in Washington, DC, at the meeting of the American Friends of the Middle East, published by the Egyptian Embassy in Washington, DC, 25 June 1953.

26 A separate administration was set up, free of the government rules and procedures and headed by a very able agricultural expert Mr Sayed Marei. He selected the best managers of the former Royal estates to administer the implementation of land reform laws at the field level. This administration was supported by a tough member of the Revolutionary Council, Gamal Salem who was given full authority to take necessary action across the machinery of the Egyptian government. At the time of implementing the reform, Egypt had a complete set of land title records and cadastral maps as well as a sufficient number of university graduates in agriculture, veterinary science and irrigation engineering. These technicians were so sufficient in number that a university graduate was assigned, on average, to 500 feddans (acres) in land reform areas and 1,500 feddans in the rest. The implementation of 1952 law was scheduled to be completed by 1958. In order to ensure meeting the targets, the President of Egypt had to distribute the landed property deeds in person to the new owners on the occasion of the anniversary of the revolution, 23 July of each year starting in 1953. See the story of implementing land reform as written by Mr Marei in 'Agrarian Reform in Egypt', *The International Labour Review*, Vol. LXIX, No. 2, February 1954, ILO, Geneva.

27 This state was created by the affected landlords' practice of sub-dividing part of their large land-ownerships into units of 10–50 acres before expropriation. Article 4 of the Land Reform Law of 1952 (amended in 1953) allowed the owners of 200 feddans and more to transfer part of the excess (area over 200 feddans) to his children (50 feddans per child) provided that the total does not exceed 100 feddans. This means each family retains 300 feddans legally. He or she was also allowed to distribute another part (by direct sale or legal deed) to tenants in 2–5 feddan units and to small owners whose ownership does not exceed 10 feddans. Through these private transactions many landlords were able to escape forced expropriation of land in excess of 300 feddans.

28 See chapter 1, p. 38 about the distorted pricing policy in Egyptian agriculture and its implications for the producers' losses and the consumers' gains.

29 These include: Marei (1957); Gadalla (1962); Warriner (1962); Saab (1967); El-Gabaly (1967); El-Ghonemy (1968); Abdel-Fadil (1975); Radwan (1977); and Hopkins (1987).

30 This survey was based on a 5 per cent random sample of the beneficiaries' households in the three land reform co-operative zones. The fieldwork was carried out in collaboration with Mrs Nabila Al-Hakim and Dr Mahmoud El-Sherif.

31 In Chapter 1, p. 38, we examined the effects of pricing policy including subsidies on the farmers as producers. In this note we show the effects on their incomes as consumers. Food subsidies have been a

significant feature of the government policy to support low income groups. Though beginning with an urban-bias, the benefits of low-cost food consumption have spread in rural areas through the network of co-operatives selling subsidised commodities particularly bread, wheat flour, sugar, tea, and edible fats and oil for cooking. The government allocation for food subsidies has dramatically increased with the population growth, from 0.3 per cent of total public expenditure in 1965/6 to 27 per cent in 1980/1 and from less than 0.1 per cent of GDP to 10 per cent in the same period. Subsidies on grain products alone amounted to an average of 15 Egyptian pounds per person per year in real terms. In addition, we estimate that about E£15 are gained per consumer per year from other commodities (cloth, fuel and transport). This average of E£30 represents nearly 20 per cent indirect increase in the real income of small farmers if they purchase the subsidised items (for a detailed discussion on the subject of food subsidies, see Taylor (1979) and von Braun and de Haen (1983).

32 It is unfortunate that despite the importance of this rural temporary emigration phenomenon, there is a scarcity of reliable data on the number, characteristics and net inflow of remittances earned by persons from rural Egypt working in Arab states. Most of the available information is either guesswork or a crude estimate. For example, there is a wide range of estimates of the total number of Egyptians working abroad from one to five million in 1980–4. The same applies to remittances. Official data of the Central Bank of Egypt underestimates the *actual* transfer of remittances entering Egypt every year. Because of the wide differential between the official exchange rate through bank transfer and the black market, about two thirds of the workers' remittances are transferred in cash and in kind outside the banking system. Official statistics tell us that remittances rose from 212 million pounds in 1975 to 3.3 billion in 1984. a sixteen-fold increase. Adams (1985) estimated that between 20 per cent and 40 per cent of total remittances have entered rural areas since 1975. The Ministry of Labour in Cairo estimated the landless workers (working in Arab states) at one million in 1986 (Al-Ahram, 30 June 1986: 3). The Department of Sociology, University of Menya, Upper Egypt studied the implications for farming of the reduction by 25 per cent of foreign workers by the Gulf countries in 1985 (after the fall in their oil revenues). It was estimated that in 1985 those who returned from Saudi Arabia alone were 160,000 workers. Dr Al-Gawhary, the head of the department reported that most of them did not return to the former status of hired agricultural worker. Instead, they were engaged in services and trade. He also pointed to the rise in child labour in agriculture which adversely affected their schooling and educational prospects (Al-Ahram, 17 June 1987: 3)

33 Despite the signals of a diminishing demand for labour in Arab states, the government policy backed by donor agencies continues to vigorously pursue mechanisation in agriculture as a substitute for the shortage of labour based on the belief that it is a permanent feature

of Egyptian agriculture. Since 1982, the policy choice is for accelerating mechanisation (Ministry of Agriculture, 'Egyptian Agricultural Mechanization Plan, 1982–1987'). Considering the size structure of holdings, ownership of farm machinery for use in private holdings is mostly concentrated in the size group of over 10 feddans. Ownership for hiring-out has emerged as a workable arrangement for use in small-holdings. Because of lack of maintenance and bureaucratic procedures in hiring tractors from co-operatives, *Gam'eya*, many small farmers resort to hiring from the private market. Given the current demand in the rental market, the financial return to capital invested in the purchase of a tractor is high.

34 In this Table, Radwan and Lee arrived at different estimates by using different sizes of household and income corresponding to a poverty line which differed from that used by Adams. Their estimates of the rural poor were 22.5 per cent (1958/9) and 17 per cent (1964/5). The three scholars used the same source of data, i.e., the results of the Egyptian Government Household Budget surveys for 1958/9, 1964/5 and 1974/5. We did not use Adams' estimate for 1974/5 at 60.7 per cent because we consider it an over-exaggeration as the poverty line was very high at 344.82 Egyptian pounds, which is almost the average expenditure per rural household in that year.

Chapter seven

The pace of poverty reduction: inter-country comparison

The purpose of this chapter is to explore the central question: given that the alleviation of poverty is a common objective in the process of rural development, are both the pace and extent of its reduction conditional upon land reform and its scale? If not, what other policy instruments can realise this objective, and under what agrarian conditions? To probe this principal question, first we compare the rural development records of the four countries whose complete land reforms were studied in Chapter 6 with a sample of ten countries which have implemented partial land reforms (including Egypt). In the latter group, we examine the implications of duality in resource use, production relations and income created by the division of reform and non-reform sectors under partial land reform. Subject to the availability of inter-temporal estimates, we then compare the speed and extent of poverty reduction in a sample of nine countries having variant rates of population growth. In examining the conditions in the initial and terminal years, we attempt to identify the types of policy instruments which differentiate the pace of reduction in the absolute numbers of the poor.

The analytical procedures

Temporal comparison between countries confronts conceptual and data problems as carefully argued by McGraham *et al.* (1985). Under our arbitrary classification of countries by relative scope of land reform and our choice of indicators this is especially true. But how is the comparison to be made? Because of the large number of interacting factors which require a series of comparable statistics going back 30–40 years, no statistical analysis of multiple regression is undertaken. Nor do we construct a single synthetic index of the quantitative information presented in Table 7.1, because this would conceal rather than reveal. Such a technique requires weighting the rural development indicators which is undesirable, unnecessary, controversial and problematic. This conclusion was reached by Hicks and Streeten (1979:

576–7) on the basis of their review of work using this method in social research.

Our analytic procedure is a combination of monographic treatment and inter-country quantitative comparison using available information. It observes variation in food productivity, nutrition, longevity and literacy over 25 years (1960–85) among a sample of 14 developing countries ranked by the degree of State intervention for restructuring private landed property. (The experience of five of these countries has already been presented.) We have used non-income indicators of the extent of public provision of command over food via secure landholding for small tenants, sharecroppers and hired agricultural workers. In abstract terms, these non-income indicators are a proxy for judging the social benefits of enhanced productive ability, and capability for participation. Although the data refer to national averages, they are comparable and useful considering that in most countries more than half of the population are rural.

To compare the variation in the pace of poverty reduction, we need to introduce the time factor and the demographic characteristics of each country. Estimates made at specific points in time are compared provided they are reliable and consistent in the criteria used for measurement. Consequently, we are restricted to comparing countries which meet these conditions. Admittedly, this approach offers a rather crude base for comparison. Nevertheless, we hope that this analytical approach will help to draw some broad lessons of interest to policy makers in LDCs with respect to rural development.

The variation in productivity and equity among CLR and PLR countries

We now compare the data in Table 7.1 between the two sampled groups of complete (CLR) and partial (PLR) reforms. With the exception of the food production performance in Iraq (as explained earlier), the data suggest that in broad terms the former group is a better performer than the latter (PLR). Throughout the period 1960–85, in China, Cuba and South Korea (where between 65 per cent and 100 per cent of agricultural land was subject to redistribution of holding rights) the performance has been notable in terms of agricultural labour productivity and *per capita* food production. Rates for China and South Korea have been consistently much higher than for Cuba and Iraq. In their early phase of land reform, Cuba experienced uncertainties with regard to the extent of curtailing the proportion of private holdings and the provision of material incentives. In Iraq, most redistributed expropriated land was unproductive in the early phase of the reforms. The group of ten PLR countries, on the other hand, did not maintain positive rates during the entire period.

253

Table 7.1 The scope of land reform and changes in productivity and other poverty characteristics in 14 selected developing countries, 1960–85

Sample countries in descending order by proportion of direct beneficiaries	Rural poverty incidence and year of estimate	Direct beneficiaries as % of total agri. hseholds (1)	Redist. privately owned land as % of total cultivable land (2)	Per capita agric. worker 1960–70	1971–80 (3)	1981–85	Food productivity per capita total population 1960–70	1971–80 (4)	1981–85	Ave. annual growth rate 1961–63 to 1979–80	As % of requirement 1960–63 (5)	As % of requirement 1985	Infant mortality 1985	1960–1985 % reduction (6)	Life expectancy 1985 In years	1960–85 % increase (7)	Illiteracy (male) % reduction 1960–85 (8)
Complete Land Reform																	
China (1948–52)	circ. 9.0 (1981)	100	100a	4.6	1.1	5.0	3.4	1.3	4.7	1.5	82	109	36	79	69	68	63
Cuba (1959, 62)	n.a.	100	95a	4.8	2.1	1.8	2.2	1.8	1.5	1.0	104	134	16	54	77	22c	89
South Korea (1945, 50)	9.8 (1980)	77	65	3.2	5.2	4.6	1.5	3.0	2.1	1.7	89	119	27	56	69	28c	80
Iraq (1958, 70)	circ. 17.0 (1976)	56	60	3.3	1.2	3.9	1.5	−2.3	−0.5	1.9	83	120	72	47	61	33	61
Partial Land Reform*																	
Mexico (1917, 34, 40)	34.0 (1982)	50	42	3.5	1.6	0.1	0.7	0.8	−1.3	0.9	109	134	50	36	67	18	63
Bolivia (1952)	n.a.	39	18	2.6	1.6	−1.1	1.2	0.1	−2.2	0.6	74	91	117	31	51	24	62
Peru (1963, 64, 69)	68.0 (1977)	28	40	0.9	−1.9	1.2	−0.5	−3.2	0.1	−0.4	95	90	95	42	59	26	70
Iran (1962, 66)	38.0 (1977)	23	22	3.0	2.6	0.3	0.6	1.3	−3.6	2.5	81	129	112	31	60	36	32
Sri Lanka (1972, 75)	26.0 (1981)	22	10	0.6	2.0	−0.5	0.6	4.2	−1.1	−0.3	96	112	36	49	70	13c	77
Algeria (1962, 70)	n.a.	22	6	4.4	2.3	4.2	−1.3	−1.9	1.5	3.6	75	116	81	49	66	28	60

Egypt (1952, 61, 69)	17.8 (1982)	10	14	2.1	0.4	1.2	0.6	−1.0	1.0	2.2	103	130	45	61	33	43
India (1953–79) b	50.7 (1979)	4	3	0.7	1.4	2.9	−0.3	0.7	2.4	0.3	93	96	45	56	30	41
Pakistan (1959, 72)	39.0 (1979)	3	4	2.8	1.0	1.4	1.6	0.7	−0.3	0.7	79	94	29	51	19	24

Notes: (a) Part of the land in the reformed sector is in State farms; 4 per cent in China and nearly 70 per cent in Cuba where about 5 per cent of land is still privately managed.

(b) Since the early 1960s, some States have passed laws fixing maximum size ceilings. For instance Kerala passed three laws, the last of which was in 1979.

(c) Percentages appear to be low because of the already high initial level in 1960.

* Years in parentheses refer to major land reform acts.

Sources: The source for the estimates of rural poverty is Appendix A.

Columns 1 and 2: These percentages do not include tenancy regulation and settlement schemes. *China, South Korea, Iraq, Egypt*, see text, *Cuba, Bolivia, India, Mexico,* Alain de Janvry, *The Agrarian Question and Reformism in Latin America,* Johns Hopkins University Press, 1981: Table 6.1 and 'The Role of Land Reform in Economic Development: Policies and Politics', Table 2 in *American Journal of Agricultural Economics,* Vol. 63, No. 2, May 1981. The percentage of Cuba's Land reformed sector is changed from 100 to 95 to reflect the privately owned farms below the ceiling. *Iran*; 'The Agrarian Question in Iran', by Homa Katouzi in *Agrarian Reform in Contemporary Developing Countries,* edited by Ajit Kuman Ghose, Croom Helm, 1983: Table 8.1. *Peru*; 'The Agrarian Reform in Peru' by Christobal Kay in Ghose. ed. *Ibid.* The percentage refer only to full beneficiaries, Table 5.10. *Sri Lanka*; The percentages do not include colonisation and plantations retained by the State, calculated from Ronald J. Herring, *Land to the Tiller,* Yale University Press, 1983: 138–52 and Shelton Wanasinghe, 'Formulation and Implementation of Land Reform in Sri Lanka' in *Land Reform: Some Asian Experiences,* edited by Inayatullah, APDACP Publications, Kuala Lumpur, Malaysia, 1980. *Algeria and Pakistan*: M. Riad El-Ghonemy, *Economic Growth, Income Distribution and Rural Poverty,* FAO, Rome, September 1984: 55–7. *Syria*: 'Alleviation of Rural Poverty Through Agrarian Reform and Rural Development in the Republic of Syria' by A.M. El-Zoobi, WCARRD Study No. 17, FAO. Rome, 1984.

Columns 3 and 4: calculated from *Production Yearbook* and *Country Tables,* several issues, FAO, Rome, Col. 3 refers to agricultural labour force and Col. 4 to total population. Both are based on index of production, 1979–81 = 100.

Column 5: The Fourth and Fifth World Food Survey, FAO, Rome, 1977 and 1985 respectively.

Columns 6, 7 and 8: Calculated from data given in *World Development Report, 1978 and 1987,* Indicators and *Statistics on Children in UNICEF Countries,* UNICEF, New York. May 1984.

Whereas the complete reform brings about an egalitarian agrarian structure, the partial reform divides the agrarian structure into two major sub-sectors: the created reform sector and the non-reform sector. The production and marketing implications of such duality start from the differential productive capacity of the land base in the reform sector as compared to the non-reform sector. Given the time and freedom to choose the land and capital equipment to retain, landlords often hold on to the best, while the expropriated portion is usually less productive. Furthermore, affected landlords keep substantial capital in proportion to the area left after expropriation. This has implications for the organisation of production and related technological change. Under such dualism, referred to as 'functional dualism' by de Janvry (1981), the employment effect of PLR is likely to be small as landless workers are often excluded, and new owners tend to rely on their family labour for cultivating their units. For their part, the effected landlords tend to operate their retained area with less hired labour particularly where absenteeism is prohibited or land is threatened by further expropriation.

In the post-reform process of rural development, the power structure behind policy formulation is likely to be determined by the residuum of partial land reform; i.e. the extent of both the land remaining as private property after curtailing the large estates and the economic activities of the landowners, traders and moneylenders. We have seen from the Egyptian experience how the residuum of landowners together with urban traders and land speculators continue to influence land transactions and related capital, thus polarising the rural economy. We shall also illustrate the implications of this duality in PLR for agricultural growth and income distribution in Mexico with special emphasis on the food producing peasants. It seems that PLR countries choose to limit the land reforms through granting generously high ceilings in the hopes of minimising damage to landlords and maintaining political support. In the marketing of crops and related pricing and credit supply, the control of mercantile interests is also relaxed. Although the economic conflicts of interest may appear to be less bitter than those before instituting the partial reforms, economically powerful members of rural communities continue to dominate local institutions and political organisations. This dominant role is likely to be manifested in the workings of the markets of land, labour and capital.

In developing human capital, the record presented in Table 7.1 shows that nutrition, life expectancy and literacy were not uniformly improved. The data do not lend themselves to a single generalisation. Given the variation in initial levels, some countries implementing partial land reform like Mexico, Sri Lanka and Algeria have performed as well as those with complete land reform. Sri Lanka (PLR) and Cuba (CLR) have dramatically reduced illiteracy and significantly raised life expectancy. The record suggests that despite a wide variation in natural endowment and *per capita* GNP, PLR countries directed a substantial share of income flow towards reducing illiteracy and infant mortality, providing safe drinking water and increasing life expectancy. Thus, both the quality and quantity of life in the countryside were improved. China remains superior in reducing infant mortality while Iran, Mexico, Egypt and Syria achieved higher rates of calorie supply *per capita* than the rest in the two groups. This comparison suggests that command over food is of primary concern to groups of both CLR and PLR.

To illustrate the implications of partial reforms for the dual organisation of production and equity in agriculture, we take a close look at Mexico, Bolivia and Peru, the three countries with the highest percentage of direct beneficiaries among PLR countries in our sample in Table 7.1. In this brief monographic treatment of three countries we do not follow a unified pattern. Instead, we emphasise the implications of duality for differential production growth in Mexico, and the institutional arrangements affecting productivity and marketed surplus in Bolivia. In Peru, we concentrate on exclusion of most of the poor and the resulting effects on income distribution and poverty reduction. Throughout we focus on the changes in food production.

Mexico, Bolivia and Peru

In these three Latin American countries, land reform policy has been a burning issue since early this century. It has been evoked by the semi-serf relations of forced labour within a socially semi-feudal agrarian system superimposed by the Spanish colonisers on the ethnic structure.[1] However, the instituted scale of land reforms and the resulting pattern of agricultural growth have fallen short of the expectations of the large indigenous population. Though the first task of their land reform laws was to abolish compulsory unpaid labour and land-grabbing and to restore and protect the Indios' property rights in land, these reforms have not benefited all. In a sense, these reforms have reinforced the duality in social structures and sources of agricultural growth. This is particularly true in Peru, where there is a marked differentiation in resource use and income between the indigenous and non-indigenous population, and among themselves.

The most unique feature of Mexico's land reform is that it has been a continual process since the first law of 1915, fixing neither a date for completion, nor a clearly fixed maximum limit on privately owned land. In the Land Reform Act of 1971, the ceiling was defined as 100 hectares per person (with exceptions up to 300 ha depending on the cropping system) of irrigated land, 200 hectares of rain-fed land and up to 50,000 hectares of arid pasture land. The traditional system of communal ownership and use of land was institutionalised by *ejidos* and *comuneros* for the indigenous population.[2] For their protection, their communal property is inalienable; it cannot be sold, mortgaged, or rented out.

In 1926 a special bank was set up to provide them credit. On average, each household received 2 and 5 hectares of irrigated land, and many did not pay for it. Thus the foundation of current duality and inequality was laid down by the established ratio of maximum to allocated irrigated land of around forty or fifty to one. According to the 1970 agricultural census, only 17 per cent of the *ejido* land was classified as cropped area (the remainder as undeveloped pasture and others). The effect on productivity of the dual system became obvious. During the period 1950–70, large privately owned farms realised a 147 per cent increase in productivity per hectare. Despite a lower quality of soil fertility, cropland in the reformed sector saw a 113 per cent increase in land productivity in the same period. Dovring (1970) found that this production gap between reform and non-reform sectors over the period 1940–60 was due partly to the differential increase in the proportion of cropped area. Between 1940 and 1960, this portion increased by 64 per cent in private holdings over 5 ha and by 27 per cent in the reformed sectors.

This feature of dualism can be explained by the regional distribution of public investment in irrigation. The data of agricultural censuses of 1950, 1960, and 1970 show that irrigation investment has been disproportionately allocated by the government with much larger shares in the States of Sonora, Sinaloa, and others in the north Pacific region where large commercial farmers in alliance with multinational corporations dominate. (The Mexican Constitution forbids foreigners to own agricultural land.) The data implies greater investment in high value cash crops, such as soya, oil seeds, fruits and sugar cane that are grown predominantly in the northern states. In the southern regions (Gulf-South, Peninsula and the Central Plateau), where *ejidos* and traditional Indian villages (*Comuneros*) are dominant, nearly 75 per cent of the cultivated land grows mostly beans and corn; two Mexican staples. During 1950–80 areas cultivated by food crops have increased by only 0.2 per cent per annum whereas the non-food crops have increased by 5 per cent (Yates, 1981: Table 3.5). There was a disparity in the use of technological advance as documented by both Yates and Dovring. Larger private farms used three times the chemical fertiliser per hectare, and twice the pesticides as did the *ejidos*. Yet, output per hectare is not correspondingly different between the reform and non-reform sectors.

Contrary to the popular belief that reduced food productivity necessarily follows redistribution, total and *per capita* food production grew rapidly in the 1950s and 1960s, despite the fact that the reform areas represented about 40 per cent of total cultivated land and the *Ejidotarios* almost half of the total agricultural households. The FAO index of food production (1952–6 = 100) shows this growth clearly (Table 7.2).

258

Table 7.2 **Index of food production in Mexico, 1956–68**

	Total food production	Per capita production
1956	116	109
1957	132	120
1958	142	125
1959	140	119
1960	145	119
1961	154	123
1962	158	122
1963	165	123
1964	175	126
1965	182	125
1966	186	125
1967	199	129
1968	206	129

Source: SOFA, 1970: Annex Table 6c

Even in the earlier period of land reform (1930–40), Dovring's study concludes that 'there is *no* evidence to show that the early land reform measures had any negative effect on production' (Dovring, 1970: 35). With the institution of the *ejido*, land reform's contribution to the indigenous population has been in its provision of an alternative to continued poverty or migration of the rural poor. Through intensified family labour and the *ejidos'* response to technological change via their application of high yield varieties of wheat and corn, they now have command over food, and through granting inalienable property rights, land reform has ensured permanent tenure security.

Gains similar to those of the Mexican rural economy have also been realised in varying degrees in Bolivia and Peru where partial land reforms left a residuum of 78 per cent and 60 per cent respectively of privately held agricultural land. The Bolivian and Peruvian reforms followed different paths in production organisation and institutional arrangements for property rights in land. Bolivia instituted privately owned individual holdings. Peru, however, chose collective ownership and use of land in most of the expropriated areas of cash crops and livestock ranches. Both reforms were swiftly implemented in response to long-standing demands of restitution of property rights by the dispossessed, destitute and exploited indigenous Indios and other landless peasants. The Peasants' Union – organised with the help of the mining workers' union – accelerated the reform implementation in Bolivia. After a period of two to three years of confusion and uncertainty, empirical evidence suggests that production, particularly that of food crops, actually increased.

At the macro-level, the FAO index used earlier for Mexico, indicates

259

satisfactory rates of annual growth of total and *per capita* food production in Bolivia during the ten-year period following the completion of implementation of the reform. While most of the food crops (barley, maize, potatoes, beans and cassava) were produced in the reformed sector, its production was able to feed the population whose growth rates rose from 2.4 per cent to 2.6 per cent between 1950 and 1970. During the decade following land reform, total food production grew at the annual rate of 3.6 per cent and *per capita* at 1.2 per cent (see Table 7.1). At the micro-level, Clark's (1968 and 1970) field study of 51 farms of the highland (Altiplano) and of the living and farming arrangements of 5,400 households before (1952), and after the reform (1966) reveals that 50 landlords had farms ranging from 355 to 9,408 hectares. They were absentee landlords, and lived in the capital city La Paz while their farms were operated by bonded labour, and managed by employed agents. Following proclamation of land reform, however, no institutional arrangements were made to take the place of those previously monopolised by the landlords in a highly controlled market network. Marketed products fluctuated because many beneficiaries refused to provide their labour to landlords in the early two years of land reform. But by 1966, production in 34 farms (of the 51 farms studied by Clark) increased following land redistribution[3] even though many affected landlords chose to retain the best land below the generous fixed ceiling of 800 hectares in Altiplano and 80 hectares in the fertile valleys. They also retained capitalised assets (machinery, cattle and trucks). Consequently, beneficiaries were decapitalised and granted less productive land in small units of 10–20 hectares in the rain-fed Altiplano, and 3–5 hectares in the valleys. Marketing arrangements for their products were not provided by government institutions. The beneficiaries made their own arrangements for transport with the help of the Peasant Union. De Janvry adds another disadvantage of the beneficiaries. 'All sources agree that the small holders, both within and outside the reform sector, have received virtually no production credit' (de Janvry, 1981: 215–16).

During my field visit to Cochabamba province in October 1959, it became clear that the 1953 revolutionary spirit of the reformers to distribute land swiftly was not matched by the readiness of State institutions to provide beneficiaries the essential complementary inputs. It seemed that the reformers wanted to avoid hurting landlords and at the same time, to satisfy as many peasants as possible along with their politically important Peasant Union. Accordingly, 18 per cent of total arable land was expropriated and redistributed in small units among a large section of the Andean Indian peasants representing 39 per cent of total agricultural households.

The revolutionary drive of the reformers in Peru was perhaps better matched by the production and marketing requirements in the 1969 land reform. Although the concentration of land and monopoly market power were as high as in pre-reform Bolivia, the cropping pattern was different, as was the production organisation after the reform. Large plantations of sugar cane and cotton on the Pacific coast and the huge livestock ranches in the Peruvian Sierra were kept intact along with their processing factories. In these areas, former workers and tenants were provided with collective rights of ownership and use of land and assets (76.6 per cent of total expropriated land were collectives). The chosen institution for production organisation was the agrarian production co-operative. Rental of land and individual farming on the collectives were prohibited.

Based on several micro-studies carried out by Peruvian scholars on the impact of land reform, Kay (1983) tells us that the reform 'did not disrupt the production and sugar industry'. Sugar yields per hectare increased by 15 per cent and its cultivated area by 24 per cent between 1969 (when the reform was quickly and effectively implemented) and 1977. In cotton areas these studies revealed a 'slight increase in output per hectare following the reform'. The reduction in the area cultivated by cotton was mainly due to unfavourable pricing policy enforced by the government which exercised complete control of cotton marketing (Kay, 1983: 218-19). With respect to impact on income distribution, the studies indicate that sugar cane workers (a minority group) obtained the largest increase in income while the Indian *Comuneros*, the largest and poorest group before the reform were largely excluded, obtaining only the smallest increases. The Peruvian partial reform, therefore, did not significantly alter inequalities in income distribution among the peasant population (Figueroa, 1976 cited in Kay, 1983: 232-3).

Such partial distributional benefits have, since 1975, been eroded by the deepening national economic problems. With inflation rising annually at the rate of 60 to 150 per cent between 1975 and 1984, real wage rates declined annually by 6 per cent. Rural poverty was as high as 68 per cent according to the UN-ECLA's estimate in 1977. Most of the poor were those excluded from the scope of land reform, i.e. the Indian *Comuneros* and *aparceros*. Illiteracy was 70 per cent in these rural communities. Their poverty was manifested in the results of the 1984 nutritional survey. The incidence of under-nutrition among the children (0-5 years) was 50-60 per cent of all children in the Sierra, and the jungle provinces where these poor indigenous people live (Figueroa, 1988: Table 6.8). Thus the Peruvian partial reform has not reduced poverty in the context of the entire rural sector.

How necessary is land reform for rural development?

To understand the impact of land reform on the pace of poverty reduction, we compare the temporal change in the incidence of poverty among

261

Table 7.3 Temporal changes in population and number of rural poor

Countries	Banking by Gini Coefficient of Land Distribution	Population			Total rural population as percentage of total population 1982	Estimates of Rural Poor	
		Average annual rate of growth %		Fertility rate		Rural poor as percentage total rural population	Number of rural poor (million)
		1960–70	1970–82	1982			
China	circ. 0.180 (1980)	2.3	1.4	2.3	79	60 (1940s) / 6–11 (1979–81)	240 / 50–80
South Korea	0.303 (1980)	2.6	1.7	2.7	39	60 (1925) / 9.8 (1980)	9 / 1.6
Iraq	0.394 (1982)	3.2	3.5	6.7	30	70 (1954/55) / 17 (1976)	2.6 / 0.8
Egypt	0.432 (1984)	2.5	2.5	4.6	55	56.1 (1949/50) / 17.8 (1982)	7.7 / 4.2
Thailand	0.460 (1978)	3.1	2.4	3.6	83	56 (1962/63) / 31.7 (1976)	13.5 / 11.6
Philippines	0.530 (1981)	3.0	2.7	4.2	62	44.4 (1965) / 42.0 (1980)	9.8 / 12.6
Pakistan	0.539 (1980)	2.8	3.0	5.8	71	51.5 (1969/70) / 39.8 (1979/80)	25.7 / 23.6
India	0.621 (1978)	2.3	2.3	4.8	76	54.1 (1956/57) / 50.8 (1977/78)	175.4 / 249.5
Sri Lanka	0.632 (1982)	2.4	1.7	3.4	76	31.7 (1969/70) / 25.6 (1970/81)	3.5 / 2.9

Sources:
Column 1 Gini Coefficient of land distribution – see Table 1.5, Chapter 1, except China, estimated as in the text under China.
Column 2 Growth rates, World Development Report, 1984, Table 19 Indicators. The year 1982 is used as the data on the Gini Coefficient and estimates of rural poverty ends in that year.
Column 3 World Development Report, 1984, Table 20 Indicators. Fertility rate represents the number of children that would be borne per woman if she were to live to the end of her childbearing years and bear children at different age-specific fertility rates.
Column 4 Calculated from World Bank data of population and urbanisation corresponding to year 1982.
Column 5 China, South Korea, Iraq and Egypt, see test, under each country historical review: Thailand: Rizwanul Islam, 'Poverty, Income Distribution and Growth in Rural Thailand', in Poverty in Rural Asia, edited by A.R. Khan and Eddy Lee, ILO, Bangkok, 1983, Table 9.3; Pakistan: Ibid, Table 1.2 and Table 2.7; India: 1956/57, Montek S. Ahluwalia, 'Agricultural Production and Prices' in J. Mellor and Desai, editors, Agricultural Change and Rural Poverty, 1985, Table 7.1, 1977/8, Planning Commission Five Year Plan 1980–5, p. 51, cited in Rizwanul Islam editor, Strategies for Alleviating Poverty in Rural Asia, ILO, Bangkok, 1985, Table 4.1; Sri Lanka: Ibid, Tables 8.1 and 8.2; Philippines, World Bank: Aspects of Policy in the Philippines: A Review and Assessment, 1980.

a small sample of nine countries in conjunction with their respective demographic characteristics. Table 7.3 presents data for those countries on which fairly reliable poverty estimates between specific points of time are available. Though estimates are based upon different periods between poverty estimates and use different price indices, most of their poverty lines are nutritionally-based (minimum food expenditure based on costing a minimum calorie requirement plus essential non-food requirements). The estimates offer a crude base for comparison. Egypt, Thailand, Pakistan, India, Philippines and Sri Lanka used minimum income to provide necessary calorie and essential non-food requirements corresponding to each country and a consistent series of periodically collected data on household actual expenditure in rural areas. In this section, we examine those countries which reduced poverty both proportionately and in absolute numbers for longer than one decade, thereby achieving rural development according to our definition (Chapter 3, p. 91). Those countries which reduced poverty proportionately, but not in absolute numbers will be examined in the following section. We shall also attempt to identify the weight of land reform relative to other policy instruments (such as fertility control) which influence the incidence of poverty.

Land reform and population growth

Despite limitations of comparability, and the absence of a uniform time series of data of poverty incidence, the set of data for the nine countries suggests that the pace and the order of magnitude of reduction in the number of rural poor is greater in countries where complete land reform is combined with reduced rates of population growth and fertility. Although it is widely recognised that the rate of population growth has a substantial effect on *per capita* income and the demand for food, it is difficult to ascertain whether the combination of land reform and fertility reduction was intentionally conceived, or if population policy was a separate instrument required for overall national development. In both cases there are feedback effects between the distribution of income/ consumption resulting from land reform, and the rate of growth of output of the agricultural labour force and the changing number of those living below the level of minimum necessity over time (see Figure 3.1). For what we know of the Chinese sequential events, land reforms and strict control of population growth are linked.

The intertemporal effect of combining complete land reform and population control is clear from the data on China and South Korea. If we accept the rough estimates available for China and South Korea for the 1940s, both countries have dramatically reduced the number of the poor with different distributional effects. Despite the natural growth of rural population between 1949 and 1981 from about 400 million to 850 million, China sustained the reduction of the number of the poor in the countryside from approximately 240 million to something between 50 million and 80 million in 1981 – a remarkable rate of nearly 15 per cent per decade. This achievement is manifested in the dramatic improvement in nutritional levels, literacy rates and the sharp rise in life expectancy from 30–40 years in the 1940s to 70 years in 1985. South Korea reduced poverty at a fast rate particularly between the initiation of egalitarian land reforms of 1945–50 and 1965 and also between 1965 and 1978. The rates were 20 per cent and 10 per cent per decade respectively. The dynamic forces in both agriculture and the national economy which contributed to the fast pace of poverty reduction in China and South Korea have been outlined earlier in Chapter 6. Cuba is not included in Table 7.3 because estimates on its poverty incidence are unavailable. Nevertheless, its indicators suggest that there has been a dramatic improvement in the standard of living in the countryside. With life expectancy rising to 75 years, infant mortality falling to less than 15 deaths per thousand live births, illiteracy almost eliminated, and daily calorie supply *per capita* rising to 134 per cent of requirements, it is no wonder that the ILO study (Ghai, 1988: 117) has concluded that absolute poverty has been 'eliminated'. This record was realised without official intervention in reducing population growth though the government subsidises contraceptives and both abortion and sterilisation are legal but not enforced by the government.

Iraq, the third country in Table 7.3 with large scale redistribution, does not have an interventionist population control policy. In fact, it has the highest rates of population growth and fertility among all countries in Table 7.3. Yet over the past two decades, Iraq has been able to reduce the incidence of poverty substantially thanks to high investment rates in agriculture and social amenities from oil revenue during the 1960s and 1970s. Based on data of poverty characteristics provided by Warriner, 1948 and Penrose, 1978, the rate of poverty incidence in the 1950s was approximately 70 per cent. In 1976, our estimate of poverty incidence, based on available data from household surveys fell sharply to nearly 17 per cent. If we accept the rather arbitrary measurements, they represent a substantial reduction in poverty incidence.

With regard to the other countries given in Table 7.3, the data do not lend themselves to a single generalisation. This suggests that the pace and extent of reduction in rural poverty cannot be explained solely by the scale of land reform. The rate of population growth, though important in influencing the number of the poor, is but one variable among others, as noted in our simple regression analysis presented in Chapter 5. The complex factors contributing to poverty alleviation in PLR countries were also noted in the review of Egypt's experience with land reform. Although birth control is practised voluntarily in most urban areas, population control is not enforced nationwide for cultural reasons. Yet, with a relatively high fertility rate of 4.6 per cent, and only 14 per cent of total agricultural households directly benefiting from land reforms, the incidence of poverty fell sharply from 56.1 per cent at the pre-reform base date of 1949–50, to 23.8 per cent in 1965 following two land reforms. By 1982 the introduction of additional policy instruments, and an increase in remittances (as discussed in Chapter 6) further reduced poverty to 17.8 per cent. During this period an expanded programme of land settlement schemes absorbed about 3 per cent of landless peasants on reclaimed, publicly-owned land, representing 4 per cent of total agricultural area.

A similar strategy was followed in Sri Lanka. Substantial food subsidies, receipts of workers' remittances and comprehensive land settlement schemes were combined with partial land reform. Yields of rice, Sri Lanka's staple food, grew, and rice farmers saw a corresponding rise in income, yet most of the rural poor remained the hired labourers in the paddy sector. In addition to the 22 per cent of total agricultural households which benefited directly from the 1972 and 1975 land reforms, 35 per cent received land from resettlement schemes which covered 19 per cent of total arable land.[4] However, Sri Lanka differs from Egypt in having achieved a higher level of education and in pursuing an active fertility control programme. Consequently, its rates of fertility and population growth rapidly diminished during the 1970s. In fact, population growth and fertility rates (1.4 per cent and 2.9 per cent respectively in 1986) in Sri Lanka are among the lowest in developing countries. The combined impact of these policies for the redistribution of income and wealth has been to reduce the actual numbers of the rural poor, as well as the proportional incidence of rural poverty, which decreased by 6 per cent between 1970–81. There are signals, however, of widening disparity in the distribution of income in the rural sector as documented by Gooneratne and Gunawardena (1983).

Let us now examine the scale of land distribution and the time trends of poverty reduction in Thailand and Pakistan, two other countries that reduced poverty both proportionately and in absolute numbers. Each did so at a different pace, with differing initial degrees of land concentration, and following opposite population policies. In the early 1960s both countries started the process of rural development with rural economies characterised by high poverty incidence. But Pakistan suffered greater inequality in land distribution, combined with higher density of agricultural population in relation to agricultural land. For easy comparison, their relevant data which are scattered in several tables in this study have been grouped in Table 7.4.

265

Table 7.4 **Agricultural growth and poverty in Pakistan and Thailand, 1960–83**

	Indicators		Pakistan		Thailand	
1.	GNP *per capita*	1976	170		380	
	$ at constant prices	1982	380		790	
2.	Agricultural GDP *per capita* agric. population $	1982	192		213	
3.	Agricultural GDP annual growth rate					
		1960–70	4.9%		5.5%	
		1973–83	3.4%		3.5%	
4.	Food Production *per capita* average index (1974–76 = 100)	1981–83	105		112	
5.	Density of agric. population, person per hectare arable land (1980)		2.5		1.7	
6.	Gini Coefficient of land concentration		0.630	(1963)	0.46	(1963)
			0.520	(1973)	0.41	(1970)
			0.539	(1980)	0.46	(1979)
7.	Agricultural landless households as percentage of total agricultural households (1981)		31		10	
8.	Rural population as percentage of total (1980)		71		82	
9.	Percentage of rural households in poverty to total rural households		41	(1962/63)	56	(1962/63)
			51.5	(1969/70)	–	
			39.8	(1979/80)	31.7	(1976)

Sources: 1,2,3,4,8: World Development Report, indicators, 1978 and 1984
        5,6,7,9: Tables 1.5, 5.4, and 7.3 in the text

When Thailand began its process of rural development, its *per capita* GNP was double that of Pakistan, and its extent of land concentration was much lower than Pakistan's. Following technology-orientated policies using high yielding varieties of wheat and rice, increased consumption of chemical fertiliser, expanded irrigation and mechanisation, agriculture grew steadily in both countries during the 1960s and 1970s. By the end of the 1970s, available estimates indicate that Thailand had reduced poverty more substantially than Pakistan. What brought about such a change in the absence of a policy to redistribute privately-owned land? Thailand's policy makers opted to follow an aggressive policy to reduce population growth rates. It also chose to expand the cultivated area by directing a substantial part of public expenditure to open up abundant lands for irrigated and diversified agriculture combined with favourable terms of trade to the agricultural sector. These measures had a significant impact on the productivity of the agricultural sector and its capacity to absorb labour. Increasing accessibility to land for all farmers, (particularly landless peasants) was achieved by doubling irrigated areas between 1960 and 1980, thus reducing the density of agricultural population from 2.1 persons per hectare to 1.7 in 1982. Consequently, only 10 per cent of agricultural households remained as landless workers.

Following an active policy for fertility control, annual rates of population growth fell from 3.1 per cent in 1960–70 to 2.5 per cent in 1970–80 and further to 2.0 per cent in 1980–6. This policy has substantially reduced the crude birth rate from 50 per thousand in the 1950s to 29 per thousand in the late 1970s, and 25 per thousand in 1986.[5] Accordingly, growth in *per capita* food production has risen from 0.7 per cent in 1960–70 to 2.5 per cent in 1970–80 (FAO 1988 Country Tables). Islam (1983) offers other explanations for the reduction of rural poverty in Thailand including: a favourable pricing policy and the rise in tourism-induced non-farming activities (silk and cotton weaving, making umbrellas and wood carving). Agricultural wage rates have increased in real terms. Labour force participation has also increased, while the share of earnings from agriculture in the gross incomes of the rural poor has been reduced.[6] Thus on the basis of availability of poverty estimates, Thailand's chosen strategy to alleviate poverty did achieve rural development by our own definition.

Though the policies introduced were successful at reducing poverty, they did not reduce inequality in the distribution of land holding as measured by the Gini Coefficient which remained virtually unchanged between 1963 and 1979 at the moderate level of 0.46. Nor was the greater inequality in the distribution of land *ownership* and agricultural income alleviated. The income accruing to many urban merchants, foreign capitalists (multinationals) and large landowners of 10 hectares and over has sharply risen (Islam, 1983: 218, Table 9.5).

For regulating the land tenure relations, policy actions were taken under popular pressure following widespread rural unrest supported by the Farmers Federation of Thailand, and the demands of students demonstrating for land reform. Through the National Assembly, a minimal law was issued in 1974 fixing farmland rents at 25 per cent of the harvest. Where rents were reduced, the income transfer from landlord to tenant was substantial. But the changes were not without social and political costs. Under land and power systems in rural Thailand, landowners were enraged and took countermeasures evicting tenants. In July 1975, the leader of the Farmers Federation and 25 peasant leaders were assassinated (Grace in Handelman, 1981: 45).

According to available estimates, Pakistan alleviated poverty over the short time frame 1962–78, but at a slower pace than did Thailand (the average rates per decade were roughly 11.5 per cent and 16 per cent respectively). This was accomplished despite the absence of population control policies, high rates of population growth (3 per cent per annum) and corresponding pressure on land. The meagre scale of the 1960 and 1972 land reforms combined with rent control reduced inequality in land distribution from a Gini Coefficient of 0.63 in 1963 to 0.52 in 1973. But these measures cannot alone be responsible for the overall development. How then did it come about? The explanation may lie in:

(a) the 'trickle down' effects of a combination of high rates of agricultural growth particularly in food grain production;
(b) the rapid expansion of irrigated land from 60 per cent to 77 per cent between 1965 and 1985;
(c) the expansion of employment opportunities under public works and rural development programmes which were intensified between 1977 and 1984;
(d) the substantial flow of remittances from migration of unskilled labour to oil-rich Arab countries; and
(e) large scale pooling of rich people's financial contributions (Zakat and Ushr) as required by the Koran (an Islamic-determined progressive taxation).

This latter type of need-based income transfer towards the poor, disabled and widows in rural areas (Mustaheqeen) has been institutionalised and targeted by the State machinery at no cost to the government. It was estimated that by 1982, nearly 45 per cent of rural poor in Pakistan were reached by this innovative institutional arrangement (Ifran and Amjad, 1983 and Ali, 1985).

Though both Thailand and Pakistan realised sustained agricultural growth, and reduced poverty, nearly one third of their rural people continue to live in deprivation. Inequalities in the distribution of income and consumption have actually worsened (World Bank, 1978: 24 and Islam, 1983: 216). Given the reliance of their national economies on the healthy performance of the agrarian system (industry employs only 10–14 per cent of the total labour force), a rapid reduction in poverty can substantially expand economic activities in the economy as a whole. Higher effective demand of the currently poor one third of the rural people of Thailand and Pakistan can, at least in the short run, accelerate domestic production. It is unrealistic to expect the slow domestic industrialisation and the international labour market to absorb the current and potential millions of poor rural youth and landless workers.[8] There is certainly a case for land reform in both countries if real incomes and consumption of the poor are to rise faster and poverty to decline rapidly.

Rural betterment: partial reforms of the Philippines and India

To illustrate empirically the implications of rural betterment as distinguished from rural development (see p. 91), we now briefly examine the experience of the Philippines and India, the last two countries in our sample presented in Table 7.3. According to the estimates on the time trend of poverty incidence, both countries have reduced poverty proportionately but not in absolute numbers.

The Philippines

The policy issue of land reform was, and still is, very heatedly debated in the Philippines. Since the 1970s a myriad of programmes for improving tenancy arrangements, and promoting employment and income have been implemented, including land settlement schemes, co-operative organisations, land consolidation, subsidised agricultural credit, farmer training schemes, integrated area projects, and programmes specifically geared to rural women.[9] But a number of Filipino scholars and non-governmental organisations questioned whether government expenditure in most of these programmes would reach the rural poor, and have forcefully argued for a genuine and comprehensive land reform programme. The call for such a programme has become more emphatic since the rise to power of the Aquino administration, whose pronounced objective is to reduce poverty and concentration of wealth in agriculture. Those calling for a massive redistribution of landed property believe that it is necessary to alleviate violent conflicts, social unrest, widespread deprivation in the rural areas, rising landlessness and falling food productivity.[10] The concern for these problems is justified in the light of increased land concentration from a Gini Coefficient of 0.50 in 1960 to 0.53 in 1981 and the rise in landlessness to nearly 40 per cent of total agricultural households. Both increases have taken place since three earlier so-called 'agrarian reforms' which left the fundamental features of the institutional frameworks of agriculture, the economic powers of landlords, multinational corporations and moneylenders virtually intact. This half-hearted legislation had serious consequences. Despite the wide application of technological advances in agriculture in the 1960s and 1970s, productivity *per capita* of the agricultural workforce has recently declined at an annual rate of minus 0.8 per cent between 1981 and 1986 and *per capita* food productivity of the total population has also declined from 2.4 per cent per year (1971–80) to minus 1.5 per cent per year during 1981–6. With capital-intensive industrialisation representing a large share in GDP of 32 per cent but able to employ only 16 per cent of the total labour force in 1986, the percentage increase of new entrants to the agricultural labour force has been as high as 1.6 per cent per year between 1970 and 1986. Apart from falling productivity, the result is increasing fragmentation of small-holdings, increasing landlessness, widening inequalities, and a rising ratio of agricultural population to cultivable land from 2.6 persons per hectare in 1960 to 3.4 in 1985 (FAO Country Tables, 1988).

The first two land reform laws of 1954 and 1963 were attempts to improve tenancy arrangements in sharecropping, to lower rents, and even to abolish tenancy altogether. But unenforceable laws are not laws. The third land reform of 1972 gave the tenants cultivating rice and corn a choice of options. The tenant could own the piece of land he tilled against payment through transferring title from landlords whose ownership exceeded 7 hectares or could rent at 25 per cent of the average net value of output, while being granted higher tenancy security. The clumsy bureaucratic procedures and the influence of the landlords significantly slowed the pace of implementation. As a Filipino scholar states:

> Outright bribery, blackmail and cheating have been reported. Peasants signing the Landlord Tenant Agreement discovered later that the price originally agreed upon has been inflated by technicians in connivance with landlords! (Po, 1980: 302)

The end result was that only about a quarter of total tenants in rice and corn land were able to purchase land from their landlords or to hold title once payment was completed after 15 years.

As in other PLR countries, landlords retained the most productive portion of their land together with substantial capital assets, leaving the new owners to purchase the less productive, and decapitalised land. New owners did, however, gain an immediate income transfer from the amortised annual payment of land price and land tax – payments which were lower than the former rent of 50 per cent of the net value of harvest. The income gain was more widespread among the tenants who continued as leaseholders and who paid 25 per cent of the harvest in addition to their prescribed security of tenure under written contract. However, these provisions were not uniformly enforced. Using results of micro-studies, Mangahas (1985: 235) reports that in rain-fed areas tenants continued to pay more than the 25 per cent legal limit. These studies indicate that

58 per cent of hired workers in sugar plantations in Negros Occidental province received wages less than the minimum required by the 1975 Wage Commission Rules. In his assessment of the 1972 land reform, Mangahas says,

> It is safe to say that the legal coverage of the land reform has set an upper limit [7 ha] to the *de facto* coverage. Many cases have been observed of evasion through transfers, sales or mortgages of the land, as well as of conversions of rice and corn areas to other crops. (Mangahas, 1985: 221)

The 1972 land reform was partial because it was limited to rented lands growing rice and corn. It excluded cash crops (coconut, sugar cane, banana, pineapples, coffee, tobacco, rubber, and cattle ranches) and the owner operated farms irrespective of their individual size. The former (cash cropped area) included 3.1 million hectares (mostly irrigated land), 170,000 tenant households and 1.1 million landless workers (Mangahas, 1985: 219). In most of this cash cropped sector, production relations and market structure are dominated by large landlords and multinational corporations. Thus, a duality in the rural economy has been created between the beneficiaries and landlords whose ownership exceeded 7 hectares within the reform sector, and between that sector and the large cash-cropping and export orientated sector. In both sectors, the market power of the landlords, traders and moneylenders has continued in terms of their share in rural banks' stock capital, the acquisition of the means of production and in their marketing of farm produce. In both sectors, the massive number of wage-dependent landless workers continue to live in poverty (Alex, 1980 and Ledesma, 1982). With inflation rising at an annual average rate of 15 to 20 per cent, *real* wage rates of the landless workers have declined, (index of 100 in 1972 to 69 in 1980).

Micro-studies cited above indicate that the annual earnings of landless workers, averaging P2,000, is less than half the minimum income fixed by the World Bank as the poverty line. In the size distribution of real income, the share of the bottom 30 per cent of the rural population fell by 20 per cent between 1970 and 1980 (Sobhan, 1983: 9 and Table 11). For those whose remunerative employment opportunities are already extremely restricted, the prospects for improvement do not appear good, with high annual rates of agricultural population growth between 1.5 and 2 per cent during 1970–85, a fall in agricultural GDP growth rates from 4.5 per cent in the 1970s to 1.7 per cent during 1980–5, and a 40 per cent fall in the share of gross domestic investment in GDP in 1986 relative to 1965.

How these dynamic forces have influenced food consumption and the time trend in poverty incidence is a difficult question to answer with certainty. Despite continuing controversy in the Philippines about the

271

mathematics of counting the poor, there is consensus that the numbers have risen, particularly in the landless labourers in agriculture. The National Nutrition Survey of 1978, the research of the Philippine Development Academy and the studies of the World Bank in 1980 indicate an upward trend in the number of the poor irrespective of conflicting views on the criteria for the cut-off point (poverty line).[11] We used the World Bank conservative estimates for 1965 and 1980/1, during which the land reform was implemented. These estimates show a small proportionate *decline* at the rate of 1.5 per cent per decade, but a rise in the absolute numbers of the poor by nearly three million persons in the countryside. The rise would be much greater if other estimates were used. How much this persistent poverty will be reduced over the next decade only time will tell. A solution to the pressing problems of the landless workers could rest with the land reform promised in 1987 that is intended to contribute to the realisation of rural development in the Philippines.

India

Our comparison of inter-country experience in land reform is incomplete without a brief reference to the rich experience of India in tackling problems of rural under-development. Here, national policy instruments have addressed most aspects of persistent poverty within a democratic process of policy formation.[12] Throughout, the fundamental principles laid down in 1947 by the Congress Party Committee on Agrarian Reform have been maintained. Private property rights in land and other means of production have been adopted within a socially complex class system, and in different States, some of which have populations exceeding 80 million. Constitutionally, each State makes independent decisions regarding land reform policy and implementation. Virtually all States have enacted numerous laws between 1952 and 1974, fixing ceilings on private land ownership, abolishing intermediaries in tenancy arrangements, controlling rental values, and fixing minimum wage rates in agriculture. Nevertheless, all of these pieces of regulatory legislation are designed with such deliberate exemptions and legal loopholes, that they could not meet the rising expectations of the mass of rural poor.[13] The end result is that only 3 per cent of privately-owned land in India has been redistributed.

Why has the fervour in advancing the cause of land reform since the early 1950s floundered in India? Clues can be found from a number of sources including official statements and academic analyses studied by the author during his visits to India in the 1960s and 1970s. Interviews with senior officials in the Planning Commission and the Revenue Department of West Bengal, and scholars at academic institutions have revealed the wide gap between idealism on the one hand, and constraining inadequacies in implementation capabilities on the other.[14] Bardhan succinctly summarised the constraints:

> These [land reform and tenancy control] laws were executed by a local bureaucracy largely indifferent, occasionally corrupt and biased in favour of the rural oligarchy. . . . Quite frequently, protective tenancy legislation may have worsened the conditions of tenants; it has led to the resumption of land by the landlords and eviction of tenants under the guise of 'voluntary' surrender of land. (Bardhan 1974: 256)

Whatever the reasons might be and ideologies apart, India is out-performed by higher populated China in terms of poverty reduction. Whereas both countries started in 1948/9 with similar conditions of rural under-development (particularly constrained by capital needs for expanding irrigated land), they chose unique institutional changes for providing accessible opportunities to the masses of tenants and landless workers. Each path has had distinct distributional implications, plans for employing the gigantic agricultural workforces, and patterns of agricultural growth. India redistributed only 3 per cent of total privately-owned land, and China radically transformed her agrarian system with complete land reform, yet both countries managed to intensify cropping, achieve self-sufficiency in food grain and to sustain growth rates in *per capita* calorie supply. Their process of planning towards an inward-looking development strategy stressed self-reliance and insulated their economies from the economic shockwaves that have battered many other developing countries since the 1970s. However, between 1960 and 1985, China's indicators of agricultural performance were almost three times those of India in terms of annual growth rates *per capita* agriculture labour force and food productivity. Despite India's efforts to improve quality and quantity of life, she is surpassed by China in terms of illiteracy reduction, increased life expectancy and nutritional improvements (see Table 7.1).

Despite their heavy investments in agricultural growth and in human capital, both countries managed to achieve high rates of gross domestic savings between 1965 and 1985 to finance their national rural development programmes (21 per cent of GDP for India and 36 per cent for China in 1986 – World Development Report 1988 Indicators). Yet, the high inequality in the distribution of land and material assets in India continues to generate skewed distribution of income, while opportunities to own land remain inaccessible for the poor cultivators and the rising number of landless workers. The concentration of landholdings (Gini Coefficient, 0.621) and the incidence of landlessness (between 31–35 per cent of the total agricultural labour force) are reflected in the proportion of poor in India being five times that of China.

The aggregative time trend of poverty incidence at the All India level is, however, misleading because of the inter-state variation in the scope of land reform. The relatively more aggressive reforms in Kerala fixed the lowest ceiling and abolished tenancy by converting tenants to owners. Table 7.5 shows the available estimates of the poverty incidence in rural areas for All India and in the State of Kerala, India's most densely populated State. In 1981, Kerala's rural population was 25.4 million with 654 persons per square km compared with 220 in all India. Kerala has also the highest percentage of redistributed land: 17.5 per cent as compared to 3 per cent in All India. Kerala is usually presented in the literature as the State that has gone as far as possible to realise an egalitarian agrarian system backed by unionised agricultural workers and progressive political organisation.

Table 7.5 **Variation in poverty reduction between All India and Kerala, 1956–78**

| | | Incidence of poverty | | |
		Rural poor%	No. rural poor (in millions)	Sen's index of poverty
*All India	1956/7	54.1	178.5	0.23
	1973/4	46.1	208.4	0.17
† State of	1961/2	50.3	7.1	0.21
Kerala	1977/8	40.9	7.4	0.15

Sources: * Ahluwalia, Montek S., Rural Poverty, Agricultural Production and Prices: A Re-examination – in Mellor and Desai (eds), *Agricultural Change and Rural Poverty*, 1985, Table 7.1
† Jose, A.V., *Poverty and Inequality, The Case of Kerala in Poverty in Rural Asia*, Khan, A.R., and Lee, Eddy, (eds), ILO, 1983, Table 5.9

Considering that Kerala is included in data on All India despite a uniformity in measurement and the time periods not being identical, the data suggest a variation in the pace of poverty reduction. Whereas poverty was reduced at the average rate of 4.7 per cent in one decade in All India, the rate was 5.9 per cent in Kerala. The more comprehensive and sensitive Sen's index also indicates a smaller poverty gap, and more equal distribution of income among the poor in Kerala than in All India. It seems that Kerala's land reform has been a main contributing factor to this differential. There are several other factors, including average size of holdings, agricultural growth in the food sector, pricing policy, higher rates of real wages in agriculture, strong labour unionism in rural areas, and the proportionately higher percentage of public expenditure on health and education in the State government of Kerala.[15] These variables have been manifested in different characteristics of rural poverty between Kerala and All India, and documented by Jose (1983). Based on official figures his findings indicate a higher quality and quantity of life in Kerala's *rural* areas as compared to All rural India as shown in Table 7.6.

274

Table 7.6 **Comparison of quality and quantity of life between Kerala and All India 1970-81**

	Kerala	*All India*
Life expectancy (years), (1978)	64	52
Infant mortality (per 1,000), (1980)	40	123
Illiteracy rate, percentage of all adults (1981)	30.8	63.9
Landless as percentage of total agricultural households (1970-5)	27	31

Source: Jose, 1983.

Concluding remarks

Other things being equal, the simple comparison between the State of Kerala and All India suggests the importance of the scale of land reform in the pace of reducing poverty incidence, as do the experiences of other countries reviewed in this chapter except that of Thailand. But the experience of the Philippines highlights another dimension in the context of economic structure. Despite its sustained economic growth of total GDP at the rate of 5-6 per cent per year from 1960 to 82, and its widely publicised green revolution, the limited scale of its land reform did not achieve rural development according to our criteria. The exempted cash-cropped areas from the 1972 reform contained most of the landless workers whose number was increasing and whose real wages were falling.

The inter-country comparison also showed how population policies can contribute to reducing the numbers of poor in the countryside. The impact of such policies is diverse. Where a population policy directly lowering fertility seems to have contributed significantly to the speedy reduction of poverty in China, South Korea, Sri Lanka and in Thailand, it did not have the same impact in India. In contrast, in Egypt, Pakistan and Iraq, all three Muslim countries whose cultural rules do not permit direct intervention to lower fertility, numbers of the poor were reduced through other methods: complete land reform and substantial technical progress in agriculture financed from the post-1973 plentiful oil revenues in Iraq; and partial land reforms combined with a notable expansion in irrigated areas and land settlement schemes and a significant rise in the landless' earnings from non-agricultural sources in Egypt and Pakistan. In each of these three countries, the dynamic forces operating in their national economies other than the rates of population growth had important influence.

The procedure followed in the inter-country comparison suggests that in order to understand the determinants of the pace of poverty reduction, it is necessary to understand how material wealth is distributed in the social setting of accessible opportunities to the poor. This varies greatly between socialism and capitalism. The comparison also suggests that the time trend in poverty incidence largely depends on the quality of the data used in measurement. This refers not only to the crucial question of the database determining who is poor and who is not, but also to the problematic definition of 'rural' as distinct from urban population in aggregative censuses in LDCs. The former is not merely technical, but makes up the rudiments of how politicians in LDCs view poverty and the prospects for the landless poor. The shared predicament of poverty among the different groups of poor has come about by different processes. While it is useful for policy makers to know the trend in the extent of poverty, planners and programmers require unambiguous classification of the simple group label 'poor' by their land tenure status and by gender. The next chapter has more to say on these issues, and their policy implications.

Notes

1   The reforms were induced by the grinding poverty of the ethnic 'Indios', Emilio Zapata revolution of 1911 in Mexico and the invasion of large haciendas in Bolivia in the 1950s and Peru in the 1960s by landless farmers.

2   *Ejido* is an indigenous system of land tenure and use. It is communally owned and operated agricultural land. The *Ejido* became a central issue in land reform since started by the peasants' leader Zapata in 1910 and 1911, and since the Spanish crown granted lands to the *Conquistadores*, the Church and noblemen '*Encomiendas*'. They expanded their lands by dispossessing native Mexican farmers from their *Ejidos*. After Mexican independence in 1821, land property of the Church in Spain, which accounted for nearly 40 per cent of total agricultural land was compulsorily put up for sale. Most of this large areas went to large estates' owners. Many *Ejidos* did not register their lands as required after independence. Their land was taken away gradually under sale of State land to large landlords and for American capitalists. By the Zapata revolution, about one quarter of the country's land was owned by foreigners mostly from the USA. Hence, the prohibition of foreigners to own land, and the restitution of the lost lands from the *Ejidos* were built into the Mexican Constitution of 1917.

  The *Comuneros* are members of very old indigenous rural communities like tribal areas in today's Africa or in some Arab states. Like the relatively more recent *Ejidos*, these communities were also subjected to dispossession of their lands. They remain not fully integrated in the market-orientated economy of rural Mexico. They are concentrated in the mountainous and remote areas as well as in forested lands.

For a detailed account of these systems and the history of their dispossession of land in the eighteenth and nineteenth centuries, see McEntire and McEntire (1969: Chapter 5). For the origin of foreign owned lands and *Comuneros* see Esteva (1983: especially pp. 36–9).

3   To judge the success of land reform by its impact on the flow of marketed surplus in the early years of implementation is a narrow concept. Clark explains in detail how the marketing functions of the affected landlords were not replaced by the government institutions in charge of land reform. During a visit to Bolivia by the author in October 1959, it became clear that the new beneficiaries in the Altiplano were like slaves in the large haciendas while marketing crops were functions of the landlords. It was also found that after five years of implementation the agricultural credit bank did not change its rules by which land title (property) was a collateral against the supply of credit. The lengthy bureaucratic procedures to issue property title to the beneficiary took on average three to four years.

It took the 'indios' of the Altiplano two years to establish themselves as producers and to struggle for marketing their products. During these years, 1953–5, uncertainty and confusion prevailed. They found themselves helpless without the necessary inputs which had been previously provided by the landlords or their agents. The decline in production which occurred in some areas were due to this created gap as well as to the fact that many landlords abandoned their farms. Clark reported that this actually happened in 11 out of the 51 farms that he studied.

The inputs were supposed to be provided by agricultural co-operatives according to articles 122–128 of land reform law. But only in 1958, more than five years after the promulgation of the law, did the government issue legislation and regulation for establishing these co-operatives.

4   In Sri Lanka the policy choice between resettlement (colonisation) schemes and tenancy regulation on one hand and redistributive land reform on the other was (and still is) a central issue in the political conflicts during the 1960s and 1970s. It was only after the landless youth insurrection in 1971 that the Land Reform Act of 1972 was issued fixing a ceiling on privately owned land ranging from 50 acres for non-paddy rice crop areas and 25 acres for paddy areas. The redistributed areas were 0.4 acre and on average in paddy land and 1–2 acres elsewhere. The ratio of maximum ownership to distributed units was nearly 62:1. Realising the limited scope of the reform, the policy makers introduced other income redistributive measures which proved to be effective but subjected the rural poor to change in government policy and in public expenditure. They included generous food subsidies followed by food stamps. The mix of land reform, large scale colonisation schemes and the income transfer measures served as a powerful mechanism for raising real incomes among the poor, reducing poverty and increasing annual growth rate of *per capita* food production from 0.6 in 1960–70 to 4.2 in 1971–80. But after removing food

subsidies in 1979 as part of the IMF induced adjustment programme, these gains have been retrogressed. Income distribution deteriorated and the number of undernourished children progressively increased (see Martins, 1983). For the impact on poverty and income distribution, see Gooneratne and Gunawardena (1983).

5   Starting in 1974, the government intervened to reduce population growth by a serious family planning programme which included a public educational campaign, heavily subsidised sterilisation and legally authorised abortion. The government also restricted migrants from Vietnam, Kampuchea and Laos.

6   This favourable development has had the greatest impact in the poor belt of north-eastern and central regions (Islam, 1985: Table 9.4). In the north and north-eastern regions, the earnings from non-farm activities represent on average, 50 per cent of gross income of rural households. Such diverse sources of employment opportunities helped to avert income instability arising from the seasonal fluctuations of rice production. In addition, female labour force participation reached 85 per cent (Chulasai *et al.*, in Hirashima, 1986).

7   It was reported that remittances from Pakistani migrant workers to their households in rural areas had a 'considerable and positive' impact on poverty in the 1970s (Ifran and Amjad, 1983: 43–4). A recent field study by Elahi and Khan reveals that remittances represented 13.8 per cent of total household income in Attock district and 55.6 per cent in Faisalabad district, both in Pakistan's rural Punjab (Hirashima, 1986: Table 3.6).

8   The trend in LDCs of capital-intensive industrialisation compounds the problems of the fast increasing number of entrants into the labour force in agriculture. The balance of unabsorbed labour must remain in agriculture at the expense of falling productivity per worker. With this structural characteristic, many LDCs with private market economies must create employment within rural areas by combining the intensification of land and labour use with non-farm activities.

9   These programmes include: Agricultural Tenancy Act, 1954; Agricultural Land Reform Code, Republican Act 3884 issued in 1963; Land settlement schemes in Minanao and Banislan where nearly 850,000 hectares were settled by former squatters on public land and landless households numbering about 50,000; associations for the beneficiaries of land reform called Samahang Nayon; rural banks for agricultural credit and the employment generating programme known as Kilusang Kibuhayan (KKK) to help landless workers, forestry workers and poor fishermen.

10   There are many who are critics of the limited land reforms and their slow implementation and who have been demanding a comprehensive land reform. They include Mangahas, Montemayor, Po, Ledesma, Umali, and Quison, just to mention a few. In addition, the numerous non-government organisations have consolidated their efforts during 1986–8 and voiced the misery of landless workers. After the announcement of the Presidential Executive order on land reform in

May 1987, the pressure has increased for a land-to-the-tiller reform abolishing absentee land-ownership and covering *all* lands irrespective of crop planted. A summary of the work of these NGOs towards land reform is published in *Information Notes*, Vol. 8 No. 6, May 1988 by the Asian NGO Coalition for Agrarian Reform and Rural Development (ANGOC), headquartered in Manila.

11   Since 1957 there have been several estimates of rural poverty derived from different poverty lines. These estimates were made by the World Bank, the Wage Commission, Philippines Development Academy and Dr Mangahas. The methodological problems in estimation are discussed in Mangahas (1985), the World Bank study on the Philippines (1980) and in Technical Appendix I of the FAO publication *The Dynamics of Rural Poverty*, 1986. The first two sources are included in the bibliography. All estimates (except that of Mangahas) are based on data given by the Family Income and Expenditure Survey conducted by the National Census and Statistics Office in 1956, 1961, 1971, and 1975. The variation in estimation is due to using different percentages of food expenditure to total, *per capita*, or household consumption per year, different pricing of the food and non-food items, inter-regional variation in consumer price indices and their adjustment to different rates of inflation. The result is a divergence of poverty lines for a rural household of six for 1975 as follows:

World Bank	4,962 pesos
The Academy	8,668 pesos
The Wage Commission	6,900 pesos

12   India's programme for rural development since the early 1960s has had several elements including: (a) community development programmes under which 100 villages with about 65,000 persons were to constitute an administrative block with service co-operatives established in villages; (b) the Intensive Area Development Programme which replaced the former programme and which concentrated mostly on irrigated areas with a technological thrust for increasing the yields of wheat using tractors and tube wells – the wheat growing areas in North India benefited most from this programme; (c) credit supply programmes (small farmers development, marginal farmers and landless labourer programmes); (d) the rapid expansion in irrigated land during the 1970s; and (e) Integrated Rural Development Programmes and a National Rural Employment Programme. Among other national programmes affecting the rural poor, the population control policy was targeted to reduce the fertility rates in the large family size groups who are mostly the poor.

13   No attempt is made here to review Indian land reform policy on which there is rich literature written by government authorities and Indian scholars. Their impact is well documented: Examples are: The Periodical reports on 'Progress of Land Reform' prepared by Land Reform Division of the Planning Commission; Rural Labour Enquiry 1974–75; Joshi (1961); Dandekar (1964); Warriner (1969); Bardhan (1970: 261–6); and Joshi (1975).

14 I visited India twice in 1964 and 1968. My visit included a field study of land reform programmes in West Bengal, and the role of Gram Panchayat. In Delhi I was informed by Prof Gadgil the then Vice Chairman of the Planning Commission on the overall progress and problems in land reform implementation. Very useful discussions with Prof Karve and Prof Dantwala were held which enlightened me on the functioning of agricultural co-operatives. Subsequently, several discussions took place with Prof Parthasarthy (Andhra University) and Dr T.C. Varghese (FAO), on a wide range of land reform policy issues in specific States in India.

15 In addition to free education at the primary and secondary levels, the State government of Kerala provides social security payments and unemployment allowances as well as monthly payments to the disabled. According to official government statistics cited in Jose (1983) in 1978 the average *per capita* expenditure on education was Rs 62.8 while the corresponding average for All India was Rs 33.7. The expenditure on education represented 45 per cent of total expenditure in Kerala during the 1960s and the 1970s. The *per capita* expenditure on health was Rs 20.6 against Rs 14.1 for All India in 1979.

Chapter eight

Policy implications and prospects for land reform

In this final chapter, an attempt is made to draw some conclusions in the light of the conceptual framework presented earlier, and the empirical evidence from country experiences studied in the preceding chapters. It is difficult for the author of a study like ours to decide precisely what to say after attempting to make each chapter comprehensive. Perhaps it is useful to begin with a retrospective assessment of how the choice of political economy has contributed to the investigation of rural development problems and policies with regard to poverty alleviation. Next, we can outline a few findings from the study of country experiences which are of interest to policy makers and analysts. From this study we present those findings which challenge commonly held beliefs frequently expressed in the analytic reasoning behind policy prescriptions, particularly in judging the necessity of land reform. We then consider how the lessons learnt from experience can be applied to assessing the impact of land reform relative to other policy choice. In the final section we discuss the prospects for land reform in the face of the current economic crises, falling food productivity, persisting poverty in many LDCs and declining concern for land reform policy.

The relevance of the analytical approach

The political economy approach was employed to systematically examine the organisation of land-based rural economies in the context of each country's own political and historical experience. The evidence presented in Chapters 4, 5 and 6 indicates how the dominance of politically and economically powerful land-based capitalists in agriculture influences not only the pattern of production growth within the rural economies, but also the perpetuation of low standards of living for a large section of the rural population. This process is viewed in this study in terms of the theory of the State and our concept of institutional monopoly of the productive forces which determine the magnitude of accumulated economic surplus, the structure of market power and the character of social organisation. This approach has enabled us to identify the institutional determinants of poverty, with particular emphasis on the barriers to entry to the land and credit markets which differ from those well-known barriers in industry. Within this context of political economy, land reform is viewed as an anti-monopoly policy manifesting the State's authority to regulate productive forces while significantly reducing the concentration of wealth and power, thus saving the society from destabilisation.

We were also able to understand the institutional determinants of malnutrition among the landless poor, investment in land productivity improvement and for accumulation of human assets (health, training and education), food productivity, terms of labour utilisation, monopoly power in the market structure, and the influence of bureaucratic behaviour. Our analytic procedure has helped to explain the erroneous view created when institutions of property rights, power relations and the role of law and government agents are excluded by the standard approach of neo-classical economics.

Our review of pre-reform agrarian systems (Chapters 5 and 6) suggests that land reform is basically a social and political issue. It cannot be convincingly justified exclusively on economic grounds or agro-technical logic of cropping intensity in land use and application of technological advance to subsistence cultivation. From whatever aspect the policy maker or development analyst approaches the problems of rural underdevelopment, the problems rest upon a host of retrogressive institutional arrangements and rural power relations.

In order to understand the relationships between land concentration, poverty incidence, landlessness and rates of agricultural growth, three hypotheses were formulated in the Introduction. We combined a qualitative approach with quantitative statistical analysis for delineating these relationships. Though our findings on the first three variables could not generalise the relationships in precise terms of cause and effect, they did show a strong positive association that should be of interest to analysts, rural development practitioners, and policy makers. Other findings on the relationship with agricultural growth is discussed later. Our combined monographic treatment and quantitative comparison of country experiences suggests that the greater the scope of land reform, the faster the pace of poverty reduction in absolute numbers. Further, the rate of reduction was even quicker when land reform was accompanied by fertility control. The wide variation in the time trend in poverty incidence is obvious in the estimated rates of poverty reduction per decade (15 per cent in China, compared with 4.7 per cent in India and 1.6 per cent in the Philippines). Our study, however, suggests the importance of the quality of the database which identifies who is, and is not, considered poor. To establish a firm relationship between these variables requires inter-temporal comparable micro-studies.

Assumptions challenged

Our intellectual excursion into country experiences suggests that a partial understanding of the determinants of poverty leads to varied perceptions of rural development. Distorted perceptions based on biased assumptions produce policies which can keep the present generation of the rural poor in persistent deprivation and malnutrition. Our study of empirical evidence leads us to challenge some erroneous, yet commonly held views which influence policy prescriptions. The first is that land reform has no place where there appears to be a shortage of land to redistribute. We have seen that, given the political will, the determinant factor is actually the ceiling on private landed property fixed according to the balance of political power in private property-market economies. In the case of South Korea, where there was significant population pressure on scarce land in 1950, very low ceilings meant that nearly 77 per cent of total agricultural households were land recipients and that 65 per cent of total cultivable land was redistributed.

The second is that there is a high extent of accessibility to land ownership through transactions in the land market. Country empirical evidence challenges the legitimacy of this assumption in terms of ownership, but not with regard to the imperfect land-lease market. Tracing the origin of large farms in Kenya and in pre-land reform Egypt and Iraq revealed that most of these large ownerships were attained by non-market transactions. Land was accumulated by institutional arrangements: grants by colonial rulers; the sovereign; concessions made by the State in exchange for political and economic support; and land-grabbing by virtue of official status and political power. The historical review also indicates that a combination of very low earnings, high land prices and capital rationing inhibited wage-dependent agricultural workers from owning or even to leasing land. Social class systems in these and many other countries were also a restrictive factor as poor tenants and landless workers could not possess property rights in land through inter-family marriage and inheritance as their families were usually a propertyless class. It was only after land reforms that tenancy and landlessness were abolished in China and reduced substantially in South Korea and Iraq, and slightly in Egypt.

The third challenged proposition views land reform not as a dynamic policy, but as a static, once-and-for-all redistribution of the existing stock of wealth in land property and other material capital, at one point in time. Our study of actual design and implementation of land reforms suggests that no single land reform policy is appropriate to all conditions. Nor does any policy, once chosen, remain static in the face of dynamic rural development and structural changes in national economies. The Mexican land reform, instituted in 1915 has no fixed date for completion, and

283

offers continual redistribution as long as the indigenous population and their descendants claim land.

Ten to twelve years after their initial reforms, both Iraq and Egypt amended latent defects in their respective legislation by substantially lowering the prescribed ceilings. Iraq realistically faced its problems in the institutional organisation of production by liquidating many inefficient State farms, and curtailing collective farms for lack of farmers' interest. We have also seen how after ten years of implementing its massive reforms, China collectivised individual holdings on a nationwide scale to ensure employment and capital formation. Twenty years later the structure of incentives and opportunities for private consumption, savings and investment were expanded by introducing cultivators' household contracts which permitted some marketable surplus to be sold in the market. We have also seen how the South Korean leadership allowed illegal tenancy arrangements in response to changing social conditions.

Fourth, it has been suggested in the literature that the origin of land reform is incompatible with parliamentary and democratic rules of law. The cases of India, Sri Lanka, and Chile (1967) challenge this view. The Philippines and Brazil are currently attempting to institute their land reforms under parliamentary majority. It is equally incorrect to claim that all authoritarian regimes bring about land reforms. Many do not. In some cases, authoritarian regimes have allied with big land owners and industrialists, for instance Paraguay, Bangladesh, Pakistan (after 1977), Nigeria and Chile (after 1973).

Fifth, our case studies have shown that governments (and their technocrats) are not neutral as usually assumed in neo-classical economic models. Nor are they to be understood as Plato's puritan 'Guardians' endowed with high moral standards and meticulous ethics. Exploitative relations and corruption prevail. Often the interests are served of those economic classes on whom governments depend for their tenure in office, while the interests of the rural poor are passed over.

Finally, our discussion and the statistical analysis (Chapters 4 and 5) challenge the belief that high rates of agricultural growth and adoption of new technology are conditional upon the dominance of large farms, and that these large farms have productive superiority over small farms. In fact, the quantitative analysis shows no clear association between concentration of land distribution and total and *per capita* agricultural growth rates. Under any degree of inequality of land distribution, productivity of both land and working labour depends on other variables. These include weather, incentives for investment to raise land productivity, adoption of labour-using technology, cropping intensity of land use, pricing systems and terms of trade between agriculture and the rest of the economy, density of agricultural population on arable land, and the soil fertility.

Issues in the evaluation of land reform

Apart from the evaluator's own ideology and personal beliefs, proper assessment of the performance of land reform encounters a number of problems. There is often confusion over whether its effects are measured against the precisely stated objectives of the policy, or against what the evaluator thinks the objectives *should* be. The starting point in the evaluation should be a clear understanding of the objectives explicitly stated at the time of the policy choice, and implicitly manifested since implementation. The rationale behind considering what has happened during the operational phase as complementary to the explicit objectives is that it mirrors the complex operative ideology of the reformers. It also reflects the way in which the primary objectives have been compromised or sustained in practice.

Country experiences in the preceding chapters suggest that two principal factors which explain the objectives and the scope need to be understood in assessing land reform's performance. The first is the initial state of rural under-development created by socially harmful and economically defective systems of land tenure and their corresponding production organisation and rural class relations. Pre-reform Iraq's undeveloped agriculture, its barriers to growth, and its unique tribal system required a policy response different from those of South Korea, Cuba, Peru and Egypt, whose agriculture was fairly developed but whose productive and political resources were monopolised by a few capitalists. The second factor is that the choice of policy scope (partial or complete) is a product of the configuration of political power and the prevailing operative ideology at the time of choice. In instituting land reform, each country leadership calculates the set of conflicting interests of different socio-economic groups in relation to their own political survival. Out of this weighting calculus, the leadership decide what is practical and relevant. Thus, the scope of land reform emerges as the net product of the balance between 'class interests and the regime interests' to use Herring's terminology (1983: 217). Historical experience indicates that land reform was the first public action taken once the balance of political power shifts towards the interests of the poor cultivators and the landless workers. This applies to diverse situations: by choice or obligation, by revolutionary change (including *coups d'état*) or by parliamentary majority.

The before-and-after statistical data on trends in agricultural production must, therefore, be analysed with specific reference to the scope of land reform policy and the time frame of its sequential stages of implementation. The rush to evaluate the production and income consequences of land reform is, therefore, unwarranted. We recall from Chapter 6, that in our field study of the impact of land reform in three Egyptian villages, a period of 15–20 years was considered adequate for before-and-after land reform comparison. A longer time frame of 30 years was used in our review of the experiences of China and South Korea and about 20 years for Iraq. This time frame is required because redistributed land is only a means for securing part or all the household income or consumption and for participation in social institutions. It also allows the evaluator to capture the effects of weather and the dynamic interaction of the beneficiaries' increased earnings from crops, newly acquired non-land assets, and from non-agricultural sources as well as their improved education. It is from such comparisons in concrete situations that we can draw some practical lessons which may be useful to policy makers, rural development practitioners and students of the political economy of land reform.

Justice and stability: the explicit objective

Land reform has not a *single* aim. Of the different objectives of land reform, social gains receive the greatest emphasis by the reformers according to our study of countries' experiences. Liberation of the exploited peasants and semi-feudal bonded labour was particularly emphatic in the objectives of the Mexican, Cuban, Bolivian, Indian and Peruvian reforms. Egypt and Iraq used the stock phrases of the abolition of 'feudalism and humiliation'. Several country leaders presented land reform as the impetus 'to raise the heads of the poor cultivators and to regain their dignity' (for example Mexico's Zapata in 1911, Iraq's Qassim in 1958, Egypt's Nasser in 1952, and Pakistan's Bhutto in 1972). In all these cases, as well as in many others, land reform was conceived as an effective approach to fairness, ending the harmful and insidious social relations which had arisen under institutional monopoly of land and other means of production. It seems that policy makers equated the economic meaning of the abolition or weakening of landlords' monopolistic power in the agricultural market structure with the ethical meaning of providing peasants with liberty, property rights, self-esteem, and eventual command over food. Because no monopolist gives up power voluntarily, the break-up of concentrated landed property, and the redistribution of property rights requires State intervention. In such circumstances, the institution of government has to extend its limits of ordinary functions, whether by democratic or authoritarian means, to adjust property rights and limit the economic freedom of entrepreneurs for the interest of the disadvantaged section of the rural population. In a sense, land reform combines the economic and ethical meaning of justice.

Government enforcement of farmland rent control, however, has proved ineffective in countries where the power of landlords remained virtually intact along with preferential access to government services. Similarly, the enforcement of laws fixing minimum wages for agricultural workers proved to be unenforceable in labour markets where the supply exceeds demand, particularly in slack agricultural seasons. Unenforced laws are no laws. Such half-hearted policies seem to have been used by policy makers as symbolic justice to pacify the discontented rural poor without harming the interests of land owners and other capitalists on whose support the regime rests. With these measures, as with partial land reforms, policy makers could gain immediate popular support, check agrarian unrest and attain political stability.

Inextricably linked to the realisation of justice and political stability is enhancement of the productive abilities of the beneficiaries, and increased employment opportunities on land. Among the necessary steps towards this goal is the removal of barriers characterising market imperfections which give larger landowners and moneylenders monopoly advantages in the market structure over small and landless farmers. According to the documented evidence presented in Chapters 4, 5 and 6, such barriers to entry increase costs borne by poor peasants seeking entry into the credit market and land transactions. Denied potential gains are manifested in the payment of high interest rates for credit obtained by informal sources, consequent indebtedness, and payment of exorbitant rental rates for scarce land. Yet another cost incurred by the wage-dependent landless workers are wages which fall below the value of their marginal and average productivity (see Chapters 4 and 5). These forms of incurred losses from institutional barriers correspond to monopoly profits gained at low risk by the landlords, middlemen, a hierarchy of labour contractors, moneylenders and owners of irrigation water pumps. Thus the emphasis placed by policy makers upon attaining social gains and political stability through land reform is well founded where it enhances the productive capacity of the beneficiaries and removes institutional barriers to agricultural growth.

Employment, investment and food productivity

While greater equity is immediately realised after land redistribution and effectively enforced rent control, the effect on employment varies according to pre-reform conditions of land use intensity and production relations. When complete land reform absorbs the masses of tenants and landless workers and combines farming with non-farming activities in rural areas, employment in rural areas is likely to increase. The aggregate effect is relatively negligible where actual tenants of land are given ownership title and continue to be self-employed.[1] Pre-reform agrarian conditions in the case studies indicate that where land concentration was initially high, and cultivation extensive, land reform combines the hitherto under-utilised labour with the intensive cultivation of land. Hence, additional investment is necessary to increase land productivity.

In our sample cases of land reforms, pre-reform yields were far below potential, and technological advances were minimally applied. The empirical evidence gathered from field studies in many LDCs by a number of scholars and presented in Chapter 4 reveals that large estates (often prevalent in pre-reform conditions) are, in general, inefficient in resource utilisation from the standpoint of the economy as a whole. Hence, there is a loss of potential gains. This does not mean that all large estates in all developing countries are inefficient. For example, the efficiency in terms of economies of scale in production in pre-land reform plantations of sugar cane and cotton, as well as of their processing factories, led the reformers in Cuba and Peru to retain and improve them. In Sri Lanka, the same was true of tea and rubber plantations. Workers participated in the management of the expropriated estates either directly or through their co-operatives. Cultivation was further intensified and the terms of employment and social benefits for workers substantially improved.

Still, there remains a fear that redistributive land reform will disrupt production and reduce the marketed surplus of food grain. This fear was not substantiated by the results of my field studies in Egypt or by evidence from the historical experience of the nine countries reviewed in the preceding two chapters. Because of the serious policy implications of this generalisation, it merits further explanation. China, Cuba, Iraq and Bolivia did experience falls in production during their early years of reform, yet in each case, contributing exogenous factors must be taken into account. Around 1957 there was a split in the Chinese Communist Party leadership over the pace of collectivisation of individual holdings and their co-operatives, with the view of Mao Zedong's faction prevailing. In a short span of two years compulsory collectivisation was swiftly implemented nationwide with the corresponding change in the cultivators' incentive structure, introducing (for the first time in the long tradition of Chinese farmers) work points dependent upon the team's net production. The primary aim was to mobilise (not voluntarily) the gigantic rural labour force at an unprecedented scale for capital formation via the construction of communal projects – notably irrigation for the intensification of land and labour use. Consequently, agricultural production fell between 1958–63. Following these dramatic changes, rice production substantially increased from 53.6 million tons in 1961 to 109.9 million tons in 1970, and further, to 175 million tons in 1987. Production of the other staple food, potatoes, also increased by 155 per cent between 1961–87 (FAO Country Tables, 1989). The ideological conflicts and administrative circumstances behind Cuba's decline in sugar cane production between 1960 and 1965, and in Iraq's wheat and rice production between 1958 and 1964 were unique for each country as explained in Chapter 6.

Our discussion suggests that apart from unfavourable weather, production can be disrupted in the early years of land reform *if and only if*:

(a) policy makers, after starting land reform, continue to fundamentally disagree about the form of property rights in land and the institutional organisation of agricultural production;
(b) State institutions are incapable of implementing the programme within the prescribed time frame, or to fulfil the promises made by politicians to potential beneficiaries;
(c) the establishment of institutions to provide necessary complementary inputs is delayed, lagging behind the abolition of the old arrangements and the speedy expropriation of land; and
(d) the distributed land is of inferior productive quality and/or without secure water for irrigation.

The facts presented in the preceding chapters show that irrespective of the political ideology behind land reform, sustaining growth rates of agricultural output and food productivity in particular requires more than reformers' rhetoric. Given the political commitment, justice, liberty, feeding people and alleviating poverty need more than the magic formula for property entitlement. For instance, the effectiveness of Iraq's land reforms depended upon higher public expenditure of bountiful oil revenue on irrigation, drainage and heavily subsidised complementary inputs (a sharp rise of 600 per cent between 1965 and 1978). In contrast to Iraq, Egypt's fertile irrigated land, intensive cropping, well-established cadastral records, and an ample quantity and quality of university trained manpower provided the necessary infrastructure to implement its policy in five years as planned. China had neither material capital, foreign aid, nor sufficient irrigated land. It accumulated capital by mobilising its gigantic labour force in agriculture for decentralised industrialisation in rural areas and for the expansion of its irrigated area from 16 per cent of total arable land in 1947 to 45 per cent in 1985.

Thus, the specific role of land reform in agricultural growth differs a good deal according to its scope the resource base, the state of agriculture productive capacity at the time of initiating the reforms, and above all the implementation capability of State institutions. This role cannot be defined in general universal abstract terms, or in terms of standardised capitalist or Marxist doctrines. Each country must be viewed specifically, and the peculiarity of its reformed institutional arrangements considered in the context of its unique pre-reform agrarian conditions.

Most of these lessons and issues of reforming concentrated private property rights in land are of less interest to policy makers in African countries south of the Sahara, where customary land tenure systems prevail and rights in land are typically defined for groups rather than individuals. Though private land concentration is of concern to a few countries with high population density on land (e.g. Kenya, Malawi, Madagascar, the Ivory Coast and some states of Nigeria), the institutional barriers to agricultural growth and increasing food production are of common concern. As cultivable land becomes relatively scarce and its produce is commercialised, investment to improve the productivity of land and people becomes linked to both land rights and the credit market. In the absence of special credit banks (as were established for the *Ejidos* and *Comuneros* in Mexico) cultivators with land use rights only, do not have land title for the collateral required for institutional credit. Thus, higher agricultural production become inseparable from greater accessibility to the land and credit markets.

In the author's meeting with scholars and development practitioners of eight African countries (Nairobi, January 1985), institutional constraints embedded in the land tenure system and changes introduced during colonial rule were identified. These include: fragmentation of farming units resulting from continual subdivision by inheritance; illegal means of land appropriation as the potential return to land rises; increasing conflicts of interest between the State and tribal chiefs over the regulations of tenure arrangements; ethnically discriminating commercial interests which result in appropriation of the highest quality land for cash crops at the expense of food crops; and the use of cheap labour. Though women are the main producers of food, their land rights are further restricted, as they are traditionally unrecognised by financing and State institutions. Still, with a shortage of rigorous micro-studies, it was difficult to establish a firm relationship between land title and productivity per unit of land. Available aggregative data suggest that in African countries where customary land tenure systems have been replaced by individual ownership and registration of title, the problems of land concentration, rising landlessness, and the combination of widespread indebtedness and loss of land become pronounced. Furthermore, access to land through the market becomes restricted. (These implications are documented in the case of Kenya, presented in Chapter 5.) During 1970–85 food production and total agricultural output have deteriorated under both systems (customary and those which introduced individual land titles in capitalist agriculture), particularly in countries with a high poverty incidence (Table 1.4). The appalling poverty and continued fall in food productivity calls for institutional reforms which are unique to each case. Where livestock is a primary source of wealth and employment, investment in improved animal husbandry would yield greater returns to the poor pastoralists, and contribute to total agricultural growth.

Although the stated objectives of land reform are social and political, we have dwelt on its role in removing the institutional barriers to agricultural growth and to greater equality in distribution of income. This we have done for five reasons. The first is to impress upon policy makers the need to sustain initial income gains for increasing the beneficiaries' purchasing power. Second, without increased food production, the net flow of marketed surplus to urban centres might be reduced. Third, though a primary factor, land reform is not the exclusive determinant of growth in agriculture. Production incentives from pricing policy and favourable terms of trade for agriculture, investment in irrigation, soil conservation and construction of rural roads, expansion of educational opportunities are all conducive to sustained growth.

Fourth, land reform is not cost-free. There are substantial expenses and financial considerations associated with its implementation, such as administrative costs and payment of compensation which incur expenditures from the national budget. Fifth, there is a positive correlation between agricultural growth and total GDP rates of growth. Accordingly, a fall in agricultural growth adversely influences the growth of the entire economy, particularly where the share of agriculture in total product and export is high. These intersectoral growth links can easily be seen from inspecting the growth records of developing countries since the 1950s (with the exception of the mineral-rich LDCs). The links are also confirmed by the historical records of the now developed (industrialised) countries.

Accessible opportunities and rapid alleviation of rural poverty

At the start of the book we asked: is the pace of poverty reduction conditional upon land reform and the scale of land redistribution and greater equity in food consumption? In Chapter 1 we presented elements of the profile of poverty in LDCs with both cross-sectional and time series types of aggregate data. The available cross-sectional data on the increasing incidence of absolute poverty, under-nutrition, and of landlessness, falling food productivity and rising land concentration in LDCs with private property-market economies is distressing (see Tables 1.2, 1.5, and Appendix A). Given the database limitations, the statistical analysis in Chapter 5 showed a positive and high correlation between poverty levels and the degree of inequality in land distribution, as well as between poverty and landlessness. The degree of association between land concentration and landlessness though lower was also positive and statistically significant. These relationships confirm the hypothesis stated earlier, that the lower the concentration of land holdings, the lower the prevalence of absolute poverty and landlessness.

In exploring policy implications for alleviating poverty, we looked closely at the ambiguity in the use of the key terms, poverty, agrarian reform, opportunities, and rural development. In Chapters 2 and 3, we stressed how the different use of these terms for political convenience or ideological reasons distorts the real issues in rural development and in the analytic reasoning behind policy prescriptions. We also questioned the widely-held assumption that opportunities for economic freedom and escape from the risk of under-nutrition can be accessible to all farmers and can be realised under the market mechanism of a *laissez-faire* land tenure policy. It has been argued that the role of land reform in leading rural development (both so defined) is in providing accessible opportunities to small and landless farmers which enhance their abilities and offer them security in direct acquisition of food without heavy reliance on the imperfect mechanism of the food-grain market. Our country historical review of pre-land reform conditions has shown that opportunities to have secured access to land were often inaccessible to poor tenants and hired labourers under *laissez-faire* land tenure policies. When these circumstances include a low demand for labour outside agriculture, landless labourers possessing no material assets (donkey, bullock and plough) have only two opportunities to choose from: to sell his or her labour for low wages, or become involuntarily unemployed and starve. Other opportunities for borrowing credit to purchase land are not opportunities because they are not accessible. Our inter-country comparison (Chapter 7) suggests that the length of time for the eradication or the alleviation of poverty and malnutrition can be considerably shortened by opportunities offered by effectively implemented land reform. This is particularly evident in situations where land is the major source of holding wealth, labour utilisation, income and power.

To realise rural development, our focus on the time trend in reducing the numbers of the poor requires careful examination of both the comparability of estimates on absolute poverty incidence, and the demographic characteristics in countries implementing land reform. For example, slowing the population growth rates in rural areas has a substantial effect in reducing the number of poor, particularly if fertility reduction policies are accompanied by complete land reform. But calculations of aggregate statistics do not necessarily reflect the true size of the rural poor population, who may or may not be reached by fertility control policies. Or, who may reject this control of their own free will.

Similarly, while the *per capita* food production may rise at the aggregate level with higher growth rates of food production and/or a slow growth of total population, it is no guarantee that food-intake will actually increase for the poor. Thus, the aggregate statistical average conceals the incidence of under-nutrition, just as average *per capita* GNP has failed to expose the magnitude of absolute poverty. Empirical evidence presented in Chapter 3 indicates that malnutrition prevailed in many countries and even famine occurred where total food supply and marketed surplus of grain increased. In this light, the implications of the variation in the views of analysts regarding agricultural growth can be seen. It is one thing to view it in terms of economic efficiency and to emphasise growth rates in total supply of food commodities; it is another to see it in the context of the poor's actual acquisition of food, and how it enhances their abilities (nutritional standards, longevity of life and participation in development). Reaching these goals is the real meaning of rural development.

The case studies have illustrated that existing inter-regional differences in poverty reduction within each country could not be captured from nationwide data. Policy makers need reliable information from field surveys on where the poor live, and why they remain poor. Variation in natural endowment, scale of non-farming activities, cropping pattern and levels of education are all present in our case studies. It is through purposeful surveys disaggregated by location and occupation that policy makers can identify the rural poor, and understand the attributes of their poverty. Thus, aggregated estimation of poverty, both for one point in time and inter-temporally, must be carefully interpreted. While useful to planners and development analysts, disaggregated data are more useful to programmers and ultimately, to different categories of the poor.

The imperativeness of land reform

If rapid reduction of poverty is the overwhelming objective of LDCs' policy makers, state intervention is imperative to reform the skewed pattern of land-ownership in favour of the propertyless. Reliance on the politically volatile sources of food subsidies, food aid, and remittances earned from the international labour market is precarious. Once remittances and food aid stop, and subsidies are removed, the rural poor are the first to suffer.

Other isolated measures to reduce poverty such as farmland rent control, progressive land taxation and the establishment of minimum wages have proved ineffective and counter-productive when power relations combined with land concentration and bureaucracy are left intact. This is also the lesson learnt from past experience in integrated rural development projects carefully reviewed by Ruttan (1984) and from my field studies in Nepal (1980) and North Yemen (1986).[2] The political economy of these ambiguously defined projects is to concentrate scarce foreign exchange and technical personnel in those rural areas that are politically chosen to satisfy the powerful members of the existing regime. In infusing these resources, progressive farmers (mostly large and middle-sized) are frequently preferred over the subsistence peasants. Under these structural characteristics, this approach neither guarantees that these projects' technical and financial resources will reach the poor, nor that income disparity will be reduced.

Although Thailand (with moderate land concentration) was able to reduce poverty by expanding irrigated land, reallocating resources, and effective fertility reduction (as discussed in Chapter 7), one-third of its rural population remained poor, and inequality in income distribution and ownership of non-land assets increased. Even the option of private land redistribution in partial land reform can be less effective when frustrated by class-biased bureaucracy, the legal and police systems and the monopoly power of local traders and moneylenders. The far-reaching power-based institutional changes necessary for reducing poverty differentiate a genuine and effectively implemented land reform policy from other income transfer programmes.

In the early stages of development in the case studies (Chapter 6) it seems that country leaders viewed land reform as the *sine qua non* of a dynamic rural economy. In turn, agricultural development was considered a leading element in their overall development strategy. Without this type of approach in the early stage of overall development, Todaro rightly says:

> Industrial growth would either be stultified or, if it succeeded would create such severe internal imbalances in the economy that the problems of widespread poverty, inequality, and unemployment would become even more pronounced. (Totaro, 1981: 252)

As a policy, land reform's fundamental function is in challenging the prevailing injustice in the appropriation of unearned income from property rights privileges. The question to raise is, 'Is the legitimisation of justice, political stability and welfare of the mass of rural poor provided by accessible opportunities impracticable, or is it a "Utopia"'? In the light of our study of country experiences, the answer is 'No'. Whether land reform is politically feasible under certain power structures is not for the social scientist or the development analyst to judge. What he or she can do is to use the faculties and professional tools to understand the totality of rural under-development problems in a specific situation, to analyse the determinants, to point out their implications for poverty, equity, economic growth and conflicts of interest, and to suggest alternatives. Throughout this book, our study of the political economy of land reform did not consider the docile maintenance of the status quo of injustice to be an alternative because it offers no choice of substitutes. Instead, this book argues that land reform is the alternative to a state of rural under-development characterised by skewed distribution of land, income and accessible opportunities, as well as by falling food productivity. Without land reform under such circumstances, the peasants and landless workers have no hope for effective participation towards their social and economic advancement.

The prospects

An alarmingly violent swing in approaches to rural under-development problems has been witnessed since 1980. This has occurred despite the persistent problems of poverty, malnutrition, landlessness and falling food productivity which were profiled in the beginning of this book. We have explored the paradoxes and puzzles surrounding the shifts in analytical reasoning behind the policy prescriptions of some economists, rich donor countries, and influential international development agencies including the World Bank and the IMF. The apparent reason for the swing is a response to the mounting problems of debt, inflation, trade and balance of payment deficits facing many LDCs. While we recognise the need for structural adjustments in LDCs to expand their exporting capacity and to ease their balance of payment deficits, we view 'fiscal and monetary medicine' as a short-term treatment of problems which themselves are long-term, deeply rooted in the prevalence of poverty associated with land-based power structures. As shown in Chapter 2, countries with a greater degree of equality in land and income distribution have, during the world economic shockwaves, managed to maintain a good record of food production and nutrition per head (see Tables 1.3, 2.1, 2.2 and 7.1). When the world economic recession deepened between 1980 and 1985, this group of countries sustained agricultural growth, food production and public expenditure on health and education.

The shift in ideology behind policy prescriptions has serious consequences: a trend away from land reform, and a declining awareness of its role in the rapid reduction of poverty and its contribution to the removal of barriers to agricultural growth and to political stability.

Though the ultimate responsibility for policy choice rests with the sovereign governments of LDCs, external factors do influence that choice. The post-1980s changes in ideological preferences of members of the OECD, particularly those of the USA, UK, and West Germany can, therefore, influence many LDC policy makers directly through the provisos attached to financial assistance and indirectly through the World Bank and IMF macro-policy dialogues with LDC governments. The power of their large shares in capital stock and their significant voting power in both of these international funding agencies cannot be underestimated. In the new scenario for rural development pursued by these capitalist powers, the market has been identified as the mechanism for efficient allocation of resources and for the distribution of income through the pricing mechanism. According to this post-1980 ideology, the market, not government intervention, is the effective means to alleviate poverty. But under which institutional systems of transactions and legal framework can the market and related incentives work in LDCs? When the distribution of both income and accessible opportunities is grossly skewed, the market works for the benefit of traders, large and medium farmers and multinational corporations, while most probably harming the landless workers and poor peasants. With neither secure tenure of land, nor legitimate access to land or credit, small tenants and landless workers can hardly respond to price incentives and profit opportunities offered by technical change.

While it is true that for the rich industrialised nations, historical structural changes have substantially lessened the relative economic importance of land, in many LDCs land continues to be of crucial importance as the major domestic food-producing and labour-using asset. This is particularly true for agrarian economies where land remains the main determinant of class structure, and of social and political power. In these countries, the labour markets outside agriculture are unable to absorb the ever-increasing entrants into the agricultural sector. With prevailing bias towards capital-intensive technology for industrialisation, no large-scale transfer of labour from agriculture into industry can be expected. Also, with the deteriorating oil revenue of the oil-rich developing countries, there is a downward trend in their demand for unskilled labour from agriculturally overpopulated countries.

As part of the current World Bank, IMF-induced adjustment programmes, public expenditure on food subsidies and increasing cultivable land and settlement schemes is being curtailed. With this in mind, as well as the declining support for land reform in both the domestic and international environments (as documented in Chapter 2), what then are the prospects for poor tenants and landless agricultural workers? It seems that the prospects for change depend upon organised non-governmental efforts to apply pressure through legal means for the introduction of land reform.

Land reform is but a single element in the wider struggle for justice and social change. Out of despair, grinding indebtedness, and wretched poverty, the hopeless poor of Ireland's Land Wars (1879–92) and of many other countries have turned to violence (Wolf, 1969). This road is currently being taken by land seizures and squatting in the Philippines, Brazil, Colombia, Kenya, Paraguay and El Salvador, just to name a few. In Peru, where partial land reforms excluded most of the landless and poorest peasants, violence has erupted in the northern provinces.

Motivated non-governmental organisations and grass roots pressure groups can help to mitigate injustice, avoid agrarian unrest and political instability and, thereby avert the disruption of production which accompanies violent rebellion. Efforts continue in the several LDCs, where agricultural trade unions, peasant organisations, youth movements and church leaders lobby peacefully for land rights and for the formulation of programmes relevant to their needs. In the Philippines, for example, non-governmental organisations (NGOs) have persistently demanded a real land reform that goes beyond the 1972 instituted land tenure regulations in areas of rice and maize, and redistribution of land and opportunities throughout the agrarian structure.[3] As mentioned in Chapter 2, the land-based power structure in the Philippines and Brazil have resulted in prolonged negotiations of the terms of the land reform, and though publicly committed to land reform, their governments have been slow to implement it, continuing to make compromises in the interest of the landlords. The success of Church leaders in Latin America and NGOs in some Asian countries is documented (El-Ghonemy, 1984; Bhaduri and Anisur Rahman, 1982, and 1984; and Handelman, 1981).[4] In a bureaucracy which should be the guardian of rights and the enforcer of law, but in reality is corrupt, these informal and collective efforts have proved to be fundamentally important.

Through legal means, NGOs, particularly agricultural labour trade unions and peasant organisations can exert pressure to restore land grabbed by influential persons, or seized by moneylenders. In alliance with the committed middle class intelligentsia, they can help mobilise public opinion, and gain support from the media locally, nationally and internationally. They can also collectively lobby for lower ceilings on land ownership and expanded agricultural land for redistribution in settlement schemes. Still, organised participation faces enormous barriers.[5] Many governments either prohibit the very existence of agricultural trade unions, or render them powerless through denying their right to strike, accounts are audited, and annual conferences approved or disapproved. Leaders have been removed from office, and even killed by landlords' hired thugs, or by the government's military. Under preferential agreements with multinational corporations, interests of agricultural workers have been compromised by many governments. To gain higher wages, better working conditions and social benefits, poor cultivators and landless workers require collective power within the law.

The effectiveness of non-statutory organisations is enhanced by occupational or gender homogeneity among their members. For example, women who constitute almost half of the agricultural workers in many LDCs, have traditionally been excluded from village organisations, trade unions and agricultural co-operatives whose membership has been the prerogative of men. With the exception of socialist countries, rural women are rarely given title to land in land reform and settlement schemes (Palmer, 1985). This hardworking silent majority have been and still are denied their legitimate rights in land to influence policies and programmes to reflect the realities of their high rate of participation in the labour force.[6] Interestingly, recent progress in furthering rural women's rights has been initiated by NGOs in the USA and Europe who have the experience and strategic ability to lobby at national and international levels. This type of support and lobbying is valuable in the broader sense: international coalitions can potentially influence policy makers, United Nations forums, regional economy co-operation organisations and international aid agencies.

The potential pressure of NGOs teamed with informal local groups and committed intelligentsia represents an ingredient of grass-root social change and democracy in practice. This is not to make a fetish of democracy, but to stress the necessity of recognising two simple and practical principles. The first is the right of expression, and the second pertains to accountability. With regard to the former, land reform beneficiaries and those millions demanding their legitimate rights in land, know what they really want, and should be heard. Amomg the share-croppers, hired landless workers and nomadic pastoralists, men and women have perceptions which may differ from those of planners and programmers. In their own interest, politicians, programmers and foreign aid-giving agencies should listen to and learn from the rural poor. Excluded from effective participation for too long, once motivated the poor can collectively articulate their perceptions of priorities and programmes. This path to social change rests on a number of assumptions:

(a) collective action is most effective;
(b) the rural poor prefer informal organisations to politically patronised and heavily bureaucratised statutory bodies;
(c) the ultimate aim of the policy makers is to increase the productivity of these excluded poor and to realise social stability; and
(d) generally speaking, the rural poor neither know how to lobby nor how the political system of their countries is organised.

As regards accountability, local civil servants working in land reform and other rural development programmes should be accountable to the beneficiaries of these programmes, instead of having a grip of power over them. Through their own local organisations, beneficiaries judge the response of the local bureaucracy to their needs and can effectively monitor corruption and misappropriation of public revenue. Jointly with local officials of government and aid giving agencies, the impact of these programmes could better be evaluated. Without this joint evaluation, the results are usually inflated.

Responding to the needs of the mass of poor cultivators is a practical necessity for the interests of politicians, government planners and programmers. Leaders of countries with capitalist agriculture should look to land reform as a means of solving the fundamental contradiction of excess accumulation of wealth coexisting with excess poverty. Policy makers should realise that the veil of ignorance has been lifted through the news of social upheavals and the lifestyle of the rich which now reaches rural areas of LDCs through mass communications media (ratio and TV). Agrarian unrest and the resulting interruption in food production is inevitable in the absence of policies rapidly to reduce poverty, alleviate inequalities in opportunities, and promote justice. In the face of increasing poverty incidence, and growing injustice, land reform is crucial, and so should regain its priority in policy prescriptions and development strategies.

Notes

1   In the case of partial land reform which transfers land title to the tenants already cultivating the land, the new owners motivated by security of tenure can intensify their family labour. Public investment in irrigation, drainage, soil conservation and construction of storage facilities can increase employment opportunities in the reform sector. Similarly, land reforms which integrate crop cultivation with non-farming activities such as processing of raw material can also raise employment. For a detailed study on the employment affects in country experiences see *Agrarian Reform and Employment*, an ILO Publication, Geneva, 1971 and Chapter 6 'Types and Consequences of Land Reform' in de Janvry (1981).

2   After carefully reviewing integrated rural development projects in LDCs, Ruttan concluded:

> The structural characteristics of most rural communities, and of the societies of which they are a part, will continue to prevent them from obtaining access to many of the development opportunities which are potentially available. Rural development programmes will rarely be able to mobilize the political and economic resources necessary for massive structural reform. . . . A major implication is that in a society in which the distribution of political resources is strongly biased against rural people, it will be difficult to mobilize the bureaucratic resources needed to make rural development programmes effective. In addition, there will be strong resistance of the evolution of local institutions that have the capacity to mobilize economic and political resources to meet the basic needs of the rural poor. (Ruttan, 1984: 399)

For a critical review of rural development programmes in Africa see, Lele (1979) third printing with new postscript. For an evaluation of field projects in Mexico, Columbia and Peru, see de Janvry, (1981: 231–54).

From my experience in the review and assessment of the large-scale rural development projects and related government programmes in Nepal (May and June 1980) and the Yemen Arab Republic (September-October 1986), a number of common features emerged:

1. They are funded by various major donor countries and the World Bank, who were experimenting with their own conceptions of rural development.
2. A major deficiency in these projects lies in their ambiguous objectives and the aggregation of rural people. Stock phrases, such as 'raising the level of living' are used and households in the areas of the projects are aggregated.
3. Monitoring and evaluation of these projects are chiefly in the form of a reporting system having an administrative character. The thrust was on judging what has been realised versus planned in terms of disbursement of materials and services during the reporting period.
4. Qualified extension staff and free technical inputs are devoted to 'contact farmers' who were mostly big and medium farmers whose farms were near tarmac roads. Whereas, the projects speak of assisting small farmers, the smaller group were not reached.
5. Female heads of households in Yemen who were farm operators in the absence of their migrant husbands in Saudi Arabia were ignored by the projects' male technical personnel for cultural reasons.

For detailed information on specific project areas, see (a) *Report of the FAO Mission on Nepal*, Follow-up to World Conference on Agrarian Reform and Rural Development FAO, Rome, 1980, and (b) *Yemen Arab Republic, Rural Development Strategy and Implementation*: An Assessment and A Review of Issues, UN-Economic and Social Commission for Western Asia, Baghdad, Iraq, 1986

3   Nearly 20 NGOs and major peasant organisations are active for the lobby for land reform in the Philippines. Peasants' organisations demonstrated and marched to Manilla in January 1987 demanding land reform. They were stopped and attacked, by police and armed forces and 18 people were killed. In May 1987, they formed the Congress for People's Agrarian Reform to lobby collectively for what they called 'Genuine Agrarian Reform'. Their efforts were co-ordinated by the Asian NGO Coalition (ANGOC) under the leadership of Dr Umali, formerly the Dean of the College of Agriculture, Los Banos. They were joined by church leaders and a number of scholars. This consolidated effort produced a plan calling for: land to the tiller; complete abolition of absentee landownership; coverage of all crops and tenure arrangement; compensation to be paid to landowners; and preferential option to the beneficiaries for organising co-operatives and collective farms. This plan states the principles for lobbying with the President, members of the Cabinet and with the Philippine Congress.

4   In Pakistan, the collective power of tenants has succeeded in withholding old rents once control was legally instituted. As an organised group, they have been able to hire lawyers to take their case through complex court proceedings, and demand their rights. Such power is effective in the face of legally prescribed reforms which remain unenforced by local bureaucracies under unaltered political systems (see Rahman (1984)). There are many examples of grass-roots efforts in countries having no fundamental land reforms. For example, the Grameen Bank work for

providing credit to homogeneous groups of landless men and women in some villages in Bangladesh, and the Small Farmers' Development Project in Nepal. In Northeast Brazil, in the Pernambuco, 55 sharecroppers and landless workers who resisted high rents and demanded higher wages were organised by the Catholic Church in a society called Ligas Camponenas which took over 600 hectares of a large sugar cane estate to grow their food crops. After a period of tension, this movement expanded and it was recognised by the government which set up an office (SUPRA) to regulate the allocation of land and its use where land seizures had taken place. Another widely publicised example is in the State of Maharashta of India. Known as the Bhoomi Sena movement, it succeeded in returning lands that had been illegally seized by the money-lenders (Sawkars). For other examples see El-Ghonemy, (1984: 1–17).

5   In my meeting with leaders of agricultural trade unions in 15 African countries held in Arusha, Tanzania during 1984, the conflicts of interests among small farmers (small owners and tenants) and hired landless agricultural workers became obvious. While there appeared to be a sense of power and self-confidence, concerns were primarily centred upon training programmes in Unionism for permanent workers in large plantations, and the possible repercussions of political confrontation with governments. The right of agricultural workers to organise is regulated by international conventions monitored by the International Labour Organization (ILO). Important among these instruments, are Conventions No. 87 and 141 on the freedom of association and protection of the right of rural workers. Only 13 developing countries ratified the first and 45 the second by 1985. Even after official ratification, it was reported that some countries violated their provisions and departed from their principles.

6   There are examples where women's organisations were able to influence policy formulation to meet the needs of rural women: India, for membership of co-operatives' management committees; Iraq for rights equal to those of men; Socialist countries including Cuba, China, Nicaragua, Vietnam, Southern Yemen for given women executive responsibilities in co-operative management and in collectives. See for example: Bronstein (1983), Palmer (1985), and Ruth B. Engo, 'Key Role of African Women in Food Production', United Nations Development Fund for Women, New York.

Appendix A

Estimates of rural poverty incidence in 64 developing countries

Country	Year of estimate	Total population (millions)	Proportion of rural population to total (%)	Percentage of rural population in absolute poverty	Estimated number of rural poor (millions)
Africa					
Benin	1979	3.4	70.7	65	1.6
Botswana	1982	1.0	75.0	55	0.4
Burundi	1978	4.0	97.7	85	1.6
Cameroon	1978	8.1	68.2	40	2.2
Chad	1978	4.3	83.6	56	2.0
Ethiopia	1976	29.7	87.7	65	16.7
Ghana	1978	11.0	64.0	55	3.9
Ivory Coast	1985	10.1	55.0	26.4	1.4
Kenya	1978	15.4	86.7	50	6.5
Lesotho	1979	1.3	95.7	55	0.7
Madagascar	1977	8.0	83.0	50	3.3
Malawi	1977	5.5	74.5	85	3.5
Mali	1975	6.3	82.8	48	2.4
Mauritius	1981	1.0	48.0	12	0.1
Niger	1975	4.7	89.7	35	1.4
Nigeria	1985	99.5	70.0	58	40.2
Rwanda	1975	4.5	96.3	90	3.6
Sierra Leone	1979	3.2	76.1	65	1.7
Tanzania	1978	17.6	98.2	60	9.0
Zaire	1975	24.7	65.2	80	12.9
Zambia	1975	5.0	30.0	52	0.8
Asia					
Bangladesh	1975/8	81.0	89.9	74–81	56.5
Burma	1978	33.1	73.8	40	9.9
China	1981	980.0	87	6–11	circ. 60.0
India	1979	674.7	78.0	50.7	265.6
Nepal	1977	13.6	95.4	61	7.7
Pakistan	1979	84.5	72.2	39	23.8
Indonesia	1980	151.0	79.7	44	52.0
Korea, Rep	1980	39.0	40.0	9.8	1.6
Malaysia	1980–2	14.2	70.2	38	4.0
Papua New Guinea	1979	3.1	73.9	75	1.7

Country	Year of estimate	Total population (millions)	Proportion of rural population to total (%)	Percentage of rural population in absolute poverty	Estimated number of rural poor (millions)
Philippines	1980–2	49.5	63.3	41	13.1
Sri Lanka	1981	15.0	72.0	26	2.8
Thailand	1978	44.4	85.9	34	13.1
Latin America					
Argentina	1975	25.5	32.0	19	1.6
Brazil	1980	122.5	32.0	68	26.5
Bolivia	1975	4.9	69.6	85	2.9
Colombia	1980	26.0	30.0	67	5.2
Costa Rica	1980	2.3	56.0	34	0.4
Dominican Republic	1978	5.3	51.0	43	1.2
Ecuador	1980–2	8.3	54.7	65	2.9
El Salvador	1978	4.5	59.4	32	0.9
Guatemala	1977	6.6	62.2	25	1.0
Haiti	1977	5.4	76.6	78	3.2
Honduras	1978	3.4	65.9	55	1.2
Jamaica	1982	2.1	50.0	51	0.6
Mexico	1982	73.1	52.0	34	12.8
Nicaragua	1978	2.6	47.9	19	0.2
Panama	1978	1.9	47.4	30	0.3
Paraguay	1978	3.0	61.2	50	0.9
Peru	1977	16.5	43.0	68	4.8
Trinidad & Tobago	1977	1.0	78.7	39	0.3
Venezuela	1980	15.0	20.0	56	1.7
Middle East					
Afghanistan	1977	14.4	86.0	63	8.2
Egypt	1982	44.2	56.0	17.8	4.2
Iran	1976	34.5	58.0	38	7.6
Iraq	1976	11.5	38.0	15–20	circ. 0.8
Jordan	1979	2.8	44.4	17	0.2
Morocco	1979	19.4	60.1	45	5.3
Somalia	1982	4.5	71.3	60	2.1
Sudan	1982	20.0	79.6	70	9.9
Tunisia	1977	5.9	50.7	15	0.4
Turkey	1986	51.0	54.0	20	5.5
Yemen, Dem	1978	1.8	64.1	20	0.2
Total					767.3

Sources: *The Dynamics of Rural Poverty*, Table 1.1, Food and Agriculture of the UN, Rome, 1986. This appendix is reproduced with authorisation from the Publication Division of the FAO. Changes have been introduced to update data for the following countries: *Nigeria*, estimate of rural poverty was made by Paul Collier, in 'Poverty, Equity and Growth in Nigeria and Indonesia', Oxford University Press, forthcoming; *Korea, Republic* estimate is cited in: Shin Dong-Wan and Choi Yang-Boo, 'Alleviation of Rural Poverty in the Republic of Korea', see text Chapter 6; *Mexico, World Development Report*, 1982, World Bank: 83; *Egypt* see text, Chapter 6. The following countries have been *added* to FAO list: *Ivory Coast*: estimate was made by World Bank, Living Standard Unit. This estimate refers to *per capita* expenditure, Table 4 in *Confronting Poverty in Developing Countries*, Working Paper No. 48, 1988; *China* and *Iraq*, see text, Chapter 6; *Turkey*, see source in Table 5.4, Chapter 5.

Appendix B–1

Statistical analysis of the relations between poverty, landlessness, agricultural growth and land concentration in 20 developing countries*

Country	LC index	Growth %	Landless %	Poverty %	
Bangladesh	0.549	0.7	31	78	
Kenya	0.770	−0.1	15	45	
India	0.621	1.0	30	51	*The equations*:
Nepal	0.602	−1.3	10	61	P = f(LC)
Sri Lanka	0.619	2.8	19	26	LNS = f(LC)
Madagascar	0.800	−2.0	na	50	AGR = f(LC)
Pakistan	0.539	1.4	31	39	
Thailand	0.460	1.8	10	34	
Indonesia	0.620	2.7	36	44	
Jordan	0.690	4.6	7	17	
Egypt	0.430	0.8	24	18	
Honduras	0.780	0.4	33	58	
Philippines	0.530	3.2	37	42	
Turkey	0.580	3.6	28	20	
Jamaica	0.815	1.8	41	51	
Panama	0.840	0.6	20	30	
Brazil	0.859	3.7	39	67	
Korea, South	0.301	3.0	4	10	
Paraguay	0.939	3.4	27	63	
Venezuela	0.920	2.7	27	56	

Notes:
- P — Rural Poverty (percentage)
- LC — Gini Coefficient of Land Concentration – independent variable
- LNS — Landlessness (percentage)
- AGR — Agricultural GDP annual rates of growth *per capita* of agricultural population 1973–83
- *Mean values of the variables*: Poverty 43%; Landlessness 24.7%; Agricultural growth 1.74%; Gini Index of Land Concentration 0.663
- d.f. — or D.F. The Degrees of Freedom
- r — The simple correlation coefficient
- r^2 — The coefficient of determination, i.e. the proportion of the total variation in Y explained by the regression (procedures of analysis of variation – ANOVA)
- na — not available
- Std. Err. — The Standard Error

*See Chapter 5: 167–77.

Results of Equation Poverty = ƒ (Land concentration)

$$P = f \text{ (LC)} \quad Y = \text{Poverty}$$
$$X = \text{Land concentration}$$

Df:	r	r^2	Adj: r^2	Std. Error:
19	0.525	0.276	0.236	16.263

		Analysis of Variance Table		
Source	*DE:*	*Sum Squares:*	*Mean square*	*F-test*
Regression	1	1815.197	1815.197	6.863
Residual	18	4760.803	264.489	p = 0.0174
Total	19	6576		

Proportion of Variation in Poverty explained by Land Concentration

$$\frac{\text{Explained variation by regression}}{\text{Total variation}} = \frac{1815.2}{6576} = 28\%$$

Figure B1.1 The relation between poverty and land concentration

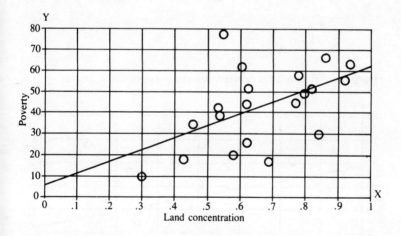

Land concentration

		Beta coefficient table		
Parameter	*Value*	*Std. Err.*	*Std. value*	*t-value*	*Probability*
Intercept	5.524				
Slope	56.508	21.57	0.525	2.62	0.0174

		Confidence intervals table		
Parameter	*95% Lower*	*95% Upper*	*90% Lower*	*90% Upper*
Mean (X, Y)	35.359	50.641	36.693	49.307
Slope	11.186	101.829	19.1	93.915

Figure B1.2 The relation between poverty and landlessness

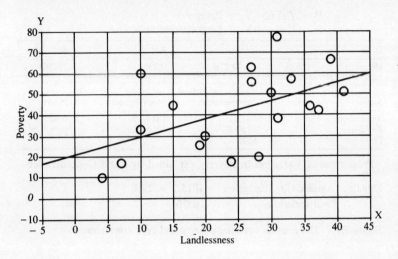

Figure B 1.3 The relation between poverty and agricultural growth

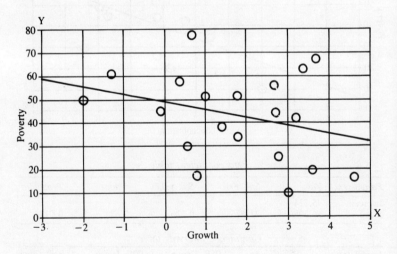

Results of Equation Landlessness = f (land concentration)

LNS = f (LC) Y = Landlessness
            X = Land concentration

DE	r	r-squared	Adj. r-squared	Std. Error
18	0.363	0.131	0.08	10.769

Analysis of variance table

Source	DE	Sum squares	Mean square	F-test
Regression	1	298.464	298.464	2.573
Residual	17	1971.641	115.979	p = 0.1271
Total	18	2270.105		

Beta coefficient table

Parameter	Value	Std. Err.	Std. value	t-value	Probability
Intercept	9.386				
Slope	23.321	14.538	0.363	1.604	0.1271

Confidence intervals table

Parameter	95% lower	95% upper	90% lower	90% upper
Mean (X, Y)	19.471	29.897	20.386	28.983
Slope	−7.354	53.996	−1.971	48.613

Results of Equation Growth = f (land concentration)

AGR = f (LC) Y = Growth
            X = Land concentration

DF	r	r-squared	Adj. r-squared	Std. Error:
19	0.035	1.241E-3	−0.054	1.783
	negative			

Analysis of variance table

Source	DF	Sum squares	Mean square	F-test
Regression	1	0.071	0.071	0.022
Residual	18	57.197	3.178	p = 0.8828
Total	19	57.268		

Beta coefficient table					
Parameter	*Value*	*Std. Err.*	*Std. value*	*t-value*	*Probability*
Intercept	1.974				
Slope	−0.354	2.364	−0.035	0.15	0.8828

Confidence intervals table				
Parameter	*95% lower*	*95% upper*	*90% lower*	*90% upper*
Mean (*X*, *Y*)	0.902	2.578	1.049	2.431
Slope	−5.321	4.614	−4.454	3.747

Appendix B–2

Sample of 19 countries including Colombia, Mexico, Peru and Morocco which were *excluded* from Table 5.4 and the statistical analysis in Appendix B–1

Relationship between rural poverty, landlessness, agricultural growth and land concentration in 19 developing countries

Country in alphabetical order	Economic level GNP per capita US dollar 1982 (1)	Agricultural GDP annual growth rates 1973–83 (2)	Gini Coefficient of land distribution and year of estimate (3)	Landless households as percentage total agricultural households/ year of estimate (4)	Rural poverty level: rural population in absolute poverty as percentage of total/year of estimate (5)
Brazil	2.240	4.2	0.859 (1980)	39 (1980)[a]	67 (1980)
Colombia	1,460	3.7	0.860 (1972)	49 (1970)[c]	54 (1975)
Egypt	690	2.5	0.456 (1975)	24 (1981)[c]	18 (1982)
Honduras	660	3.3	0.780 (1974)	33 (1974)[c]	58 (1980)
India	260	2.2	0.621 (1977)	30 (1981)[a]	51 (1979)
Indonesia	580	3.7	0.620 (1973)	36 (1973)[a] Java	44 (1980)
Jamaica	1,330	–0.2	0.814 (1980)	41 (1972)[b]	51 (1980)
Kenya	390	3.4	0.802 (1970)	15 (1976)[c]	50 (1976)
Korea. South	1,910	1.5	0.301 (1980)	4 (1978)[c]	11 (1978)
Mexico	2,270	3.5	0.747 (1970)	49 (1979)[b]	49 (1975)
Morocco	870	0.7	0.642 (1962)	33 (1980)[a]	45 (1979)
Nepal	170	1.0	0.602 (1980)	10 (1983)[a]	61 (1978)
Pakistan	380	3.4	0.539 (1980)	31 (1980)[c]	39 (1980)
Paraguay	1,610	6.0	0.930 (1982)	60 (1972)[c]	63 (1980)
Peru	1,310	0.9	0.776 (1972)	24 (1972)[c]	68 (1977)
Philippines	820	4.3	0.530 (1981)	37 (1982)[a]	42 (1982)
Sri Lanka	320	4.1	0.623 (1982)	19 (1982)[a]	26 (1981)
Thailand	790	3.8	0.460 (1978)	11 (1980)[c]	28 (1976)
Venezuela	4,140	2.6	0.920 (1973)	27 (1973)[b]	56 (1980)

Sources:
Col. 1 & 2   Tables 1 and 2 of basic indicators – World Development Report 1984 and 1985 respectively.
Col. 3   FAO. The 1970 World Census of Agriculture. *A Statistical Analysis*, publication No. 47, 1984, and preliminary results of 1980 Census of Agriculture – the Figure of Egypt in Richard H. Adams, 'Development and Structural Change in Rural Egypt 1952–82' *World Development*. Vol. 13, 6, 1985: 705–23.
Col. 4a.   'The rural Landlessness: Dynamics, problems and Policies', September 1985. Table 14, FAO, Rome
   b.   ACRD IX/1979/11: 20–1, ILO, Geneva.
   Kenya: Collier and Lal (1986: 79), Honduras: Peter Peek. 'Agrarian Structure and Rural Poverty – The Case of Honduras, ILO, September 1984 Egypt and Pakistan: El-Ghonemy, M. Riad. 'Economic Growth, Income Distribution and Rural Poverty in the Near East' FAO, 1984 Table 20, p. 57 Peru and Colombia. FAO/ECLA. 'Studies on Rural Poverty'. Santiago, 1984 – Table 22, p. 169 (English edition) – Thailand. NGOC. 'Marginalization of Agric. Labour' 1984 p. 40.
Col. 5   Compiled from different sources cited in 'The Dynamics of Rural Poverty', an FAO publication 1987, Table 1. except Brazil, Columbia, Venezuela. Honduras, Jamaica and Paraguay. FAO/ECLA *ibid* Table 3.

Summary of results of regression analysis and simple correlation between poverty, land concentration and landlessness, and between agricultural growth rates and land concentration in a sample of 19 developing countries

Poverty and land concentration	$(Y = a + bx)$
Regression coefficient (poverty is the dependent variable)	78.26 (positive and statistically significant at 99 per cent)
Standard error of the regression	17.37
Coefficient of determination	$r^2 = 69$ per cent
Simple correlation	$r = 0.828$ positive
Poverty and landlessness	
Simple correlation	$r = 0.49$ positive
Land concentration and landlessness	
Simple correlation	$r = 0.64$ positive
Agricultural GDP growth rates and land concentration	
Regression coefficient (growth rates is dependent variable)	0.26 (positive but statistically insignificant at 95 per cent)
Standard error of the regression	1.56
Simple correlation	$r = 0.014$ (negative)
Mean values of variables	
Absolute rural poverty (percentage)	46.4
Gini Coefficient of Land Distribution	0.679
Landless agricultural households (percentage)	30.1
Agricultural GDP annual growth rates (percentage)	2.86

Appendices

Figure B2.1 Rural poverty at various degrees of land concentration

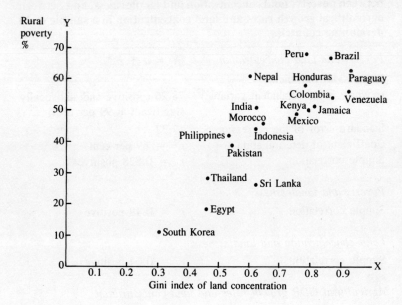

Bibliography

Abdel-Fadil, M. (1975) *Development Income Distribution and Social Change in Rural Egypt 1952-70*, Cambridge University Press.

Adams, D. (1958) *Iraq's People and Resources*, University of California.

Adams, R. (1985) 'Development and structural change in rural Egypt 1952-1982', *World Development* **13**, 6, June.

Adams, R. (1986) *Development and Social Change in Rural Egypt*, Syracuse University Press, New York.

Adelman, I. (1974) 'South Korea' in Chenery, Hollis *et al.* (eds) *Redistribution with Growth*, Oxford University Press.

Adelman, I. and Robinson, S. (1978) *Income Distribution Policy in Developing Countries – A Case Study of Korea*, Oxford University Press.

Adelman, I. (1987) *Practical Approaches to Development Planning – The Case of Korea*, Johns Hopkins Univ. Press, Baltimore, USA.

Ahluwalia, M. (1985) 'Rural poverty, agricultural production and prices' in J. Mellor, and G. Desai, (eds) *Agricultural Change and Rural Poverty*, Johns Hopkins University Press, Baltimore and London.

Ahluwalia, M. *et al.* (1978) *Growth and Poverty in Developing Countries*, World Bank Staff Working Paper No. 309, World Bank, Washington, DC.

Alamgir, M. *et al.* (1977) *Famine 1974: Political Economy of Mass Starvation in Bangladesh* Bangladesh Institute of Development Studies, Dacca.

Alamgir, M. (1980) *Famine in South Asia – Political Economy of Mass Starvation in Bangladesh*, Bangladesh Institute of Development Studies, Cambridge, Massachusetts, Oelgesclager, Gunn and Hain.

Alex, J. and Almeda, J. (1980) *Wage Rates of Farm Workers in the Philippines*, Bureau of Agricultural Economics, Manila.

Ali, M.S. (1985) 'Rural poverty and anti-poverty policies in Pakistan' in R. Islam, (ed.) *Strategies for Alleviating Poverty in Rural Asia*, ILO, Bangkok.

Altimir, O. (1984) 'Poverty, income distribution and child welfare in Latin America: a comparison of pre- and post-recession data' in R. Jolly, and G. Cornia (eds) *The Impact of World Recession on Children*. Pergamon Press, Oxford.

313

Alwan, A.S. (1961) *Studies in Agrarian Reform*, Al-Tijariya Press, Baghdad, *(Arabic)*.

Alwan, A.S. (1985) *Agrarian Systems and the Alleviation of Poverty in Iraq*. United Nations Economic and Social Commission for Western Asia, Baghdad.

Anand, S. (1983) *Inequality and Poverty in Malasya: Measurement and Decomposition*, Oxford University Press (published for the World Bank).

Anand, S. and Kanbur, S. (1984) 'Inequality and development: a reconsideration' in H.P. Nissan (ed.) *Towards Income Distribution Policies – From Income Distribution Research to Income Distribution Policy in LDC's*, EADI, Tilburg University, The Netherlands.

Anisur-Rahman (ed.) (1984) *Grass Roots Participation and Self Reliance*, Oxford and IBH Publishing Co., New Delhi, ILO.

Azam, K.M. (1973) 'The future of the green revolution in west Pakistan', *International Journal of Agrarian Affairs* 5, 6, March.

Aziz, S. (1978) *Rural Development: Learning From China*, Macmillan, London.

Backman, K. and Christensen, R. (1967) 'The economics of farm size', *Agricultural Development and Economic Growth*, Cornell University Press, Ithaca.

Baer, G. (1962) *A History of Landownership in Modern Egypt 1800–1959*, Oxford University Press.

Bain, J.S. (1956) *Barriers to New Competition*, Harvard University Press, Cambridge, Mass. USA.

Bakir, M. (1979) 'The development of level of living in Iraq', unpublished Ph.D Thesis, University of Leeds.

Bakir, M. (1984) 'Distribution of income in Iraq during the 'seventies' (Arabic), UN/ECWA Expert Group Meeting, Income Distribution Statistics in Arab Countries, Baghdad, ECWA.

Ban, S.H. *et al.* (1980) *Rural Development*, Harvard University Press.

Bardhan, P.K. (1970) 'Trends in land reform' *Economic and Political Weekly*: 261–6.

Bardhan, P.K. (1974) 'India' in H. Chenery *et al. Redistribution with Growth*, Annex: 255–62, Oxford University Press.

Bardhan, P.K. (1984) *Land, Labor and Rural Poverty – Essays in Development Economics*, Oxford University Press, Delhi.

Barraclough, S. (ed.) (1973) *Agrarian Structure in Latin America – A Resume of the CIDA Land Tenure Studies*, Lexington Books. Massachusetts, USA.

Baumel, W.J. (1965) *Welfare Economics and the Theory of the State*, Bell and Sons, Ltd., London.

Becker, G.S. (1970) 'Investment in human capital: a theoretical analysis', *Journal of Political Economy* **78**.

Becker, G.S. (1980) *Human Capital*, Columbia University Press, New York.

Berry, A.R. and Cline, R.W. (1979) *Agrarian Structure and Productivity in Developing Countries*, Johns Hopkins University Press, Baltimore, USA.

Bhaduri, A. and Anisur-Rahman, M. (1983) *Studies in Rural Participation*, International Labour Organization (ILO), Geneva.

Bigsten, A.I. (1983) *Income Distribution and Development: Theory, Evidence and Policy*, Heinemann, London.

Booth, A. and Sundrum, R.M. (1985) *Labour Absorption in Agriculture*, Oxford University Press, UK.

Bromley, D. (1982) *Improving Irrigated Agriculture: Institutional Reform and Small Farmer*, World Bank Staff Working Paper No. 531, Washington, DC.

Bronstien A. (1983) *The Triple Struggle: Latin American Peasant Women*, War on Want, London.

Bruce, W. (1972) *The Market in a Socialist Economy*, Routledge & Keegan Paul, London.

Cassen, R., and Associates (1986) *Does Aid Work?*, Clarendon Press, Oxford.

Chamberlain, E. (1983) *Theory of Monopolistic Competition*, Harvard University Press.

Chambers, R. (1985) *Rural Development: Putting the Last First*, Longman.

Chenery, H. (1979) *Structural Change and Development Policy*, Oxford University Press.

Chenery, H. *et al.* (1974) *Redistribution With Growth*, Oxford University Press.

Chenery, H. Ahluwalia, M.S., Duloy, J.H., Jolly, R. (1981) *Redistribution with Growth* fourth edition, Oxford University Press.

Clark, R.J. (1968) 'Land reform and peasant market participation on the north highlands of Bolivia', *Land Economics*: 153–72, May.

Clark, R.J. (1970) *Land Reform in Bolivia*, USAID, Spring Review, Washington DC.

Clark, C. and Haswell, M. (1964) *The Economics of Subsistence Agriculture*, Macmillan, London.

Cleland, W. (1939) 'A population plan for Egypt', *L'Egypte Contemporaine* No. 185.

Coats, A.W. (1969), 'Is there a structure of revolution' cited in K.R. Ranadive, (1978) *Income Distribution: the Unsolved Puzzle*, Oxford University Press: 331.

Cohen, J.M. and Uphoff, N. (1980) 'Participation's place in rural development: seeking clarity through specificity' *World Development* **8**: 213–35.

Cohen, S.I. (1978) *Agrarian Structures and Agrarian Reform*, Leiden, Boston.

Collier, P. (forthcoming) *Poverty, Equality and Growth in Nigeria and Indonesia*.

Collier, P. and Lal, D. (1986) *Labour and Poverty in Kenya 1900–1980*, Clarendon Press, Oxford.

Commander, S. and Hadhoud, A.A. (1986) *Employment, The Labour Market and the Choice of Technology in Egyptian Agriculture*, Overseas Development Institute, London.

Commons, J.R. (1923) *Legal Foundations of Capitalism*, Macmillan, New York.

Commons, J.R. (1934) *Institutional Economics, Its Place in Political*

Economy, Macmillan, New York.

Corbett, P. (1965) *Ideologies: Philosophy at Work*, Hutchinson, London.

Cornia, G.A. (1985) 'Farm size, land yields and the agricultural production function: an analysis for fifteen developing countries', *World Development,* **13**, 4: 513–34.

Cornia, G.A., Jolly, R., and Stewart, F. (eds.) (1987) *Adjustment With a Human Face: Protecting the Vulnerable and Promoting Growth.* A UNICEF study, Vol. 1, Clarendon Press, Oxford.

Cornia, G.A. *et al.* (1988) *Adjustment with a Human Face* Vol. II, Country Case Studies, a UNICEF Study, Clarendon Press, Oxford.

Cox, T. (1986) *Peasants, Class and Capitalism: The Rural Research of L.N. Kritsman and his School*, Clarendon Press, Oxford.

Crouchley, A.R. (1938) *The Economic Development of Modern Egypt*, London.

Currie, J.M. (1981) *The Economic Theory of Agricultural Land Tenure*, Cambridge University Press.

Dandekar, V.M. (1964) 'From agrarian reorganisation to land reform', *Artha Vijnama* **6**, 1, Gokhale Institute, Poona, India.

Dandekar, M.M. (1962) 'Economic theory and agrarian reform,' *Oxford Economic Papers,* **14**, February.

Dasgupta, P. (1987) 'Inequality as a determinant of malnutrition and unemployment: policy', *The Economic Journal,* **97**: 177–88, March.

Dasgupta, P., and Ray, D. (1986) 'Inequality as a determinant of malnutrition and unemployment: theory', *The Economic Journal,* **96**: 1011–34, December.

Deane, P. (1989) *The State and Economic System: An Introduction to the History of Political Economy*, Oxford University Press (Opus Book).

de Janvry, A. (1981a) *The Agrarian Question and Reformism in Latin America*, Johns Hopkins University Press, Baltimore, USA.

de Janvry, A. (1981b) 'The role of land reform in economic development: policies and politics', *American Journal of Agricultural Economics,* **63**, 2, May.

Demsetz, H. (1982) 'Barriers to entry', *The American Economic Review,* **72**, 1, March.

Dey, J. (1980) 'Women and rice in Gambia: the impact of irrigated rice development projects on the farming system,' Unpublished Ph.D thesis, University of Reading, UK.

Dong-Wan and Yang Boo, (1984) 'Alleviation of rural poverty in the republic of Korea', WCARRD Studies No. 12, FAO, Rome.

Dorner, P. (1964) 'Land tenure, income distribution and productivity interactions' *Land Economics* **XL**, 3, August.

Dorner, P. and Kenel, D.R. (1971) 'The economic case of land reform: employment, income distribution and productivity', *Land Reform, Land Settlement and Cooperatives*, FAO, Rome.

Dovring, E. (1970) *Land Reform in Mexico*, Agency for International Development, Spring Review, Washington, D.C.

Dumont, R. (1964) *Cuba: Socialism et Development*, Editions du Seuil, Paris.

Duncan, O.D. and Artis, J.W. (1951) 'Some problems of stratification research,' *Rural Sociology* **16**, 1, March.

Dunning, J.H. (1981) *International Production and the Multinational Enterprise*, Allen and Unwin, London.

Dunning, J.H. and Stopford, J.M. (1984) *Multinationals Company Performancce and Global Trends*, Macmillan, London.

Edgeworth, F.Y. (1881) *Mathematical, Psychics: An Essay on the Application of Mathematics to the Moral Science*, London.

Egyptian Government, *Bulletin of Agricultural Economy*, Ministry of Agriculture, Dokki, Giza, (several issues), (*Arabic*).

Egyptian Government, (1986) *Statistical Yearbook, 1952–1985*, General Agency for Public Mobilization and Statistics, Cairo, June.

El-Gabaly, M. (1967) 'New trends in land policy in the UAR (Egypt)' in M.R. El-Ghonemy (ed.) *Land Policy in the Near East*, FAO, Rome.

El Ghonemy, M.R. (1953) 'Resource use and income in Egyptian agriculture before and after land reform', unpublished Ph.D thesis, State University of North Carolina, Raleigh, USA.

El Ghonemy, M.R. (1955) 'Capital formation in Egyptian agriculture', *L'Egypte Contemporaine*, (February).

El Ghonemy, M.R. (1968) 'Land reform and economic development in the Near East', *Land Economics,* **CLIV**, Feb.

El Ghonemy, M.R. (1968) 'Economic and institutional organization of Egyptian agriculture since 1952' in P.J. Vatikiotis, (ed.) *Egypt since the Revolution*, Allen and Unwin, London.

El Ghonemy, M.R. (1980) *The Concept of Land Reform and its Role in Rural Development*, Dar et Gil Publishing House, Cairo. (*Arabic*).

El Ghonemy, M.R. (ed.) (1984) *Development Strategies and the Rural Poor*, Economic and Social Development Paper No. 44, FAO, Rome, Italy.

El Ghonemy, M.R. (1984) 'The crisis of rural poverty: can participation resolve it?', *Studies On Agrarian Reform and Rural Poverty*, FAO, Rome.

El-Imam, M. (1962) *A Production Function For Egyptian Agriculture 1913–1955*, Institute of National Planning Study, No. 259, Cairo.

Esman, M. and Uphoff, N. (1984) *Local Organisations: Intermediaries in Rural Development*, Cornell University Press, Ithaca and London.

Esteva, G. (1983) *The Struggle for Rural Mexico*, Bergin and Garvey, Mass, USA.

Fage, J.D. (1978) *History of Africa*, Hutchinson & Co., London.

Food and Agriculture Organisation of the United Nations, Rome, (FAO) *Production Yearbook,* **24**, 1970; **30**, 1976; **31**, 1977; **34**, 1980, **35**, 1985.

FAO (1961) *Report of the Regional Land Reform Team for Latin America.*

FAO (1970) *The State of Food and Agriculture 1945–1970.*

FAO (1977) *Fourth World Food Survey.*

FAO (1979) *Report*, World Conference on Agrarian Reform and Rural Development, (WCARRD).

FAO (1981a) *1970 World Census of Agriculture.*

FAO (1981b) *Agriculture: Toward 2000.*

FAO (1983a) *Women in Food Production.*

FAO (1983b) 'Women in developing agriculture', in *The State of Food and Agriculture 1983.*

FAO (1984) *Agricultural Holdings in the 1970 World Census of Agriculture: A Statistical Analysis.*

FAO (1985a) 'Agricultural price policies' Document No. C85/19.

FAO (1985b) *Fifth World Food Survey.*

FAO (1985c) *State of Food and Agriculture* (SOFA).

FAO (1985d) *Report of the WCARRD Follow-up Inter-Agency Mission to Mozambique.*

FAO (1986a) *The Dynamics of Rural Poverty.*

FAO (1986b) 'Land reform, land settlement and cooperatives', *Bulletin no. 1/2.*

FAO (1987a) 'Second progress report of WCARRD programme of action involving the role of women' in *Rural Development Document C 87/19,* August.

FAO (1987b and 1988) *Country Tables: Basic Data on the Agricultural Sector.*

Fei, J., Ranis, G. and Kuo, S (1979) *Growth with Equity: The Taiwan Case*, Oxford University Press, published for the World Bank.

Fenelon, K. (1970) 'Iraq national income and expenditure 1950–1956' in *National Income in Iraq: selected studies*, Central Statistical Organization, Baghdad.

Fields, G. and Fei, J. (1978) 'On inequality comparisons' *Econometrics.*

Fields, G.S. (1980) *Poverty, Inequality and Development*, Cambridge University Press.

Figueroa, A. (1976) *Estudi Por Paises subre el Empleo Rural: Peru*, ILO, Geneva.

Figueroa, A. (1988) 'Economic adjustment and development in Peru: towards an alternative policy' in Cornia *et al* (eds.) *Adjustment with a Human Face, Vol, II, Country Case Studies*, Clarendon Press, Oxford.

Frank, C.R. Jnr and Webb, R.C. (eds.) (1979) *Income Distribution and Growth in the Less Developed Countries*. The Brookings Institute, Washington, DC.

Gabbay, R. (1978) *Communism and Agrarian Reform in Iraq*, Croom Helm, London.

Gadalla, S.M. (1982) *Land Reform in Relation to Social Development in Egypt*, University of Missouri Studies No. 5.

Galbraith, J.K. (1984) *The Anatomy of Power*, Hamish Hamilton, London.

Gayoso, A. (1970) *Land Reform in Cuba*, Agency for International Development, Spring Review, Washington, DC.

Georgescu-Rogen, N. (1960) 'Economic theory and agrarian economics' *Oxford Economic Papers*, **xii**: 1–40.

Ghai, D. and Smith, L.D. (1987) *Agricultural Prices Policy and Equity in Sub-Saharan Africa*, Lynne Rienner Publications, Boulder, Colorado.

Ghai, D., Kay, C. and Peek, P. (1988) *Labour and Development in Rural Cuba*. An ILO Study, Macmillan.

Gooneratne, W., and Gunawardena, P.J. (1984) 'Poverty and inequality in rural Sri Lanka', A.R. Khan and E. Lee (eds.) *Poverty in Rural Asia*, ILO, Geneva.

Gordon, D. (1965) 'The role of the history of economic thought in the understanding of modern economic theory', *American Economic Review*, May: 119–27.

Graaf, J. (1957) *Theoretical Welfare Economics*, Cambridge University Press.

Gray, A. (1931) *The Development of Economic Doctrine*, Longmans, Green, London.

Griffin, K. (1984) *Institutional Reform and Economic Development in the Chinese Countryside*, Macmillan.

Griffin, K. (1986) 'Communal land tenure systems and their role in rural development', in D. Lal and F. Stewart (eds) *Theory and Reality in Development – Essays in Honour of Paul Streeten*, Macmillan, London.

Griffin, K. (1985) 'Rural poverty in Asia: analysis and policy alternatives' in R. Islam, (ed.) *Strategies for Alleviating Poverty in Asia*, an ILO-ARTEP publication, Bangkok.

Guevara, E.C. (1964) 'The Cuban economy: its past and present importance', *International Affairs*, **40**, 4, October.

Haidar, S. (1944) 'The problem of the land in Iraq', unpublished Ph.D Thesis, The University of London.

Hansen, B. and Marzouk, G. (1965) *Development and Economic Policy in the UAR, Egypt*, North-Holland Publishing Company, Amsterdam.

Harris, B. (1984) *State and Market*, Concept Publishing Co., New Delhi.

Hassan, M.A. (1955) *Land Reclamation and Settlement in Iraq*, Majlis Al-Imar, Baghdad.

Hasseeb, K. (1964) *The National Income of Iraq, 1953–61*, Oxford University Press.

Hayami, Y. and Kikuchi, M. (1985) 'Directions of agricultural change: a view from villages in the Philippines', in J. Mellor, and G. Desai (eds) *Agricultural Change and Rural Poverty*, Johns Hopkins University Press, Baltimore, USA.

Hayek, F. (1986) *The Road to Serfdom*, Ark Paperbacks, Edition, London.

Handelman, H. (ed.) (1981) *The Politics and Agrarian Change*, Indiana University Press, Bloomington, USA.

Henry, C.M. (1986) 'Economies of scale and agrarian structure', *Oxford Agrarian Studies*, Institute of Agricultural Economics, Oxford.

Herring, R.J. (1983) *Land to the Tiller*, Yale University Massachusetts, USA.

Hicks, N. and Streeten, P. (1979) 'Indicators of development: the search for a basic need yardstick', *World Development*, **7**, 6, (June): 567–80.

Hicks, N. (1980) 'Economic growth and human resources', *World Bank Staff Working Paper*, No. 408, Washington, DC, July.

Hirashima, S. (1978) *The Structure of Disparity in Developing Agriculture*, The Institute of Developing Economies, Tokyo.

Hirashima, S. and Muqtada, M. (eds.) (1986) *Hired Labour and Rural Labour Markets in Asia*, an ILO publication, New Delhi.

Hirschleifer, J. (1985) 'The expanding domain of economics', *American Economic Review*, December.

Hirschman, A.D. (1981) *Essays in Trespassing: Economics to Politics and Beyond*, Cambridge University Press.

Hopkins, N. (1987) *Agrarian Transformation in Egypt*, Westview Press, Boulder, Colorado.

Hopkins, R. and Vander Hoover, R. (1981) *Economic and Social Policy Synthesis Programme*, ILO, Geneva.

Hunt, D. (1984) *The Impending Crisis in Kenya*, Gower, England.

Hussein, M. (1985) 'Fertilizer consumption, pricing and food grain production in Bangladesh', Bangladesh Institute of Development Studies, Dhaka (mimeographed).

Hymer, S. (1960) *The International Operations of National Firms: A Study of Direct Foreign Investment* MIT Press, Cambridge, Mass, USA.

Hymer, S. (1971) 'The multinational corporation and the law of uneven development' in J. Bhagawati (ed.) *Economics and World Order*, Macmillan, New York.

International Labour Organisation, (ILO) (1971) *Agrarian Reform and Employment*, Geneva.

ILO (1972) *Employment, Incomes, and Equity –A Strategy for Increasing Productive Employment in Kenya*, Geneva.

ILO (1979) *Poverty and Employment in Rural Areas*, ACRD, IX, Geneva.

ILO (1983) *Rural Labour Market Issues Relating to Labour Utilization, Remuneration and the Position of Women*, Geneva.

Ifran, M. and Amjad, R. (1983) 'Poverty in rural Pakistan' in A.R. Khan and E. Lee (eds) *Poverty in Rural Asia*, International Labour Organization, Geneva.

Institute of Development Studies at the University of Sussex, *Register of Research in the UK, 1981–83*.

Institute of Pacific Relations (1939) *Agrarian China: Selected Source Materials from Chinese Authors*, George Allen and Unwin, London.

Iraqi Government, *Statistical Abstract* (several issues), Central Bureau of Statistics, Ministry of Planning.

Iraqi Government, (1970) *National Income in Iraq*, Selected studies, Central Statistical Organisation, Baghdad.

Islam, R. (1983) 'Poverty, income distribution and growth in rural Thailand' in A.R. Khan, and E. Lee (eds) *Poverty in Rural Asia*, an ILO publication, Bangkok.

Islam, R. (ed.) (1985) *Strategies for Alleviating Poverty in Rural Asia*, ILO, and Bangladesh Institute of Development Studies, Bangkok.

Issawi, C. (1947) *Egypt: An Economic and Social Analysis*, Oxford University Press.

Issawi, C. (1982) *An Economic History of the Middle East and North Africa*, Columbia University Press.

Johnson, E.F. and Kilby, P. (1975) *Agriculture and Structural Transformation*, Oxford University Press, London.

Jose, A.V. (1983) 'Poverty and inequality – the case of Kerala', in A.R. Khan and E. Lee (eds) *Poverty in Rural Asia*, ILO, ARTEP, Bangkok.

320

Joshi, P.C. (1961) 'Prospects and problems of ceilings on land holdings in India' *Agricultural Situation in India.*

Joshi, P.C. (1975) *Land Reforms in India: Trends and Perspectives,* Allied Publishers, Delhi.

Kaldor, N. (1935) 'Market imperfection and excess capacity', *Economica,* **II**, February.

Kalecki, M. (1934) *Theory of Economic Dynamics,* Unwin University Books, London.

Kaufman, H.F. *et al.* (1953) 'Problems of theory and method in the study of social stratification in rural society', *Rural Sociology,* **18**, March.

Kay, C. (1983) 'The agrarian reform in Peru: an assessment: in A.K. Ghose (ed.) *Agrarian Reform in Contemporary Developing Countries,* ILO-WEP study, Croom Helm, London.

Keidel, A. (1981) *Korean Regional Farm Production and Income 1910-1975,* Korea Development Institute, Seoul.

Kelley, A., Khalifa, A. and El-Khorazaty, N. (1982) *Population and Development in Rural Egypt,* Duke University Population Studies, Durham, North Carolina, USA.

Keynes, J.M. (1936) *The General Theory of Employment, Interest and Money,* Harcourt Brace and Company, New York.

Khan, A.R. (1984) *The Responsibility System and Institutional Change,* in K. Griffin (ed.) *Institutional Reform and Economic Development in the Chinese Countryside,* Macmillan.

Khan, A.R. and Lee, E. (eds.) (1983) *Poverty in Rural Asia,* ILO, ARTEP, Bangkok.

Kifle, H. (1983) *The Role of State Farms in Agrarian Transformation in Centrally Planned Economies of Africa.* A study prepared for a Regional Workshop organized by FAO in Arusha, Tanzania, 17-22 October 1983.

Kim, Wan-Soon, and Yun, K.Y. (1988) 'Fiscal policy and development in Korea', *World Development,* **16**, 1: 65-83,

King, T. (1980) *Education and Income,* World Bank Staff Working Paper No. 402, Washington, DC.

Lal, D. (1983) *The Poverty of 'Development Economics',* London Institute of Economic Affairs, Hobart Paperback, 16.

Lardy, N.R. (1983) *Agriculture in China's Modern Economic Development,* Cambridge University Press, England.

Ledesma, A.S. (1982) *Landless Workers and Rice Farmers,* International Institute for Rice Research, Los Banos, Philippines.

Lee, E. (1979) 'Egalitarian peasant farming and rural development: the case of South Korea' in Dharam Ghai *et al.* (eds) *Agrarian Systems and Rural Development,* Macmillan.

Lee, H.K. (1936) *Land Utilization and Rural Economy in Korea,* Greenwood Press, New York.

Lele, U. (1975) *The Design of Rural Development: Lessons From Africa,* The Johns Hopkins University Press, Baltimore.

Leys, C. (1975) *Underdevelopment in Kenya: The Political Economy of Neo-Colonialism,* Heinemann, London.

Lipton, M. (1974) 'Towards a theory of land reform', in D. Lehman, (ed.) *Agrarian Reform and Agrarian Reformism*, Faber & Faber, London.

Lipton, M. (1977) *Why Poor People Stay Poor*, Temple Smith, London.

Lipton, M. (1983) *Demography and Poverty*, World Bank Staff Working Paper No. 623, The World Bank, Washington, DC.

Lipton, M. (1985) *Land Assets and Rural Poverty*, World Bank Staff Working Paper No. 744, Washington, DC.

Livingston, I. (1986) *Rural Development, Employment and Incomes in Kenya*, ILO Study, Gower, England.

Longhurst, R. (1983) 'Agricultural production and food consumption: some neglected linkages', *Food and Nutrition*, **9**, 2, FAO, Rome.

Lowe, J.W. (1977) 'The International Finance Corporation and the agribusiness sector' *Finance and Development*, **26**, March.

Lugogo, J.A. (1986) 'The impact of structural changes in Kenya plantation sector', *The Socio-Economic Implications of Structural Changes in Plantations in African Countries, Working Paper*, ILO, Geneva.

Lunven, P. and Sabry, Z. (1981) 'Nutrition and rural development' *Food and Nutrition*, **9**, 3, FAO, Rome.

MacLeod, H.D. (1867) *The Elements of Economics*, London.

Mangahas, M. (1985) 'Rural poverty and operation land transfer in the Philippines', in R. Islam, (ed.) *Strategies for Alleviating Poverty in Rural Asia*, ILO, ARTEP, Bangkok.

Mangahas, M., Barros, B. (1980) *The Distribution of Income and Wealth*, The Philippines Institute for Development Studies.

Marei, S. (1957) *Egyptian Agrarian Reform*, Cairo.

Marshall, A. (1952) *Principles of Economics*, Macmillan, London, 8th edition.

Martins, B. (1983) *Nutrition and Malnutrition in Sri Lanka*, WEP Working Paper, ILO, Geneva.

Marx, K. (1906) *Capital: A critique of Political Economy*, The Modern Library Edition, New York.

Matthews, R.C.O. (1986) 'The economics of institutions and the sources of growth', *The Economic Journal*, **96**, December: 903–18.

McCormic, C. (1956) 'It can be solved', in K.H. Parsons, R.J. Penn and P.M. Raup (eds) *Land Tenure – Proceedings of the International Conference on Land Tenure*, held at Madison, Wisconsin.

McEntire, D., McEntire, I.L. (1969) 'Agrarian reform in Mexico', *Toward Modern Land Policies*, University of Padua, Italy.

McGraham, D. *et al.* (1985) *Measurement and Analysis of Socio-Economic Development*, United Nations Research Institute for Social Development (UNRISD), Geneva.

McSweeney, B.G. (1974) *Learning about Rural Women*, Population Council, New York.

Mellor, J. (1975) *Agricultural Price Policy and Income Distribution in Low Income Nations*, World Bank Staff Working Paper No. 214, Washington, DC.

Mellor, J. and Desai, G. (eds.) (1985) *Agricultural Change and Rural Poverty*, Johns Hopkins University Press, Baltimore and London.

Mellor, J. and Johnson, B. (1984) 'The world food equation: interrelations among development, employment and food consumption' *Journal of Economic Literature*, **22**, June.

Melville, B. (1988) 'Are land availability and cropping pattern critical factors in determining nutritional standards', *Food and Nutrition Bulletin*, The United Nations University, Tokyo.

Mill, J.S. (1948) *Principles of Political Economy*, Penguin Books 1970, (Books IV and V) reprinted from Routledge and Kegan Paul (1965).

Ministry of Agrarian Reform of the Philippines (1982) *Agrarian Reform Programme: Highlights of Accomplishments*, Manila, September.

Montgomery, J.D. (ed.) (1984) *International Dimensions of Land Reform*, Westview Press, Boulder, Colorado, USA.

Morowitz, D. (1977) *Twenty-Five Years of Economic Development, 1950–1975*, World Bank, Washington, DC.

Morrow, R.B., Sherper, K.H., (1970) *Land Reform in South Korea, United States Agency for International Development, Spring Review*, Washington, DC.

Myers, R. (1982) 'Land property rights and agricultural development in modern China' in R. Barker *et al* (eds) *The Chinese Agricultural Economy*, Westview Press, Boulder Colorado and Croom Helm, London.

Myrdal, G. (1944) *An American Dilemma: The Negro Problem and Modern Democracy*, Harper, New York.

Myrdal, G. (1956) *An International Economy, Problems and Prospects*, Routledge & Kegan Paul, London.

Myrdal, G. (1960) *Beyond the Welfare State*, Yale University Press, New Haven, Connecticut, USA.

Myrdal, G. (1968) *Asian Drama, An Enquiry into the Poverty of Nations*, Twentieth Century Fund, New York, USA.

Nicholls, W. (1941) *A Theoretical Analysis of Imperfect Competition with Special Application to the Agricultural Industries*, The Iowa State College Press, Ames, USA.

Nozick, R. (1974) *Anarchy, State and Utopia*, Basil Blackwell, Oxford.

Oakley, P. and Marsden, D. (1984) *Approaches to Participation in Rural Development*, ILO, Geneva.

Olson, G.L. (1974) *US Foreign Policy and the Third World Peasant*, Praeger Special Studies.

Palmer, I. *et al.* (1983) *The North East Rainfed Agricultural Development in Thailand: A Baseline Survey of Women's Roles*, Population Council, New York.

Parsons, K.H. (1962) *Agrarian Reform and Economic Growth in Developing Countries*, US Department of Agriculture, Economic Research Service, Washington, DC.

Parsons, K.H. (1979) 'The challenge of agrarian reform' in G. Johnson, and A. Maunder (eds) *Rural Change, The Challenge for Agricultural Economists*, Proceedings, 17th International Conference of Agricultural Economics held at Banff, Canada, published by Gower, England.

Bibliography

Parsons, K.H. (1984) 'The place of agrarian reform in rural development policies', *Studies on Agrarian Reform and Rural Poverty*, FAO, Rome.

Parsons, K.H. (1985) 'John R. Commons: his relevance to contemporary economics', *Journal of Economic Issues*, September.

Peek, P. (1984) *Collectivizing the Peasantry: The Cuban Experience*, International Labour Organization, Geneva.

Penrose, E. and Penrose E.F. (1978) *Iraq Interntional Relations and National Development*, Earnest Benn, London.

Perisse, J. (1983) 'Heterogeneity in food composition – table data', *Food and Nutrition* **9**, 1, FAO, Rome.

Perkins, D. and Yusuf, S. (1984) *Rural Development in China*, a World Bank Publication, Johns Hopkins University Press, Baltimore, USA.

Phelps, E.S. (1965) 'A critique of naturalism' Chapter 4 in *Fiscal Neutrality Towards Economic Growth*, MacGraw Hill.

Pinstrup-Anderson, P. (1983) 'Export crop production and malnutrition' *Food and Nutrition,* **9**, 2, FAO, Rome.

Po, B. (1980) 'Land reform policies and their implementation in the Philippines', in Inayatullah (ed.) *Land Reform: Some Asian Experiences*, APDAC, Kuala Lumpur.

Radwan, S. (1977) *Agrarian Reform and Rural Poverty: Egypt, 1952-1975*, ILO, Geneva.

Radwan, S. and Lee, E. (1986) *Agrarian Change in Egypt: An Anatomy of Rural Poverty*, Croom Helm, London.

Rajkrishna, K. (1982) 'Some aspects of agricultural growth, price policy and equity in developing countries', *Food Research Institute Studies,* **XVIII**, 3, Stanford, USA.

Ranadive, K.R. (1978) *Income Distribution: The Unsolved Puzzle*, Oxford University Press.

Ravallian, M. (1987) *Markets and Famine*, Clarendon Press, Oxford.

Rawls, J. (1973) *A Theory of Justice*, Oxford University Press.

Robinson, J. (1933) *Economics of Imperfecct Competition*, Macmillan.

Roemer, J.E. (1982a) *A General Theory of Exploitation and Class*, Harvard University Press.

Roemer, J.E. (1982b) 'Exploitation, alternatives and socialism', *The Economic Journal,* **92**, March, 87-107.

Russell, B. (1938) *Power: A New Social Analysis*, Norton, New York.

Ruttan, V.W. (1984) 'Integrated rural development programmes – a historical perspective', *World Development,* **12**, 4, April: 393-401.

Ruttan, V. (1982) *Agricultural Research Policy*, University of Minnesota Press, USA.

Saab, G. (1967) *The Egyptian Agrarian Reform, 1952-62*, Oxford University Press.

Safilos-Rothchild, C. (1982) *The Persistence of Women's Invisibility in Agriculture: Theoretical and Policy Lessons from Lesotho and Sierre Leone*, The Population Council, New York.

Safilios-Rothchild, C. (1983) 'Women and the agrarian reform in Honduras' *Land Reform, Settlement and Cooperative,* **1/2**, FAO, Rome.

Samaranayake, T. (1982) 'Effects of inflation on income distribution' *Economic Review*, April.

Sanyal, S. (1984) 'Trends in landholdings in rural India' in B. Bardhan and T.N. Srinivasan (eds) *Poverty in South Asia*, Columbia University Press, New York.

Saith, A. (1984) 'China's new population policies', in K. Griffin (ed.) *Institutional Reform and Economic Development in the Chinese Countryside*, Macmillan, London.

Schultz, T.W. (1964) *Transforming Traditional Agriculture*, Yale University Press.

Schultz. T.W. with Ram, R. (1979) 'Life span, health, savings and productivity', *Economic Development and Cultural Change*, 27 April: 399–42.

Schultz, T.W. (1981) *Investing in People: the Economics of Population Quality*, University of California Press, Berkeley.

Sears, D. (1969) 'Challenges to development theory and strategies' *International Development Review*, December.

Sen, A.K. (1966) 'Size of holding and productivity' *Economic Weekly*.

Sen, A.K. (1975) *Choice of Techniques: An Aspect of the Theory of Planned Economic Development*, Basil Blackwell, Oxford, Third edition.

Sen, A.K. (1981) *Poverty and Famine: An Essay on Entitlement and Deprivation*, Clarendon Press, Oxford.

Sen, A.K. (1983) 'Development: which way now?' *The Economic Journal*, **93**, December: 745–62.

Sen, A.K. (1984) *Resources, Values and Development*, Basil Blackwell, Oxford.

Sen, B. (1970) 'The future of the green revolution in West Pakistan', *International Journal of Agrarian Affairs* **5**, 6, March.

Singer, H. (1972) *Employment, Incomes and Equity – a Strategy for Increasing Productive Employment in Kenya*, ILO, Geneva.

Singer, H. (1985) 'What Keynes and Keynesianism can teach us about less developed countries', 7th Keynesian Seminar, University of Kent, Canterbury, 15 November.

Singer, H. and Ansari, J. (1982) *Rich and Poor Countries*, George Allen and Unwin, London.

Singh, A. (1986) 'The world economic crisis stabilization and structural adjustment', *Labour and Society*, **11**, 3, (September) International Institute of Labour Studies, Geneva.

Smith, Adam. (1776) *The Wealth of Nations*, Random House Inc. 1937 edn.

Smith, T.L. (1947) *The Sociology of Rural Life*, Harper and Brothers, New York.

Sobhan, R. (1983) *Rural Poverty and Agrarian Reform in the Philippines*, series of Poverty Studies, No. 2, FAO, Rome.

Southall, R. (ed.) (1988) *Labour and Unions in Asia and Africa: Contemporary Issues*, Macmillan, London.

Stewart, F. (1971) 'Appropriate intermediaries or inferior economics' *Journal of Development Studies*, **7**, April.

Bibliography

Stewart, F. (1985) 'The fragile foundations of the neoclassical approach to development', *Journal of Development Studies*, **21**, January: 282–92.

Stigler, G. (1982) 'The economists and the problem of monopoly', *The American Economic Review*, **72**, 2, May: 1–11.

Streeten, P. (1972) *The Frontiers of Development Studies*, Macmillan, London.

Streeten, P. (1981) *Development Perspectives*, Macmillan, London.

Streeten, P. *et al.* (1981) *First Things First: Meeting Basic Needs in Developing Countries*, Oxford University Press.

Suh, Sang-Chui (1965) *Growth and Structural Changes in the Korean Economy Since 1910*, Ph.D. Thesis, Harvard University Press, USA.

Sukhatme, P. (1978) 'Assessment of adequacy of diets and different economic levels', *Economic and Political Weekly*, August.

Szal, R. (1984) 'Trends in income distribution in South Korea and their relationship to policy and planning', in H.P. Nissen (ed.) *Towards Income Distribution Policies*, European Association of Development Research and Training Institute (EADI), Book Series 3, Tilburg University, Netherlands.

Tai, Hung-Chao (1975) *Land Reform and Politics*, University of California Press, Berkeley.

Taussig', M. (1982) 'Peasant economies and the development of capitalist agriculture in the Cauca Valley, Colombia' in J. Harriss (ed.) *Rural Development: Theories of Peasant Economy and Agrarian Change*. Hutchinson University Library, London.

Taylor, L. (1977) 'Research directions in income distribution, nutrition and the economics of food'. *Food Research Institute Studies*, **XVI**, 2: 29–45.

Thirtle, G. and Bottomley, P. (1988) 'Is publicly funded agricultural research excessive?' *Journal of Agricultural Economics*, **39**, 1, January.

Todaro, M.P. (1981) *Economic Development in the Third World*, Longman, New York, Second Edition.

Toye, J. (1987) *The Dilemmas of Development*, Blackwell, Oxford.

Tyler, G.J. (1983) *Somalia: Case Study on Rural Poverty*, Poverty Study No. 7, FAO, Rome.

UNICEF, (1984) *Statistics on Children in UNICEF Countries*, New York.

United Nations Centre on Transnational Corporations (1983), *Transnational Corporations in World Development*, New York.

United Nations Department of Economic and Social Affairs (1984) *Data Base of Mortality Measurement: 'The Matlab Project and the Campaniganj Health Project – two models from Bangladesh*, Population Series No. 84, New York.

United Nations Economic and Social Commission for Western Asia (1986) *Yemen Arab Republic, Rural Development Strategy and Implementation: An Assessment and Review of Issues*, Baghdad, Iraq.

United Nations, *National Account Statistics*, several issues, New York.

United States AID (1986) *Policy Determination of the Agency for International Development, Land Tenure*, PD-13, 9 May.

Usher, D. (1981) *The Economic Prerequisite to Democracy*, Basil Blackwell, Oxford.

Uphoff, N. and Ilchman, W. (eds) (1972) *The Political Economy of Development*, University of California Press, Berkeley and Los Angeles, California, USA.

Uphoff, N. *et al.* (1979) *Feasibility and Application of Rural Development – Participation: A State of the Art*, Rural Development Committee, Cornell University, Ithaca, USA.

Usher, D. (1978) 'An imputation to the measure of economicc growth for changes in life expectancy' in Milton Moss (ed.) *The Measurement of Economic and Social Preference* National Bureau of Economic Research, New York.

Visaria, P. (1981) *Size of Land Holding, Living Standards and Employment in Rural Western India*, World Bank Staff Working Paper No. 459, Washington, DC.

Voelkner, H. and French, J. (1970) *A Dynamic Model for Land Reform Analysis and Public Policy Formulation*, Spring Review Background Paper 7, Agency for International Development (AID), Washington, DC.

Von Braun, J. and DeHaen, H. (1983) *The Effects of Food Price and Subsidy Policies on Egyptian Agriculture*. Research Report, No. 42, International Food Policy Research Institute, Washington, DC.

Walker, K. (1965) *Planning in Chinese Agriculture, 1956–1962*, Frank Cass.

Wan Dong, S. and Yang-Boo, C. (1984) 'Alleviation of rural poverty in the republic of Korea', a study on poverty prepared for FAO, No. 12, Rome, Italy.

Warriner, D. (1948) *Land and Poverty in the Middle East*, Royal Institute of International Affairs, London.

Warriner, D., (1969) *Land Reform in Principle and Practice*, Clarendon Press, Oxford.

Wheeler, D. (1980) *Human Resources Development and Economic Growth in Developing Countries: A Simultaneous Model*, World Bank Staff Working Paper, No. 407, Washington, DC.

White, G. (ed.) (1983) 'Chinese development strategy after Mao', *Revolutionary Socialist Development in The Third World*, Wheatsheaf, Brighton, UK.

Wickramasekara, P. (1985) 'An evaluation of policies and programmes for the alleviation of poverty in Sri Lanka' in R. Islam, *Strategies for Alleviating Poverty in Rural Asia*, ILO.

Williams, S. and Karen, R. (1985) *Agri-Business and the Small-Scale Farmer*, Westview Press, Colorado, USA.

Wolf, E.R. (1969) *Peasant Wars of the Twentieth Century*, Harper & Row, New York.

World Bank (1975) *Land Reform Policy Paper*, Washington DC.

World Bank (1978) *Thailand: Toward a Development Strategy of Full Participation*, East Asia Regional Office.

World Bank (1979) *Growth with Equity – The Taiwan Case*, by J.C.H. Fei, G. Ranis, and S. Kuo, Oxford University Press.

World Bank (1980) *Aspects of Poverty in the Philippines, a Review and*

Assessment, 2, Washington DC.
World Bank (1983) *Focus on Poverty,* Washington DC.
World Bank (1984) *Social Indicators Data Sheets,* Washington DC.
World Bank (1978 and 1984), *World Development Report, Development Indicators,* Washington DC.
World Bank (1987 and 1988) *World Development Report,* Washington DC.
World Bank (1986, 1987) *Annual Report,* Washington DC.
Yates, P.L. (1981) *Mexico's Agricultural Dilemma,* The University of Arizona Press, Tucson, Arizona, USA.
Yeh, K.C. (1973) *China, a Handbook* Yuan-lium, (ed.), Newton Abbot, Devon, UK.

Name index

329

Name index

Cornia, G. 14, 70, 73, 128–9, 136–7, 138
Cox, T. 150, 179
Currie, J. 112, 135

Dandekar, V. 135, 246, 279
Dasgupta, P. 108–9, 116
Dawson, E. 210
De Haen, H. 38, 250
de Janvry, A. 67, 241, 255, 256, 260, 299
de Mandeville, B. 112
Demsetz, H. 145
Desai, G. 42
Dey, J. 32
Dong Wan, 52, 205, 207, 209, 303
Dorner, P. 113, 128–9
Dovring, E. 258, 259
Dumont, R. 246
Duncan, O.D. 114
Dunning, J. 143
Duran, M.A. 246

Edgeworth, F. 123
El-Gabaly, M. 249
El-Ghonemy, R. 4, 21, 34, 35, 36, 48, 58, 68, 77–8, 98, 115, 130, 131, 136, 156, 180, 181, 182, 212–13, 216, 224, 226, 227, 232, 234, 237, 239, 244, 246, 247, 249, 255, 260, 277, 280, 290, 293, 297, 299–300, 301
El-Imam, M. 180
El-Khorasaty, M. 40
Elliot, C. 160
Engels, F. 95, 102
Engo, R.B. 301
Esman, M. 105, 115
Esteva, G. 277

Fage, J.D. 161
Fei, J. 52
Fenelon, K. 221
Fields, G. 114
Figueroa, A. 261
Filmer, T. 179–80
Frank, C.R. Jnr. 114
Frei, President 65, 66, 67, 77
French, J. 241
Frisch, R. 52

Gabby, R. 212
Gadalla, S. 249
Galbraith, J. 83, 113
Gayoso, A. 224
Ghai, D. 42, 126, 224, 225, 264
Ghose, A. 255
Gooneratne, W. 116, 265, 278
Gordon, D. 47
Graaf, J. 14
Gray, A. 33
Griffin, K. 125, 130, 136, 137, 138, 195, 198
Guevara, E.C. 246
Gunawardena, P.J. 116, 265, 278

Hadhoud, A. 130, 131, 237, 238
Haider, S. 210
Handelman, H. 268, 297
Hansen, B. 234
Hasseeb, K. 219
Haswell, M. 115
Hayami, Y. 130, 132–3, 137
Hayek, F. von 84, 113
Henry, M. 130, 132, 137, 138
Herring, R. 285
Hicks, N. 110, 117, 252
Hirashima, S. 278
Hirschleifer, J. 75
Hirschman, A. 75
Hopkins, N. 237, 249
Hopkins, R. 105, 115
Hume, D. 64
Hunt, D. 28, 161, 166, 183
Hussein, A. 77, 248–9
Hussein, M. 38
Hymer, S. 143

Ibrahim, A. 42
Ifran, M. 268, 278
Ilchman, W. 48
Islam, R. 262, 267, 268, 278
Issawi, C. 180, 210

Jefferson, T. 56
Jiminez, A. 224
Johnson, L.B. 59
Johnston, B. 115
Jolly, R. 14, 73
Jose, A. 274–5, 280

Subject index